The Story of the Roman Amphitheatre

The Roman amphitheatre was a site both of bloody combat and marvellous spectacle, symbolic of the might of Empire. Yet it had significance beyond mere entertainment; to understand the importance of the amphitheatre is also to understand a key element in the social and political life of the Roman ruling classes.

Generously illustrated with 141 photographs and plans, *The Story of the Roman Amphitheatre* offers a comprehensive picture of the origins, development, and eventual decline of the most typical and evocative of Roman monuments.

With a detailed examination of the Colosseum, as well as case studies of significant sites from Italy, Gaul, Spain and Roman North Africa, the book is a fascinating gazetteer for the general reader as well as a valuable tool for students and academics.

D. L. Bomgardner is Head of Classics at Elstree School, Berkshire.

The Story of the Roman Amphitheatre

D. L. Bomgardner

London and New York

First published 2000
by Routledge
11 New Fetter Lane, London EC4P 4EE

Simultaneously published in the USA and Canada
by Routledge
29 West 35th Street, New York, NY 10001

Routledge is an imprint of the Taylor & Francis Group

First published in paperback 2002

© 2000, 2002 D. L. Bomgardner

Typeset in Garamond by
Keystroke, Jacaranda Lodge, Wolverhampton
Printed and bound in Great Britain by
Bell & Bain Ltd, Glasgow

British Library Cataloguing in Publication Data
A catalogue record for this book is available from the British Library

Library of Congress Cataloging in Publication Data
A catalog record for this book has been requested

ISBN 0–415–16593–8 (Hbk)
ISBN 0–415–30185–8 (Pbk)

For Helen, Kathryn, Albert, Joyce and Tom.

Contents

Plates

Figures

Tables

Preface

In this book I shall try to tell the story of that most typical of Roman monuments, the amphitheatre, from its origins through its heyday and on into its death throes and beyond, in such a way as to be of interest both to the specialist and to the general reader. Due to limitations of time and resources available for this research, the material and monuments discussed have had to be highly selective. They were chosen either because of their undoubted importance or else because of personal interest or personal experience of them. The vast dispersal of the amphitheatres within the empire makes it virtually impossible for anyone to visit more than a select subset of these monuments.

This book is not intended to be a comprehensive discussion of this architectural genre; one already exists: a vast compendium of recent research and a comprehensive architectural survey and analysis in French by Jean-Claude Golvin.[1] Nor does my own experience allow me to attempt such an investigation; there are far too many amphitheatres that I have not seen and research has had to be crammed into the school holidays between terms of teaching. The result must inevitably be a *mélange* of carefully chosen case studies, general principles, impressions and conclusions linked together by a running commentary.

In the first chapter I investigate how the amphitheatre formed a central element in the social and political life of the ruling classes of ancient Roman society. By examining the seating arrangements in the Colosseum (Flavian Amphitheatre, Rome) in detail, I intend to show how this monument epitomises the functions of social status and conspicuous display of wealth and power. To be seen to be in attendance at the Colosseum and one's particular location *vis-à-vis* the emperor's box were vital social and political markers of status and the progress (or otherwise) of one's official career. Here I also attempt to investigate some of the psychological interactions between architecture and spectator. I do not intend to say anything new about the actual structural details of the Colosseum, nor do I intend to give a detailed overall architectural summary. There is a great need for a comprehensive modern study of the Colosseum and efforts to this end are afoot elsewhere by other hands, most notably the team of archaeologists, architects and architectural historians led by Dottore Moccheggiani Carpano. This book has neither the scope nor the research resources to attempt such an ambitious project. I use the Colosseum in the light of the published resources available as illustrative of wider principles. I make no claim to pushing forward our knowledge of the architectural history or delineation of the structure of this monument, but I shall try to provide insight into its social functions in Roman society.

I also intend to rectify the popular misconception that 'the Roman mob of unemployed, welfare-coddled proletariat' filled the amphitheatre watching spectacles. As will be shown, the vast majority of the seating in this arena was reserved for the cream of society with only a limited portion for what might be called popular seating. It is as if the vast majority of the best seats at a football stadium were reserved for hugely expensive corporate boxes with only a few terraces for standing spectators in the upper reaches of the structure.

In Chapter Two, I trace the probable origins of the amphitheatre and then look closely at several of the earliest examples, in particular the Pompeii arena. I shall try to show both how it reflected the social composition of its community and the way in which the details of its construction and design reflected the tensions and status of the constituent elements of the Pompeian polity.

Then in Chapters Three and Four I will examine several of the most important monuments as case studies of their type. First I will look at the largest examples of this genre, including the amphitheatres at Verona, Puteoli, Capua, Arles and Nîmes. Next I shall look in detail at the amphitheatres of the North African provinces, in particular Carthage and El Jem. The development of the spectacles and their final fall before the pressures of the late empire, not least the Christian opposition, form an integral part of this story. The final abandonment and reuse of the arena in other guises forms an enthralling postscript to this study. Finally I shall attempt to suggest possible lineal descendants of the amphitheatre spectacles down to the present day and the modern bullfights.

This book represents the fruits of some twenty years of research (part-time during the last fourteen years) and investigations that began with my doctoral dissertation from the University of Michigan. For ten months I lived at Carthage and travelled widely in the zone extending from central and eastern Algeria, through Tunisia and western Libya. With the generous assistance of research funding from the American Schools of Oriental Research and with the kind permission of Dr Azzeddine Beschaouch, then director of the Institut National d'Archéologie et d'Art de Tunisie, and M. Abdelmajid Ennabli, Conservateur du Site de Carthage, I studied most of the amphitheatres within this area, where I was able to do so, the notable exceptions being those at El Jem and Lepcis Magna. I presented this research as my doctoral dissertation, 'An Analytical Study of Roman North African Amphitheatres' (Ann Arbor, MI: 1985).

Acknowledgements

I wish publicly to acknowledge the help of the following individuals and organisations: the American Schools of Oriental Research and its then president, Dr Phillip King, and the Inter-Departmental Programme for Classical Art and Archaeology, University of Michigan, Ann Arbor, MI, for generous financial support to enable me to undertake the study of North African amphitheatres; the Institut National d'Archéologie et d'Art, Tunis, and its former director, Dr Azzeddine Beschaouch, as well as M. Abdelmajid Ennabli, the Conservateur du Site de Carthage, for permissions to undertake this study; Professor Margaret Alexander and Dr Aisha ben Abed for their unstinting generosity in encouraging me to undertake the study. I also wish to express my appreciation for the help of John and Stephanie Betlyon, and Mme Genevieve Darghouth during my sojourn as Research Fellow at the Carthage Research Institute.

I also wish to thank John H. Humphrey, the supervisor of my dissertation, and the members of my dissertation committee, John Eadie, John Pedley and Fred Albertson, as well as Elaine K. Gazda and Bruce Frier for their part in this work.

I wish to acknowledge the generous help of Richard Linsley Hood, Michael Vickers, K.D. White and Mark Wilson Jones, my headmaster Syd Hill, my colleague Simon Stagg, and the Governors of Elstree School, towards the completion of this study. Needless to say all errors that remain are my own responsibility. I also wish to thank the editorial staff at Routledge for their tireless assistance.

Most of all I wish to express my deeply felt thanks to my wife Helen for the countless instances of good humour and patience in the face of a husband made even more insufferable through pressures of finishing such a work.

The illustrations used in this study have come from the following sources: J.-Cl. Golvin, *L'amphithéâtre romain* (de Boccard: Paris 1988): Figures 1.5, 1.6, 1.8, 2.1, 2.4, 2.5, 3.2, 3.4–3.9, 4.1, 4.3–4.14, 5.1. Mark Wilson Jones: Figures 1.10–12, 3.3, 3.10. J.B. Ward-Perkins and Yale University Press: Figures 1.1, 1.3. Cambridge University Press: Figures 1.4, 1.7. Bayerischer Schulbuch Verlag, Munich: Figure 1.2. Adam & Charles Black, London: Figure 1.9. C.K. Williams II (ASCS, Athens): Figure 2.2. Frank Sear: Figure 2.3. Rainer Graefe: Figure 2.6. Museo Nazionale Archeologico, Naples, and John Ward-Perkins and Amanda Claridge, *Pompeii AD 79* Exhibition Catalogue (London 1976): Figure 2.7. Electa Archive/Electa Einaudi Mondadori: Figure 2.8. Gennaro Pesce: Figure 3.1.

Abbreviations

MSNAF	*Mémoires de la Société Nationale des Antiquaires de France*
*OCD*³	S. Hornblower and A. Spawforth, eds., *The Oxford Classical Dictionary*, 3rd edn (Oxford 1996)
PBSR	*Papers of the British School at Rome*
PECS	R. Stillwell et al., eds, *The Princeton Encyclopedia of Classical Sites* (Princeton 1976)
RA	*Révue archéologique*
RAfr	*Révue africaine*
RANarb	*Révue archéologique Narbonnaise*
REL	*Révue des études latines*
RevTun	*Révue Tunisienne*
RIA	*Rendiconti dell'Istituto archeologico*
RM	*Römische Mitteilungen des deutschen archäologischen Instituts, Römische Abteilung* (1886–)
t.a.q.	*terminus ante quem*
t.p.q.	*terminus post quem*

Chapter One

The Colosseum

In answer to the request, 'Name one example of a Roman amphitheatre', most people would reply, 'The Colosseum'.[1] It represents, as no other monument, the amphitheatre. The powerful associations and images conjured up by the words 'The Colosseum' convey both the majesty and might of the Roman empire. It dominates the space it occupies, towering above the surrounding streets and buildings. It is at once both a symbol and a metaphor for the imperial might of the Roman empire that dominated the ancient Mediterranean world. The story of the amphitheatre and its spectacles from their origins through the zenith of their development and into the decline and eventual fall provides a unique insight into the evolution and fall of the Roman empire itself.

Plate 1.1 Colosseum (Flavian Amphitheatre), Rome: the interior of the monument and the substructures surviving in the arena.
Photograph by D.L. Bomgardner.

'While stands the Colisseum [*sic*], Rome stands. . . . When Rome falls, so falls the world.' These memorable words were written in the eighth century AD by the Venerable Bede.[2] They refer to the colossal bronze statue of the emperor Nero standing 120 ft. high in the vestibule of his palace, the Domus Aurea, on the Velian Hill. By the end of the millennium the term had come to refer to the equally colossal amphitheatre that had been built at the command of the emperor Vespasian and which rose majestically in proximity to this Neronian colossus. After the collapse of the statue, the term 'colisseus' or 'colosseum' had become associated with the amphitheatre itself. However today most people would link the amphitheatre with Bede's words.

It is not hard to understand why this association between Rome and its most famous ancient monument should be so intense. In the fifth century AD Rome fell before the barbarian onslaught. The towering mass of the Flavian Amphitheatre, to give it its official name, had impressed itself upon the minds of visitors as a distant, yet powerful, echo of the former greatness of Rome. Throughout the dangerous years of the early Middle Ages, this mighty monument served as a fortress to some of the most powerful families of Rome. Amidst chaotic political in-fighting between powerful rival families and their factions, it stood as a crumbling, yet proud reminder of the former glory of Rome. By this time the amphitheatre had lost its historical context as the Flavian Amphitheatre and had become a monument for all ages, the Colosseum.

The popes began the process of repairing the crumbling façade of this monument and consecrated the structure to the memory of the Christian martyrs who died there. During the Enlightenment the Colosseum figured prominently among the ruins re-examined and copied in the nascent neo-Classical style of architecture. No visit on the 'Grand Tour', so popular with the gentry of Europe, would have been complete without an atmospheric tour of the Colosseum. In the mid-eighteenth century the Italian artist Gian Battista Piranesi made a famous series of prints of the monuments of ancient Rome, including the Colosseum. So impressed was he that he used the sketches of its internal structural details as the basis for imaginative reconstructions of other long-vanished ancient buildings. The Romantic movement of the nineteenth century found in the Colosseum's crumbling majesty the perfect blend of grandeur, decay and brooding menace, particularly by moonlight, as in Lord Byron's evocative lines from his verse-drama *Manfred*. Even in modern Rome the Colosseum remains one of the few ancient monuments that have not been overshadowed and dwarfed by recent architecture.

THE ACCESSION OF VESPASIAN AND THE ORIGINS OF THE FLAVIAN AMPHITHEATRE

This monument was the showpiece of the new Flavian dynasty of emperors (Vespasian, Titus and Domitian), who reigned from AD 69 to 98. It was the largest stone amphitheatre in the world and was designed to impress onlookers with the power, worth and beneficence of the Flavian dynasty. The need to impress was particularly important. The Flavians had recently come to power after a short, but vicious, civil war. The year AD 69 saw four other emperors (Nero, Otho, Galba and Vitellius) all lose their lives in violent circumstances. Vespasian had been successful in picking up the pieces of the shattered fabric of society, but he was now trying to establish his own reign and line of succession on a firm, lasting basis.

The location chosen for the new amphitheatre was most significant. It was built on the site of the infamous Golden House (Domus Aurea) of Nero. This fabulous pleasure palace, complete with its own self-contained lake and parkland setting, had been built in the very heart of the city of Rome. After the Great Fire of AD 66, Nero's original palace, the so-called *Domus Transitoria*, extending from the Palatine to the Esquiline Hill, was severely damaged. Vast tracts of the fire-damaged city were cleared to make room for his new architectural fantasy, the Golden House.

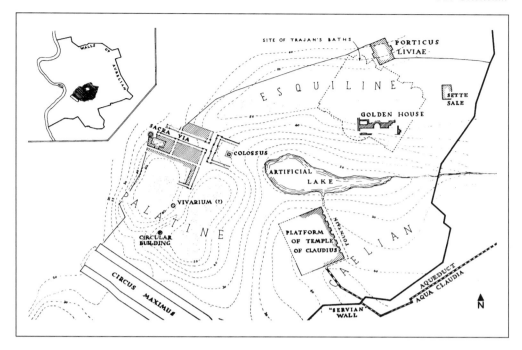

Figure 1.1 Rome, Nero's Golden House, sketch-plan of the probable extent of the park, showing the known structures.
Source: J.B. Ward-Perkins, *Roman Imperial Architecture*, The Pelican History of Art Series (Harmondsworth 1981), 60, fig. 26. Copyright Yale University Press.

What had been the private property of Rome's inhabitants was now turned into a gigantic, private imperial estate. Huge sums of money and enormous resources were poured into its construction. Every conceivable luxurious convenience adorned it, including dining rooms in which, if the description given by Suetonius is taken literally, the ceilings rotated, from which scented water sprays and rose petals rained down upon the banqueters beneath. When the palace and its lake and gardens were finished, Nero is reported to have said, 'At last, I can live as befits a human being.' In one sense Nero's Golden House may be seen as an attempt to compete with the opulence and majesty of Oriental potentates. Nero's 'Royal Palace', in both its scale and magnificence, befitted the most powerful ruler and the most important political centre in the Mediterranean world.

Symbolic of the self-glorification which this complex represents was the colossal statue of the Sun God, some 120 ft. high, fitted with the head of Nero himself. This stood in front of the atrium of the palace, beside the lake. Nero rightly realised that he was one of the greatest rulers of his world and contact with Hellenistic monarchies had taught him the traditions of self-aggrandisement commensurate with such status. Such sentiments proved abhorrent to the Roman Senate and people.

Extravagances such as these and a public preference for all things Greek made Nero intensely unpopular in Rome and the west. When, finally, he was overthrown in a *coup d'état*, nearly all traces of his hated reign were obliterated. The Golden House, however, survived until fire damaged it in AD 104, when Trajan levelled the site and erected his huge Baths complex atop one of its wings.

In the ebb and flow of power at Rome, each new dynasty had two imperative priorities: first, to establish quickly its own authority and legitimacy, and second, to discredit the previous dynasty, particularly the last emperor of the line. By portraying the previous emperor as an incompetent, debauched, unfit ruler, the new dynasty was putting itself into a stronger position. Vespasian must have wondered if he, too, might not succumb to the dogs of war as so many of his immediate predecessors had done. He had, however, several factors in his favour. First, the paroxysm of bloodletting during the previous months had exhausted the Roman world. It was ready for peace, almost at any price. Second, he had two sons: Titus, the elder, an able general like his father, and the younger son, Domitian, still virtually unknown and untried. Two male heirs apparently in good health, with at least one of them of proven ability, seemed to bode well for a stable succession. Third, Vespasian's track record showed proven abilities as a civil servant and soldier. In addition his personal traits of modesty, industry, common sense, good judgement and a strong sense of humour were well suited to the job in hand. Vespasian also had powerful allies among his fellow military commanders, particularly the governor of Syria, Licinius Mucianus, who commanded the powerful strike force that guarded the eastern frontiers of the empire against the Parthians. However, one crucial factor was missing. Vespasian was not a senator. He was of equestrian stock and he had risen in the military command structure of the empire through his skills as a general. As such he depended almost entirely upon the good will and support of the legions to maintain his position as emperor. This alongside some senatorial support, probably led by Mucianus, made up the alliance of his power base.

Vespasian's choice of a permanent stone amphitheatre as the single monument that would most signify his new imperial dynasty reflected the realities of his power. Vespasian was a soldier's soldier with a long and glorious military record of distinction. In his early campaigns in Britain, where he distinguished himself as commander of the southern corps of the invasion forces, including the capture of the heavily fortified hill forts of the south-west, he earned triumphal decoration. And later, when he was appointed to the command in Syria-Palestine,[3] where a successful rebellion of the Jews and the threat of a protracted, gruelling guerrilla war made the task thankless and often unattractive, Vespasian proved himself the master of the situation. Thus, with growing support from the eastern army groups of Palestine, Syria, Egypt and the Danube, as well as promises of help from Vologaesus, king of the Parthians, Vespasian received word of the defeat of Vitellius' forces at Cremona and Vitellius' own assassination in Rome. The legions proclaimed him emperor on 1 July AD 70. Vespasian's debt to the Roman legions was incalculable.

The early history and development of the amphitheatre have been closely linked with the Roman army and with the distinctively Roman military virtues encompassed by the Latin term *virtus*.[4] It is, therefore, significant that the first of the soldier-emperors of the Roman empire should choose to commemorate his accession and the dynastic succession of his sons, Titus and Domitian, by the decision to erect a permanent, monumental stone amphitheatre in the heart of Rome. These facts should be borne in mind alongside the above-mentioned political motives that were designed to distance Vespasian from the unpopular Neronian building programme in Rome and also, at a stroke, to rectify it.

With these considerations in mind Vespasian chose the site of the lake of the former Golden House as the location for his new stone amphitheatre. In one stroke he was righting the wrong that had so angered the Roman populace – the appropriation of public land for the emperor's personal use. Vespasian was returning this land to the people of Rome (*populus Romanus*); henceforward the amphitheatre would be an adornment for the city as well as a public venue for imperial beneficence and not a secluded, exclusive preserve of imperial despotism as previously. At the same time he was recognising the military virtues by which he had risen to achieve 'the purple'.

Thus the Colosseum was the hallmark of a new policy of conciliation and integration. It was also an extravagant gesture of goodwill and generosity towards the Roman people and the Roman legions, a magnificent ornament befitting the splendour and power of the capital of the Mediterranean world, but of a very different kind from the Golden House of Nero.

VISITING THE COLOSSEUM

Let us imagine a spectator making his way towards the Colosseum. The time is shortly after the completion of the monument: in the reign of the emperor Domitian. Let us imagine further that our spectator is coming from the direction of the Roman Forum and proceeding along the *via Sacra*. As he approaches, the tall roof lines of the basilicas and temples lining the way would partially obscure the view of the Colosseum. The spectator would catch tantalising glimpses of its enormous stone mass, even from as far away as the Forum.

As the spectator approached, the multiple arcades of the façade would be framed by the triumphal archways along the *via Sacra*. A feeling of excitement and anticipation would grow in his mind as he glimpsed fleetingly this massive structure.

Finally, when he had passed through the confines of the narrow streets surrounding the Forum, the spectator would suddenly emerge into the large open area surrounding the Colosseum. Immediately ahead lay the *Meta Sudans*, a monumental fountain in the shape of a circus turning-post (*meta*). Nearby the colossal statue of Nero towered above its surroundings. After the death of Nero, Vespasian replaced Nero's head with that of the Sun God.

A ring of bollards (small stone blocks, five of which still survive *in situ* on the eastern side)[5] marked the outer edge of the travertine pavement that surrounded the monument. Like sentinels they barred access to vehicular traffic as well as acting like a filter to slow down, direct and control the converging streams of pedestrians. Thus the first visual impressions of

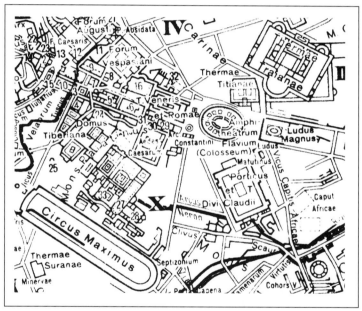

Figure 1.2 Rome: area around the Forum and Colosseum.
Source: Grosser Historischer Weltatlas. Ier Teil. Vorgeschichte und Altertum, 5th edn (Munich 1971), overlay 'Rom zur Kaiserzeit' to Karte 35. Copyright Bayerischer Schulbuch Verlag.

the monument would be a field of hard, repetitive images, which converged towards the edges of the structure and disappeared behind its massiveness.

When he had passed the barrier of the bollards, the spectator entered the vast travertine piazza (some 17.5m wide). Its circular space presented the spectator with a convergent visual field that, like a magnet, tended to hold one's gaze within the space defined, on the outside, by the bollards and, on the inside, by the façade of the amphitheatre. It made movement towards the façade and access to its eighty arcades at ground level easy. The piazza was paved to heighten the monumental character of the setting as well as to provide an area free from mud. Here peddlers, sausage-sellers and drinks and souvenir vendors hawked their wares, while pickpockets plied their trade amongst the unwary. Here the thousands of people about to attend the spectacles would search for the proper arcade entrance.

To organise this potentially chaotic and dangerous activity, at ground level a series of Roman numerals (I to LXXVI) were inscribed above the arcades of the façade. Only the four main entrances (on the major and minor axes of the ellipse) were not numbered. Each spectator had a ticket (or *tessera*), on which was the number of an arcade. This indicated the arcade that provided the most direct route to the spectator's seating area.

The details of the distribution of these tickets are poorly understood and poorly documented. However, by analogy with other well-attested social institutions, one can attempt to reconstruct the system. The patron–client relationship is well known in ancient Rome. Society was organised into a social pyramid: a small number of first-rank patrons supported a much larger number of less important clients. Each of these clients might be in his own right a patron to clients of a lower social status, and so on down the social scale. Such patronage took the form of material assistance as well as other, less tangible, forms of support. A patron's clients would, in their turn, publicly show their allegiance, loyalty and respect for their patron. Such forms of help might include the organisation of political support and other services requested by the patron. Since the emperor was ultimately the sole patron for the rest of Roman society, he alone was responsible for the organisation and financing of such spectacles. It is, therefore, sensible to assume that he would have control over the distribution of the tickets. Large numbers of tickets would probably be given to his most important clients: the most consequential citizens and politicians in Rome. In turn they would probably have distributed batches of tickets to their own clients, and so on until the lowest levels of society were reached. It is assumed that the precise number of tickets that a client received depended upon his social status. The more important the client, the larger the number of tickets he received.

THE FAÇADE

The majestic façade of the Flavian Amphitheatre rose 48.5m in three superimposed tiers of arcades and an attic storey (Figure 1.3). The attic itself was crowned by a series of tall masts. These masts secured the rigging for the vast awning (*velarium*) that protected the audience from the scorching sun or pouring rain. Each mast was supported upon a stone socket at its base; it was firmly bonded into the masonry of the façade and then it passed through the crowning entablature of the attic storey, which gave it stability.

Each tier of arcades was decorated by the addition of applied Classical orders of engaged semi-columns: Tuscan (Doric columns with bases), Ionic and Corinthian (in ascending order). The lofty attic storey had applied Corinthian pilasters. The overall effect would be to frame each archway between a pair of attached half-round columns, thus providing a rhythmical, horizontal articulation of the façade. In addition each storey was separated from the next by a prominent, projecting entablature. This design, besides providing an aesthetically pleasing, rhythmic modulation based upon well-established Classical practice, also linked the interior layout of the seating (in four separate vertical zones) with the exterior in a similar segregated, four-fold division. Thus the rigid hierarchies of Roman society were reinforced both inside and outside the amphitheatre. The Colosseum was much more than a massive building. It was a political statement: the Flavian emperors were identifying themselves with the existing social order, the *status quo*, and also consciously distancing themselves from the radical policies of Nero.

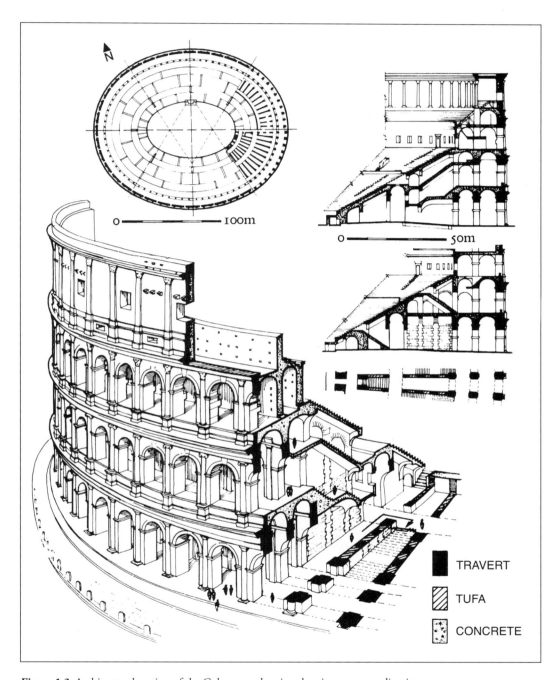

TRAVERT

TUFA

CONCRETE

Figure 1.3 Architectural section of the Colosseum showing the piazza surrounding it.
Source: J.B. Ward-Perkins, *Roman Imperial Architecture*, The Pelican History of Art Series (Harmondsworth 1981), 69, fig. 31. Copyright Yale University Press.

The technique of framing arches within a framework of engaged half-columns supporting an entablature is also known in Etruria, where this motif has been found on a painted cinerary urn (*c.* 150 BC from Clusium). The use of a simple row of arches to decorate a monumental façade is attested in the Greek world (at Lindos, Rhodes) very early in the second century BC.[6] Thus it seems likely that both Greek and Etruscan influences were at work, contributing to the origins of the so-called *fornix* system of architectural ornamentation.

The Romans, however, developed this system of architectural decoration to its highest degree. Early examples of this technique include a portico in the enormous terraced Temple Complex of Fortuna Primigenia at Praeneste (late second century BC or Sullan era) and at Rome in the façade of the Capitoline Tabularium (*c.* 78 BC). During this time indigenous Etruscan and Italic elements were blending with Greek influences to create a hybrid late republican architecture.[7] However, the boldest and most monumental uses of this method of ornamenting an arcuated façade are to be found in the entertainment buildings of early imperial Rome: the Augustan Theatre of Marcellus and the Flavian Amphitheatre.

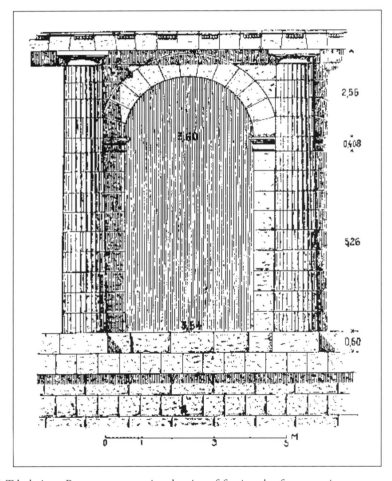

Figure 1.4 Tabularium, Rome: reconstruction drawing of *fornix* style of construction.
Source: D.S. Robertson, *Greek and Roman Architecture*, 2nd edn (Cambridge 1971), 242, fig. 101. Copyright CUP from R. Delbrück, *Hellenistische Bauten in Latium*, 1, Strasburg, 1907, fig. 30 a.

An interesting early parallel for the system of alternating applied Classical orders (Doric/Tuscan, Ionic and Corinthian) decorating the façade of the Colosseum may be found in the above-mentioned Temple Complex at Praeneste. Doric columns are used to support the barrel-vaulted roof of the twin ramps connecting the lower and middle terraces, Ionic columns are used in the portico and hemicycle colonnade of this middle terrace and Corinthian columns are used in the double colonnades of the upper terrace and the massive semicircular exedra.

CIRCULATION PATTERNS AND SOCIAL STATUS

It is hard to imagine a more effective method of controlling spectators and ensuring maximum, efficient circulation than that employed in the Colosseum. As mentioned above, the broad, travertine-paved circular piazza that surrounded that Colosseum allowed easy access to every part of the façade. From there an elaborate series of circular galleries (or *ambulacra*) provided effective lateral movement. Each of the eighty bays along the monument's façade gave access to a convergent radial passageway; each of these led straight into the interior vaulted spaces below the seating. These radial passages either led to stairways (for vertical movement between different levels) or to arched entryways (*vomitoria*) that provided access to the seating, or else they interconnected with circular galleries deeper within the structure. Only rarely did they end in a cul-de-sac. In addition the spacious exterior galleries of the ground, first and second storeys (double-arcaded for the ground and first floors) provided welcome sheltered passageways for stretching the legs during intervals in the programme. In Roman theatres a series of rectangular porticoes behind the stage (*porticus post scaenam*) served the same purpose.

What follows is an attempt to reconstruct the patterns of access used by different social classes as they entered the Colosseum and took their seats.

The four main entrances corresponding to the major and minor axes of the arena were marked out for special treatment. None of these was numbered like the other bays of the façade. The major axis entrances gave direct unrestricted access to the arena itself. In contrast both of the minor axis entrances gave direct access to special, reserved boxes. Three aspects of the northern (minor axis) entrance merit attention. First, the numbering of the outer bays of the façade began here and continued anti-clockwise. Second, a shallow distyle columnar porch, including a pediment adorned with a four-horse chariot group (*quadriga*) above it, stood in front of this entrance. Finally, a subterranean gallery (the so-called 'gallery of Commodus') gave access to the box on this side ('G' on Figure 1.5).[8] These pieces of evidence allow us to identify the box on the northern side of the arena as the imperial box (or *pulvinar*). Here the emperor and his immediate retinue, that is male members of his family and specially honoured guests, reclined on their couches to watch the spectacles. The empress, her female entourage, the Vestal Virgins and the magistrates, in whose name the games were being officially given, occupied the box opposite (*tribunal editoris*) (see Figure 1.6: the two boxes are located directly above the two chambers labelled 'A' on the plan). These two locations (at the ends of the arena's short axis) were the best seats to occupy in order to see and be seen – both functions extremely important in this, the principal amphitheatre of the Roman empire.

As part of his programme of social reform legislation, the emperor Augustus rigidly segregated the seating arrangements in the theatres of Rome by social classes. Later the emperor Domitian again vigorously enforced these enactments, which had obviously grown lax in observance and enforcement in the intervening years.[9]

Senators[10] and specially honoured foreign guests sat in the orchestra of Roman theatres on special ivory seats (*subsellia*). The order of knights[11] sat in the first fourteen rows of the theatre, the section known as the *ima cavea*. Roman citizens (*cives Romani*) sat in the next block of seats, that

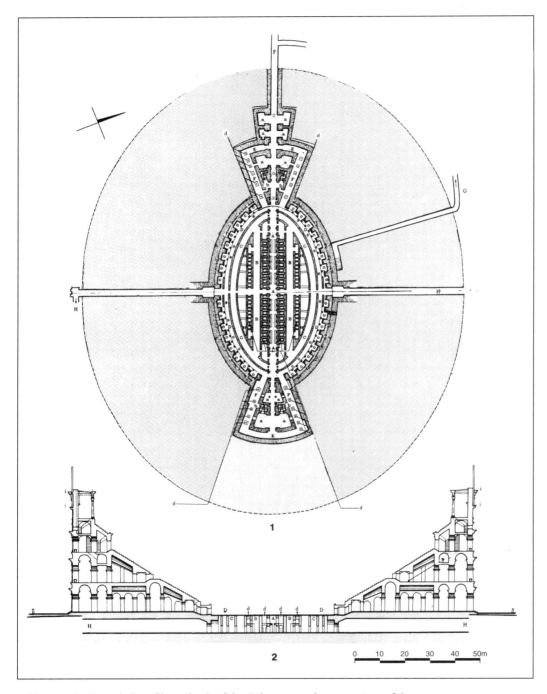

Figure 1.5 Ground plan of lower levels of the Colosseum and cross-sections of the monument.
Source: Golvin, Planche XXXVII. Copyright J.-Cl. Golvin.

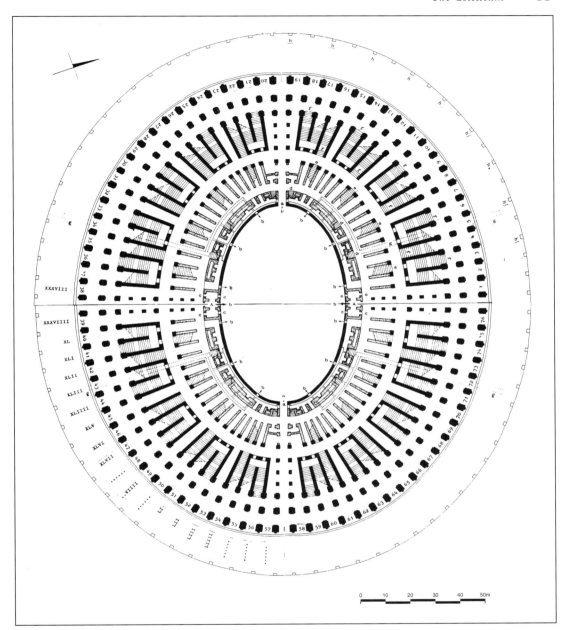

Figure 1.6 Architectural plan of the Colosseum, Rome.
Source: Golvin, Planche XXXVI. Copyright J.-Cl. Golvin.

is the *media cavea*. Augustus even went so far as to subdivide this section into further block reservations, for example married men, soldiers, minors and their tutors (*paedagogi*) in adjacent blocks of seats. These subdivisions corresponded to the natural horizontal subdivision of the seating into wedges (*cunei*) made by the radially-aligned steps running from top to bottom of each vertical zone of seating. The rest of the population were apparently lumped together.[12] This category included the urban poor, foreigners in residence at Rome, freed slaves, slaves, etc. They sat in the highest block of seats, the *summa cavea*. Finally, women, presumably the 'respectable' wives and daughters of Roman citizens, were expected to sit under the protecting shelter of the colonnade that usually crowned the theatre seating area. This precaution ensured that these women of quality kept their pale complexions. A suntan denoted low social status, indicating that the woman in question had to go outside to work to support herself.[13]

The rigid separation of the Colosseum's seating into distinct vertical zones and the remains of inscriptions recovered from the stone seats (*gradus*) themselves, show that the same, or very similar, seating restrictions applied here as in the theatres of Rome. Thus, senators, priests of the most important religious cults (such as the twelve Arval Brethren responsible for the rites ensuring the fertility of the soil) and distinguished foreign visitors or ambassadors would have sat on the podium of the amphitheatre, at the very brink of the arena itself. Higher up sat the knights in the *ima cavea*, while farther up still the Roman citizens occupied the *media cavea*. The rest of the undifferentiated mass of spectators crowded together into the *summa cavea*. Finally, at the pinnacle of the seating, protected by a tall colonnade, sat the ladies of quality in the region known as the *summum maenianum in ligneis*.

Let us now try to trace the routes used by each of these groups and then to analyse the resultant patterns.

Important spectators would reach the podium from the innermost *ambulacrum*. From this tunnel twelve stairways led up directly through *vomitoria* and out onto the podium (labelled 'd' on Figure 1.6). These twelve stairways formed a symmetrical array of two groups of six, about the main east and west entrances to the arena.[14] The innermost *ambulacrum* itself could be reached directly from any one of forty-four of the exterior bays of the façade.[15] (Interestingly, the four main underground drains evacuating water from the arena (labelled 'g' on Figure 1.6) also seem to be grouped into a similarly symmetrical pattern.) Thus each quadrant of the façade contained twelve bays (forty-eight in total) suitable for use by senators and others seated on the podium.

It seems natural to assume that the most important people would get the best seats. The seats closest to the arena and nearest to the ends of its minor axis would have a much better view than those higher and farther away and closer to the ends of the major axis. Thus the best seats were on the podium and at the ends of the minor axis (the imperial box and the *tribunal editoris*) and the worst seats were in the upper gallery and at the ends of the amphitheatre's major axis. The podium contained seven rows of marble seating divided into fourteen wedges (or *cunei*). Elaborate gradations of status existed among senators: for example, those of patrician or plebeian ancestry, those who had an ancestor who had held the consulship and thus given the family *nobilitas*, etc. Each of these would influence the order in which each senator gave his opinions (*sententiae*) about issues before the Senate and also doubtless reflected his seating at the public spectacles. The layout of the podium provided ample scope for the working out of such delicate decisions of protocol as regarded seating allocation.

Spectators reached the lower zone of the *ima cavea* from the middle *ambulacrum* on the ground floor, from which sixteen stairways[16] (labelled 'e' on Figure 1.6) led up through *vomitoria* and out onto the lowest *praecinctio* of the *cavea*. These stairways formed groups arranged symmetrically about both the major and minor axes of the monument, distributed every fourth or fifth bay around the façade. Others reached the upper part of the *ima cavea* by a more indirect route. First one climbed up one of the thirty-six stairways (nine in each quadrant of the structure: labelled 'f' on Figure 1.6) that led the spectator to the double-arcaded gallery which lay on the outside of the first floor. Once here the spectator passed on into the inner *ambulacrum*, from which twenty short stairways (five in each quadrant) led up through *vomitoria* and out onto the top *praecinctio* of the *ima cavea*. Here too the spectator's seating would reflect his social status and importance. The *ima cavea* had twelve rows of marble seating divided by stairways into sixteen wedges (or *cunei*). Each wedge had two *vomitoria* – one at the top, the other near the bottom. Thus a knight would choose his route according to two criteria. First he needed to know the precise location of the wedge in which his seat lay, and then whether his seat was in the upper or the lower part of the *ima cavea*.

Doubtless differentiation of seating by status, similar to that for senators, also occurred here. There were apparently as many gradations of status among equestrians as among senators. Knights in the imperial civil service were classified according to their salaries, political clout and other honorific distinctions. The gift by the emperor of a horse (*equus publicus*)[17] or the appointment to serve on one of the five equestrian jury panels (*decuriae*) at Rome conferred great honour. So much care was taken to reflect discriminations in status that in the earliest known legislation (*lex Roscia*, 67 BC) about the reservation of the seats in the theatres of Rome for the knights, there was even special provision for a block of seats for a very particular class of knights, namely those who had gone bankrupt[18] – separated, of course, from their still solvent brethren. In the case of both senators and equestrians, it would be clear for all to see at each performance in a theatre or amphitheatre exactly whose careers or fortunes were on the rise and vice versa by following the location of their seating over several years. Thus, an improvement in the quality of one's seat would indicate advancement or preferment and the opposite would also be true. This feature of the spectacles was perhaps nearly as important as the entertainment itself: after all possessing superior status is only half the prize; being publicly seen to possess it is the other half.

A series of twenty stairways led from the small *ambulacrum* that skirted the masonry fabric of the vaulting on the inside (at the first-floor level) to another small covered gallery, between the first and second floors (+19.5 m) and tucked into the uppermost vaulting space directly above the inner gallery of the double-gallery of the first floor (see Figure 1.7)[19]

Spectators could then pass straight on from this intermediate covered gallery up one of a series of sixteen stairways to reach the arcaded gallery of the second floor. From there one passed through one of sixteen *vomitoria* inside into the *praecinctio* that circled the top of the *media cavea*. The *media cavea* had nineteen rows of marble seating divided into sixteen *cunei*. Here sat Roman citizens with sufficient wealth to enable them to wear the *toga*. As mentioned above, Augustus subdivided this large group by additional criteria: marital status, soldiers on active duty, young men below the age of majority accompanied by their tutors (*paedagogi*) in an adjacent block of seats, etc. Each subdivision was supposed to sit together in a block of seats reserved for them. Rank and status were probably represented to a certain extent here too, although it is far from clear how far this may have been applied.

The arcaded gallery of the second floor as well as its inner *ambulacrum* led by stairways to the covered gallery,[20] which lay directly above (see Figures 1.7, 1.8 and 1.9). From this covered gallery a series of sixteen T-shaped stairways (consisting of two lateral, ascending branches both feeding into a single inward, ascending branch) led through *vomitoria* to the *praecinctio* circling the top of the *summa cavea*. Here there were seven rows of limestone seating divided into sixteen *cunei*. The urban poor, slaves, freed slaves and humble foreign residents of Rome (and perhaps women of similar status) sat here. It is possible that here too rank and status may have regulated the seating, but it seems more likely that it was unreserved. The earliest arrivals probably got the best seats. There is no evidence that these seats were reserved, unlike the situation in the lower zones of the *cavea*.

Sixteen stairways led from this covered gallery[21] to the attic gallery[22] and thence by twenty-four T-shaped stairways led to the lofty, wind-swept gallery[23] that crowned the *cavea* (see Figures. 1.7 and 1.9). Here wooden seating (perhaps six rows high), divided into eighty *tabulationes* (corresponding to the number of bays in the façade of the amphitheatre), was tucked beneath the colonnade that crowned the summit of the *cavea*, the *summum maenianum in ligneis*. Here sat the

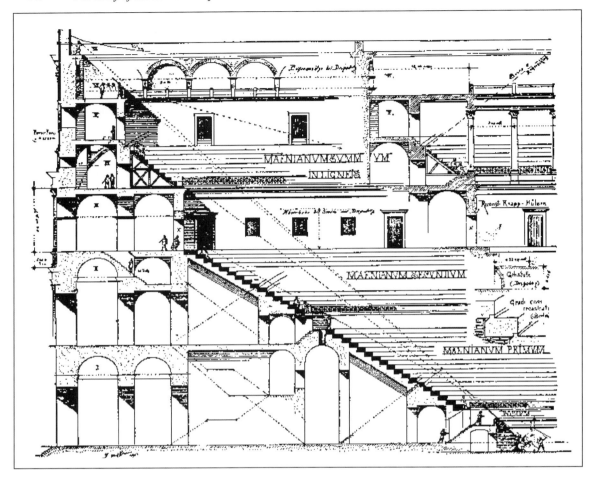

Figure 1.7 Cross-section of *cavea* of the Colosseum, Rome.
Source: D.S. Robertson, *Greek and Roman Architecture*, 2nd edn (Cambridge 1971), 286, fig. 118a. Copyright CUP from Durm, *Die Baukunst der Römer*, 2nd edn (Leipzig 1905), fig. 745.

ladies of fashion, the wives and daughters of senators, knights and important Roman citizens, protected from the sun and rain. Perhaps, here too, rank and status determined the seating.

Several patterns emerge from the bewildering routes of access to the various zones of the seating. First, the principle of four-fold symmetry ensured that each quadrant of the monument had roughly equivalent access to all regions of the *cavea*. Second, there seems to have been a segregation of the ground floor by social status. Only high-status spectators would go deeply within the framework of the overarching vaulting and passageways: the higher the social status, the more deeply one travelled within the labyrinth of galleries, passageways and tunnels. Senators reached their seats by means of the innermost *ambulacrum*, fully within the bowels of the substructures. Similarly the knights would go to the intermediate *ambulacrum*, midway between the inner and outer zone, to reach their reserved tiers of seating. Everyone else had to climb the vertiginous stairways of the outer double-arcaded galleries. Such patterns, whether conscious or coincidental, created an elaborate filtration system. The inner sanctum of power and privilege was reserved for the elite of Roman society; access to these innermost spaces was strictly reserved. It

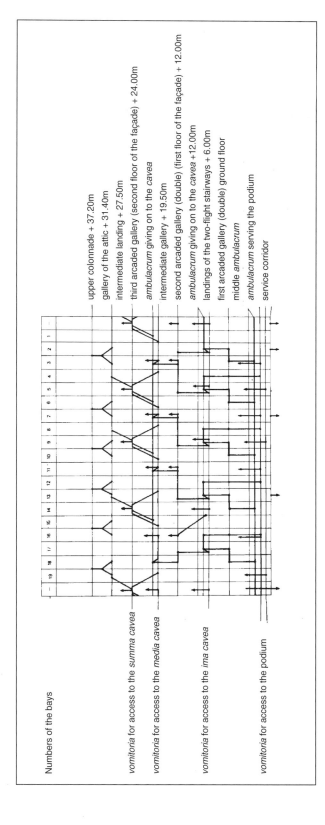

Figure 1.8 Diagram depicting the inter-relationships of the access passageways to the seating of the Colosseum.
Source: Golvin, Planche LX. Copyright J.-Cl. Golvin.

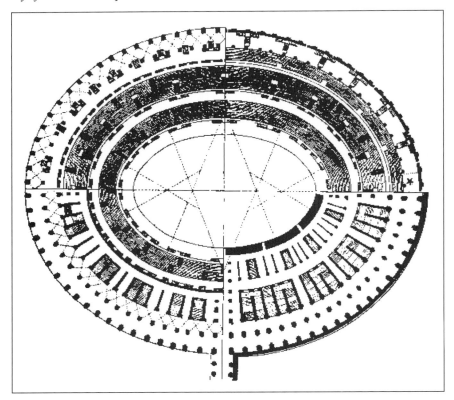

Figure 1.9 Colosseum, Rome (restored): plan at four different levels.
Source: J.H. Middleton, *Remains of Ancient Rome*, II (London 1892), 88, fig. 59. Copyright Adam & Charles Black, London.

has even been suggested that the stairways leading off the inner as well as those leading off the outer of the two double galleries on the exterior of the monument at ground level were reserved for separate social classes. In this scheme only Roman citizens and the 'ladies of quality' who needed to reach their seating in the *media cavea* and in the covered gallery at the top of the seating beneath the crowning colonnade would use the inner stairways. Similarly the undifferentiated mass of spectators sitting in the *summa cavea* would use only the outermost stairways leading off the outermost gallery of the ground floor. Although this would make excellent sense, there is no evidence to support such a hypothesis.[24]

The treatment of high-status women in this scheme merits further discussion. By placing their seats in the highest echelons of the *cavea*, the *summum maenianum in ligneis*, a kind of 'purdah' was achieved: a segregation by sex. Furthermore, the women in this sector, as in 'purdah', sat in a position that was screened from the eyes of the men. At the rear of the *summa cavea* a sheer wall (some 5m high) rose up forming the footing for the covered seating within the colonnade above. This method of construction provided a guarantee of privacy for those sitting within the colonnade, for the men, who sat far below them, would be unable to view anything within this cool shaded zone. In the modern bull rings of Spain, those who are disturbed by the sight of blood sit in the highest reaches of the seating. From there the drama below takes on an almost surreal quality due to the greater distance and diminished view of details. Unlike men, toughened in battle to the sight of bloodshed, such women were deemed more sensitive and in need of protection from such sights. More cynically, however, there is the possibility that, by placing them in such a position (making necessary the climbing of something like 220 stair treads to reach this height), women would be discouraged from attending such spectacles at all. Additionally, gladiators were well known as 'heart-throbs' and potent symbols of virility. Perhaps the seating was also intended to minimise the possibilities for interactions between the socially despised slave gladiators and these women of quality, who might begin to think the unthinkable, if they were allowed to get too near 'the forbidden fruit' of illicit passion. For whatever reasons, high-status ladies were segregated within a zone where they were both remote from the actions of the arena and from the potentially unwelcome attentions of the mob seated below them. The regular practice of providing ring-side seats for the Vestal Virgins would seem to be a striking contradiction to this practice. However, the rigid restrictions upon the guaranteed chastity of these most sacred priestesses of the hearth of Vesta, including burial alive if they transgressed, provided the necessary safeguards to their behaviour. The supreme honour of being seated near the emperor and in the best seats provided some reward for their enforced sexual continence.

Such a system of reserved seating by rank and status required the presence of attendants both to supervise the initial seating and to ensure that no violations occurred later. Such attendants (*dissignatores*) are well attested in the theatres of Rome.[25] They summarily and unceremoniously ejected any would-be gate-crashers.

DESCRIPTION AND ANALYSIS OF THE *CAVEA*

As mentioned above, the *cavea* of the Colosseum contained five segregated seating areas (from bottom to top): the podium, *ima cavea, media cavea, summa cavea* and the *summum maenianum in ligneis*. Seating in each zone was restricted by social status as described above.

The podium (5.04m wide) comprised two elements: a wide platform (2 m) and behind this seven tiers (each *gradus* was 0.72m wide) of marble seats divided into fourteen *cunei*.[26] If a single row of seats of honour (*subsellia*) occupied the platform, then it could seat approximately 250 senators and other VIPs. If, on the other hand, a double row of such seats had existed (a reasonable assumption, given the width of the platform), then it could have accommodated some 500 spectators.[27] The seven rows of marble seats were probably also designed to accommodate *subsellia*, which made it necessary to allocate a double portion of space (0.8 m) for each spectator. On these assumptions, some 1,750 onlookers could have watched from these broad steps.[28] The suggestion has been made that senators sat on the platform of the podium, while the Order of Knights sat behind on the seven tiers of marble seating.[29] Although this suggestion may sound appealing, a thorough analysis of the evidence will reveal that it is unlikely.

It is well known that the first fourteen tiers of seating in the theatres of Rome were reserved for the equestrian order. If one analyses the seating capacity of the *ima cavea* of the Theatre of Marcellus in Rome (the region allocated to the knights by the *lex Roscia*), one finds that some 6,800 spectators could sit in it.[30] In the light of evidence for the equestrian order at Rome in the reign of Augustus this seems a reasonable estimate. In the Colosseum the seven tiers of seats behind the platform of the podium could not accommodate such a multitude. Thus alternatives must be sought to the suggestion that senators and knights both shared the podium.

Those areas which are nearest the arena and nearest the uppermost reaches of the seating are precisely those most likely to have been altered later. It is therefore possible that the podium as described above is not the original construction, but one from a later phase of construction. The Senate under Augustus numbered about 600 members. However, by the later fourth century AD, the number of senators had swelled to something approaching 2,000.[31] If one allowed a double width allocation for the senators, as would befit their status, then the combined seating capacity estimates of the platform and the seven marble tiers of seating behind it (excluding the combined areas of the *tribunalia*) are approximately 2,070 spectators – an estimate well in agreement with the figure for the enrolment of the Senate. It is, therefore, tempting to view the podium as an addition to the Colosseum contemporary with the vastly enlarged size of the Senate of the late fourth century and not as an early imperial feature for the seating of both the senators and the knights behind them.

The *ima cavea* (13m wide) had oval-shaped gangways (*praecinctiones*) at the top and bottom of the twelve tiers of marble seating divided into sixteen wedges (*cunei*) by stairs.[32] The seating capacity for this region was about 11,700 spectators. In these seats the Order of Knights sat. The role and numbers of the equestrian order were expanding with the evolution of the Principate, culminating in the era of the Antonine emperors of the second century AD.[33] The enlarged provision of the *ima cavea* should perhaps indicate that, already by the Flavian era, the equestrian order had attained an enhanced status and importance. Alternatively, the enormous popularity of gladiatorial contests may have made necessary a larger reserved seating zone for the knights in the arena than in the theatre since more, on average, may have been expected to attend a single performance here. Terence complained bitterly about the fickleness of the spectators, who far preferred the gladiatorial combats. They ruined the second performance of his play, *Hecyra*, when they suddenly rushed into the theatre in mid-performance mistakenly thinking that a gladiatorial combat was going to take place there.[34]

The *media cavea* (17m wide) had three oval-shaped gangways (*praecinctiones*) at the bottom, middle and top of the nineteen tiers of seating (*gradus*), either in marble or limestone, divided by stairways into sixteen *cunei*. Some 20,400 spectators drawn from the class of full Roman citizens (*cives Romani*) sat here. As mentioned earlier, inscriptions carved on to the seats themselves indicate that there were block seating reservations for special groups within this category. The toga was the physical sign of such status and distinguished this vast section from the *pullati* who sat above in the *summa cavea*. This region had seven tiers of limestone seating divided by stairways into sixteen *cunei* and could accommodate a mere 10,100 seated spectators. Here those of undifferentiated status sat: slaves, freed slaves, foreigners of no special status, the urban poor of Rome who couldn't afford the toga and such like.

Above the *summa cavea* there rose a sheer vertical masonry barrier, some 5m tall, that marked the beginning of the zone known as the *summum maenianum in ligneis*, where the 'ladies of quality' of Rome sat in their remote seclusion, unseen by the eyes of those below. Places for some 10,300 spectators were provided beneath the shelter of the overhanging colonnade within which the wooden seating was divided into eighty sectors (*tabulationes*). It is quite probable that this sector of the Colosseum was reorganised or rebuilt at least once during its long history.[35]

THE EVIDENCE FROM THE INSCRIPTIONS RESERVING PLACES FOR THE ARVAL BRETHREN

During the reign of the emperor Augustus, an ancient college of priests, the twelve *Fratres Arvales* (Arval Brethren), concerned with ensuring the fertility of the soil, was re-established under imperial patronage. Indeed the reigning emperor was always one of the twelve, the remainder being chosen from among the most pre-eminent members of the senatorial aristocracy. The cult was based upon a grove sacred to the goddess Dea Dia, located at the fifth milepost on the *via Campana* outside the *porta Portuensis*. There a large series of inscriptions recording details about this cult were uncovered (the so-called *Acta Fratrum Arvalium*). Among them there was an inscription, assigned a date of AD 81, which recorded, in great detail, blocks of seats in the Colosseum that had been set aside for members of this college and their families.[36]

The twelve Arval Brethren themselves would doubtless have shared a position of honour near the imperial box on the platform of the podium. The inscription begins by recording the reservation of portions of a block of eight marble seats in the twelfth *cuneus* of the first *maenianum*. This can be easily identified with the *ima cavea* of the Colosseum, the only amphitheatre in Rome at that time.[37] The college occupied a precisely measured amount of space (1.5725 m)[38] on each of the eight tiers of marble seats. The average allocation for each spectator was about 0.4m of seating space. Thus this amount of space would correspond to four spectators each in the eight tiers or a total of thirty-two in all. It was necessary to specify the amount of seating in this way since there were no armrests or other methods of marking off individual seats. A short inscription in abbreviated form and a couple of straight lines, marking the limits of the allocation, cut into the marble seats themselves would also probably have assisted seating attendants. Thus thirty-two members of the equestrian order would probably have sat in this block. Their precise relationship to the college of Arval Brethren is not clear.

The next section of the text, dealing with the seating arrangements in the *media cavea*, is unfortunately garbled. The most sensible interpretation would seem to be that sixteen *cives Romani* (four in each of the four rows mentioned) had seats reserved for them.[39]

Finally the allocation in the *summum maenianum in ligneis* is given. Here, in the fifty-third *tabulatio*, portions of eleven wooden *gradus* were apportioned. Interestingly, the amount of space allotted in each row increases from bottom to top, so that the ladies sitting in the highest tier had about 10 per cent more space than those on the bottom. Perhaps this was intended to compensate for the longer climb to the seats or perhaps simply reflected the circular geometry of each of the blocks (be they *cunei* or *tabulationes*) of seating in the amphitheatre. Once again it would seem that four people sat in each of the eleven rows, giving a total of forty-four ladies.

Table 1.1 indicates the relative percentages of seating allocation by social status. Not unexpectedly, senators and equestrians made up the majority of the college's manpower (73 per cent). Roughly one-quarter of the remaining members were represented by Roman citizens of good standing. The most probable interpretation of the seating in the *summum maenianum in ligneis* is that it was for the wives of members of the college. In Rome priests were not usually required to lead a celibate life, and, if our assumptions are correct, then three-quarters of the members of the college will have been married. This is only one of several alternative conclusions for these data.

Table 1.1 Allocation of seating at the Colosseum for the *Collegium Fratrum Arvalium*

SECTION OF *CAVEA*	Seating estimate	Percentage of total
Podium	12	12%
Ima cavea	32	31%
Media cavea	16	15%
Summum maenianum in ligneis	44	42%
Total	104	

Table 1.2 shows the seating capacity estimates for each individual section of the *cavea*. The popular image, promulgated by Hollywood extravaganzas, of the Roman mob packed into the Colosseum to witness almost daily carnage simply cannot be supported by these data. What the data do clearly show is that there was a positive bias against such an element's attendance. A mere 18 per cent of the seating allocation, and that of poor quality, was provided for the fringe

Table 1.2 Seating capacity estimates for each section of the Colosseum[40]

Section of *cavea*	Seating estimate	Percentage of total
Tribunalia[a]	60	0.1
Podium (excluding *tribunalia*[a])	2,190	4
Ima cavea	11,680	21
Media cavea	20,430	37
Summa cavea	10,100	18
Summum maenianum in ligneis	10,300	19
Total	54,760	

[a] *tribunalia* (12 m wide) probably covered only the platform itself (2 m wide) and not the seven tiers of marble seating behind.

elements of Roman society: the urban poor, slaves, freed slaves, foreigners. First and foremost the Colosseum was a monument dedicated to the social contract of Roman society: the symbiotic relationship between the emperor and the senatorial and equestrian classes, on the one hand, and the relatively well-to-do Roman citizens, on the other. These groups held some 62 per cent of the total seating allocation. Women sat in the cloistered seats beneath the colonnade at the top of the *cavea* – a mere 19 per cent of the total seating capacity and with a very poor view.

Older boys, those who had attained the age of seventeen and thus were qualified to wear the *toga virilis*, probably sat with or near their fathers. Certainly the elder sons of senators accompanied them to the meetings of the Senate. Younger boys, those young enough to require a *paedagogus* (a kind of private tutor cum child-minder), were encouraged by the Augustan legislation mentioned above to sit together, with their tutors, in another block of seats, at their elbows to oversee their behaviour. Young girls and women would probably have sat with or near their mothers in the *summum maenianum in ligneis*. The small proportion of space reserved for women in the Colosseum indicates that they were not normally expected or even encouraged to attend in large numbers.

THE ARENA

In its mature form the arena of the Colosseum had a remarkable system of defensive measures designed to protect spectators from the inherent dangers of the contests that took place there, the gladiatorial contests (*munera gladiatorum*) and the wild beast hunts (*venationes*).

Big feline species, such as lions, leopards, panthers and even occasionally tigers, were extremely popular spectacles. Leopards, in particular, have an amazing ability to climb trees in the wild. Therefore, it was necessary to take precautions so that none of these animals escaped from the arena. Furthermore, due to the geometry of the arena-wall towering some 3.6m above the sandy floor of the arena itself, the region immediately below its brow and around the periphery of the arena could not be seen by most of the spectators in the *cavea*, except for those few on the podium. Animals or combatants that happened to stray into this so-called 'blind zone' would be invisible to a large proportion of the crowd, and, as George Jennison (both a Classical scholar and manager of Bellevue Zoological Gardens in Manchester) perceptively pointed out, a wild animal ejected into the blazing sunshine and awesome din of the arena, would instinctively seek a dark corner at the foot of the podium wall and cower there in fear and bewilderment.[41]

An ingenious solution was devised. Massive posts were inserted into the floor of the arena and between them a sturdy net barrier was strung. This barrier not only helped spectators to view the drama unfolding in the arena safely, but also kept the combatants and animals out of the 'blind zone'. This net formed the first line of defence for the spectators. Behind it there was a broad gangway paved in marble. From here attendants patrolled the gangway to coax reluctant animals back towards the centre of the arena. The arena-wall itself was covered with slabs of polished marble. This served both to add a luxurious decorative element to the monument and to provide an extremely slippery surface to minimise the dangers of an animal climbing out of the arena. Atop the arena-wall there was a substantial bronze balustrade (of which unfortunately no trace now remains), in front of which an elaborate series of horizontally positioned ivory rollers was placed. These rollers overhung the arena-wall at its crest so that any animal that succeeded in scaling the slippery wall would be unable to get a purchase; the rollers simply turned freely on their shafts. Positioned along the front of the arena-wall there was also a series of crow's nests. Archers, stationed in them, provided a last line of defence against the possibility of escape from the arena.

Plate 1.2 Colosseum (Flavian Amphitheatre), Rome: details of the two phases of construction in the subterranean structures of the arena: Domitianic and Severan. Photograph by D.L. Bomgardner.

The arena itself, an ellipse measuring 76.96 × 46.18 m,[42] was covered with fine-grained sand. This material absorbed the blood shed there and prevented the combatants from slipping. In addition it provided a hygienic medium to ensure the cleanliness of the arena. Soiled sand would be removed and fresh sand deposited after each series of spectacles. This was an important factor, particularly for the animals which were trained there in preparation for an upcoming spectacle. Diseases would spread rapidly among captive species that were not at the best of their condition after the long journey from their native habitat. The arena floor was probably made of wooden planks that spanned the two-storey deep substructures beneath it.

The precise date at which these subterranean galleries and machinery were added to the Colosseum is still debated. However, it is certain that they did not form part of the original monument dedicated by Titus in AD 80, but were later additions in the reign of Domitian (AD 81–96). Before each spectacle animals were transferred from long-term storage and breeding menageries (the so-called *Vivarium*, just outside the *Porta Praenestina*) into the underground chambers of the Colosseum. Two underground tunnels (at either end of the minor axis of the monument) (see Figure 1.5: labelled 'H') led from the outside down into these subterranean galleries. Here, on the lower storey of this complex, the animals were kept in a series of thirty-two self-contained iron cages, each enclosed in its own rectangular holding pen (eight in each quadrant). Just before the performance, these cages were hoisted up to the upper level. From here, at the appropriate signal, the animals were released from their cages and driven up inclined ramps and through trap doors into the arena. Similarly stage props and massive wooden mechanical devices (*pegmata*) could also be introduced suddenly into the arena by means of trap door mechanisms and counter-weighted hoists. The cumulative dramatic effect of such manoeuvres, if executed with co-ordinated precision, would have held an audience enthralled.

The Romans loved dramatic reversals and fantastical mechanical devices in their spectacles. For example Orpheus, portrayed by a condemned criminal, instead of charming the wild beasts with his music would be devoured by them. Another spectacle had a stage prop resembling a huge whale that opened its mechanical maw and disgorged dozens of animals into the arena for a wild beast hunt. This fascination with the bizarre, the unusual and the fantastical illustrates the importance of the behind-the-scenes work teams, who laboured unseen at supplying the beasts for the arena as well as manhandling the props and sets into position, and then, with split-second timing, hauling them up and into the arena. That this did not always go according to plan and thus reflected poorly upon the emperor, the patron of each spectacle, can be seen in the fact that the emperor Claudius was known to have forced some of the carpenters and other technicians responsible for the stage props and scenery to fight in the arena as a punishment for the failure of any pieces of apparatus to work effectively during the spectacles for the public.[43]

Plate 1.3 Colosseum (Flavian Amphitheatre), Rome: the façade. Photograph by D.L. Bomgardner.

Gladiators were trained and accommodated in four imperial gladiatorial training schools (or *ludi*): the *Ludus Dacicus, Ludus Gallicus, Ludus Magnus* and the *Ludus Matutinus*. These schools, built in the reign of Domitian (AD 81–96), were situated immediately to the east of the Colosseum. An underground tunnel (see Figure 1.5: labelled 'F') along the eastern branch of the Colosseum's major axis probably provided unseen communication with this complex. Each of these imperial schools specialised in producing a different kind of gladiator: the Dacian and Gallic Schools, were linked with gladiators representing these national fighting styles and armour types. The *Ludus Matutinus* trained wild beast fighters (*venatores*).[44] The *Ludus Magnus* (overall: *c.* 75.4 × 54.4; arena: 63 × 42 m) was apparently the most important and largest of these training academies, where the other major categories of

Plate 1.4 Ludus Magnus, Rome: note the shape of an external rectangle of chambers with an inscribed oval inside for the arena; also the Colosseum looming in the distance.
Photograph by D.L. Bomgardner.

gladiators were prepared. Six months of intensive training was the minimum period required before a gladiator could be classed as a rank amateur (*tiro*).

THE ADMINISTRATION OF THE SPECTACLES

During the late republic an elaborate bureaucratic administration gradually arose to organise and supply all the constituent elements necessary for the spectacles.

During his lifetime, Julius Caesar amassed an extensive network of gladiators and training schools. In particular, he established a famous (his political opponents would have called it an infamous) *ludus* at Capua in which he had 5,000 gladiators.[45] By so doing, Caesar wisely cut out the profits for the middlemen who supplied gladiators and wild beasts to the spectacles of prospective political candidates at Rome. A large part of Caesar's political strategy involved the production of spectacles on the most lavish scale to boost his popularity and to ensure electoral success. He was able to furnish his own needs from his own sources of supply. When Caesar was assassinated (44 BC), his adopted son and heir, Octavian, the future emperor Augustus, inherited this large-scale organisation. The network, centred upon Capua, remained the personal property of the emperors and was inherited by each in turn from his predecessor. Gladiators trained in this premier training school of the empire were given the honorific title of *Iuliani*, until Nero's reign, when they were styled *Neroniani*. This epithet marked them out as the elite of their profession: the emperor's own gladiators. Another imperial establishment was located at Laurentum, just south of the mouth of the Tiber on the Tyrrhenian coast. Here elephants were kept, trained and probably bred in a special menagerie (*vivarium*). The emperors were served by an ever-expanding 'civil service' of highly trained and educated slaves and freedmen. This situation had obvious advantages in that such personnel owed their sole allegiance to the emperor himself. Many of these men became involved in the management of the spectacles. Tiberius Claudius Speculator was just such a man. He was one of the emperor Tiberius's freed slaves (a *libertus Augusti*, an imperial freedman), and was the manager (*procurator Laurento ad elephantos*) of the elephant menagerie at Laurentum known to us from his funeral inscription found in Rome.[46]

A whole range of administrative bureaux administered by this 'private service' of imperial slaves (*familia Caesaris*) and freedmen (*liberti Augusti*) arose to deal with every aspect of the imperial spectacles in the arena. From epigraphical evidence we know of the existence of a Department for Gladiatorial Clothing,[47] a Department for Clothing for Beast Fighters,[48] a Department for Providing Tragic Choruses for Spectacles[49] and a Department for the Decoration and Adornment of the Spectacles.[50] Individual officials are also attested, for example an imperial freedman was the supervisor in charge of the supply of herbivorous animals for the spectacles[51] and an assistant for the supply of wild beasts,[52] probably feline species, to the games is also attested.

The emperor had not only the services of his own household slaves and freedmen, but the Roman army itself was involved in supplying the beasts necessary for the emperor's spectacles in Rome. Inscriptions attest the existence of soldiers seconded to the duty of hunting down and trapping alive wild beasts for the shows in Rome.[53] These troops were probably supplied from the Praetorian Guards and Urban Cohorts, chiefly stationed in Rome. However, two of the Urban Cohorts were stationed abroad, one each at Lyon and Carthage. Both of these sites were key intersections on long-distance trade routes. It is quite possible that these two cohorts were involved in the trans-shipment of wild beasts collected in the hinterlands by the legionary trappers on seconded duty.

This situation changed dramatically under the Flavian emperors. During the dedication of the Flavian Amphitheatre (AD 81) under Titus, 9,000 animals and hundreds of gladiators were exhibited in a hundred days of games on an unparalleled scale. It soon became obvious that an organisational network, based largely upon Capua and the Bay of Naples area, was inadequate for the new demands placed on it by the construction of the Colosseum in Rome. And so Domitian (who reigned AD 81–96), Vespasian's younger son, established a major new supply and training network based on Rome and situated just to the east of the Colosseum. Chief among the new constructions was the *Ludus Magnus*, which was designed to replace the imperial gladiatorial training school in Capua as the main centre for training imperial gladiators. The director of this establishment (*procurator Ludi Magni*) was one of the more senior appointments in the career structure of the equestrian order.[54] From what is known of the holders of this senior position, long service in the military and particularly an appointment with the Praetorian Guards in Rome seem to have been prerequisites for this posting. The *Ludus Magnus* seems, on the basis of these qualifications, to have been run along military lines of discipline and organisation. Three other training schools were also built (as mentioned above): the *Ludus Matutinus*, for the training of wild beast fighters (*venatores*), the *Ludus Gallicus* and the *Ludus Dacicus*, for the training of gladiators belonging to the classes known as Gauls (*Galli*) and Dacians. The directors of these schools were less prestigious and a member of the equestrian order might expect to hold one of these procuratorships in mid-career.[55] One of the procurators of the *Ludus Matutinus*, whose name is not known,[56] probably came from Alexandria in Egypt and had previously held the procuratorship of the imperial gladiatorial training schools in Asia Minor. From the time of the Hellenistic kingdom of the Ptolemies (third century BC), Alexandria was recognised as the main centre in the ancient world for the training, handling and breeding of captive species. The imperial gladiatorial training schools of Italy, probably including the original Capuan establishment, were from the start placed under the direction of an equestrian procurator, who was subordinate to the procurator of the *Ludus Magnus*.[57] By the second century AD, at the latest, a series of imperial gladiatorial schools existed throughout the empire. They were often grouped into regional administrative districts, each region supervised by its own equestrian procurator.[58] This empire-wide network operated in a manner similar to the bush league, minor and major league recruitment schemes in American baseball. Talent spotters would draft promising performers from their local training schools into provincial training barracks and then finally into the imperial schools in Rome.

Thus by the end of the Flavian dynasty (AD 96) in Rome, the essential framework of the imperial administrative network for the organisation and supply of gladiators, wild beasts and their specialised professional huntsmen was already in position. The first steps taken by Julius Caesar to remove the extra expenses incurred by dealing with middlemen in this trade were finally completely rationalised under Domitian. The Roman army took over an unspecified part of the role of live capture of animals for the arena. In addition specialised menageries (*vivaria*) were established for the safe storage, training and probably captive breeding of these species. The imperial service of slaves and freedmen administered the details of supplying and equipping the spectacles. Finally the equestrian order held the senior management positions that administered the various imperial training institutions, such as the procurator of the *Ludus Magnus* in Rome. By these measures, the emperors attempted both to limit their costs by cutting out middle-level suppliers and to retain control of this potentially politically sensitive area in their own hands. The immense popularity that was possible for the giver (*editor*) of a lavish spectacle must be reserved almost solely for the emperor himself. Indeed imperial permission was required for an individual to give such games. No easy opportunity would be given to a potential rival to establish his popularity with the people through the giving of such games.

BUILDING MATERIALS AND CONSTRUCTION TECHNIQUES

Laying-out and building the Colosseum

Although the Colosseum is often described as an ellipse or an oval, in fact it is made up of segments of circles (of different radius and with different centres) joined together smoothly to produce a 'polycentric pseudo-ellipse'. The simplest combination possible is one in which there are four circular segments (see Figure 1.10). Two segments (on the ends of the major axis of the 'ellipse') would have a rather small radius and their centres (actually on the major axis) would be within the arena itself. The other two haunch segments (at the ends of the minor axis of the 'ellipse') would have a much larger radius and their centres would be located along the minor axis. More complex and complicated constructions are theoretically possible in multiples of four centres (eight, twelve, sixteen, etc.) for the vertices of the circular segments needed to construct the perimeter of the monument. However, the constraints of practical necessity usually limited the series to, at the most, twelve centres.[59]

There are two theories regarding the design of the Colosseum.

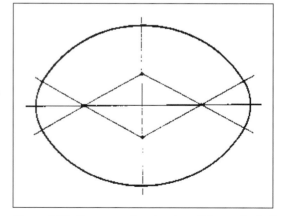

Figure 1.10 Reconstruction drawing of the method of laying out the perimeter of a simple four-centred arena. *Source:* M. Wilson Jones, 'Designing Amphitheatres', *MDAI(R)* 100 (1993), 395, fig. 2. Copyright Mark Wilson Jones.

1. Hallier's reconstruction

On the basis of recent studies undertaken by M. Gilbert Hallier, the Colosseum was laid out according to a simple four-centred polycentric plan. The 'module', or the basic unit of measurement used in its construction, was 26 Roman feet. The constituent elements were the arena, 10 modules long by 6 wide (260 *pedes* × 156 *pedes*, or 76.96 × 46.18 m), the *cavea* ,7 modules wide (182 *pedes* or 53.87 m) and the overall dimensions, 24 modules long by 18 wide (624 *pedes* × 520 *pedes*, or 184.70 × 153.92 m).

This system of using segments of circles to form an elliptical structure had very practical advantages. If the structure had been a true ellipse, the inner wall of the arena would not have been parallel to the outer wall of the façade. Continuous adjustments would have been necessary in the laying-out and construction of the monument to ensure that connecting walls between the inner and outer walls ran true. This difficulty was avoided by the use of polycentric circular segments. In this system the arena-wall, intermediate *ambulacra* and exterior façade walls were segments of circles with a common centre and thus were automatically parallel. In addition any walls that interconnected the inner and outer elements of such a structure were all radii of a common circular segment. These characteristics facilitated economies of design, laying-out and construction.

Surveying and marking out the plan of the structure on the ground would also have been simplified by such a system. First the major and minor axes would be laid out perpendicular to one another. Then the four centres of the circular segments would be laid out on these axes. Next, by attaching the appropriate lengths of rope to one of these centres, wall lines could be marked out in both a radial and annular direction. Thus the entire labyrinthine structure of the Colosseum was based upon a very simple design principle.

2. Wilson Jones's reconstruction

A more recent survey of the design principles involved in the planning and laying-out of amphitheatres has been undertaken by Mark Wilson Jones.[60] Starting from the same basic premises as Hallier, Wilson Jones has extended his enquiry to elucidate both the initial principles involved in the design of the Colosseum and the subtle adjustments that were made on site in order to complete this monument as a viable architectural structure.

Wilson Jones attributes the Colosseum as one of the amphitheatres that follow a scheme based upon Pythagorean triangles and inscribed circles as the basis of their design. Here, the minor axis is divided into three equal lengths: the inner third, i.e., the width of the arena, and the two outer thirds, i.e., the *cavea*, whose width is the same as that of the arena. This scheme produces the well-rounded shapes of amphitheatres.

In detail it involves the construction of a Pythagorean triangle (whose sides are in the ratios 3:4:5) (see Figure 1.11).[61] This initial stage of planning produced a four-centred oval. Perhaps to smooth the trace further, suitable modifications were introduced by the introduction of four additional circular segments, thus making a total of eight circular segments in all (Figure 1.12).

Wilson Jones proposes that a module of 30 Roman ft. was used in the initial planning stages of this monument. The original Pythagorean triangle would be 3 by 4 by 5 modules (90:120:150 Roman ft.). This design would produce an arena of 10 by 6 modules (300 × 180 Roman ft.) and a *cavea* width equal to that of the arena (6 modules or 180 Roman ft.). The overall dimensions would be 22 by 18 modules (660 × 540 Roman ft.), and the radii of the four-centred polycentric trace of the arena would be 7 modules (210 Roman ft.) for the haunches and 2 modules (60 Roman ft.) for the ends; the radii for the façade would be 16 modules (390 Roman ft.) for the haunches and 8 modules (240 Roman ft.) for the ends. However, this was merely the initial stage of design and planning.

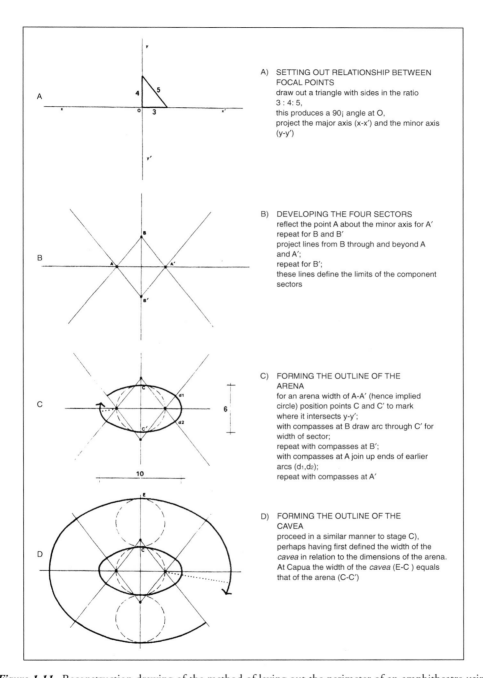

A) SETTING OUT RELATIONSHIP BETWEEN FOCAL POINTS
draw out a triangle with sides in the ratio 3 : 4: 5,
this produces a 90¡ angle at O,
project the major axis (x-x') and the minor axis (y-y')

B) DEVELOPING THE FOUR SECTORS
reflect the point A about the minor axis for A'
repeat for B and B'
project lines from B through and beyond A and A';
repeat for B';
these lines define the limits of the component sectors

C) FORMING THE OUTLINE OF THE ARENA
for an arena width of A-A' (hence implied circle) position points C and C' to mark where it intersects y-y';
with compasses at B draw arc through C' for width of sector;
repeat with compasses at B';
with compasses at A join up ends of earlier arcs (d₁,d₂);
repeat with compasses at A'

D) FORMING THE OUTLINE OF THE CAVEA
proceed in a similar manner to stage C),
perhaps having first defined the width of the *cavea* in relation to the dimensions of the arena.
At Capua the width of the *cavea* (E-C) equals that of the arena (C-C')

Figure 1.11 Reconstruction drawing of the method of laying out the perimeter of an amphitheatre using the Pythagorean-triangle-and-inscribed-circle-scheme.
Source: M. Wilson Jones, 'Designing Amphitheatres', *MDAI(R)* 100 (1993), 404, fig. 13. Copyright Mark Wilson Jones.

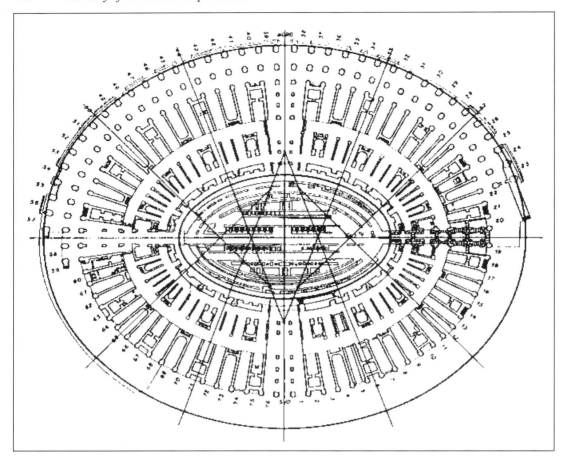

Figure 1.12 Reconstruction drawing of the final system of laying out the trace of the Colosseum.
Source: M. Wilson Jones, 'Designing Amphitheatres', *MDAI(R)* 100 (1993), fig. 22 c. Copyright Mark Wilson Jones.

Probably, in order to 'fine tune' the circumference of the façade of the *cavea* so that its eighty bays would each have an intercolumniation of 20 Roman ft., the arena was compressed to a module of 28 Roman ft.,[62] while the *cavea* itself retained its original width of 180 Roman ft. Finally, this plan was converted to an eight-centred polycentric curve trace (see Figure 1.12) for both the arena and *cavea* façade. Yet another subtle modification occurs in the trace of the arena-wall. The curvature of the end segments is not constant, but increases quite markedly immediately prior to reaching the major axis entrance passageways. This feature may have been intended to make the junction with this passage closer to a right angle (90 degrees).[63] Finally the trace of the arena-wall is not concentric with that of the basement retaining wall below it. This may be due to different schemes for the laying-out of these two regions of the arena, and thus perhaps evidence for different phases of construction.

Comparison of schemes for the design of the Colosseum

Perhaps the most important conclusion to be drawn from the two schemes presented above is that a range of choices is always possible for any modern attempt to reconstruct the, now lost, design processes that governed the planning and actual laying-out of an amphitheatre. The endeavour is not an exact science, but a combination of meticulous architectural surveying and formal analysis, coupled with an intuitive understanding and a thorough grasp of the methods and techniques at the disposal of the Roman engineers and architects of the day. Having said this, Hallier and Wilson Jones are certainly the most competent modern practitioners of this art. Gilbert Hallier, the pioneer in this field of study, brings a certain Classical elegance and a detailed knowledge of Greco-Roman mathematical treatises to his analyses.[64] Wilson Jones, on the other hand, trained as an architect and a resident of Rome, brings a rigorousness and attention to detail that characterises his analytical technique as well as a novel methodology that concentrates on the final state of the façade as a critical determinant in the planning and laying-out of these monuments. Both approaches have advanced this emerging discipline and substantially increased our knowledge of the ways in which ancient architects, engineers and builders designed, laid out and built their structures.

The foundations

The foundations for this monument were staggering. Recent estimates place the amount of earth removed to excavate them at 30,000 tonnes. Enormous amounts of concrete and cut stone were then laid down to stabilise the upper structures. The Italian engineer Giuseppe Cozzo has studied the construction of this monument and revealed that it too followed simple building principles. The entire edifice was built around a network of massive, solid travertine piers to carry its prodigious weight. Seven concentric 'elliptical' rings with eighty piers in each ring formed the skeleton upon which everything else was built. The piers rose into the air and suspended from them, like some fantastical three-dimensional spider's web in concrete, the floors, vaulted tunnels and annular passageways took shape.

In order to complete the monument, begun only in AD 75, in time for its dedication in AD 80 under Titus, a radical construction strategy was adopted. The exterior façade and the next two annular walls (going towards the interior of the monument) were built up to the height of the second storey (that is, two arcades high). Only the exterior façade itself was completed with the addition of a third storey of arcades. The four interior 'elliptical' rings of piers were built to their complete height. However, only the uppermost vaulting, at the level of the seating of the *cavea*, was constructed upon these four rings of piers. Thus the podium, *ima cavea* and *media cavea* were built before the corridors, stairways and *ambulacra* beneath them. As the inscription regarding seating allocations for the Arval Brethren (AD 80/81) indicates, the uppermost seating in this proto-*cavea* of the Colosseum was constructed in wood (the so-called *summum maenianum in ligneis*). This wooden seating was apparently in the region of the later *summa cavea*.[65] The rationale behind this scheme was to provide a covered *chantier*, under which workmen could get on with the enormous task of construction year-round in all weather.

Building materials and construction techniques

The building materials used in the Colosseum were well-known local products with a long history of use. Some 100,000 cubic metres of travertine blocks, quarried at Tivoli in the Sabine hills east of Rome, were used in the major load-bearing parts of the structure (the network of seven concentric 'elliptical' rings of piers) and in those areas where decorative carved stonework was required (for example, the façade). Marbles from various quarries were used mainly as thin facing slabs to adorn the monument (for example, the facing of the arena-wall), but large blocks of marble were also used for the seating (*gradus*) of the podium, *ima* and *media cavea* as well as for the columns of the crowning colonnade. Brick was used in the construction of arches for concrete vaulting (to make sloping concrete vaulting for stairways) and for building short stretches of walling between travertine piers (to make radial passageways). Concrete was used in conjunction with brick arches to provide the vaulting that formed the basis of the seating areas and the internal stairways. It has been pointed out that concrete must be laid down in reasonably temperate conditions (above 10 degrees Celsius) and that the Romans were well aware of this fact.[66] Some 300 tonnes of iron were used in the crampons which bound the blocks of travertine firmly together into their courses. Much of the damage to the Colosseum during the Middle Ages, when the arts of metallurgy were in abeyance, was caused by scavengers prising apart the stone fabric of the monument in search of the smelted iron within its walls.

The highly symmetrical nature of this structure may have helped in the actual construction process. It is suggested that work gangs may have been trained in the specialised construction of a particular feature of the monument, for example in the construction of one of the types of stairways used beneath the seating. Specialisation would bring the inherent advantages of expertise and speed of construction. Furthermore, the large numbers of virtually identical construction processes in this monument would have made this approach logical. The labour force used in the construction of the Colosseum consisted in part at least of the Jewish prisoners of war brought back to Rome following the brutal suppression of the Jewish revolt by Titus in AD 70.

The phases of construction

As mentioned above, by the time of its dedication under the emperor Titus in AD 80, the Colosseum had three storeys of external arcades, a podium, *ima cavea, media cavea* and a *summum maenianum in ligneis*. It is probable that Titus added the third storey of arcades to the façade. Vespasian had died in AD 79 without seeing the completion of more than the first two storeys of the amphitheatre's façade. It was left to Domitian (AD 81–96), the younger son, to complete the monument in virtually its final form. He added the towering attic storey to the façade. Here tall Corinthian applied pilasters framed bays which alternately contained a small square window or a large bronze shield. The holes and supporting brackets for the masts that supported the awning (*velarium*) were located in this part of the façade. It is estimated that the masts themselves would have towered far above the crown of the attic itself. It is also probable that the subterranean galleries, chambers, hoists and mechanisms beneath the arena floor were added at this time. Domitian's other architectural schemes, such as the new imperial residence on the Palatine, the so-called *Domus Transitoria*, reveal the broad sweep of his architectural vision. The strikingly innovative nature of the subterranean additions to the Colosseum would seem to be more in keeping with Domitian's other projects rather than the more conservative, mainstream contributions of his father and elder brother to Rome. Recent research has confirmed this picture while eliciting a bewildering array of further alterations and additions in this region of the substructures, the most important later phase being the transition from the massive cut-stone (*opus quadratum*) piers with wooden frameworks of the Domitianic era to the brickwork (*opus latericium*) substructures of the Severan era (see Plate 1.2 above).[67]

There is a long history of the reconstructions and rebuildings of the Colosseum in its later years.[68] Lightning is known to have struck it at least twice in antiquity necessitating rebuilding in the uppermost wooden parts which were apparently burnt by this action. The fate of the monument in the Middle Ages was to serve first as a quarry for both stone and mainly for the metal crampons used to fasten blocks of stone together. Then too the marble was hauled out either for reuse elsewhere or else to be burnt for quicklime. Finally the skeleton was fortified as a stronghold for the Annibaldi and the Frangipani in the internecine struggles of medieval Rome. However, its ultimate preservation was due to the timely intervention of Pope Benedict XIV (1740–58). He ordered it partially rebuilt and, perhaps most importantly, its structure to be supported and consolidated. It was made a memorial to the Christian martyrs killed in Rome during the persecutions of the first three centuries AD.

Recently much work has been done to analyse and catalogue the later interventions in the fabric of the Colosseum under the auspices of Dr Moccheggiani Carpano, in whose official care this monument resides.[69] Traffic vibration, over the past decades, has become an increasing problem threatening parts of the remaining structure. Dr Moccheggiani Carpano has led the recent efforts of conservation of its structure and a re-evaluation of the significance of the Colosseum. Under his direction, a comprehensive study and publication of the monument is under way.

CONCLUSION

The Colosseum was the most impressive monument of its genre ever constructed: the largest amphitheatre the Roman world had ever seen, and a fitting monument for the capital of the Mediterranean world. Yet the Colosseum was not the haunt of howling mobs of the unemployed urban masses of Rome drinking in debauchery and lewdness with their eyes and ears as they watched the spectacles in the arena below them. This view is based largely upon hostile Christian testimony and rhetoric. The principal charge levelled against all spectacles was that they were pagan, idolatrous and demonic rituals, part of the old religion of the Roman state, and a very important part, too.

The historian's task is to try to assess the evidence, to present it clearly without bias and then to attempt to understand its significance in terms of contemporary values. It would have been unfair to the Romans and their culture to adopt a politically correct posture: prejudging and condemning by our own values, not their own.

This monument had a multitude of functions and social values attached to it. 'Being seen' was almost as important as 'seeing' the spectacles. The predominant amount of seating space devoted to the upper and middle classes of Roman society segregated rigidly by class status in this structure leads to the following conclusions.

First, the Colosseum was a conservative monument extolling the traditional male virtues of courage (*virtus*), discipline (*disciplina*) and skill at arms (*ars militaris*). Vespasian, like Augustus before him, was attempting to re-educate the Roman citizenry and to re-direct and re-channel the potentially destructive energies unleashed in the arena. Vespasian was trying to re-instil into the ruling classes of Rome the traditional military virtues and traditions which had made Rome triumphant over all the neighbouring lands of the Mediterranean. The dissolution and dissipation of these classes during the late republic had both personally and collectively nearly brought Rome to the brink of collapse. Vespasian was a soldier, a no-nonsense, hard-headed pragmatist sprung from the rich soil of sturdy, hardworking Italian peasant stock. His solutions to problems were usually straightforward and effective, for example his successful re-organisation of the economy after the bankruptcy of Nero's reign. The vivid lessons of supremely professional military skill, courage and discipline even to the death represented in the gladiatorial contests of the Colosseum would have been approved by such an emperor. In addition, the long tradition of hunting as 'warfare without the armour' and as being worthy of adoption by the ruling classes for the lessons it could teach about courage, skill, endurance and co-operative manoeuvres would also not have been lost on such an emperor. The gladiators and hunters of the arenas, often drawn from the underclasses of society, could in the arena become legends in their own lifetimes, adored by a mass audience of fans. The sheer dramatic power of a life-and-death contest, executed with consummate skill and courage, has few comparable experiences in life. The Colosseum was not a monument to depravity and vice; it was a testimony to the power and stability of the social order of Roman society and the cardinal position of traditional military virtues within that society.

Chapter Two

The origins and early development of the amphitheatre

THE ORIGINS OF THE GLADIATORIAL COMBATS

The origins of the gladiatorial combat (*munus gladiatorum*) may never be discovered. At present the best working hypothesis for the origins of these spectacles assumes that the Etruscan civilisation adopted this custom from the Samnites of southern Italy, Campania and Lucania.[1] The Etruscans then passed it on to the Romans during the period of the Etruscan kings (sixth century BC). Our first historical references to this practice among the Romans come from the difficult times at the beginning of the First Punic War (264–241 BC).

In 264 BC at the public funeral of Decimus Brutus Pera in the *Forum Boarium* (the cattle market of Rome), his two sons staged a spectacle in which three pairs of gladiators fought simultaneously.[2] Human sacrifices at the funeral of an important man were nothing new. During the funeral of Patroclus (a popular artistic motif among Etruscan tomb paintings), Homer's *Iliad* depicts the sacrifice of Trojan prisoners to the fallen hero's shade. The new element was the introduction of an armed combat ending in the deaths of the warriors.[3] The blood of the victims was believed to enliven and sustain the shades of the departed, who without such sustenance would wander insubstantially through the Underworld without strength or memory.[4] Polybius, the third century BC Greek historian, who chronicled the rise of Rome to dominance in the Mediterranean world, describes in vivid detail the funeral rites for a prominent Roman aristocratic head of family (*paterfamilias*).[5] A procession of mourners and family members solemnly processed to the Forum. Among the procession, individuals chosen for their striking similarity (in terms of physical attributes: body type, height, age, etc.) to prominent male ancestors of the family (*gens*) wore death masks of these illustrious progenitors. At the obsequies themselves, the glorious achievements of these, the most famous members of the family, were remembered through a series of set-piece speeches. Polybius adds that it was as if they themselves were present in the persons of the look-alikes. Then the newly deceased's achievements were chronicled and added to those of his forebears. Thus the continuity of the family and its sense of tradition and cumulative glory were emphasised above all else. Grief was not uppermost in the ceremonies, but rather communal pride in the family and its role in shaping the glorious destiny of the nation (*patria*). Polybius well understood the effect of these powerful forces upon the history of Rome. Thus individuals and their purely personal ambitions were effectively absorbed into the larger units of the family (*gens*) and the state (*patria*).

The introduction of armed combat to the death into such funeral rites must be seen in this light. A commander's military prowess and success in battle conveyed glory to the individual, but also importantly to the family and the nation. An armed duel to the death would mirror the courage (*virtus*), skill (*ars*) and success (*fortuna*) of the departed commander. In addition, such a practice could be seen, in one sense, as a compression into a single symbolic act of both the funeral games in honour of the illustrious dead (the 'agonistic' element) and the blood sacrifices (the 'sacrificial' element) that attended the funeral itself. Furthermore, the associations of human sacrifices with the 'heroic' past of the Homeric epics would also, in one sense, elevate the recently deceased to the glorious status of a 'hero'. Initially, these *munera gladiatorum* would have been intended to enhance the prestige and glory of the dead man as part of his family's and nation's glorious tradition. The intention to provide an entertainment for those attending the funeral would surely have seemed, at best, secondary, and at worst, repulsive, to the family. Armed combat to the death would have been a sobering reminder of the transitory nature of human existence. Nevertheless, these combats did make a profound impact upon the public who attended such funerals. It should be noted that only the most eminent, male members of the most important Roman families would have been given such a signal honour.

Electoral bribery (*ambitus*)

During the later republic, intense competition among eminent Roman families for a limited number of high political positions eventually led to the degeneration of these original funeral rites into flagrant bribes for political support. The intense popular interest in these funeral spectacles led at first gradually to an increase, and finally to a rapid inflation, in the number of pairs of gladiators exhibited. There had always been a certain amount of competition among the pre-eminent families of Rome for high office, but it reached a peak of feeding frenzy during the late republic. In addition to the glory and honour attached to such magistracies, Rome's extensive overseas conquests meant that huge private fortunes could also be amassed through election to high political office. The Senate tried to regulate these practices by potential candidates through a series of laws concerning electoral bribery (*ambitus*). In 63 BC Cicero introduced a bill to prevent prospective electoral candidates from exhibiting gladiatorial spectacles in the two years preceding their attempt to win election to office.[6] Nevertheless the problem remained insoluble, by the very nature of Roman society, and the legal safeguards were somehow contravened: 'where there's a will, there's a way'.[7] Too much was at stake: the rewards outweighed the risks.

Private enterprise initiatives

Entrepreneurs arose who were eager to supply the ever-increasing demand for highly trained professionals to fight as gladiators. Campania, in particular, had a certain *cachet* in this regard and the city of Capua became the unrivalled centre of a regional network of gladiatorial training schools and barracks. It was from such an institution in Capua owned by such an entrepreneur, one Cnaius Lentulus Batiatus, that the slave revolt led by the slave gladiator Spartacus erupted (73–71 BC). Julius Caesar himself, in 49 BC, established his own training school here; it could accommodate 5,000 gladiators (*secutores*).[8]

Gladiators were recruited from the slave populations of the ever-expanding Roman empire. The huge sums of money that the best gladiators commanded were paid to their owners/trainers (*lanistae*) by Roman citizens hopeful of recouping such enormous sums when they successfully stood for public election.

Julius Caesar and the origins of the imperial gladiatorial training barracks

Julius Caesar, in particular, was remarkably successful at gauging the public's tastes and preferences in these matters. The Roman ruling classes were sensitive to charges of acting in a way that was not according to tradition (*mores maiorum*). Since their inception, the *munera gladiatorum* had always accompanied the public funeral of an eminent nobleman, albeit on an ever-increasing scale. Caesar was the first to contravene this unwritten rule. In 52 BC, on the death of his daughter Julia, he promised a magnificent series of spectacles (*munus*) and a public feast (*epulum*) to honour her memory.[9] In 46 BC, at the time of his quadruple triumph in Rome, Caesar staged the most lavish spectacles that had ever been seen in the city. He was a master showman with an unfailing intuition of what would be a crowd pleaser. His rather luckless political opponent, Pompey the Great, was at times unsuccessful in this respect. Pompey ended his triumphal games (55 BC) in the Circus Maximus at Rome with an exhibition of elephants. These elephants immediately captured the hearts of the crowd with their turns and tricks that imitated human activities. However, the spectacle ended with the elephants being hunted down in the arena by native tribesmen using javelins. Not only did some of the elephants stampede causing blind panic among the spectators nearest them, but the action, far from eliciting the desired effect, rebounded badly upon Pompey. The crowd had become so taken with the near human qualities of these gentle giants that they were repelled by the brutality of their slaughter.[10] This is a rare example of a sense of fellow-feeling for creatures of the animal kingdom.

This era witnessed the transition of these spectacles from a religious rite for the illustrious dead to a popular entertainment of exploitation: votes being given to the politicians who could make good on the promises of bigger and better spectacles. Nobody did it better than Caesar. His massed spectacles of 46 BC blew the competition away both for their sheer size and for his incomparable showmanship.

THE ORIGINS AND EARLY DEVELOPMENT OF THE *VENATIONES*[11]

The origins of the *venationes* consist of two separate strands: one, an indigenous Italic tradition of ancient religious rituals and ceremonies, the other, an import from the former Punic domains of North Africa.

Animals were used as sacrificial victims in connection with religious festivals at Rome from a very early date. However, certain festivals, in particular the *Cerealia*, the *Floralia* and the *ludi Taurei*, involved their use in a more dramatic role as part of a public spectacle. In the *Cerealia* animals, including hares and roe deer, were hunted before spectators as a part of the religious pageant. During the *Floralia*, foxes were released into the Circus with burning bundles of straw attached to them. Before the immolation of the bulls in the *ludi Taurei*, it has been suggested that they were first hunted as part of a spectacle. The institution of these games has been seen by some as due to the impact of Greek religious influences on Roman society in the later third/early second century BC. It is possible that such influences might also have contributed to the origins of the spectacles known as the *venationes*.[12] It is quite clear that the Hellenistic monarchies of the Middle East, particularly the Seleucid kings of Syria and the Ptolemaic kingdom of Egypt, used animals as a regular feature of their processions and religious festivals. Indeed the most impressive menagerie in the Mediterranean world was to be found in Alexandria dating from the time of Ptolemy II (283–246 BC).[13]

After the defeat of the Carthaginians in the First (264–246 BC) and Second (218–202 BC) Punic Wars, the Romans began to import wild animals from the former Punic domains and from other native allied kingdoms of North Africa. The first elephants, captured in Sicily, to appear in Rome in the Circus were part of triumphal games (252 BC). They formed part of a spectacle in their own right and were not killed.[14] Similarly ostriches made their first appearance in the Circus at Rome in about 197 BC.[15] The first recorded instance of the hunting of wild animals (*venatio*) in the Circus as part of votive games (*ludi votivi*) occurred in 186 BC.[16] Marcus Fulvius Nobilior, following his victories in Greece, celebrated games there which he had vowed in return for victory. As part of the fulfilment of that vow, Fulvius sponsored a staged hunt of lions and leopards.[17] This is our first recorded instance of such a *venatio* where animals were actually killed. It is sometimes difficult to distinguish between these two types of *venationes*, the exhibition-type and the hunting-type, since the Romans referred to both as simply a *venatio*. Soon after contacts were established with Egypt, the hippopotamus, crocodile and giraffe were exhibited at Rome.[18]

In addition to the import of wild animals from North Africa it has been suggested that the idea of using wild beasts as part of a staged hunting spectacle may have been imported alongside the animals from North Africa. This idea has much to commend it on circumstantial evidence, but there is no hard proof yet that its origins lay in this part of the world.[19]

The earliest attested exhibitions of animals (*venationes*) at Rome, as seen above, were usually either in conjunction with the celebration of a triumph (as part of the procession or the games which usually accompanied the other festivities) or as part of *ludi votivi* in fulfilment of a particular vow usually associated with a specific victory in war. At this early stage of development, it was almost as likely that the animals would merely be exhibited in a menagerie (particularly if they were a new species seen for the first time) as that they would be killed in a hunting display. By the end of the third century BC, following the final defeat of Hannibal and Carthage in the Second Punic War, the supply of wild animals from North Africa to Rome began to show a vast increase. In particular, the big cats (*Africanae*) proved extremely popular and were much sought after.

By 169 BC the first recorded *venatio* (sixty-three *Africanae*, forty bears and forty elephants) as part of the regularly scheduled *ludi circenses* given by the annually elected curule aediles took place.[20] This marks a new stage in the development of *venationes* in that they now appear integrated into the fabric of spectacles of the Roman religious calendar, unlike the irregular triumphal games and *ludi votivi*, which were *ad hoc* performances.

The first reference to non-Roman condemned criminals being thrown to the beasts for execution (*damnatio ad bestias*) at Rome took place in 146 BC.[21] Following the celebration of his triumphal games for his victory over Carthage, Scipio Aemilianus put to death the foreign auxiliary deserters from his army by throwing them to wild beasts (*feris bestiis*), presumably in the Circus. Aemilianus's adoptive father, L. Aemilius Paulus, following his victory over Perseus in the Macedonian wars, had in like manner executed foreign troops who had deserted from his army. Elephants trampled the hapless soldiers under foot, presumably as part of the triumphal games held at Amphipolis in 167 BC.[22]

The earliest recorded instance of a *venatio* in which multiple hunting displays with lions took place simultaneously (probably in the Circus) is recorded for the period about 100 BC.[23] Similarly the earliest recorded example of the import of specialised natives to hunt the species with which they had particular expertise took place in 93 BC.[24] King Bocchus of Mauretania sent native spearmen (*iaculatores*) to assist at the games given by Sulla. They probably hunted large felines in the Circus.

It is here necessary to digress upon the place of hunting in the ancient world, especially in Greco-Roman society. As in many other cultures, hunting was the activity, *par excellence*, of the ruling classes of the ancient world, the aristocracy. It was thought that hunting developed essential skills for warfare as well as encouraging the formation of character, endurance and approved psychological attitudes. Xenophon called it 'the image of war'. Skill, endurance, courage, enjoyment of vigorous physical activity and the love of the countryside were all important elements in the hunting ethos. It was an excellent opportunity for a nobleman or king to display his prowess at the manly pursuits of hunting and his courage in the face of potential physical danger. It is completely appropriate that, in keeping with the essentially aristocratic spirit of *munera*, *venationes* should have eventually come to be combined with them.

THE ORIGINS OF THE AMPHITHEATRE

Curio's revolving double theatre/amphitheatre

In his encyclopaedic compendium of knowledge about the known world, the *Historia Naturalis*, Pliny the Elder discussed the origins of the architectural form known as the amphitheatre.[25] According to Pliny, the amphitheatre was born fully developed, like Athene sprung from the head of Zeus, during the spectacles given by C. Scribonius Curio in 52 BC.[26] Curio's father, an

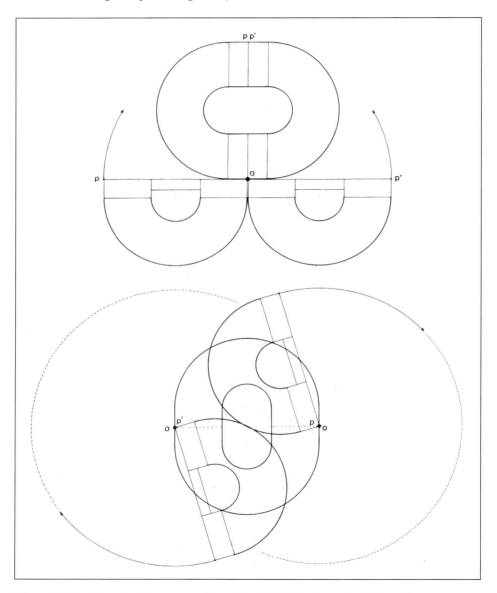

Figure 2.1 Two hypothetical reconstructions of Curio's 'double theatre/amphitheatre'.
Source: Golvin, Planche IV. Copyright J.-Cl. Golvin.

illustrious statesman (consul in 76 BC) and general, had died in 53 BC and in his own will had laid the charge upon his son of giving a magnificent funeral spectacle in his honour. It has been suggested that Julius Caesar helped defray the expenses for these games, thus winning Curio, a former political opponent, but not a wealthy man, over to his side. Curio was to prove of use to Caesar on many occasions.

The culmination of these spectacles was an elaborate and ingenious mechanical construction. Two full-scale wooden theatres were constructed back to back. Entertainments appropriate to the theatre (mimes, pantomimes, comedies, tragedies) took place in them on the first day (*ludi scaenici*). The next day, however, while spectators were still seated in them, the twin theatres began to rotate upon two massive pivots so that at the end of their rotation they had joined together orchestra to orchestra to form an 'amphitheatre' (see Figure 2.1). Gladiatorial combats (*munera gladiatorum*) then took place in this new structure. On the final day athletic competitions (*certamina athletarum*) were held on the joined stages of the new 'amphitheatre'. Finally the planking for the stages was removed and the winners of the previous day's gladiatorial combats fought again in the arena thus created. It is recorded that the monument was manoeuvred back and forth between its two configurations several times until the strains upon the mechanism proved too great and it was left probably in the amphitheatre position for the rest of its relatively short lifetime.

It is impossible for this account to be the true origin of the amphitheatre for such monuments had already existed in stone for over a generation in Campania. Doubtless the event described took place; Cicero also refers to it in one of his letters.[27] But Pliny's interpretation leaves much to be desired. It is more probable that the spectacles given by Curio were intended to elicit a response from the spectators of amusement and delighted wonder. The amusement would come from the intentional pun of the construction of an 'amphitheatre' from 'two theatres'. The word 'amphitheatre' means a 'theatre all around'. The wonder would come from the delight of the crowds as they witnessed 'at first hand' the mechanical cleverness of this huge mechanical toy: a double theatre that could rotate upon pivots to form an enclosed structure while the audience remained in their seats. What is a distinct possibility is that this was the birth of the architectural term 'amphitheatre' (*amphitheatrum*). Previously, such structures were called either *amphitheatra* or *spectacula* as at Pompeii, the earliest dated example of an amphitheatre.[28] The main point of the building seems to have been to provide the spectators with yet another novelty never before seen and the thrill of experiencing a seemingly impossible engineering feat take place under their very feet. Evidently Curio did not have the contacts and resources to make a sensational impact in any other way, for example, by exhibiting never-before-seen animals. It is also significant that by this time the amphitheatre is regarded in Rome itself as an appropriate venue for gladiatorial combats, which previously had only ever been seen in the forum or a circus at Rome.[29]

As shown above, Pliny was mistaken about the origins of the amphitheatre. In Campania amphitheatres had already existed for at least a generation: probably from the end of the second century BC and certainly from 70–65 BC, the secure date for the construction of the amphitheatre at Pompeii.

An alternative theory from Classical/Hellenistic architectural antecedents

During the on-going American excavations at Corinth, recently an intriguing structure was uncovered in the area near the Roman forum of the city.[30] In Classical times this area accommodated the stadium used in the running events during the civic athletic festivals, an important part of the religious observance of the city. Near it and to the south-east there was a structure dubbed the 'Platform for Physical-Contact Sports' by the excavators. Here, probably in the late fifth or early fourth century BC, an oval arena was laid out (*c.* 18.0 × 16.5 m). Then it was dug into the soft bedrock of a sloping hillside and surrounded by a porous limestone kerb and a cobbled 'walkway'. At a later date (the third quarter of the third century BC has been suggested) a water channel and three water basins were added to the inner edge of this walkway. A series of post-holes extending from the periphery of the walkway for a distance of some 15m over the surface of the racecourse itself has been interpreted by the excavators as foundations for wooden bleachers (in Greek *ikria*) from which spectators could watch the contact sports events (boxing, wrestling and the pankration, otherwise known as all-in wrestling) – always very popular – in

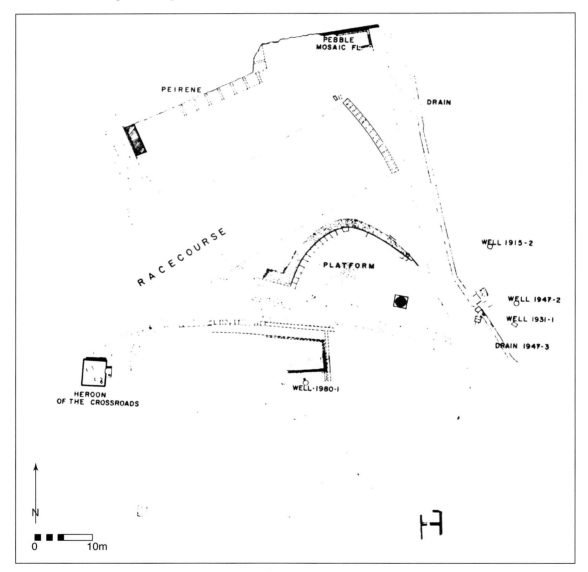

Figure 2.2 Platform for physical-contact sport in the area of the later Roman forum, Corinth
Source: C.K. Williams III et al., 'Corinth: 1980 Excvs.', in *Hesperia* 50/1 (1981), 1–21, fig. 2. Copyright C.K. Williams III, et al., Corinth Excvs. reports.

some comfort and with an improved view. These bleachers extended over nearly three-quarters of the circumference of the arena, but did not apparently rest upon the hillside to the south-east. It was common practice at Greek athletic competitions for conveniently situated hillsides to be used by spectators who either stood or sat directly upon the ground.[31] Thus it is likely that this hillside was used by the spectators too, so that the seating would have effectively been continuous all around the arena.

This monument both in its form (a roughly oval arena surrounded on all sides by seating) and in its function (a venue specifically designed to accommodate a 'spectacle' and its viewers) is an important antecedent in the architectural traditions of Classical and Hellenistic Greece that led to the development of the amphitheatre in Italy itself. It is indeed significant that the probable centre for the origins of the amphitheatre in Italy, as will be seen, was in Campania around the fringes of the Bay of Naples. This area was saturated in Greek culture and contacts.[32] It formed an important part of the Greek colonisation of southern Italy or Magna Graecia as it was known.

THE EARLY CAMPANIAN TRADITION OF PERMANENT AMPHITHEATRES

Any discussion of the earliest amphitheatres must, at present, remain tentative in its conclusions. For there are a series of problems associated with this aspect of the study of amphitheatres. First there is no commonly agreed list of the earliest representatives of this monument. Nor is there likely to be such in the near future. The second problem concerns the state of preservation of such monuments. Since they are the oldest examples, they have suffered more than many the depredations of the years and are, in general, very poorly preserved. Another problem is the lack of general interest in these earliest arenas. In general they do not represent the grandest examples, usually later in date, and thus have been largely overlooked for excavation. Indeed some are probably now irrecoverable, except by large-scale, deep excavations of later, larger amphitheatres where an earlier precursor has either been amalgamated into the fabric of the larger structure',[33] or else completely levelled and built over by the later amphitheatre.[34] Without a detailed architectural study, in the first instance, and at least stratigraphic sondages, in the latter, there can be little hope of unravelling the intricacies of such structures. It may well be that many temporary or even semi-permanent structures of wood from the second century BC remain to be discovered. It remains to present the results of our current state of knowledge about the earliest surviving examples of amphitheatres.

The Pompeian amphitheatre (see Plate 2.1) is unique in this class. It is a well-preserved, well-published monument that can be assigned a secure date shortly after 70 BC. It must be the benchmark by which all other early monuments are judged as to whether they should be included in this list of early arenas.

Pompeii

Pompeii and nearby Herculaneum are among the best-studied archaeological sites in the Mediterranean world. Their remarkable fate, destroyed and entombed in volcanic ash or mud in a single day and night in AD 79, by the violence of the eruption of nearby Mount Vesuvius, has meant that they became a time capsule of the Flavian era in southern Italy. On-going excavations since the late eighteenth century have uncovered their history in unique detail, including touching vignettes of domestic life, such as the carbonised remains of the last meal prepared just before the eruption occurred. The excavators have even managed to recover plaster casts of the bodies of the ill-fated inhabitants who died on that terrible day.

The truly remarkable degree of preservation of their ruins has meant that unprecedented details about construction techniques, building materials, inscriptions, graffiti on walls, painted wall

Plate 2.1 Overview of the Pompeii amphitheatre with Mount Vesuvius in the background.
Photograph by D.L. Bomgardner.

frescoes and details of interior decor and decoration have come to light during the excavations.
During the early nineteenth century these discoveries were as influential upon the decorative
tastes of Europe as the discoveries of King Tutankhamen's tomb and regalia in the Valley of the
Kings were to be upon the early twentieth century.

The amphitheatre at Pompeii is unique among early arenas. It has been preserved and frozen in
time at a well-defined date (24 August AD 79) and, by means of its inscriptions, which are still *in
situ*, can be assigned a date for its initial construction in about 70 BC (soon after the foundation
of the Sullan veteran colony here)[35] (see Plate 2.2).

The Social War (91–88 BC) was a bitter struggle fought against Rome by its former Italian allies
in central and southern Italy for the prize of equality of social status and opportunity with Roman
citizens. Pompeii, with its strong fortifications, was a centre of resistance against Rome in
Campania. The city finally fell to L. Cornelius Sulla Felix, one of Rome's ablest generals, following
a short siege. Sulla later marched upon Rome itself and had himself made dictator. As part of his
reorganisation of the Roman empire, he confiscated much land, both from powerful political
opponents, whom he had proscribed and killed, and from towns which had opposed Rome
(during the Social War) or himself (in the ensuing civil war in Italy). Large estates were sold to his
chief political supporters at knock-down prices and the confiscated municipal lands were used as
the basis for the allocation of land to retired Roman legionary veterans, who had served Sulla
faithfully. Such veteran colonies served the double purpose of both rewarding Sulla's veterans and
providing tightly-organised pockets of loyal, armed supporters in potentially hostile regions of the
Italian mainland. Just such a veteran colony was established at Pompeii. Estimates of its size range
from 2,000 to 5,000 soldiers,[36] who were officially installed as the new masters of the city,
henceforth known as the *colonia Cornelia Veneria Pompeianorum*. The local Oscans (otherwise

known as Samnites) lost control of their own affairs and the best of their lands to the hated new-comers.

In this tense political situation lies the background to the construction of the amphitheatre at Pompeii. Both Porcius and Valgus, the donors of the amphitheatre, had been rewarded handsomely for their loyalty to Sulla. They had both probably bought large estates in this region of Campania for a pittance. Porcius had probably arrived in Campania before the new colony's foundation. He may be the same Marcus Porcius whose name is found embossed on the countless wine amphorae exca-

Plate 2.2 The dedicatory inscription of the Pompeii amphitheatre. Photograph by D.L. Bomgardner.

vated in the corridor that stretches from Narbonne to Bordeaux which are contemporary with this era.[37] If so, his Campanian vineyards produced vintages for the lucrative provincial export market in the Bordeaux region. Valgus probably arrived with the new colonists, for he originally came from the Samnite district of Hirpinia, where he owned vast estates. He was the wealthy and powerful protector (*patronus municipii*) of the city of Aeclanum immediately after the Social War[38] and held the chief magistracy with censorial powers (*duovir quinquennalis*) in an uniden-tified municipium near Abellinum.[39] Like Porcius, Valgus acquired extensive tracts of land in Campania and in southern Latium near Casinum. With such a similar political pedigree and history, it is not surprising that we find Porcius and Valgus teaming up as two of the most important political leaders of the new Roman veteran colony at Pompeii.

Probably in the mid-seventies BC Porcius and Valgus were first elected as chief magistrates (*duoviri*) for the colony. At this time they had the second of Pompeii's stone theatres, the so-called *theatrum tectum*, or Odeon, built (probably underwriting the cost partly from their own pockets). The same pair paid for the construction of a new stone amphitheatre during their tenure of the town's chief magistracy, the duovirate with censorial powers (*duoviri quinquennales* in *c.* 70 BC).[40] As censors, Porcius and Valgus had the authority to revise the citizen rolls of Pompeii as well as the roll of the membership of the local town council, the *ordo decurionum*. This was a powerful political opportunity to neutralise opponents and to benefit supporters. At this early stage of the Pompeian colony, there is little evidence of efforts to conciliate the local population; instead all power in the community appears to have been in the hands of the Roman newcomers.

This new stone amphitheatre (referred to in the dedicatory inscription by the term *spectacula*[41]) was built on land owned by Porcius and Valgus in the south-eastern corner of the city. Both the monument and the land were given *to the colonists* in perpetuity. The dedicatory inscription makes it quite clear that the amphitheatre was built primarily for the use and enjoyment of these new colonists. Such benefactions to the local community during one's term of office were a common practice; indeed, in some communities, it was a legal obligation.[42] Often it took the form of the gift of a series of gladiatorial spectacles,[43] but sometimes a more lasting architectural addition to the town's public monuments and amenities was funded instead. Valgus and Porcius combined both these functions in a single benefaction.

Pompeii had witnessed gladiatorial spectacles for many years before this. But they had taken place in the town's forum – an elongated rectangular public market square surrounded by monumental porticoes probably, as at Rome above the *tabernae* of the *Forum Romanum*, surmounted by balconies (*maeniana*).[44] Vitruvius states that it was customary for gladiatorial combats to be staged in the municipal *fora* of Italy.[45] The owners of such balcony seating used it to enhance their prestige and status through the gift of seats to individuals or else to make a profit by letting out the seats during the spectacles. Thus it was not necessary to have an amphitheatre in order to have gladiatorial spectacles.

Pompeii had done without an amphitheatre for many years. Why build such an expensive monument at this time? The most obvious answer seems to be two-fold. Other important cities in Campania (the fertile plain bordering the Bay of Naples), such as Puteoli[46] and Cumae,[47] and at Paestum[48] in Lucania, the region bordering Campania to the south, had either already built an amphitheatre or were soon to do so. Thus in order to be seen to be 'keeping up with the Joneses' in municipal terms, Pompeii needed to have the newest prestige monument, an amphitheatre. Furthermore, on the basis of the text of the dedicatory inscription quoted above, the new colonists seem to have associated a new amphitheatre in their own minds with their own identity as Roman citizens. A recent study has attempted to demonstrate a link between Roman veteran colonies (of the Sullan, Augustan and triumviral eras) and the inception of the widespread construction of stone amphitheatres in Campania.[49] It was a monument built by, and intended mainly for, the enjoyment of the Roman citizens of the new colony. Like the Colosseum in Rome, discussed in Chapter 1, the amphitheatre at Pompeii was intended as a place to go to see and be seen, a place of visible social status and rigid social hierarchies. The best seats, nearest the arena, were undoubtedly reserved for the most important of the Roman citizens of the new colony: the chief magistrates, local town councillors (*decuriones*), their sons (*praetextati*), honorary members of the local senate (*patroni*) as well as important members of local and imperial priesthoods, all occupied the podium. The rest of the Roman colonists would have probably occupied the *ima cavea*, being *de facto* of superior status to the locals through their Roman citizenship. The *media cavea* was probably reserved for seating for the newly enfranchised Oscans of Pompeii, who were now nominally Roman citizens too, although probably assigned to a different voting tribe from the colonists.[50] The rest of the seating would have served for the remainder of the population in the higher seats, farther away from the arena. Thus, the amphitheatre and its seating arrangements would be a constant reminder of the new social order and the dominance of the new colonists vis-à-vis the local Oscans. In addition, the cultural milieu of the amphitheatre would suit the tastes of recently demobbed veteran soldiers eminently well. Since the beginning of the first century BC, gladiatorial instructors (*doctores*) had been used in the weapons-drill training of new Roman legionary recruits.[51] The new monument undoubtedly symbolised the quintessential qualities of the new Roman veteran soldier-colonists: a monument designed to flaunt the *Romanitas* of the new colony.

This association between the traditions of the Roman military and the amphitheatre is an important aspect of this monument and one which has only recently been adequately stressed. Most modern theories about the amphitheatre tend to postulate its origins in the Hellenistic architectural traditions of second-/first-century BC Campania. The clear evidence of the dedicatory inscriptions from the Pompeian amphitheatre is that the new colonists saw their stone amphitheatre not as a Campanian monument, but as a quintessentially Roman one.

And yet the displaced and aggrieved local Oscans shared in its use and also enjoyed the spectacles performed in it. The intentions behind the construction of an ancient monument are difficult to reconstruct today, but it seems probable that a blend of self-aggrandisement, ostentation and perhaps even a degree of conciliation may best describe the motivation behind the construction of the Pompeian amphitheatre.

The arena

The amphitheatre[52] is located in the south-eastern corner of the city, where it nestled snugly against the city ramparts to the east and south. Recent limited excavations beneath the arena have revealed traces of structures, perhaps houses, which existed on this site prior to the construction of the amphitheatre. Thus, the view that this region of the city was largely open and given over to market gardens and orchards must be revised in the light of this recent evidence. An elongated arena (66.8 × 34.5m) was dug into the ground to an average depth of about 6m. The arena-wall was 2.18m high and was probably originally decorated with frescoes to imitate slabs of expensive marbles. Two large vaulted tunnels (4.26m wide: see Figure 2.4, labelled 'A' and 'B') gave access to the arena from the north and south (at the ends of the arena's long axis). Just within the entranceway of each of these tunnels into the arena, there lay a pair of small vaulted rooms (*carceres*: 3.00 × 2.85m, internal dimensions; see Figure 2.4, labelled 'c') that gave access by a single doorway (0.87m wide) to the open-air portions of these tunnels. These chambers were used to store props and as waiting rooms for the gladiators who were to perform in the arena. Due to the lack of security in these areas, it is unlikely that wild beasts would have been stored here.

The auditorium

The spoil from this excavation, banked up around the arena and stabilised on the south and east by the ramparts of the city and elsewhere by the construction of a continuous terrace wall, formed the basis for the tiers of stone seating. The seating for the three separate zones of the *cavea* (*ima cavea, media cavea, summa cavea*) rested directly upon this geologic basis. The exterior of the monument consisted of a series of lofty, shallow arcades (see Plate 2.3) constructed from polychrome tufa ashlars. This produced a decorative effect of alternating light and dark voussoirs in the arches; the rear wall was built of Roman concrete faced with small, roughly shaped, ashlar blocks laid in a pattern somewhat resembling a net (the so-called *opus quasi-reticulatum*).

A series of tunnels led from the exterior façade to the inner parts of the monument. There were two large tunnels, one (see Figure 2.4, labelled 'A') ran straight into the northern entrance to the arena. The other (see Figure 2.4, labelled 'B'), due to the presence of the city ramparts to the south, ran parallel to the rampart wall for most of its length and then finally made a right-angled turn to the left to lead into the southern arena entrance tunnel. Two other large tunnels (see Figure 2.4, labelled 'H' and 'I'), located in the western façade of the exterior, led straight down to large barrel-vaulted corridors, the so-called *cryptae* (see Figure 2.4, labelled 'D', 'E', 'F' and 'G'). These *cryptae* ran beneath the *media cavea* and gave access to the podium and *ima cavea*. By means of a series of sixteen doorways (see Figure 2.4, labelled 'e') the spectator would enter the moat-like trench that separated the inner ring of the *cavea* from the rest of the auditorium. From here stairways led directly onto the inner ring (the podium and *ima cavea*). Spectators who wanted to go on to the *media cavea* would use one of the series of sixteen double stairways (see Figure 2.4, labelled 'f') located in the moat.

Attached to the exterior façade of the amphitheatre there was a series of six grand stairways, two double (see Figure 2.4, labelled 'K' and 'L', 'M' and 'N') and two single (see Figure 2.4, labelled 'J' and 'O') (see Plate 2.3). These stairways provided access to the broad terrace surrounding the monument, which acted as an *ambulacrum* for access to the upper regions of the *cavea*. From this terrace, a series of forty arched doorways (*vomitoria*: see Figure 2.5, indicated by arrows) led directly down into the *summa cavea*. As described below, this region of the auditorium was later modified.

Beneath one of the double stairways (see Figure 2.5, labelled 'K' and 'L') a narrow tunnel (see Figure 2.4, labelled 'C') led straight down to a small entranceway into the arena. Near the inner end of this tunnel, if a spectator turned to the right just before entering the arena, he would climb up a small stairway (see Figure 2.4, labelled 'b') leading into the *tribunal* (3 × 1.79m) on the

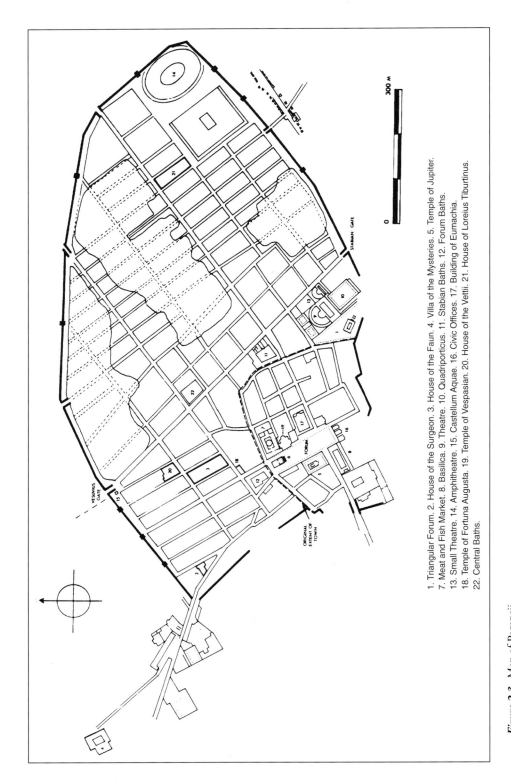

1. Triangular Forum. 2. House of the Surgeon. 3. House of the Faun. 4. Villa of the Mysteries. 5. Temple of Jupiter.
7. Meat and Fish Market. 8. Basilica. 9. Theatre. 10. Quadriporticus. 11. Stabian Baths. 12. Forum Baths.
13. Small Theatre. 14. Amphitheatre. 15. Castellum Aquae. 16. Civic Offices. 17. Building of Eumachia.
18. Temple of Fortuna Augusta. 19. Temple of Vespasian. 20. House of the Vettii. 21. House of Loreius Tiburtinus.
22. Central Baths.

Figure 2.3 Map of Pompeii.
Source: F. Sear, *Roman Architecture* (London 1982), 104, fig. 56. Copyright Frank Sear.

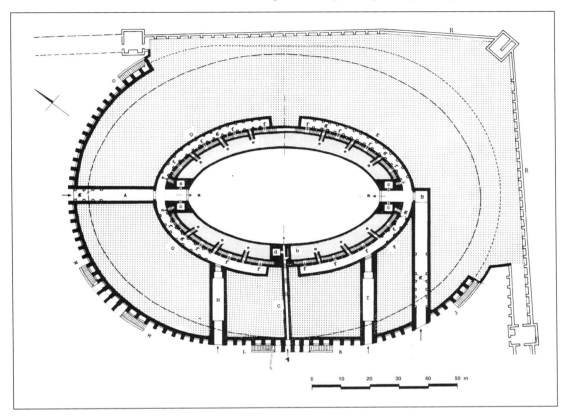

Figure 2.4 Plan of the Pompeii amphitheatre: features below the *cavea*.
Source: Golvin, Planche XXIII, 1. Copyright J.-Cl. Golvin.

Plate 2.3 The shallow exterior arcades and external stairways on the façade of the Pompeii amphitheatre.
Photograph by D.L. Bomgardner.

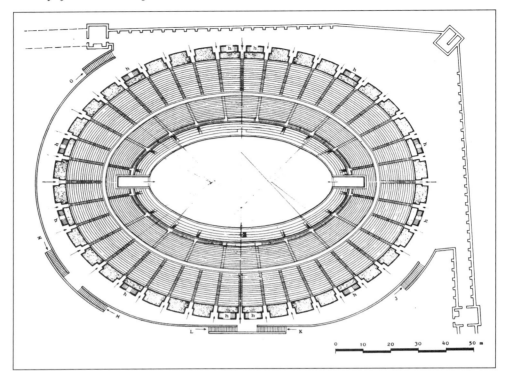

Figure 2.5 Plan of the seating of the Pompeii amphitheatre.
Source: Golvin, Planche XXIII, 2. Copyright J.-Cl. Golvin.

podium. On the other hand, if he turned left, he would enter a small chamber (see Figure 2.4, labelled 'd') beneath the *ima cavea*. Dead gladiators were probably dragged from the arena through this narrow doorway (*porta Libitinensis*), into the tunnel and then into this chamber. If this interpretation is valid, this chamber would be a *spoliarium*, a small room where the equipment would be stripped off a gladiator prior to his burial. From the *spoliarium* dead gladiators would have been taken up the tunnel and through the façade for burial. At Pompeii, as in every Roman town, the main cemeteries lined the main roads leading out of the town. There were major cemeteries lining both the Sarno and the Nucerian Gates, those nearest to the amphitheatre.

Thus spectators of a particularly high status gained their access to the podium, *ima cavea* and *media cavea* solely via the four large tunnels (see Figure 2.4, labelled 'A', 'B', 'H' and 'I') underneath the mass of the seating banks. Only the highest-ranking citizens of Pompeii would have had any reason to enter these tunnels and it is reasonable to assume that some form of admission control operated at their mouths. The most restricted access would have occurred at the mouth of the small tunnel (see Figure 2.4, labelled 'h'), for only the magistrate(s) paying for the games or presiding *ex officio* at the spectacles and their honoured guests entered the amphitheatre by this route. The common crowd gained access to the *summa cavea* only from the upper terrace, which was reached by the series of external stairways attached to the amphitheatre's façade (see Figures 2.4 and 2.5, labelled 'J', 'K', 'L', 'M', 'N' and 'O'). It is probable that here, as in the Colosseum (see Chapter 1), reputable women sat in the sheltered individual boxes (*cathedrae*) at the top of the *cavea*. The *summa cavea* would have held the great mass of Pompeian society. Once again, as in the Colosseum, status, social hierarchies and their public segregation were uppermost in the layout and design of the seating in the amphitheatre at Pompeii.

With these considerations in mind, it is possible to suggest that the innermost ring of the *cavea* (including both the podium and the *ima cavea*) was originally intended to accommodate only the Roman veteran colonists of the newly-founded Sullan colony. The substantial moat-like trench (see Plate 2.5) separating this region from the rest of the *cavea* could be explained in terms of a social barrier. If this hypothesis is correct, then the seating capacity estimate for this section of the *cavea* provides a valuable index for

Plate 2.4 Pompeii amphitheatre: the deep trench separating the *ima* from the *media cavea*.
Photograph by D.L. Bomgardner.

the size of the original veteran colony of Pompeii at about 2,100 spectators.[53] If this approach is valid, an important new detail about the size of the original Sullan colonisation of Pompeii may have been revealed by an analysis of the seating capacity of its amphitheatre.

Table 2.1 Analysis of the seating capacity of the Pompeii amphitheatre

	Double width allocation (0.8m per person)	Single width allocation (0.4m per person)
Podium	589[a]	
Ima cavea		1,475[b]
Subtotal for podium and *ima cavea*		2,064
Media cavea		7,466
Summa cavea		13,607
Cathedrae		1,120[c]
Total		24,257

a The seats (*gradus*: 88cm wide) in the podium were flat, double-width honorific seats, a sure indication that *bisellia* were meant to occupy this space.

b These seats (*gradus*: 70cm deep), in section, were 30cm high at the front and consisted of two horizontal zones: the front part was 38cm wide and the rear part was a shallow channel 32cm wide. The front part of the seating was for the bottoms of the spectators; the rear part was a walkway and foot rest area, for those who sat behind. This was the normal configuration for seating blocks. *Bisellia* required a totally flat surface area. Thus it is assumed that these seats were given a single width (i.e., 40cm) allocation.

c Each theatre box was roughly 1.5 × 3.0m; there were eighty of them, giving a surface area of 360m^2 available for seating. Their floor spaces were flat indicating that seating was either on wooden benches or individual chairs. No more than fourteen persons would have fitted into each box.

Plate 2.5 The various divisions of the seating (podium, *ima, media* and *summa cavea*) in the Pompeii amphitheatre.
Photograph by D.L. Bomgardner.

The later life of the amphitheatre

During the course of the first century AD, a number of important alterations and changes in the fabric and structures of the amphitheatre took place. The auditorium itself, originally probably consisting of wooden seating, was replaced in stone. Each wedge (*cuneus*) was paid for by individual benefactors, often local magistrates, whose contributions were recorded in a series of inscriptions carved on the low 60cm wall (*balteus*) that separated the lowest ring of the auditorium from the rest of the seating. In addition, the special boxes (*tribunalia*) reserved for the magistrates giving the shows and other highly honoured guests and celebrities were added to the podium at the ends of the short axis of the arena. We cannot assign a precise date to these changes; they were gradual and piecemeal, but they were certainly finished by the time of the eruption of Vesuvius in AD 79.

While the auditorium was being replaced in stone, the uppermost part of the amphitheatre was itself undergoing radical alterations. A series of eighty individual vaulted boxes (*cathedrae*) was added to the top of the auditorium. This change was possibly linked with the emperor Augustus' social legislation that forbade women to watch such spectacles, unless they sat in the uppermost seats of the auditorium. Such 'ladies of quality' would have gained access to these private boxes from the upper terrace. A series of doorways (see Plate 2.7 and Figure 2.5, labelled 'h') led onto a small landing, to the right and left of which stairways led up (*c.* 3.4m) to a gangway (1.5m wide) that circled the top of the structure (see Plate 2.4).[54] This gangway (see Figure 2.6, labelled 'A') ran along the outside of the theatre boxes and was itself bordered on the outside by a low wall to prevent people falling down onto the upper terrace. Every third theatre box was fitted with an arched doorway so that spectators could enter it from this outer gang-

Plate 2.6 The reserved boxes added to the top of the amphitheatre at Pompeii.
Photograph by D.L. Bomgardner.

way. Entry to the other two intervening boxes was by way of a smaller gangway located in front of the boxes (see Figure 2.6, labelled 'C'). The relative isolation of these boxes would fit the interpretation that they were reserved for the 'women of quality' of Pompeian society. These boxes were built from a combination of *opus incertum* and alternating courses of Roman concrete faced in small ashlar blocks and one or more courses of brick (the so-called *opus vittatum*). This building style did not come into general use in Pompeii before the Augustan period (*c.* 27 BC–AD 14) and thus gives us a date before which it is most unlikely to have been built.

Closely linked with the construction of these boxes was the addition of an awning (*vela*) to the top of the structure. In order to support the tall wooden masts that spread the awning over the spectators, a series of stone sockets (17–21cm wide × 17–24.6cm thick) and ring consoles (19.5cm wide × 21cm in section) were added to the rear wall of the boxes. Thus the awning, securely anchored, offered welcome shade from the scorching sun and protection from the occasional spring or autumnal shower.

As we shall see below, there exists a unique wall fresco that includes a view of the amphitheatre and this awning – a rare confirmation of archaeological conjecture. There is also good archaeological evidence for the introduction here at Pompeii of awnings to the amphitheatre before the amphitheatre riots took place. On the basis of inscriptions painted on walls that advertised forthcoming spectacles at Pompeii, a likely date for their construction is during the Julio-Claudian era (prior to AD 59), but probably after the Augustan age (27 BC–AD 14).[55] As illustrated by the fresco (see below, Figure 2.7), these awnings were simple mechanisms that suspended billowing folds of canvas above the top of the auditorium. The fresco is probably inaccurate in its depiction of only part of the auditorium with an awning, since it is quite certain that masts were fitted all around the outside of the theatre boxes that crowned the seating. Such an accurate depiction would have blocked the view into the arena and *cavea* of the amphitheatre where the focus of the action took place.

Plate 2.7 The archway leading to the stairways leading left and right up to the region of the reserved boxes atop the *cavea* at Pompeii. Note the construction in mixed ashlar and brick courses (*opus latericium*) characteristic of the period after the earthquake.
Photograph by D.L. Bomgardner.

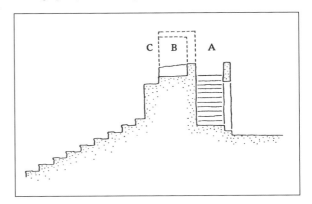

Figure 2.6 Reconstruction drawing of the upper reconstructed zone of the Pompeii amphitheatre, showing the reserved boxes and the access ways to them.
Source: J. Graefe, *Vela erunt* (Mainz 1979), I, Abb. 82. Copyright Rainer Graefe.

The amphitheatre riots of AD 59

In the year AD 59 an event occurred in Pompeii's amphitheatre that captured front-page headlines in Rome and turned into one of the biggest scandals ever to come out of this provincial town, ultimately ruining the lives of many of the chief protatgonists. Spectacles paid for by a former Roman senator, one Livineius Regulus, featuring the performance of a troupe of gladiators, took place in the amphitheatre. Livineius Regulus had been expelled from the Senate and had retired to Pompeii, perhaps choosing a smaller pond since he was no longer such a big fish.

In addition to the usual home town crowd, visitors from the nearby town of Nuceria were there in large numbers. The Roman historian Tacitus[56] recorded the horrific details of what happened. An argument broke out between the locals and the Nucerians. Hard words led to violent actions. At first stones flew, then swords were drawn and fighting broke out. The Pompeians, having the advantage of reinforcements to hand, soon got the better of it. Many Nucerians, both adults and children, were either killed or severely wounded. An official deputation of Nucerians who had been thus assaulted went to Rome and complained to the emperor Nero, who referred the matter to an official enquiry by the consuls. As a result of their investigations, the Senate imposed the following penalties. The Pompeians were found to be guilty of public disorder offences and were banned from having public performances of gladiators for ten years. Furthermore, the 'clubs' (*collegia*) that had been illegally organised at Pompeii, and which had probably supplied the 'muscle' during the riot, were abolished. Finally, Regulus and his fellow-instigators of this violent disturbance were banished, judged to have been guilty of deliberately planning and executing the affair.

There had been much bad blood between the inhabitants of Pompeii and Nuceria for generations. Pompeii had traditionally been a member of the Nucerian confederation, composed of the Samnite settlements in the Sarno valley. But this confederation gradually lost its cohesion and with the destruction of Nuceria (216 BC) in the war against Hannibal in Italy, the league disappeared. Nuceria was soon re-established and during the Social War (91–88 BC) took the side of the Romans, while Pompeii revolted. From this time, their outlooks and interests differed dramatically. The neighbouring town of Stabiae had been totally destroyed by Sulla and its territory annexed to that of the loyal Nucerians. As described above, a colony of Roman veteran legionary soldiers was established at Pompeii by Sulla. Similarly, veterans were also established at Nuceria on two occasions: first, an Augustan settlement, the *colonia Nuceria Constantia*, then in AD 57, Nero settled another veteran colony here.[57] It is quite possible that this latest settlement of veterans may have sharpened old hatreds, especially if the lands assigned to the new colonists were disputed by their Pompeian neighbours. Land hunger and disputes have perennially been the source of trouble in the Mezzogiorno (south of Italy).[58]

The riot in the amphitheatre at Pompeii, less than two years after the new colonial settlement at Nuceria, is surely not coincidental. Indeed the words used by Tacitus to describe those involved are the '*coloni Nucerini Pompeianique*', which can mean simply the inhabitants of both towns, or more precisely Roman veteran colonists. I feel that the words were chosen with the latter sense specifically in mind. On the basis of the outcome of the inquiry and the punishments dealt out, it is reasonable to assume that the Pompeians, organised into quasi-political associations (*collegia*) and led by Livineius Regulus and a group of like-minded colleagues, laid a trap for their new neighbours. They invited the Nucerians to the amphitheatre at Pompeii to watch some spectacles, where the trap was sprung with devastating effect. It is not surprising that Nero's newly discharged veterans should have felt in a strong position to appeal personally to the emperor in Rome. Indeed, Nero acted with restraint in referring the matter to the consuls for an official inquiry.

One must ask the question why Tacitus should include such relatively unimportant news of provincial squabblings in his history of imperial Rome. I believe the answer is two-fold. First,

Tacitus obviously had a personal dislike of Livineius Regulus – he goes out of his way to refer us to the episode, sadly now lost, in his history where Regulus was thrown out of the Senate. To record his further disgrace and exile from Italy would have been nearly irresistible. Second, I think that Tacitus wished to show the Roman Senate, and particularly the consuls, operating effectively in a crisis. Republican government, the exercise of authority by the Senate unfettered by the emperor, was the dearest desire of Tacitus. Here was an instance of the emperor deferring to the authority of this august body and as such it was not to be missed as an example of correct procedure. It surely also served as a counter-example to cynics and sceptics who thought that the old order and its re-establishment were effectively dead in the water; such an example of effective republican administration showed tantalisingly the possibilities for the future under an 'enlightened' despot. This episode also serves as an effective counter-point to those later bad years preceding Nero's fall from power and ultimate death.

There is fascinating archaeological testimony of these bloody events. In the peristyle garden of the so-called House of the Gladiator Actius Anicetus (I.3.23) a fresco depicting the riot in the amphitheatre was painted on one of the walls (see Figure 2.7). The wall painting clearly shows us a bird's eye view of the region of the amphitheatre including the city walls and the adjacent Large Palaestra. The amphitheatre is sketchily depicted showing the theatre boxes (*cathedrae*) and the awnings (*vela*). In addition the arena-wall is shown decorated with what appears to be a pattern in

Figure 2.7 Wall fresco from the house of the gladiator Actius Anicetus (I.3.23) depicting the amphitheatre riots of AD 59.
Source: J. Ward-Perkins and A. Claridge, *Pompeii AD 79* Exhibition Catalogue (London 1976), 35. Copyright Museo Nazionale Archeologico, Naples.

imitation of marble. Some of the minor details of the amphitheatre are incorrect, for example, the number of arches beneath the double staircase leading up to the terrace around the upper auditorium (the painting shows eleven, in fact there were six). Care must be taken to interpret this archaeological document with due sensitivity to its limitations. An attempt to prove or disprove minor points of structural detail of this monument cannot be supported by this evidence. On the other hand, the depiction of its major components does seem to agree well with what has survived of this monument.

It is possible that the amphitheatre at Pompeii may not have been shut down for the entire ten years of the original senatorial ban. It has been suggested that perhaps Poppaea, the second wife of Nero, whose mother's family were important residents of Pompeii, owning both the House of the Menander and that of the Golden Cupid, interceded successfully at a later date to reinstate the gladiatorial spectacles here.[59] The local magistrate, Decimus Lucretius Satrius Valens, a local priest of the imperial cult (*flamen perpetuus*) of the young prince Nero (during the reign of his adopted father the emperor Claudius), has also been proposed as a successful pleader on behalf of Pompeii.[60]

We are ignorant of many details of this ban, but thanks to the pioneering efforts of the Italian epigrapher, Sabbatini Tumolesi, in her study and publication of those inscriptions relating to amphitheatres and their spectacles, new interpretations of old evidence have been produced. She argues that beast hunts (*venationes*) and athletic competitions, but not gladiatorial combats (*munera gladiatorum*), continued to be held at Pompeii soon after the imposition of this ten-year ban.[61] Sabbatini Tumolesi's study reveals that the period of the Claudio-Neronian era, roughly the two decades preceding the riots in the amphitheatre (AD 59), produced the vast majority of the evidence for spectacles in the amphitheatre at Pompeii. The inscriptions have revealed no fewer than eight major benefactors who paid for spectacles (*munerarii*). There were two mayors (*duoviri*), A. Clodius Flaccus and that incomparable benefactor, Cnaius Alleius Nigidius Maius, who also provided another series of games as priest of the imperial cult for the emperor Vespasian (*flamen Caesaris Augusti Vespasiani*); three important municipal politicians, Marcus Tullius, Tiberius Claudius Verus, and Numerius Popidius Rufus; one deputy mayor (*aedilis*), Aulus Suettius Certus; one priest of the imperial cult for the emperor Nero (*flamen Neronis Caesaris Augusti fili*), Decimus Lucretius Satrius Valens; and finally an extremely wealthy freedman, who served the local cult of the emperor (*augustalis*), Lucius Valerius Primus. Such important local figures in both the political life of the town (chief magistrates: *duoviri* and *aediles*) and also its religious life (both as citizen-priests, *flamines perpetui*, and as freedmen, *seviri augustales*) were normally able to act as donors (*munerarii*) of amphitheatre spectacles. Because of the enormous popularity of spectacles and thus the potential political implications of giving them (the cult of personality, demagogy, rival political ambitions, etc.), the right to present such spectacles was tightly controlled and stringently regulated. Either the emperor himself or the local town council (*ordo decurionum*) had to give permission for the spectacles to take place. Successful election to the chief magistracies implied the necessity of giving such spectacles out of one's own funds (sometimes with help from a wealthy patron or colleague). On the other hand appointment as a priest of the imperial cult in a municipality of Italy probably merely gave one the opportunity to display one's munificence 'for the emperor's safety' (*pro salute imperatoris*).

The assumption that most of the inscriptions that recorded amphitheatre spectacles would be of the latter days of Pompeii, the Flavian era, has been shown to be mistaken. This last phase of Pompeii's history was a period of few attested *munera*. On the one hand the ten-year ban (AD 59–69) on gladiatorial combats restricted the opportunities for such games. We soon find athletic contests replacing gladiators in the published programmes of spectacles datable to this era. And, on the other, following the cataclysmic earthquake of AD 62, the funds that would normally have been spent on such games would probably have been diverted into rebuilding the city's monuments that were damaged in the catastrophe.

The earthquake of AD 62

This disaster, a foretaste of the city's catastrophic end under the tonnes of ash from Mt Vesuvius, struck Pompeii on 5 February, AD 62. A violent earthquake nearly demolished both Herculaneum and Pompeii. Severe damage and loss of life were recorded as far away as Nuceria and Neapolis (Naples). The scene has been vividly captured for posterity on two reliefs that the banker Lucius Caecilius Iucundus had sculpted for the private shrine (*lararium*) in his house, perhaps as a thank-offering for having survived.[62] Both Tacitus and Seneca described the quake and its ruinous results.[63]

There is an easily identifiable phase of construction at Pompeii, characterised by the predominant use of bricks and brick-faced Roman concrete (*opus testaceum*), associated with the repairs made following this devastating earthquake. The amphitheatre suffered damage to its vaulted passageways and repairs were completed before its destruction in AD 79. A series of brick buttressing-arches were inserted like ribs beneath the vaulting inside the *cryptae* and also into the vaulted tunnels of the amphitheatre (see Plate 2.8 and Figure 2.4, labelled 'g'). It was probably at this time that the arena-wall was also redecorated with new frescoes that depicted a detailed series of scenes showing gladiatorial combats (*munus gladiatorum*) and wild beast hunts (*venationes*) in the arena.[64] The original frescoes have sadly been lost and are now only known from a series of water-colours made by F. Mazois at the time of their discovery.

Plate 2.8 The brick arches used to reinforce the amphitheatre following damage suffered in the earthquake of AD 62. Photograph by D.L. Bomgardner.

Gladiatorial training schools at Pompeii (Ludi Gladiatorii)

An earlier, but smaller-scale building,[65] where gladiators were at least housed if not trained, existed at the so-called 'House of the Gladiators' (*Caserma dei gladiatori*). This structure, built sometime within the period from the reign of Augustus to that of Claudius (27 BC–AD 54), contained numerous graffiti about gladiators written around the walls of the courtyard which identified its function. Its use did not apparently survive the earthquake of AD 62.

After the catastrophic earthquake of AD 62, the large *quadriporticus* that lay directly behind the stage of the Large Theatre in Pompeii was converted into a gladiatorial training barracks (*ludus*

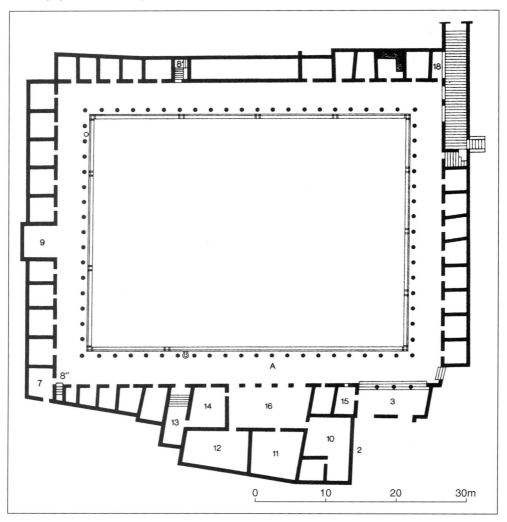

Figure 2.8 Plan of the *quadriporticus* behind the Large Theatre at Pompeii.
Source: La Rocca et al. (Rome 1976), 154. Copyright Electa Archive/ElectaEinaudiMondadori.

gladiatorius) (see Figure 2.8).[66] There can be no doubt as to this identification for not only were abundant graffiti and wall paintings (4th Style) found in its interior that dealt with gladiatorial themes, but also a large store of gladiatorial equipment, including fifteen helmets, some greaves, belts, the shoulder-armour of a net-fighter (*retiarius*) and the skeleton of a horse with rich trappings. Grisly details included the discovery in one cell of the remains of two gladiators in leg irons, obviously still serving their sentence for some infraction of the rules of conduct when the volcanic eruption entombed them for eternity.

Gladiators were almost as popular with the ladies as with the amphitheatre crowds (predominantly male), and there are abundant graffiti about the sexual prowess and conquests of individual gladiators attested at Pompeii. In one of the rooms of the *quadriporticus* was found a couple locked in a last embrace, a lady, richly adorned in all her finery and jewels, and her gladiator lover, preserved forever in their last tryst by the eruption of Vesuvius.

The *quadriporticus* itself consisted of a large rectangular courtyard (*c.* 46.9 × 36.5m, interior dimensions) surrounded by colonnaded walkways (4.4–4.9m wide) on to which individual cells (*c.* 3.5m square, inside) opened. This large number of small rooms on both ground and first floors, a courtyard whose surface area was nearly the same as that of the arena of the amphitheatre (courtyard: 1,810m²; arena: 1,788m²) and the restricted access (one easily guarded entrance, #3 on Figure 2.8) to this building made it an obvious choice for a gladiatorial training school. Further modifications included the construction of a flat for the manager[67] of this troupe of gladiators (*lanista*) on the second floor, in the kitchen (#12 on Figure 2.8) the addition of a massive hearth for cooking for a large number of people and a remodelling of the large, trapezoidal-shaped, communal dining hall (*c.* 12.3 × 6.5m inside: #16 on Figure 2.8) – large enough for at least a hundred to dine. The entrance area underwent modifications to make it more secure. A guard chamber (#15 on Figure 2.8) was installed and the entranceway itself (#3 on Figure 2.8) was narrowed and fitted with a gateway.

It is easy to imagine the dreary, claustrophobic existence of the wretched souls forced to endure the rigours of training as gladiators for the arena here. At night they would be locked securely away in their cells. There was room in each cell for up to six gladiators, but it is not known how many were locked in together. During the daytime, they would train in the courtyard, breaking their regime for meals in the mess hall or a rest in the shade of the colonnades. If the gladiators displeased their owner, they would be punished, for example, by being locked up in leg irons. Most gladiators were slaves, but there were also freed slaves (*liberti*) and even free-born fighters, who signed on voluntarily, agreeing to submit to the unbending harshness of the discipline of the gladiatorial code. The gladiator agreed to submit to being whipped, burnt with hot irons and even to suffer death itself.

It is difficult to estimate the number of gladiators comprising this troupe (*familia gladiatoria*). However, the dining hall could accommodate no more than two hundred and this seems a reasonable maximum figure. It is estimated that between one hundred and two hundred gladiators would have occupied this school. This is in agreement with the evidence for the number of pairs of gladiators exhibited in the local spectacles in the Pompeii area, where from ten to forty-nine pairs of gladiators are mentioned on the inscriptions advertising the gladiatorial combats, although twenty pairs appears to have been the norm.[68] At Rome, on the other hand, 120 pairs had long been the legal limit. It is reasonable to assume that the provincial maximum numbers would be much lower than those for the capital. One *lanista*, such as the owner of this troupe of gladiators at Pompeii, would be able to supply all of the gladiators for each local spectacle. The inscriptions make it clear, however, that the most popular supply of gladiators at Pompeii was from the nearby imperial gladiatorial barracks at Capua. These gladiators are clearly identified on the inscriptions (*Iuliani* [prior to Nero's reign]; *Neroniani* [after Nero, who reorganised the institution and gave his own name to the new imperial barracks[69]]). With an unlimited power to recruit the finest talent, the gladiators from the imperial training schools of the empire were the finest money could buy. Capua had also had a long reputation for distinction in this area, even before the institution there of Julius Caesar's troupe of 5,000 gladiators (*secutores*) in 49 BC, which later became the imperial barracks of the *Iuliani*.[70]

It is perhaps fitting to close this section with an inscription found scrawled on one of the walls of the dining hall: 'The philosopher Annaeus Senecas (*sic*) is the only Roman writer to condemn the bloody games!'[71] A grim reminder of the almost universal acceptance of this form of 'entertainment', with rare moral objections being raised. Obviously Seneca's high moral stand struck a deep, resonant chord in at least one gladiator's heart. It would perhaps have disheartened him if he had known the true basis of Seneca's Stoic objections – that the spectacles degraded the free-born citizen spectators. Seneca, as with most Romans, would not have cared deeply about the fate or suffering of slaves. He was concerned with the dehumanising influence of these spectacles upon the people of quality who really mattered. It would take a Christian revolution many years in the future to turn concern away from the welfare of the 'haves' of society and towards the 'have nots'.[72]

The spectacles in the arena

Two basic types of spectacles (*munera*) took place in the amphitheatre at Pompeii. One type of spectacle (*ob honorem*) consisted of contests paid for by either newly-elected municipal politicians (*duoviri, aediles*) or else municipal priests of the imperial cult of a particular emperor (*flamines Augusti*). Both arose from a sense of obligation for the special honour the individual achieved by his elevated social status. By the foundation charters of some veteran colonies, the chief magistrates (*duoviri*) and their deputies (*aediles*) were actually obliged to pay for a fixed number of full days of spectacles. The late republican veteran colony of Urso in Spain required that *duoviri* give four full days – two of chariot racing (*ludi*) and two of gladiatorial contests (*munera*), while their deputies were required to provide three full days – two of theatrical performances (*ludi scaenici*) and one of gladiatorial combats (*munus*).[73] At Pompeii, the evidence shows that during the Augustan era, four days of spectacles was the average requirement of the *duoviri*, but that by the Neronian era this figure had dropped off to two days.[74]

The second type of spectacle (*munera assiforana*) had a commercial motivation. An organiser (*lanista*) exhibited a troupe of professionals at which an entry fee was charged in the hope of making a profit. The evidence for both types of spectacles exists at Pompeii, although the municipal spectacles provided many more examples of preserved graffiti on the exterior white-washed walls of houses (*edicta munerum*). It has been suggested that handbills and possibly public criers advertised the private games, leaving no tangible evidence today.[75]

The evidence for gladiatorial combats at Pompeii

Having been sealed by the eruption of Vesuvius in AD 79, Pompeii is a time capsule of the Flavian era and has a unique stockpile of evidence for all aspects of daily life. A rich variety of material survives about the gladiators who fought in the amphitheatre. We have already mentioned the archaeological materials uncovered in the *quadriporticus* behind the Large Theatre, which was converted into a gladiatorial training barracks after the earthquake of AD 62. A large number of graffiti advertising forthcoming shows in the amphitheatre (*edicta munerum*) also survive. Professional sign painters (*scriptores*) daubed these announcements on to the exterior white-washed walls of private houses. Some seventy-three such notices have survived.[76] They usually announced the name of the donor (*editor muneris, munerarius*), the number of pairs of gladiators and often the troupe from which they come and its owner/trainer (*lanista*), the date of the performance, the location, and sometimes even the reason for the spectacles. A small number of inscriptions give us a far more detailed glimpse into the life of the arena. One particular inscription details the complete programme and roster of the gladiators who fought in two series of gladiatorial shows given by the *lanista* Marcus Mesonius during the month of May probably sometime between AD 54 and 62.[77] This is a unique permanently preserved example of what must have been a common feature of the *munera*. Papyrus programmes, similar to those painted on walls as graffiti, described below, would have been on sale before the spectacles, probably in the piazza surrounding the amphitheatre. Each gladiator in a papyrus programme is identified by his name, his troupe affiliation (only the finest gladiators, the *Iuliani* and the *Neroniani*, appeared), the type of gladiatorial armament he is wearing and the number of combats he had previously fought. At a later date, another hand has added the outcome of each man's encounter: whether victorious (*vicit*), vanquished but granted his life (*missus*) or dead (*periit*).

The best preserved section of the inscription records the twenty pairs who fought in the second series of games. Of these twenty gladiators, ten were victorious, eight were beaten but spared, while only two died. The popular preconceptions about 50 per cent kill rates must be re-examined in the sober light of factual evidence. Only 10 per cent of the gladiators who fought in this exhibition met their death. Two gladiators had over fifty contests each under their belts. For the courageous, the skilful and the lucky the arena could be the passport to fame, fortune and freedom for a slave. The risks were grave, but the rewards were commensurately high. For the born optimist and the compulsive risk-taker, the arena must have seemed a golden opportunity, not the graveyard of all hope.

Broadly speaking, gladiators belonged to one of two classes: the heavies and the lights. The inscriptions record an amazing variety of gladiatorial armaments. Samnites (later called *secutores*), *hoplomachi* and *murmillones* are all types of heavily-armed gladiator. They had a more or less complete set of body armour, a helmet, a shield and a sword, differing only in details of equipment design. The *murmillo*, for instance, often had a distinctive fish emblem on the crest of his helmet and was often pitted against the net-fighter (*retiarius*): an obvious pun intended about the use of a net to 'catch a fish'. The heavily-armed gladiator had the advantage of better protection, but a short-range weapon, a sword, as well as reduced speed, endurance and agility from the added weight of his armour. He played the waiting game, biding his time, husbanding his reserves of energy and strength. He parried the blows of his nimble enemy, and perhaps played at being helpless to lure his lightly-armed opponent in close, where he would be vulnerable without heavy defensive armour.

The lightly-armed gladiator had his own advantages. Being unencumbered by heavy armour, his extra speed, endurance and agility allowed him to adopt 'hit-and-run' attacks to wear down his opponent and exploit any openings in his defence. Often the light gladiator had either longer-range offensive weapons, for example, the net and trident of the net-fighter (*retiarius*) or the long curving sabre of the Thracian, or else a greater offensive armament, such as the two swords carried by the *dimachaerius*. The chariot-gladiator (*essedarius*) had the mobility of his chariot with the long-range offensive capability of his javelins. The horseman-gladiator (*eques*) had a small round shield and full-visored helmet and carried a lance.

The finely balanced interplay between the varied strengths and weaknesses of light against heavy provided the most exciting combats. And at Pompeii the inscriptions record combats between *dimachaerii* and *hoplomachi*, Thracians and *murmillones*, Thracians and *hoplomachi*, *hoplomachi* and *murmillones*. However, those classes involving horses tended to fight with others of the same kind, either chariot-gladiators (*essedarii*) or horsemen (*equites*).

The wild beast fights (*venationes*)

No gladiatorial spectacle (*munus*) would have been complete (*iustum atque legitimum*) without the wild beast fights (*venationes*) that always accompanied them. Hunting was a daily activity for many of the inhabitants of the countryside. For the poor peasant, it provided a much-needed supplement for the pot. For the wealthy landowner, it provided an aristocratic pastime of vigorous physical activity, highly demanding skills of horsemanship and marksmanship, the excitement of the chase and a proof of the male virtues most valued in Roman society. Other than success in battle, success in the hunt was the other prized attribute of a successful man. As practising hunters themselves, the spectators probably most enjoyed the degree of skill demonstrated by the huntsmen (*venatores*) in the arena. Thus in one single day all of the cardinal virtues (courage, strength, skill, discipline) most prized by Roman society were presented for the edification as much as the enjoyment of the spectators.

The *venationes* took place in the morning before the main event of the gladiatorial combats in the afternoon. At Pompeii the evidence suggests that normally these events were considered a poor second best to the gladiators. For the most part, they seem to have been modest affairs using only local animals, such as bears and bulls. The usual variations in the format would occur. Trained professional huntsmen (*venatores*) would take on the animals let loose in the arena. The use of hunting dogs is recorded. Sometimes beasts were forced to fight one another by being tethered together.

The tomb of the important local citizen, Aulus Umbricius Scaurus (a former chief magistrate of Pompeii, i.e. a *duovir*), has a rich decoration of sculptured frescoes in bas-relief. The reliefs represent a full gladiatorial spectacle, probably given at Scaurus's funeral and paid for by his father who hired the gladiatorial troupe of the lanista Numerius Festius Ampliatus.[78] Unusually for Pompeii they depict *venationes* of lions and leopards, as well as the more accustomed boars, bears, bulls, wolves, hunting dogs and stags. It is not therefore surprising that such a lavish and spectacular contest should be deemed worthy of commemoration for posterity.

Nigidius Maius, 'Prince of Benefactors'

Cnaius Alleius Nigidius Maius was one of the most prolific benefactors of his fellow citizens among the annals of the spectacles of Pompeii.[79] He rose impressively into the heights of Pompeian society, probably achieving the position of *aedilis* by the reign of Claudius. He held the chief magistracy twice, the second time with censorial powers (*duovir quinquennalis*) in AD 55/56. There is also good reason to think that he was a priest of the local imperial cult for Vespasian (*flamen Vespasiani Augusti*). He appears to have used this position to appeal to the emperor for an overturning of the ten-year ban on gladiatorial spectacles at Pompeii. At the height of his powers, he purchased the luxurious house known as the 'House of Pansa' (Region I, insula 7, #1), probably shortly before the eruption of Vesuvius.

He was hailed on local inscriptions as both the '*princeps coloniae*' ('the most important man of the colony') and '*princeps munerariorum*' (the chief of the donors of spectacles). Throughout the third quarter of the first century AD, we find evidence of his numerous spectacles given to the citizens of Pompeii. Perhaps the most unusual of his gifts was the dedication of a series of painted wooden panels (*opus tabularum muneris*) depicting the highlights of a recent series of spectacles. Literary references[80] have made known such representations, but actual epigraphical evidence is quite rare. Such a desire to perpetuate the memory of a successful spectacle and to commemorate it in a durable form is also well known on mosaic pavements all over the empire, particularly North Africa.[81]

Nigidius Maius epitomises both the costs and the rewards associated with the giving of spectacles. The costs were exorbitant and only the wealthiest could hope to compete for the honour of giving a series of gladiatorial contests. Totally alien to us is the concept that magistrates should pay for their election through a public munificence, costing a small fortune, the so-called *summum honorarium*, the funding either of spectacles or of public monuments. The reward which Maius received was the public honour both of having his statue on horseback erected in the forum at public expense and also of being acclaimed the best, the greatest of the benefactors of the colony, '*princeps munerariorum*'.

THE EARLIEST AMPHITHEATRES IN STONE

As mentioned above, there are considerable problems associated with any review of the evidence for the earliest amphitheatres. Recently Golvin has published a list of the earliest amphitheatres known at present.[82] Here is a list of these monuments with the relevant date or the best estimate for their dates of construction:

- Capua, the early amphitheatre (towards the end of the second century BC)
- Cumae and Liternum (towards the end of the second century BC)
- Pompeii (*c.* 70 BC; *cavea* completed during the Augustan era)
- Abella (probably built during the Sullan era, i.e., the first quarter of the first century BC)
- Teanum and Cales (probably Sullan era)
- Puteoli, early amphitheatre (probably mid-first century BC; consolidated in the Augustan era)
- Telesia (typologically similar to the Puteoli and thus dated similarly)
- Paestum, Phase I (probably first century BC)
- Sutrium (probably 40–30 BC)
- Ferentinum (probably before the reign of Augustus)
- Carmo, Spain (*c.* 30 BC)
- Ucubi, Spain (*c.* 30 BC)
- Antioch, Syria (Caesarean era, i.e., mid-first century BC).

Plate 2.9 Paestum amphitheatre: the exterior of the monument clearly showing both the earlier (first century BC) phase of construction in rough-hewn *opus quadratum* and its later (second century AD) brick phase. Photograph by D.L. Bomgardner.

In addition to these stone monuments we know of temporary wooden structures, the best known being that built for Caesar's Quadruple Triumph at Rome (46 BC). There is good reason to believe that the origins of this architectural type ultimately derived from these temporary wooden structures erected in the *Forum Romanum* for the performances there of gladiatorial spectacles from the second century BC onwards.

A recent reinterpretation of the available evidence by Welch argues for a purely Roman, not Etruscan or Campanian, origin for the amphitheatre.[83] There is a flaw in the traditional argument used to establish the origins of the amphitheatre in Campania. The earliest examples of wall paintings apparently depicting *munera* are found in this region in the fourth century BC and similarly the earliest established date for an amphitheatre (at Pompeii, *c.* 70 BC) is also here. This is in a very real sense circumstantial evidence for a Campanian origin for the amphitheatre, there being no link between the two phenomena lying some three centuries apart.

The original architectural form of the amphitheatre probably took shape in wood in the middle of the Roman Forum during the course of the second and first centuries BC. This spot was the traditional venue for gladiatorial combats in Rome and there is evidence that people watched them from balconies (*maeniana*) constructed especially for this purpose above the boutiques (*tabernae*) that lined the two long sides of the Forum itself. Rome is certainly the location where the earliest attested gladiatorial combats occurred.

What does seem to be the case is that the earliest examples of the amphitheatre in stone do appear first in Campania. In reviewing the locations where the earliest stone amphitheatres are found, Welch notes that they share either a Roman colonial origin (e.g., Pompeii) or especially close links with Rome (Latin or maritime colonies). In addition, during the 40s BC, Caesar's troops were stationed in Spain at both Carmo and Ucubi, and in Syria at Antioch. Perhaps the earliest phase of the amphitheatre at Roman Corinth (a Roman colony of 44 BC, described as initially 'a self-conscious enclave of *Romanitas*') should also form a part of this group of Caesarean amphitheatres.[84] A Roman military origin for these monuments is a reasonable assumption.

All of these early examples of this genre share several features in common. Their exterior façades are bare walls, functional and without attached orders of columns or pilasters. The seating is supported for the most part by earth fill consolidated between retaining walls or else by simple vaulting or some combination of the two. At this early date, the arenas lack subterranean galleries and service areas: a simple layer of sand covered the arena floor. The sophisticated cells (*carceres*) for releasing beasts directly into the arena have not yet been developed or incorporated into these structures. The awnings (*vela*) which would later cover spectators did not come into use in the amphitheatre much before the mid-first century AD (Claudian era). The colonnaded galleries which later crowned the summit of the seating are not found in these earliest examples.[85] They are severely functional and business-like in their form and use. The role of the Roman legions in the design and construction of these monuments merits further investigation.

We shall now turn our attention to investigate the best-known and most fully developed examples of the amphitheatre: the imperial amphitheatres of the empire.

Chapter Three

Imperial amphitheatres

AN INTEGRAL PART OF THE MONUMENTAL URBAN LANDSCAPE

There are basically two types of amphitheatre: those that were chiefly functional and had little or no architectural adornment or decoration and those that were among the architectural jewels in the array of civic monuments that adorned the greatest cities of the Roman empire. This latter type of amphitheatre is an 'amphitheatre in the imperial style'. Let us look at those features that characterise such monuments.

Imperial amphitheatres formed an integral part of the complex of impressive monuments that adorned every major city in the empire. They provided a luxurious focus for civic pride and inter-city competitiveness. Each major city had its own monumental public buildings. Sumptuous bath complexes, towering temples, august basilicas, splendid colonnaded market squares (*fora*), luxurious theatres, awesome amphitheatres, stadia and perhaps a massive circus for chariot racing graced the monumental centre of every city of consequence.

There were fierce rivalries between neighbouring metropolises, each vying for pre-eminence in its civic monuments, either in sheer size or perhaps in the degree of luxuriant decoration or in the costliness of the building materials used. The Campanian rivalry between Capua, long pre-eminent for its famous gladiatorial training schools, and Puteoli, the premier port of the western Italian coast and chief entrepôt for imported corn and luxury items for Rome, included the addition of a second amphitheatre at each site in a bid to outdo the competition.[1] The Augustan amphitheatre at Puteoli was the largest permanent stone structure of its day. The later Flavian amphitheatre at Puteoli, modelled closely upon the recently completed Colosseum in Rome, fittingly crowned the pre-eminence of this remarkable cosmopolitan port.[2] About the earlier amphitheatre at Capua there is virtually no information. However, not to be outdone, Capua constructed a second amphitheatre, the so-called Anfiteatro Campano, and in the Hadrianic era redecorated this already imposing monument with a sumptuous sculptural programme, including arches whose keystone blocks were carved to represent the upper torsos of Olympian deities in high relief.[3] Such civic rivalries, cities attempting to outdo one another in their civic monuments, are a constant thread in the history of the development of the architectural monuments of the Roman empire and especially in the history of the imperial-style amphitheatre.

THE ARCHITECTURE

Sheer monumentality, both in scale and degree of ornamentation, is the key to the characterisation of these monuments. They fit easily within the framework of impressive constructions that formed the monumental heart of every major Roman city.

An important part of their size is their enormous seating capacities. They could easily accommodate 40,000 to 60,000 spectators in relative comfort. The upper limit for a standing-room only, packed house can only be guessed at, but must be at least 10–20 per cent above these figures, reaching nearly 100,000 spectators in the largest venues. In this respect an important criterion for categorising such an amphitheatre is the relative ratio of the surface areas of the arena to that of the seating. For imperial amphitheatres this ratio is relatively small (the arena is rarely more than a quarter of the total surface area of the monument and often less). These buildings were designed to hold a very large number of people; indeed, only the vast hippodromes of the empire were designed to hold larger crowds as they watched the ever-popular chariot races.

A highly decorated and architecturally elaborate external façade is also an important criterion for inclusion in this category. Imperial amphitheatres had multi-storeyed, arcaded façades that were adorned with applied Classical orders of semi-columns and/or pilasters. Often these Classical orders formed a progression from the bottom to the top of the façade. The example of the Colosseum (in Chapter One) has already been discussed in detail. Here the ground storey had an applied Tuscan order of semi-columns, the first storey had an applied Ionic order, the second storey had an applied Corinthian order and the top storey had an applied order of Corinthian pilasters which framed the huge bronze shields that adorned the attic of the façade.

Sometimes these massive structures had much more elaborate schemes of decoration, such as life-size or greater than life-size statues, fitted securely within the arcades of the upper storeys and picturesquely framed by these same arches. Sculptural adornment might also include the addition of sculpted torsos of divinities to the keystones of the arcades of the façade, such as on those at Capua, Carthage and El Jem.

Such sumptuous treatment of the exterior of the monument was frequently matched by an even more luxurious scheme of decoration in the interior spaces of the *cavea* and arena. Ultimately the degree of elaboration depended solely upon the resources available to the community.

Decorative material

Marble

The most extravagant decorative material was precious marble, varying in quality and appearance from the glistening white purity of Italian Carrara and Greek island Parian marble to the richly variegated and highly prized marbles of Numidia and Phrygia. Other costly stone materials were equally valued, such as Egyptian porphyries and granites.

Roman builders used these materials in a variety of ways. They might fashion monolithic semi-columns, architraves and pilasters with which to adorn the façade, or they might add a free-standing marble colonnade to crown the top of the *cavea*. In order to emphasise the high social status of certain zones of the seating, such as the podium and the *ima cavea*, entire ranges of seating might be added in solid marble. In a similar way marble sculptures might adorn the handrails of balustrades in the *cavea*, for example, in the amphitheatre at Capua, where the graceful figures of hounds at full stretch are frozen in the midst of the chase (see Figure 3.1). At other sites such marble sculptural elaboration adorned the balustrades, *vomitoria* archways and walkways in the *cavea*.

As noted above, free-standing statues often adorned the arches of the arcades of the exterior façade. They might also grace the interstices of the colonnade crowning the summit of the seating or even the gables of the monumental entrance porches around the base of the monument's façade. These sculptures were often carved from the most costly of marbles.

Carvings in high relief might adorn the pediments of monumental entrance porches with further sculpture in the round atop, for example, a four-horsed chariot (*quadriga*). The torsos of divinities carved nearly in the round on the keystones of the exterior arcades at Capua and elsewhere had to be executed in materials other than marble for practical reasons. The tensile strength of marble is relatively weak compared with many other stone building materials and it has a tendency to fracture. In the important load-bearing role of the keystone in an archway, marble would be liable to fail, causing structural damage.

Often the *summa cavea* held a small temple nestled into the fabric of this highest range of seats. Sometimes the temple itself would be fashioned of marble, but the cult statue of the deity would always have been so honoured. The small temple to Ephesian

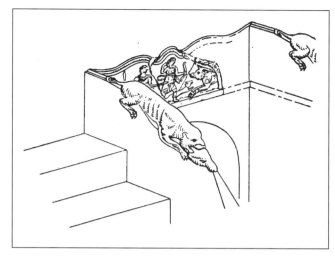

Figure 3.1 Marble sculptural decoration of the balustrades of the *cavea* in the Anfiteatro Campano, Capua. Hunting hounds with their prey and the huntress goddess Diana hunting a boar with her bow. *Source:* G. Pesce, *I relievi dell'Anfiteatro Campano*, Studi e Materiali del Museo dell'Impero Romano, N. 2 (Rome 1941), 47. Copyright Gennaro Pesce.

Diana that graced the summit of the amphitheatre at Lepcis Magna in Libya is an excellent example of this type of scheme.

While solid marble was used in many constructions, some amphitheatre builders chose to adopt a more economical approach: to cut the precious blocks of stone into thin slabs and to apply these as merely a decorative veneer, but giving the illusion of more opulent ostentation. Even communities with very limited resources wished to appear grander than they really were and often local stone quarries were worked to produce the building materials for an amphitheatre. But then, the builders exercised their ingenuity. They would apply a thick plaster coating, partly made from powdered marble, to all of the decorative features that they intended to resemble marble, but at a small fraction of the cost of the real thing. The marble rendering glistened in the sun in much the same way as genuine marble would have done. Another way to cut costs was to paint the arena-wall in such a way that it would resemble the variegations and veins in genuine marble – not however a very convincing substitute.

Stucco

The most lavish examples of this genre had intricately carved plaster ceilings even in the galleries, staircases and chambers under the seating. Here swirling tendrils of elaborate plant-life tracery intermingled with figures of mythological significance enlivened the otherwise drab and dingy interiors of vaulted passages, stairwells and barrel-vaulted rooms. The Colosseum in Rome has some of the best-known examples of this kind of ornamentation.

A SELECTIVE SURVEY OF IMPERIAL AMPHITHEATRES IN THE ROMAN EMPIRE

The Verona amphitheatre[4]

The historical and architectural background

The Roman city of Verona lay curled within a bend on the banks of the Adige (*Atesis*) river, just within the foothills leading up to the Brenner Pass over the Alps. The fertile plain of the Po (*Padanus*) river valley spread out before it providing rich farmland and excellent vineyards and wines in its immediate region. It lay some 104km west of Venice in the Tenth (Venetic) Region of Italy. It was perfectly situated to take full advantage of its central location astride both the main east-to-west road of Cisalpine Gaul, the *via Postumia* (148 BC) that led from Genoa (*Genua*) in the west to Aquileia in the east, and the important military road, planned by Drusus and completed by Claudius, the *via Claudia Augusta*, that led from Mutina (on the strategic *via Aemilia*) going north through Verona and following the course of the Adige over the Brenner Pass into the lands of the Vindelici.[5]

This region of northern Italy between the Apennines and the Alps, so-called Cisalpine Gaul, was of crucial strategic significance to the Romans. It provided a military staging area rich in resources for logistical supply as well as furnishing a military buffer zone against both the hostile Alpine and Dalmatian tribesmen to the north and north-east and also against incursions from raiding Gallic or Germanic tribes. This fertile region had once been home to the Celtic tribes that had emigrated here at the beginning of the fourth century BC. However, by the middle of the second century BC, there were few Gauls left here. Rome had vigorously pursued a policy to reduce Gallic influence both by official colonisation (e.g., Placentia and Cremona, 222 BC) and by its encouragement of 'reverse immigration' of southern Italians and Romans into the region. By the first century BC, it is jestingly referred to as 'Gallia Togata', or 'The Gaul where only Roman citizens live'.[6] Only in the highland region of the Apennines between Bologna (*Bononia*) and Genoa (*Genua*) did large numbers of Ligurian tribesmen still dwell, largely in peaceful and useful service to the Romans as auxiliary cavalry units in their army. Similarly in the rugged upland zone of the Transpadane region, i.e., north of the Po river, large numbers of native Venetic tribesmen (to the east) and Cenomani (to the west) survived.[7] In 89 BC the remaining non-Roman tribal contingents were awarded the *ius Latium* (Latin rights – roughly half way towards full Roman citizenship) and their major settlements, such as Verona, were given the status of Latin colonies (*coloniae Latinae*). By this measure, the final stages towards annexation of this region into Italy were put into effect. By means of Latin colonial status, the aristocratic element in the native population were encouraged to become Roman citizens. If they successfully ran for election to one of the chief magistracies in the Latin colony (*duoviri* or *aediles*: two of each annually), at the end of their year in office, they received Roman citizenship for themselves and their families. Within less than two generations, Caesar (in 49 BC) conferred the Roman citizenship upon the remaining tribesmen and granted municipal Roman status to their cities (*municipia*). In 42 BC, all of Cisalpine Gaul became officially part of Italy proper.[8]

In his study of the architecture of the Roman empire, Ward-Perkins makes clear the seminal importance of the cities of northern Italy in working out the details of the processes for the laying-out of urban landscapes imported from central Italy into this tribal, cantonal countryside bereft of a tradition of large urban settlements.[9] Among the many strands of influence at work in this process, there is a distinctive contribution from the realm of the Roman military camp and its architecture. The most striking example of this interaction is the distinctive forum-basilica complex, where the basilica is set crosswise at the long end of the forum, found in these northern

Italian cities. This type of forum bears a striking resemblance to the headquarters building complex (*principia*) of the Roman legionary fortress with its courtyard and apsidal basilical hall in a similar arrangement. The predominantly military nature of this region during its formative years makes such interactions between civil and military architecture almost inevitable. Indeed, in tribal provinces that lacked a pre-existing urban infrastructure and its attendant architectural traditions, the Roman legions were the repositories for architectural and civil engineering skills. Compare the situation when Pliny the Younger was governor of Bithynia under Trajan. When he needed an architect to survey the proposed route of a canal to link a lake near Nicomedia with the sea, he had to apply to the governor of the neighbouring province of Moesia Inferior, the most convenient region where legionary troops were stationed, to get the necessary military architectural expertise for the proposed project.[10]

The Roman legions were busy in this region of Italy during the reign of the emperor Claudius, building the main military road from Verona north across the Alps, the *via Claudia Augusta*. In addition, it was probably during this reign that the provinces of Rhaetia and Noricum, which lay just the other side of the Alps, received their definitive provincial organisation.[11]

Having sketched the historical and geographical background of this distinctive region of northern Italy it is now time to turn to an examination of the amphitheatre at Verona and to see how it fits into its larger context.

The amphitheatre

Overall dimensions	152.43 × 123.24m
Arena dimensions	75.68 × 44.43 m
Width of *cavea*	39.4m
Area of arena	2,641m^2
Area of *cavea*	12,113m^2
Total area	14,754m^2
Estimated perimeter	866m
Percentage of total area devoted to seating	82 per cent
Estimated seating capacity[a]	28,200
Estimated seating capacity[b]	38,900

a Assuming that the third storey was given over entirely to a crowning colonnade and portico behind the windows of the attic storey. This is the more probable figure (see below).
b Assuming that seating occupied the third storey of the amphitheatre, similar to the wooden bleachers of the attic storey of the Colosseum.

The vast amphitheatre at Verona, famous today for its regular season of *al fresco* operatic performances, still provides an impressive reminder of its former glory and importance. Of the major northern Italian amphitheatres, Verona is the major surviving example.[12]

Situated on the southern side of the settlement, just to the south of and outside the early defences that provided protection only to this side of the city, which was not protected by the loop of the Adige river, the amphitheatre formed an impressive monumental focus. The amphitheatre is in perfect alignment with the rectilinear street grid of the Roman settlement (commonly dated to *c.* 49 BC) and must therefore have been built after the street grid was laid out. In addition, the proximity of the arena to the walls (*c.* 80m south of the defences) has led scholars to propose that its construction must be later than the troubled times of the Civil Wars (i.e., later than *c.* 27 BC), otherwise its nearness to the defences would have posed a security risk for Verona, if it had been occupied by hostile forces. Two other pieces of archaeological evidence are able to define more closely the date of its construction.

Plate 3.1   Verona amphitheatre: view of the interior of the amphitheatre as used for modern operatic productions. By kind permission of Dr Ivan Johnson.

The amphitheatre, much like the Colosseum, has a massive external skeletal framework of the durable, slightly pinkish local stone. It consists of three storeys, the lower two of arcades with applied Tuscan half-columns and an upper attic with large windows in line with the lower arcades and delineated into panels by plain, engaged Tuscan pilasters. The individual blocks of stone of this façade have been left rough-hewn with projecting bosses on their faces, being finely dressed to fit together only at their horizontal and vertical joints. This style of architectural decoration, known as 'rusticated' masonry, was popular in Rome only for a short time during the reign of the emperor Claudius (AD 41–54).[13] Claudius, having suffered from a severe physical disability since childhood, adopted a reclusive, bookish, intellectual bent, instead of the career of public service and military training usual for a prince of the imperial house. He was a student of the historian Livy and, doubtless under Livy's guidance, wrote a history in Greek of the Etruscan and Carthaginian peoples, both unfortunately now lost. Since this style of masonry seemed to hark back to the distant past before the architectural refinement of neatly coursed and finely dressed cut-stone work (*opus quadratum*), it perfectly reflected Claudius's well-known, distinctly 'antiquarian' tastes.[14]

The second piece of archaeological evidence is the series of sculptured bas-reliefs recovered from the clearance of this amphitheatre over the years. In particular, the series of reliefs depicting gladiatorial combats has been studied by Coarelli,[15] who finds, in the carefully depicted body armour and particularly the helmets, evidence for a Julio-Claudian date.

This evidence for the date of the amphitheatre taken in conjunction with the historical and topographical evidence, particularly the activity of the Roman legions in and around Verona under Claudius during the construction of the military road, the *via Claudia Augusta*, cumulatively points to a Claudian date of construction for this amphitheatre.

Construction technique

As mentioned above, the main load-bearing framework of this monument was the massive three-storeyed, arcaded façade composed of seventy-two arches. As in the Colosseum, the radial walls and barrel vaulting that supported the seating of the *cavea* were in concrete, but of a distinctively local and economical style.[16] It used large river cobbles from the Adige laid in a mortar matrix to form thick bands of concrete (*opus caementicium*: varying from 95 to 150cm thick). These concrete bands alternated with levelling courses of brick (24cm thick and composed of three courses of brick, each brick being roughly 45cm long and 6cm thick) which corrected and controlled the irregularities of the cobbles so that the wall rose true. The only drawback to this construction technique was that any corners or other architectural members that required a sharp profile had to be executed in cut-stone work. The arena-wall, and the inner and outer corners of each of the radial walls, as well as the series of thirty-two piers that flanked the outer portion of both sides of each of the major axis entrances (see Figure 3.2), were rendered in cut stone for this reason.

The façade

The façade had seventy-two arches, of which only four now survive in the north-east sector, mainly due to the destruction caused by an earthquake in 1183, followed by the reuse of the fallen debris elsewhere. The applied decoration of half-columns and half-pilasters is uniformly Tuscan throughout the three superimposed storeys of the façade.[17] The arches of the façade themselves are simple archivolts, whose voussoirs, including those that spring from the impost blocks, are simple segments of the single-centred arch. This is an early stage in the architectural development of the archway.[18] Each of the upper storeys of the façade shows a decrease in height of about 25 per cent, which is in accord with the Vitruvian rule for superimposed orders.[19]

Organisation and access of the seating

The amphitheatre at Verona is the earliest example of the use of Roman numerals above the arches of the ground floor to indicate the most direct route to one's seat. From the evidence of the four surviving arches (LXIIII to LXVII), the northern entrance bore the Roman numeral 'I' and the sequence continued anti-clockwise to 'LXXII'. Four bays, two flanking each of the main entrances, led directly from the exterior of the monument into the arena via small doorways through the arena-wall (see Figure 3.2, labelled 'b').[20] These passageways probably provided access as service corridors to supply the arena with combatants, cageloads of animals and stage props. The positions of these entry points are where you find small rooms or chambers (*carceres*) in later examples of amphitheatres. Such cells are clearly intended for the release of caged animals into the arena, particularly in North African amphitheatres such as at Thuburbo Maius (see Chapter Four).

There is also evidence that individual stone blocks for seating (*gradus*) bore a precise 'grid reference' in relation to the *cavea* as a whole.[21] It is clear that the allocation of seating was highly organised even at this early date. Due to the near total alteration of the *cavea* during the Renaissance, it is not now possible to gather further details concerning the seating or its precise arrangement. However, the existence of 'boxes' for presiding magistrates and dignitaries may be inferred on the basis of two small stairways (on the ends of the minor axis of the arena: see Figure 3.2, labelled 'c') that led from the arena up to the podium, and doubtless to these 'boxes' as found in many other amphitheatres. As usual in an amphitheatre of the size and complexity of this one,

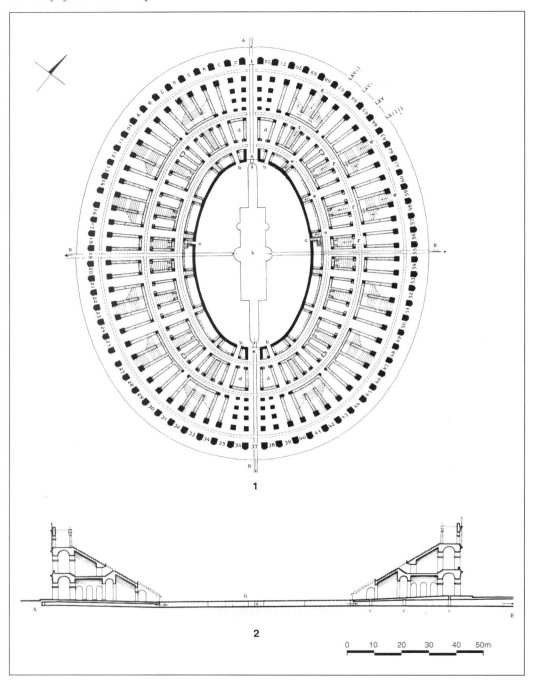

Figure 3.2 Architectural ground plan and cross-section of the Verona amphitheatre.
Source: Golvin, Planche XXXIII, 1 and 2. Copyright J.-Cl. Golvin.

Plate 3.2 Verona amphitheatre: view of the exterior of the monument showing how most of the original façade (visible on far left) has fallen away revealing the inner wall of the peripheral arcade.
By kind permission of Dr Ivan Johnson.

a sophisticated system of stairways and covered passageways conveyed spectators from the exterior of the monument to the proper sector of the *cavea* for their seating. Three ring-galleries enabled rapid movement around the periphery of the monument, and each of these ring-corridors had connections to the seating above. The inner ring had twelve stairs that led to the podium and *ima cavea*, the middle one had sixteen leading to the *media cavea*, and the outer one had twelve multi-landing stairways leading to the upper seating and colonnaded portico that crowned the *cavea*. There are surprisingly few stairways leading from the outer portico to the upper seats. Other monumental arenas had many more. Perhaps this fact should support the hypothesis that the entire upper storey of the amphitheatre was given over to a large colonnaded portico with no seating. This reconstruction would lower the seating capacity of the upper storeys and require fewer stairways for spectators. Another possible explanation is that, at this early date, the design features of the monumental amphitheatre were still being worked out. In later monuments, this lack of adequate provision of access to the upper storey was rectified. The traces of corbels on the upper portions of the façade are evidence for the provision of a permanent awning (*vela*) for the comfort of spectators.[22]

The subterranean structures of the arena

The arena held a large, shallow basin (36.13m long, 8.77m wide and less than 2m deep: see Figure 3.2, labelled 'h')[23] fed by a branch of the aqueduct (see Figure 3.2, labelled 'A') that entered the amphitheatre beneath the northern entrance passageway (Bay I).[24] Three large drains (see Figure 3.2, labelled 'B'), each located beneath a branch of the three remaining axes of the arena, took care of the drainage of this basin.[25] The southern branch formed the main channel. Three concentric ring-drains (2m deep and covered by large slabs of stone) ran beneath the three ring-corridors described above.[26] When this basin was not in use, a flooring of timber planks covered it.

The subject of the staging of mock sea battles (*naumachiae*) in the arenas of amphitheatres has been much debated, and, in recent years, has tended to pass out of favour. The literary accounts of such performances have tended to be discredited on the grounds that they confused amphitheatres with the true venues – purpose-built water-filled artificial lakes (also called *naumachiae*). In a recent article, Coleman has argued forcefully for the credibility and veracity of the literary descriptions of *naumachiae* taking place in amphitheatres, particularly those in the Colosseum during the inaugural games of Titus.[27]

The amphitheatre at Mérida had a long, narrow, shallow basin (50 × 7.1m, 1.25m deep) in the centre of the arena; an aqueduct filled it and two large drains emptied it. The Mérida amphitheatre is Augustan in date[28] and could therefore be a precursor of the Verona arena's basin system.

The Verona basin has a large central pool with a smaller linear, lozenge-shaped extension along each branch of the major axis of the arena, extending right up to the arena-wall (see Figure 3.2). The narrow width of the basin and the shallow depth meant that actual warships could never have fought a mock re-enactment of a famous naval battle here. It is possible that mock sea battles involving a small number of scaled-down ships may have been fought here. Perhaps each opposing fleet started out in line astern formation in the lozenge-shaped extensions and then, when they had reached the larger central basin, manoeuvred into battle formation to close with one another. Or perhaps aquatic *venationes* took place in the basin: hunters, either in small boats or standing around the edge of the basin, attempted to net or harpoon their prey, perhaps seals or other local game. Or perhaps a pair of gladiators in small boats, starting at opposing ends of the basin, engaged in a mixture of long-range and hand-to-hand combat, similar to the analogous chariot gladiators, the *essedarii*. Perhaps the shallow lagoons of the Veneto with their small shallow-draft boats are the best place to look for the possible origins of the water spectacles performed here. None the less the shallowness of the basin as well as its proportions make its use difficult to assess.

Design principles

A recent monograph by Mark Wilson Jones on the principles of design involved in the laying-out of amphitheatres has broken new ground in this area of amphitheatre studies.[29] Wilson Jones has studied the geometry of the monument in Verona and has reconstructed the principles involved in its design and the method of laying out its ground plan.

The Verona amphitheatre follows what Wilson Jones terms the equilateral-triangle-and-inscribed-circle-scheme' of design (see Figure 3.3). Through the use of simple geometric principles and simple design instruments, such as the compass, the architect produces the arena and exterior façade perimeters. The trace of the curve is based around a pair of equilateral triangles with an inscribed circle whose centre is the centre of the arena.[30] These are the design principles involved in the preliminary planning stages of the monument. Wilson Jones has carried his process of analysis much farther and has elucidated even the subtle adjustments that the architect has made to achieve the final harmonious plan of the amphitheatre. In this process the arcaded façade of the monument played a critical role.

The concept of 'modular design' was integral to the Greco-Roman architectural tradition. Here a 'module', a specific unit of length (in whole numbers of Roman feet), is adopted as a unifying principle in the design of an architectural space. Every dimension of the monument is in harmonious ratio with this 'module' in simple, whole number multiples. This is the theoretical basis. However, in practice, things did not always work out so neatly and exactly as planned.

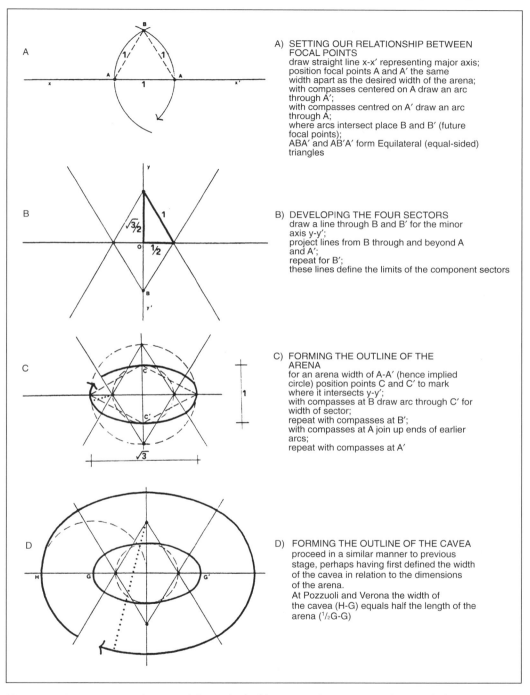

A) SETTING OUR RELATIONSHIP BETWEEN
   FOCAL POINTS
   draw straight line x-x' representing major axis;
   position focal points A and A' the same
   width apart as the desired width of the arena;
   with compasses centered on A draw an arc
   through A';
   with compasses centred on A' draw an arc
   through A;
   where arcs intersect place B and B' (future
   focal points);
   ABA' and AB'A' form Equilateral (equal-sided)
   triangles

B) DEVELOPING THE FOUR SECTORS
   draw a line through B and B' for the minor
   axis y-y';
   project lines from B through and beyond A
   and A';
   repeat for B';
   these lines define the limits of the component sectors

C) FORMING THE OUTLINE OF THE
   ARENA
   for an arena width of A-A' (hence implied
   circle) position points C and C' to mark
   where it intersects y-y';
   with compasses at B draw arc through C' for
   width of sector;
   repeat with compasses at B';
   with compasses at A join up ends of earlier
   arcs;
   repeat with compasses at A'

D) FORMING THE OUTLINE OF THE CAVEA
   proceed in a similar manner to previous
   stage, perhaps having first defined the width
   of the cavea in relation to the dimensions
   of the arena.
   At Pozzuoli and Verona the width of
   the cavea (H-G) equals half the length of the
   arena (¹/₂G-G)

Figure 3.3 Reconstruction drawing of the method of laying out the perimeter of an amphitheatre using the equilateral-triangle-and-inscribed-circle-scheme.
Source: M. Wilson Jones, 'Designing Amphitheatres', *MDAI(R)* 100 (1993), 404, fig. 14. Copyright Mark Wilson Jones.

Wilson Jones rightly stresses the conscious effort, on the part of the architect, to produce a façade whose arcaded bays would each work out to be a whole number of Roman feet, and thus avoid fractions. However, the theoretical scheme of design (outlined above) rarely produced this desired outcome. Thus, it was necessary to adjust the circumference of the façade to produce such an effect. In Verona this was achieved by lengthening the radii of the four circular segments of the oval trace. Thus the circumference would be able to be divided equally into bays (60, 64, 68, 72 and 80 bays were quite usual for monumental amphitheatres[31]) that were each a whole number of Roman feet in width (measured from the centre of each pier). Another modification occurred in the arena's trace, where the width was increased from 144 to 150 Roman ft., probably so that the radius for its haunch segments would be 200 Roman ft. Thus the *cavea* width became 128 Roman ft. (again just a bit more than the theoretical 125 Roman ft., half the length of the arena) and the width of individual bays on the façade became more than 20 Roman ft.[32]

Nearly the same theoretical principles and proportions as those used in the Verona amphitheatre were also employed in the design of the Flavian amphitheatre at Puteoli (see p. 89).

Gladiatorial barracks (ludus publicus)

An inscription found in Verona records the existence of an imperial (*publicus*) gladiatorial barracks here.[33] Lucilius Iustinus, who was a citizen of equestrian rank and had held his city's highest magistracies, paid for four columns, including their adornment and the mosaic paving surrounding them in the public portico 'that leads to the gladiatorial barracks [*ludus publicus*]'. The inscription probably dates from the early imperial era (certainly not earlier than the Augustan era).[34] No trace of this barracks has yet been uncovered.

It is tempting to see this gladiatorial barracks as having supplied, at least in part, the 2,000 gladiators that are recorded as having fought valiantly alongside the troops supporting Otho in this region of Italy in AD 69 against Vitellius and his Rhenish legions.[35] Tacitus sneers at the use of gladiators, but Otho was desperate for every fighting man he could muster, fearing the imminent invasion of northern Italy in the early spring before his forces had had time to prepare. Verona was an important centre of support for Otho in this region, providing a buffer zone that kept open the route from Aquileia, in the hope that the Dalmatian, Pannonian and Moesian legions would link up with Otho's forces in northern Italy. This was a hope only partly fulfilled and ultimately dashed with the total defeat of Otho's force in the first battle of Cremona.

The Flavian amphitheatre, Puteoli[36]

Overall dimensions	149 × 116m
Arena dimensions	74.8 × 42m
Width of *cavea*	37m
Area of arena	2,467m²
Area of *cavea*	11,107m²
Total area	13,575m²
Estimated perimeter	832.5m
Percentage of total area devoted to seating	82 per cent
Estimated seating capacity	35,700

During the Flavian era when it was at the peak of its power, Puteoli, as part of its programme to commemorate its status as the most important port and the second city of Roman Italy, decided to build a second monumental amphitheatre. Until then, no Italian city had possessed two permanent monumental amphitheatres;[37] Rome had had the stone and timber amphitheatre of

Statilius Taurus (built in the reign of the emperor Augustus) later replaced (when it was destroyed in the fire of AD 64) by the little known wooden amphitheatre of Nero.[38] At a stroke Puteoli was announcing its claim as one of the most important and cosmopolitan cities of the empire.

There is nothing surprising in a Campanian city having a passionate interest in the spectacles of the amphitheatre. As seen in Chapter Two, the most famous gladiatorial training schools were native to Capua and its vicinity and the detailed epigraphical evidence recovered from Pompeii makes clear the intense dedication of its citizens to these pursuits. Indeed, from an early date, virtually every major centre in Campania had its own amphitheatre.[39]

Another factor that influenced the decision to build a second monumental arena in Puteoli was the fact that it lay astride the main coastal route to Rome. Every major vessel bound for Rome from the southern or eastern shores of the Mediterranean would have passed Puteoli. This critical fact of political and economic geography meant that Puteoli lay astride the main artery of the trade in wild beasts for the arenas of Italy, chiefly Rome. It is not coincidental that this new amphitheatre should have been purpose-built for *venationes* (spectacles involving wild beasts) so that it might take full advantage of this situation.[40]

The floor of the arena had a series of forty-six trap doors through which animals could be quickly and dramatically introduced into the arena during a *venatio* (see Plate 3.3). The effect would have been electric during a performance: to see scores of animals suddenly appear, as if by magic, was similar to the special effects that we so take for granted in the modern cinema. Roman stage-producers were acutely aware of the necessity to avoid boring the spectators by too many repetitions of similar spectacles. Variety, ingenuity, dramatic impact and a sensitivity to the

Plate 3.3 Flavian amphitheatre, Puteoli: overview of the amphitheatre and the arena showing the trap doors in the floor of the arena. Monte Solfatara looms in the background. The concrete flooring is a modern reconstruction of an ancient timber floor.
Photograph by D.L. Bomgardner.

sensibilities of the audience were all essential elements for a successful series of games. As mentioned in Chapter Two, Pompey the Great to his cost underestimated the compassionate sympathies of the crowd during one of his *venationes*, when the slaughter of performing elephants who had shown they were much more than brute beasts so disgusted and sickened the spectators that a lasting negative impression was formed.[41]

This is an excellent example of the need to bear in mind that popular images of the games as blood-soaked orgies of carnage are popular stereotypes, bearing little resemblance to the truth. The purpose of these exhibitions was to evoke public wonder (*admiratio*), enjoyment and approval. Rare species of exotic animals were always the favourites of the crowd – a sight few others would have had the privilege and pleasure of witnessing. The spectators had an innate appreciation of the grace, beauty and strength of the prey that heightened the moment of truth when a man pitted himself against the full fury of nature in tooth and claw. As Professor Wiedemann has pointed out, by the appearance of subduing the natural world in the *venationes*, the Roman populace would receive powerful messages of consolation that Roman power was able to control both death and the forces of nature.[42] The donor of shows that could offer these aspects would receive both popularity and a lasting favourable response from the crowd of spectators. The episode from the triumphal games of Pompey demonstrates the potential damage that could be done to these aims by an ineptly conceived exhibition. Another important aspect of this episode is that, when the Roman crowd was given an opportunity to learn at first-hand about the kindred nature of the animal kingdom to humanity, they responded with compassion and outrage at the wanton destruction of animals. Thus, as with much of human life, education, or rather the lack of it, played a crucial part in the attitude of the Romans towards animals and the spectacles in the arena.

The dedicatory inscription

As mentioned above, Puteoli is an unusual example of an Italian city that possessed two monumental amphitheatres. This is yet another indicator of the pre-eminence of Puteoli among Italian ports, until the construction of the harbour complex at Portus near Ostia under Trajan.[43]

During his study of this monument, Amadeo Maiuri recorded the discovery of four monumental marble dedicatory inscriptions positioned one above each of the four main axial entranceways of the amphitheatre. One of them was substantially complete and there is no doubt about the text, which records that the Roman colony of *Flavia Augusta Puteolana* paid for this amphitheatre out of its own resources.[44] This simple dedication reflects the obvious pride with which the port was able to finance this ambitious project without the need for imperial subventions or the intercession of a powerful municipal *patronus*.[45] Golvin has speculated that the wealthy corporations of Puteoli, enriched by the profits of Italy's premier port, may have been the ultimate source for the funding of the amphitheatre.[46] It is certainly true that some of these corporations had their own private club rooms or *sacella* (chapels) in rooms tucked beneath the stairways of the ground floor of the monument, thus emphasising their close connection with this structure, if they did not actually fund its construction.[47]

Another important observation concerning the wording of the dedicatory inscription is that here too, as at Pompeii, the amphitheatre is consciously associated with the essence of *Romanitas*, a monument prototypically Roman in its every association. Puteoli was a remarkably cosmopolitan city and port, containing strong Greek and overseas influences in its history and society. And yet it is as the Roman colony of *Flavia Augusta Puteolana* that it associates itself with this monument.

This inscription clearly indicates that this monument was built after AD 69, the date of the colony's foundation.[48] It is possible, however, on the basis of the construction techniques employed, to supply a tentative date for its initial construction and for the major phases of its development.

The cavea

On the basis of the construction techniques utilised in the earliest phase of this monument, Maiuri has assigned to it a date of the Flavian era (AD 69–96). This early phase comprises the *cavea* (up to the level of the colonnade at the top of the seating), the substructures of the arena and the façade.

Unlike the earlier amphitheatre at Puteoli which utilised part of an adjacent hillside to support its seating, this *cavea* sprang from a deliberately levelled terrace and rested upon a series of seventy-two radial walls interconnected by concrete barrel vaulting (see Figure 3.4). These

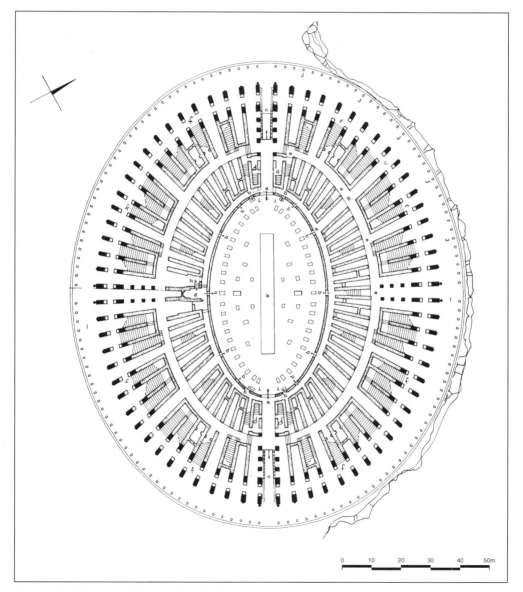

Figure 3.4 Flavian amphitheatre, Puteoli. Ground plan of the amphitheatre.
Source: Golvin, Planche XXXVIII. Copyright J.-Cl. Golvin.

radial walls were built of Roman concrete with a fine outer skin of carefully cut, roughly square tufa blocks (*c.* 8cm on each side) arranged in a neat pattern to resemble the diagonals of a fishing net, hence its Latin name *opus reticulatum*, meaning 'net-work'. The outer ends of these radial walls were finished off by the addition of brickwork (*opus testaceum*). Two brick levelling courses within each of the radial walls (one at the base and the other at mid-height composed of rectangular bricks: 20 × 25 × 3.5cm) ensured that the concrete construction rose evenly and true. A thick coating of stucco, decorated to imitate cut-stone work (*opus quadratum*), covered the whole.

The façade

The outer ends of these radial walls terminated in seventy-two stone piers built from the local trachytic stone which formed the bases for the arches of the façade. An arcaded gallery (*c.* 4m wide) comprised the ground and first floor of the amphitheatre, while an attic storey finished off the façade. Like the Colosseum, on the cut-stone piers between adjacent arches, engaged columns (probably constructed from a stone core with applied stucco decoration that included the column capitals themselves) adorned the façade. It is not now possible to determine whether the applied orders of the façade were the same for each of the levels or whether there was a regular progression upwards as in the Colosseum.

The façade of this amphitheatre shares a very rare architectural feature with those at Arles and Nîmes. Each of the engaged columns of the first storey rests upon a socle that projects some 38cm from the vertical profile of the façade. Such idiosyncratic design features must surely indicate a common linkage for these monuments, at least in the design phase. Such conclusions are further strengthened by the research of Mark Wilson Jones into the architectural design processes used in the construction of amphitheatres.[49] He groups these three amphitheatres, as well as the one at Verona, into a family based on the design principles used in their construction. Closely related monuments include the Colosseum and the amphitheatres at Capua (Anfiteatro Campano), El Jem, Pola and Salona.

Architectural fragments have been recovered which indicate that the amphitheatre was provided with a purpose-built awning system.[50] In addition, a broad elliptical piazza paved with the local volcanic trachytic stone (*c.* 7.75m

Plate 3.4 Flavian amphitheatre, Puteoli: the actual state of preservation of the façade. Note the various construction materials clearly visible and the bases of the external piers of the arcaded façade.
Photograph by D.L. Bomgardner.

wide) surrounded the amphitheatre (see Figure 3.4). At its edge two steps led down to the surrounding street level. A series of stone bollards (*c.* 3m apart) bordered the edge of this piazza. Two uses have been suggested for such bollards, first that, in conjunction with removable wooden barriers, they served as a means to facilitate crowd control and limit access to the piazza itself and the amphitheatre, and second that they acted as stanchions to secure the ends of ropes from the awning masts at the top of the attic of the amphitheatre. The broad paved piazza would have been an integral part of the monumental appearance of the amphitheatre. This theme of monumentality would be carried through in the architectural decoration of the four major axial entrances into the amphitheatre. The remains of two free-standing columns, bearing either an architrave and pediment or perhaps, as in the Colosseum, free-standing statuary groups, attest the adornment of each of the four main axial entrances.

Club rooms and cult shrines

A remarkable series of chambers (installed beneath the sloping barrel vaulting that carried the stairways from the outer portico up to first-floor inner gallery) provides a unique insight into the larger context of the cultural life of this amphitheatre. Only those vaults that opened outwards, on to the brightly illuminated exterior portico, provided evidence for the specialised use of these architectural spaces. Those that opened inwards, on to the dimly lit internal *ambulacrum* beneath the seating of the *media cavea*, were not selected for such special adaptations. Both the element of adequate levels of exterior illumination and the greater accessibility and visibility of these chambers appear to be important in their selection. Being seen to have special status and privileges is nearly as important as the possession of these social distinctions. In addition, only the southern half of the *cavea* contained these specially adapted spaces; this may be significant, for this side of the arena faced the centre of the city, or it may be merely a result of a better preservation of the evidence on this side of the monument.[51]

The southern axial entranceway into the arena was the most important of the four axial entrances. For it led, as described in more detail below, to the municipal equivalent of the imperial box (*pulvinar*) in the Colosseum. Indeed, tucked away beneath this 'royal box' lay a remarkable, richly decorated shrine, added probably during the second century AD (see Figure 3.4, labelled 'g').[52] The entrance to this shrine was either directly from the arena through a doorway (2.25m wide), or by one of two lateral stairways that led down from the intermediate *ambulacrum* of the *cavea*. Certainly the most dramatic access was from the arena itself. Here the inner corners of each of the interlocking rectangles that formed this chapel's plan converged upon two diagonal lines that focused upon either side of the apse at the far end of the chamber. The architect's conscious manipulation of physical space has heightened the psychological tension of a three-dimensional space. In addition to the design elements that point to a ritual function for this chamber, the rich adornment of the walls with marble slabs and the floors with marble pavements (*opus sectile*) also points to a special use and status for this chamber. No trace of a cult statue or dedication has remained. However, it is possible, on the basis of comparative evidence, to suggest that Nemesis, the goddess controlling one's fate for good or ill, may have been worshipped here as in so many other amphitheatres.[53] It is easy to envisage the last act of a gladiator before stepping into the arena to face his deadly foe: the offering of an appropriate sacrifice on the altar together with the correct form of supplication in order to propitiate this savage goddess. From here, the gladiators would have marched out into the arena to face their fate – for good or ill. Surely, on one level, the fascination of the spectators for these contests lay in the fact that they represented a symbolic microcosm of the struggles of human existence, including the inexorable role of good and bad luck.

As seen above, Puteoli, particularly during the early empire, was the second city of Italy: the cosmopolitan, wealthy port of Rome. As such it had a large number of powerful, professional guilds of traders and merchants that controlled the commerce and business of this bustling port. It has long been known that, in addition to their professional activities, these guilds played an important, active part in the social life of the city. At Ostia, in the so-called *Piazza delle*

Plate 3.5 Flavian amphitheatre, Puteoli: one of the 'club room' chambers tucked beneath a staircase just within the exterior arcaded gallery.
Photograph by D.L. Bomgardner.

Corporazione (Plaza of the Corporations), these professional guilds from all over the empire had offices near the capital's port at Portus. A similar situation may be postulated to have occurred at Puteoli during its heyday.

It is interesting that these specialised rooms for the guilds were added during the second century AD; there is no trace of such adaptations in the original construction phase. In general, each of these chambers had two distinctive architectural parts. First, there was a roughly rectangular exterior space bounded by two massive piers of the exterior façade and the two corresponding members on the inside of the outer portico. This space was often blocked off by lateral partitions running between the corresponding piers of the façade and inner portico, thus emphasising the private nature of these spaces. Next came the inner chamber, tucked beneath the diminishing and steeply sloping vaulting that supported the staircase above it. The low inner end of these chambers often contained an apse and a low base, probably intended as the architectural setting for statuary, either cult or honorific statues. No statues or fragments have been found *in situ*, so that it is difficult to attempt to assign an attribution of the deity (or deities) worshipped here.

Four of these chambers were probably chapels.[54] Three others were more ambiguous in their interpretation, suggesting private club rooms, rather than shrines.[55] The distribution of these shrines and club rooms perhaps reveals the intention of their founders. A plot of their locations around the periphery of the *cavea* reveals that the southern entrance to the arena forms a plane of symmetry around which these chambers cluster.[56] Furthermore, those arcades nearest the southern entranceway reveal architectural traces of cult practice,[57] while those farthest from this axis seem to have been used as assembly rooms.[58] Those shrines nearest the southern entranceway were the more important by virtue of their superior location. This observation is borne out by the archaeological evidence.

One shrine contained a podium (0.93m high, 0.83m deep and 3.7m wide) spanning the entire width of the rear of the chamber.[59] Behind this shrine, a large cistern (7.3m deep) took up the majority of the rear area of the sub-stairway vaulting, in much the same way that many houses have an oddly shaped under-the-stairs cupboard or storage area. The podium bore traces of the attachment of marble slabs and probably formed the base for statuary. The outer foyer, blocked off on the west by a low wall in tufa, had a utilitarian pavement of waterproof plaster (*opus signinum*). The inner room was paved with a sumptuous cut-marble floor (*opus sectile*) composed of white, red, and Numidian marbles and serpentine, into which four marble discs were inserted along the edge of the floor next to the foyer. Two of these four discs carried a dedicatory inscription recording the private gift of the marble paving by one Gaius Stonicius Trophimianus.[60]

The Stonicii are attested among Puteolan inscriptions and this inscription almost certainly represents a local dignitary's record of his gift to the refurbishment of this chamber. It is tempting to speculate on whether Trophimianus had some connection with the guild of marble suppliers who operated out of Puteoli.[61]

Another shrine[62] extended along the entire interior space (a depth of 13.33m) and ended in a crosswall for buttressing, behind which lay a small cistern (3.09 × 2.65m). The outer foyer, like the previous shrine, had only the western side of the portico blocked off; its pavement was composed of large slabs of cipollino marble. The inner room had a cut-marble floor (*opus sectile*): a pattern of rhombuses within a rectangular panel, while the walls carried traces of nails for affixing marble revetment slabs. Two altars (a: 0.7 × 0.72m and b: 0.6m each side) stood before a podium (0.8m high, 3.2m wide and 1.8m deep) that formed the base for cult statues and/or cult objects. Within the fill of the podium was found an earlier fountain basin and associated lead piping in a shallow channel leading towards the exterior of the monument. Two deities, whose identities are otherwise unknown, were worshipped in this shrine.

Maiuri has identified a third chamber as a shrine.[63] It shared the rich marble decoration of floors and walls with the previous examples described. The rear of the shrine ended in an apse, in front of which stood a statue base revetted with marble (1.8m wide, 1.5m deep and 0.9m high). Traces exist here too of a fountain in the right-hand wall, probably from the earlier phases of this monument. The iconography of the deity venerated here is unknown.

Not every shrine was decorated with marble revetment. Another chapel[64] contained stucco decoration of the sloping barrel vault of the ceiling, similar in style to that found in the chamber tombs along the *via Campana* of the first and second centuries AD.

In addition to the shrines described above, Maiuri also identified a series of rooms, located farther away from the southern axis of the arena, which he calls the '*sedi degli corporazioni*' or the club rooms of the corporations or guilds of Puteoli. One imagines that they were rather like the hospitality pavilions of major British businesses at important sporting events today. These were probably areas where the members of the guilds and their invited guests could have suitable refreshment during the intervals of the spectacles. Unlike those chambers designated as shrines, there is little evidence to suggest religious ritual here.

One club room had the same two-part plan as the shrines above.[65] Its outer foyer was paved in large white marble tesserae and separated by side-walls from the portico itself. Traces of a small cross-wall (3m from the rear of the chamber) along with marble revetment were also found. At the boundary between the foyer and the inner room, a polychrome mosaic garlanded with

Plate 3.6 Flavian amphitheatre, Puteoli: the stucco decoration on the vaulting of a chamber inserted beneath the vaulting of the *cavea*. Photograph by D.L. Bomgardner

an inscription inside (For Pulvis [?], the heart throb of the *scabillarii*') appears in the mosaic paving, set so as to be read from the foyer looking into the chamber.[66]

This inscription names a guild, the *scabillarii*, musicians who played a type of large wooden or metal castanet attached to a shoe (*scabillum*) to accompany dramatic performances and other spectacles, where musical accompaniment would be appropriate. To us today, it seems amazing that such a highly specialised subset of the modern percussion section of an orchestra should, in effect, have its own official headquarters, central office or hospitality pavilion in this amphitheatre. However, it is possible that this overestimates the evidence.

Two other inscriptions found in the debris cleared from the amphitheatre by Maiuri record important sociological information. One inscription, forming part of the lintel of an architrave, bore the letters: *SCHOLA ORG[IOPHANTORUM]*, i.e., the meeting place of the association or organisation (*collegium*) of the priests who initiated new cult members into the orgiastic rites of Dionysus, the god of wine and intoxication, defined as either inebriation through the agency of wine or ecstatic possession by the godhead.[67] Maiuri associates this inscription with the cult of Liber Pater, an Italian deity of fertility usually associated with the Greek god Dionysus, at Puteoli. Large numbers of people originating in the eastern Mediterranean lived and worked in Puteoli and this inscription bears testimony to their religious rituals here, either in the amphitheatre itself or nearby. The second inscription, found near the eastern entrance to the arena in 1926, is a fragmentary dedicatory inscription that mentions the professional guild of the master mariners of Puteoli (*navicularii*). These men formed the backbone of the port's prosperity, providing employment and trade opportunities for the rest of the community. Their ships carried the grain shipments from Alexandria and Carthage that fed the multitudes of Rome's urban population. Their cargoes on the return leg of the voyage included Campanian oil and wine, as well as the locally manufactured glass and early imperial red tableware pottery (*terra sigillata*) for the luxury markets of the provinces. Maiuri proposes that the inscription may have graced the marble decoration of the club room of this guild in the amphitheatre (but without being able to specify its location). In any case, these master mariners would certainly have had special reserved blocks of high-status seating and also an official meeting place among the chambers such as Maiuri has described. The fantastically rich decor of these chambers is an indication of the opulence which the individual colonists as well as the guilds of Puteoli had to invest in such displays of conspicuous wealth.

The drainage system

Every amphitheatre tended to be liable to flooding on account of two factors. First, since most arenas sank deeply below the prevailing ground level of the surrounding terrain, there was a tendency for rising groundwater to accumulate in the arena itself. Second, whenever there was a heavy shower of rain, because of the amphitheatre's funnel-shaped geometry, the run-off water also tended to pool into the arena. Therefore, it was essential for every viable amphitheatre to have a more or less elaborate drainage system. Even the simplest sunken amphitheatres, such as that at *Calleva Atrebatum*, the tribal capital of the Atrebates at Silchester in Berkshire, had its own series of wooden-lined drains.[68]

When one remembers that most Classical archaeologists of the past were primarily concerned with the recovery largely of the artistic heritage of the Greco-Roman world, it is not surprising that the drainage systems of the amphitheatre should not have issued a sirens' call for their investigation. Additionally, by the nature of the inquiry, before the age of remote-controlled robotics and associated fibre-optical television cameras, it would have been extremely difficult and costly to have probed the deeply buried and probably silted-up remains of the drainage system of an arena. It is, therefore, much to the credit of Maiuri that he included a detailed study of the elaborate system of conduits, ducts, sumps, settling pits, piping and drains of this amphitheatre in his publication of 1955.[69] In general the drainage system consisted of two parts. The first part of this network carried surface water away from the arena, its subterranean galleries, the podium, *ima* and *media cavea*. The second part drained the *summa cavea*, external façade and its portico and the broad elliptical piazza surrounding the monument. The water collected from the uppermost parts of the seating was partly channelled into a series of cisterns located symmetrically beneath the *media cavea*. Both parts of the drainage system carried the run-off rainwater and overflow from the cisterns deeply beneath the surface of the monument's paving to a network of radial drains, disposed much like the bones radiating from the backbone of a fish. Each of these radial drains fed into the main axial (east to west) sewer, which comprised the backbone of the fish using the above analogy. From here the waste water flowed via sewers into the sea.

The fountains

Allied to the problems of the removal of unwanted water are those relating to the provision of an adequate water supply for the various needs of the amphitheatre. Among these needs is the provision of drinking water for the tens of thousands of spectators in the seating and for the beasts confined beneath the arena. In addition it was important to provide an adequate supply of water for public hygiene (e.g., for the flushing of toilets and the regular washing of passageway floors and seating areas) and for the maintenance of a clean, healthy environment in the subterranean galleries, where regular mucking out and washing down of both the cells and the passageways would be necessary. The bulk of the water supply for the subterranean galleries of the arena came from the *aqua Campana*, an aqueduct that entered the lower reaches of the arena by a channel positioned beneath the northern axial entranceway of the monument. Maiuri has refuted Dubois' arguments that this aqueduct was intended to supply the water for mock sea battles (*naumachiae*) in this arena.[70] The aqueduct supplied the substantial requirements of the underground warren of cells and passages beneath the arena (see Plate 3.7).

Plate 3.7 Flavian amphitheatre, Puteoli: the two-storey complex of subterranean passages and cells beneath the arena in brick construction. This is the inner annular corridor with trap doors into the arena above it. See Figure 3.5.

Photograph by D.L. Bomgardner.

Maiuri uncovered and recorded the existence of six fountains located along the outer wall of the middle *ambulacrum* of the *cavea*.[71] These fountains were fed from cisterns located beneath the sloping barrel vaulting of the outer ring of masonry radial walls of the amphitheatre. Using the highly symmetrical distribution of these fountains, at least two more may be confidently expected to have existed.[72] Thus the pattern that emerges is two-fold: along the minor axis, arcades three positions to the right or left held fountains, while, along the major axis, arcades six positions to right or left provided water. Maiuri points out that, in addition to these internal fountains, an equal number of external fountains would also have existed, nestled beneath the sloping barrel vaulting that opened outward on to the external portico of the amphitheatre. Examples of this may be found in the earlier phases of the shrines and club rooms as described above.[73] Thus we have a grand total of at least sixteen fountains for the ground floor alone. There must have been many more than this number, partly on the grounds of sheer necessity, when one considers the tens of thousands of spectators, and partly on the grounds of sufficient numbers to permit the substitution of cult chambers and assembly rooms in place of those fountains in the outer ring of the amphitheatre.

A monumental fountain, known as a *nymphaeum*, was discovered along the southern axis of the arena some 15m to the south of the outer edge of the paved elliptical piazza at this point. This open space was perhaps a cross-roads junction to the south of the major entrance into the arena and therefore the monumentalisation of this space would have been appropriate. The fountain consisted of a large rectangular basin (*lacus*: 9m wide and 3.08m long) and behind this a hemicycle (7m wide and 2.83m in diameter). The entire fountain was revetted in marble slabs and a marble protome in the shape of a lion's head mask formed the spout from which the water streamed down into the basins.[74] The fountain was built at the same time as the amphitheatre itself or else shortly afterwards.

The subterranean structures of the arena: chronology and function

Maiuri assigns the construction of the elaborate series of vaulted galleries, passageways, ramps and chambers on two levels beneath the concrete floor of the arena to the Domitianic, or at the latest, the early Trajanic period see (Plate 3.7).[75] The entire nature of the architecture in this region is utilitarian and non-decorative. The large expanses of brick walls there are left unadorned by any trace of a stucco coating, unlike the walls of the interior of the *cavea*, where every visible trace of wall surface is thickly plastered with stucco and then painted in bright monochrome colours (red used for the lower register and white for the upper).

These substructures were all to do with business – the business of storing securely and then delivering animals and stage props efficiently into the arena at the right moment in the course of the spectacles unfolding there. There is a wonderful sense of unifying organisation and efficiency about the layout of this zone, every element contributing to the overall effect. Here at Puteoli, these substructures are much better preserved than in the Colosseum and deserve a closer examination.

The three arches of the façade at either end of the major axis formed a complex entranceway. The central bay was largely occupied by a ramp leading steeply down into the subterranean galleries of the arena (see Plate 3.8 and Figures 3.4 and 3.5, labelled 'c'). It is clear that all the heavy equipment, stage props (*pegmata*) and caged animals entered the subterranean structures by these ramps prior to the day of the performances. In order to provide alternative access to the main axial entranceway, the bays on either side were interconnected with it beyond the point where the ramp plunged dramatically down into the depths of the arena. This ramp could be covered by stout planking so that, on the day of the spectacles, the *pompa* that inaugurated every religious festival could proceed unhindered through this central bay and on into the arena.

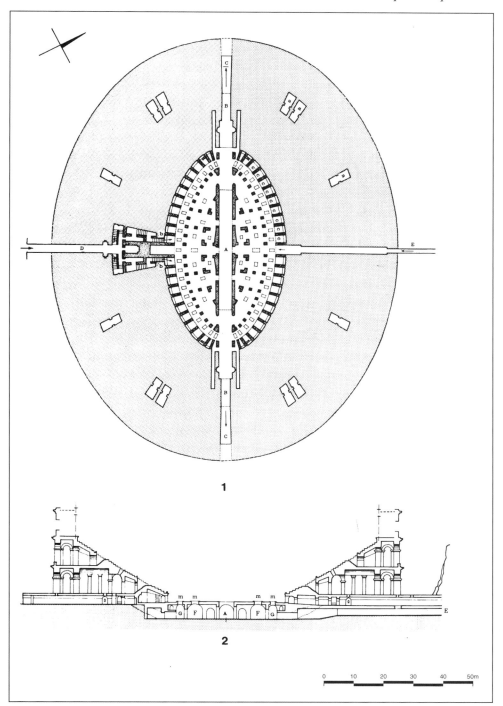

Figure 3.5 Flavian amphitheatre, Puteoli. Ground plan of the substructures of the arena and cross-section of the amphitheatre.
Source: Golvin, Planche XXXIX, 1 and 2. Copyright J.-Cl. Golvin.

Plate 3.8 Flavian amphitheatre, Puteoli: the subterranean structures of the arena. View looking back from the central gallery towards one of the major axis entranceways into the substructures.
Photograph by D.L. Bomgardner.

On the southern end of the minor axis, another vaulted gallery gave access to the subterranean regions of the arena. However, here, no ramp plunged steeply down into its bowels, but rather two symmetrical stairways (see Figure 3.5, labelled 'b') gave access to its nether regions. From this same gallery, stairs led upwards to the box (*pulvinar* or *tribunal editoris*), where the *editor* (provider or donor of the spectacles) and the most honoured dignitaries sat during the spectacles. With this circulation plan in mind, it may be possible to reconstruct the route that the *pompa* followed on the day of the solemn inauguration of the spectacles.

Following the analogy of the sun's path, the *pompa* probably entered the arena by the entranceway at the eastern end of the major axis. Then the solemn procession either did a lap of honour around the arena, or else processed straight across and out the western entranceway. There the procession either halted or more probably continued anti-clockwise around the broad *piazza* surrounding the amphitheatre to the southern entrance of the minor axis. Here the procession probably broke up into its constituent parties of honourable dignitaries and arena personnel, including the gladiators and beast fighters. Both parties could reach their respective destinations from this gallery: the dignitaries climbing up their segregated stairway into the box of honour, the arena personnel descending into the murky bowels of the arena by the lower stairways.

The fundamental plan of the entire complex revolves around the two main axial galleries: the larger central gallery (90m long and 4.75m wide) and the shorter transverse gallery (55m long and 4m wide). The two ramps leading down from the major axis galleries each had a kind of small vestibule at the lower level. These vestibules (see Figure 3.5) had a semi-circular apse in each of the flanking walls. Such apses are often associated with religious purposes, such as a cult statue in a niche. The goddess Diana was worshipped in this amphitheatre,[76] although it is not possible to specify the exact location(s) and precise number of her shrines here. These vestibules could be closed off by a door. Further concern for safety and security is evident in the provision of a sliding wooden portcullis, the grooves for which still survive in the side-walls farther along the tunnel.

It is easy to visualise the process of manhandling the numerous stage props and cages (*carceres*) down these ramps and into the main central gallery. The central portion of this main gallery was not vaulted in concrete, but covered by a series of wooden beams spanning its width (4.75m) (see Plate 3.9). Such a scheme would allow maximum flexibility so that the gap could either be closed or open to allow truly monumental stage sets and follies (*pegmata*) to emerge during the spectacles. We hear from literary sources of entire artificial mountains covered in trees being used in the performances in the arena to re-enact mythical *tableaux vivantes*, such as the legend of

Orpheus taming the beasts, but with a cruel twist in the tale: Orpheus (a condemned criminal, almost certainly a slave condemned by the courts to a sentence of public execution in the arena) fails and is torn limb from limb by the savage, very much untamed, wild beasts.[77] Such cruel and ironic twists of popular myths and legends were apparently popular spectacles in the arena and specially modified theatres and stadia of the Roman empire.

The subterranean passageways and cells

All circulation originated from the central gallery of the substructures. A series of ten broad archways opened symmetrically to left and right along the central gallery (see Plate 3.9). These archways led into a series of highly irregularly shaped storage areas (two storeys high) that were sandwiched between the axial galleries and two concentric peripheral annular galleries (the inner 2.5m wide, the outer 1m wide) (see Figure 3.5 and Plate 3.7). Trap doors opened into the arena above these annular corridors.

Access to these annular galleries was either by means of the transverse and central galleries or through one of the irregularly shaped chambers. The outer annular gallery existed only on the upper level, the inner annular gallery only on the lower (see Plate 3.10). A large number of stairways led from the lower to the upper level of the substructures for the easy movement of personnel (see Plate 3.11). Animals in cages were hoisted from the lower to the upper level by means of an elaborate series of hoists with ingeniously counter-weighted mechanisms. The lower level gave access to a series of forty large storage chambers (4m deep, 2.3m high and from 2.15 to 2.30m wide, positioned beneath the outer edge of the arena), probably designed to provide longer-term storage facilities for the animals destined for the spectacles (see Plate 3.7). The upper level gave access to a series of forty smaller chambers (2.93m deep, 1.9m high and 2.1m wide) positioned directly above the lower level chambers (see Plate 3.10). These chambers probably housed the cages of animals immediately prior to their appearance in the arena. The cages on the upper level were shunted forward on some form of roller system into the inner annular gallery, where a series of modillions were mounted along the interior walls at this height (see plate 3.7) to take the weight of this assembly. Above each

hoisting station, there was a trap door positioned overhead (of varying dimensions, some 1 × 1.3m, others 1.9 × 1.25m or 2.7 × 2m). When the mechanism was engaged, the cage sprang upward and through the trap door into the arena, so that the animal was delivered dramatically into the setting of the arena above. Burning straw was probably placed in the back of each cage to force the animals out of this relative safety and into the harsh glare of the sunlight and the din of the crowd in the arena.[78] It goes without saying that the cages and trap doors would have had to be lowered as soon as possible, both to ensure that the animals did not re-enter them and also to remove obvious obstructions to the view of

Plate 3.9 Flavian amphitheatre, Puteoli: the subterranean structures of the arena. View showing the central gallery in the middle of the arena, originally roofed with timber beams.
Photograph by D.L. Bomgardner.

Plate 3.10 Flavian amphitheatre, Puteoli: the outer annular corridor which existed only on the upper level of the substructures. See Figure 3.5. Photograph by D.L. Bomgardner.

Plate 3.11 Flavian amphitheatre, Puteoli: the stairways that connected the lower with the upper level in the subterranean chambers of the arena.
Photograph by D.L. Bomgardner.

the spectators. Also here at Puteoli (with the Colosseum in Rome) is the earliest known appearance of the net barrier designed to keep animals and gladiators out of the 'blind zone' at the foot of the podium wall, probably dating to the Domitianic era.

The floor of the arena rested upon an enormous expanse of concrete vaulting, sloping gently downward towards its outer perimeter (6.7m above the bottom of the subterranean zone in the centre of the arena, but only 6.25m at the edges). This slope will have encouraged efficient drainage of this large flat expanse, which would have been prone to partial flooding, especially during heavy seasonal rains.

It is interesting to note that the film *Spartacus* (1960) used the architecture of these subterranean brickwork galleries and stairways as the inspiration for the stage sets of the gladiatorial barracks in Capua from which the gladiatorial revolt of 79 BC started (see Plate 3.11). This is an obvious architectural anachronism, since such brickwork is never found before the Augustan era, but Hollywood has never been overly concerned for accuracy in such matters.

In conclusion, one can see a distinctive advance in the planning and execution of the subterranean structures in the Flavian amphitheatre of Puteoli. Unlike the 'forced fit' nature of the Colosseum and the Anfiteatro Campano at Capua, where the architect is trying to force a rectilinear array of substructures to fit into an oval hole, the substructures here are more typologically developed and more competent. They reflect a smoother accommodation between rectilinear and oval elements of the architectural space, where the dividing partitions of the galleries themselves curve to fit into their space more efficiently. As such, these subterranean galleries and chambers should be later than those of the Colosseum and Capua, and should, therefore, perhaps best be considered as part of the Domitianic/ Trajanic programme of alterations to this structure, rather than an integral feature of the initial Flavian construction.

Corinthian colonnade atop the cavea

Like the Colosseum in Rome, this amphitheatre had a crowning colonnaded portico atop the seating. All traces of this uppermost part of the seating have long since been destroyed, but the existence of a monumental Corinthian colonnade there may be deduced from the numerous architectural fragments of columns, bases and capitals uncovered during excavation (see, e.g., Plates 3.7–3.9 where the remnants of column shafts remain visible). The fragments reveal a bold, deeply cut technique, somewhat lacking in refinement, but eminently suited to be seen at a great distance as part of the crowning colonnade of the superstructure. Only one complete column has survived (4.72m high). There are also fragments of the column capitals (0.87–0.88m high) and one well-preserved fragment of a column base (1.17m wide, 0.43m high). These dimensions provide an estimate for the overall height of the columns as just over 6m high (6.03m).

The major phases of construction

Since Maiuri's original study and publication of this monument (1955), much additional work has taken place in the study of the development and the chronological significance of various Roman construction techniques. Nevertheless his chronological framework for the major phases of this monument has withstood the test of time.

Here is a brief summary of Maiuri's architectural phasing and chronology of the Flavian amphitheatre.

1 *Phase I (Flavian era, after AD 69)*. The bulk of the *cavea* and at least some of the substructures of the arena.
2 *Phase II (Domitianic/early Trajanic era)*. The addition of the Corinthian colonnade to the top of the *cavea*. Possibly the elaborate galleries and cells in brickwork of the substructures of the arena.
3 *Phase III (probably the latter half of the second century AD)*. The addition of the internal buttressing piers and arches beneath the continuous barrel vault of the external portico in brickwork; the raising of the level of the stairways; the renovation of the chambers beneath the sloping barrel vaulting in the outer ring of radial walls of the *cavea* for shrines and assembly rooms; the insertion of a major chapel (*sacellum*) beneath the *pulvinar* at the southern end of the minor axis of the arena. And perhaps the brickwork subterranean structures of the arena, if not part of the earlier phase of construction.

This amphitheatre reflects a monument that is characteristically Roman in its plan, its design features and its building materials and construction techniques. Nevertheless there is good evidence that every aspect of this edifice's construction made use of local manpower and craftsmanship as well as local materials. We see here a wealthy, self-reliant, technically sophisticated metropolis adopting Roman traditions and monument types in a conscious imitation of Rome. It is also intriguing that the Flavian colony should build an amphitheatre, the chosen dynastic monument of the first of the soldier-emperors, Vespasian. May we, perhaps, see the influence of Vespasian's close association with his military origins, the soldier's soldier, brought to power through the agency of the Roman legions, at work here too?

The local patrons of Puteoli

We have already seen above that the important guild of ship owners, the *navicularii*, was involved in providing contributions to the adornment of the amphitheatre. We have even seen evidence for such small guilds as that of the *scabillarii*, the musicians who played the foot-castanets, paying for an assembly room beneath the seating of the *cavea*. Wealthy individuals, such as Gaius Stonicius Trophimianus, also paid for parts of the adornment of the amphitheatre, the re-paving in marble of the shrine beneath the arcades of the portico.

There is also important epigraphical evidence for some of the individuals who gave gladiatorial spectacles at Puteoli and their fascinating reasons for doing so. Caius Julius Apollonius gave a gladiatorial spectacle lasting for three days.[79] Apollonius served in the imperial civil service at Rome where he first held a post in the *decuria* of attendants who were at the service of the *aediles* and tribunes (perhaps the tribunes of the *vigiles*). He then achieved the honoured position of *accensus velatus* (a personal attendant who accompanied a senior magistrate, possibly the emperor himself, alongside his lictors).[80] Whether Apollonius himself was originally from Puteoli is not certain. The inscription, found in Puteoli, is from the tomb of his wife, Annia Agrippina. Apollonius may have presented the three-day series of gladiatorial spectacles commemorated in it here at Puteoli. It would have been an occasion of sacrifice for the emperor's well-being and safety (*pro salute Imperatoris*) and also requiring his special permission.[81]

Marcus Gavius Puteolanus was a well-known citizen who had held the chief magistracy (*duovir*) as well as that of deputy chief magistrate (*aedilis*).[82] He paid for a display of gladiators lasting for four days, probably at Puteoli. The inscription itself was found at Naples, which, however, had no amphitheatre: Puteoli had the nearest one. Gavius probably gave these games when he was elected chief magistrate (*duovir*) in fulfilment of his obligation to give such an exhibition upon his successful election.[83]

By far the best-known benefactor was a star of the Roman theatre in the time of the emperor Marcus Aurelius, the freedman Pylades.[84] He was a *pantomimus*, an actor who mimed all the roles in an essentially serious dramatic presentation while the chorus and orchestra accompanied him and narrated the tale to the audience.[85] Tremendous versatility and consummate talent were needed to achieve such a difficult feat successfully. 'Pantomimes' were amongst the highest paid and most celebrated performers in the Roman theatre. Pylades was a local slave boy made good. Although he was born a slave, he received his freedom from the emperor at the peak of his fame. He was patron of the guild of actors (*parasiti Apollinis*) and was the foremost pantomime of his age (*pantomimo temporis sui primo*), showered with honours (normally reserved for free-born Roman citizens) by his native Puteoli. He was entitled to wear the regalia appropriate to citizens who had held the chief magistracy (*duovir*) and who were members of the town council (*ordo decurionum* [*honorato Puteolis, d(ecreto) d(ecurionum), ornamentis decurionalib(us) duum-viralib(us)*]). He was given the honorary municipal title of *augur* for his devotion to his home town (*patria*) and his unstinting generosity in presenting gladiatorial shows with a beast hunt of assorted types of animals (*in edendo muner(a) gladiatorum venatione passiva*) with the express permission of the emperor Commodus. The gladiatorial spectacle may have been given in response to the award of the right to wear the regalia and insignia of a *duovir* and a member of the town's senate, i.e., as if he had been elected *duovir* (in which case he would have had to give such games).

Repairs to the main structure

The region of the Bay of Naples is one of much volcanic and seismic activity. In antiquity such activity was identified with a close connection with the Underworld and one of the direct entrances from the world of the living to the world of the dead was considered to be in this region, among the Phlegraean Fields (*campi Phlegraei*). As a result of such frequent and violent activity as well as the inherent instability and the slow sinking of the ground relative to sea level (*bradysism*), the major monuments of Puteoli have suffered considerably. This amphitheatre was no exception, and Maiuri reckons that by the latter half of the second century AD it was in need of immediate and radical repair to counteract these destructive forces of nature. Such repairs took several forms to underpin the basic structure.

The continuous barrel vaulting of the external porticoes of both the ground and first floors had evidently shown signs of cracking and instability. To counteract the distortions of the structure's geometry and to shore up the underside of this vaulting, a series of substantial brick reinforcing piers (1.8–1.82m wide × 1.22–1.24m thick) in pairs were added internally to each existing pier and were linked together by a brickwork arch (see Plate 3.4 where the bases of these brick piers are still visible).[86] This internal buttressing system effectively reduced the internal width of the *ambulacrum* from 4.8m to a mere 2.42m. A thick coating of stucco, painted red in the lower zone and white above, was applied to these brick pilasters and arches as well as the original interior members of the architecture in an attempt to hide the repairs. In effect the stucco masked the vertical joints where the new piers were abutted on to the old ones.[87]

As a result of the decrease in the width of the external portico, the stairways would now have fallen quite visibly short (by more than a metre) of the interior space of the ground-floor arcade. In a further effort to disguise the repairs, all the stairways of the ground-floor arcade were re-laid in new stone risers at a higher level and extended by some three additional treads at the bottom so that now there was a conjunction between the ends of the stairways and the beginning of the open space of the *ambulacrum*.[88] In consequence the floor levels of the intermediate landings of the stairways, the *ambulacrum* beneath the seating as well as that of the upper exterior arcade had to be raised accordingly.

Design principles

As described above (see p. 70) for the Verona amphitheatre, Wilson Jones has recently undertaken an analytical study of the detailed way in which Roman architects planned and laid out monumental amphitheatres.[89]

Like Verona, the arena at Puteoli is based upon the so-called 'equilateral-triangle-and-inscribed-circle-scheme' (see above, p. 70f., for a detailed description of this method of planning an amphitheatre). The initial stages and principles involved in the planning and design of both monuments are remarkably similar.[90] Both arenas share similar proportions in that the width of the arena and of the *cavea* is half that of the arena's length in both monuments.

The actual dimensions of the Puteoli arena were 250 × 140 Roman ft. Its trace was generated from a four-centred arc system with radii of 200 and 50 Roman ft. respectively. The *cavea* width turned out to be 131 Roman ft. and the overall dimensions, 512 × 402 Roman ft. The façade consisted of seventy-two arcaded bays, each measuring 20 Roman ft. in width. The laying-out and design of this monument seem, in comparison with Verona, more adept, particularly in the success with which the bays of the façade achieved the desired width of a simple whole number of Roman feet. Perhaps this may be explained by the fact that Puteoli was built a generation later than Verona, during which time much practical experience of constructing monumental amphitheatres was gained.

The Anfiteatro Campano, Capua[91]

Overall dimensions	165 × 135m
Arena dimensions	76.12 × 45.83m
Width of *cavea*	44.4m
Area of arena	2,740m²
Area of *cavea*	14,755m²
Total area	17,495m²
Estimated perimeter	942.5m
Percentage of total area devoted to seating	84 per cent
Estimated seating capacity	47,426

Among the most important arenas that were direct copies of the Colosseum in Rome is the Anfiteatro Campano at Santa Maria Capua Vetere (the site of ancient Capua). Its superstructure has suffered much in the course of time and much of the seating and the vaulting upon which it rested are now missing. Furthermore, very little more than a few individual arches now remain of the once impressive double-gallery of the ground floor, or indeed of the upper storeys of this once imposing façade (see Plate 3.13). Yet, its subterranean structures remain well preserved and the impressive series of finely executed, high-quality sculptural decorations that once adorned it adds much to our knowledge of how monumental amphitheatres were embellished, as well as to our knowledge of the architectural context of such sculpture.

Like the Colosseum, the Anfiteatro Campano was girded by a broad, paved piazza. Robust stone bollards for fastening the ropes of the awning system (*vela*) and also probably for fixing

Plate 3.12 Anfiteatro Campano, Capua: overview of the amphitheatre showing the poor state of preservation of portions of the *cavea*.
Photograph by D.L. Bomgardner.

Plate 3.13 Anfiteatro Campano, Capua: the paved piazza encircling the amphitheatre. Note the bollards at its outer edge and the few remaining arcades of its façade.
Photograph by D.L. Bomgardner.

wooden crowd-control barriers regularly dotted its outer edge. Like the Colosseum, it too had a double external *ambulacrum* as well as two interior annular passageways (see Figure 3.6).[92] By using these annular galleries, spectators could choose the right combination of stairways and interior galleries so that eventually they would emerge from beneath the seating through the appropriate portal (*vomitorium*) out into the proper tier (*maenianum*) and wedge-shaped block (*cuneus*) of the seating. The same principles regarding status and access probably operated here as in the Colosseum. In general the higher the status of the spectators, the deeper they penetrated into the passages and annular corridors that lay beneath the seating. Spectators of low status reached their seats from the outermost regions of the exterior colonnade.

The façade consisted of eighty arches (*en tas de charge*), rising in three storeys and crowned by an attic.[93] Half-columns adorned the piers between adjacent arches and these applied orders probably alternated (Tuscan, Ionic, Corinthian in ascending order) just as in the Colosseum. Unlike the Colosseum, however, where a series of large Roman numerals were engraved on the keystones of the arches of the ground-floor façade, at Capua the keystones bore detailed sculpted busts of deities (see Plate 3.14). Both systems, Roman numerals and sculpted busts, aided spectators by giving each bay of the façade a unique identification and thus assisting them in their choice of which arcade to enter in order to take the most direct route to their seats.

The subterranean structures

The subterranean structures of the Anfiteatro Campano bear a striking resemblance, in their layout, organisational principles, plan and building materials, to those of the Colosseum.

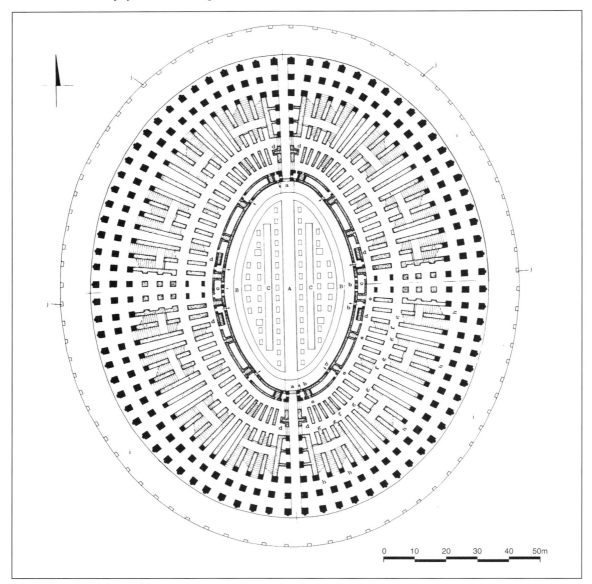

Figure 3.6 Anfiteatro Campano, Capua. Ground plan of the amphitheatre.
Source: Golvin, Planche XL. Copyright J.-Cl. Golvin.

However, at Capua there are many more transverse galleries parallel to the minor axis of the arena than in the Colosseum, where only a single central crossway existed. Once again one sees the architect's essentially futile attempt to insert a square peg into a round hole. The rectilinear ground plan of the subterranean galleries simply does not fit easily into the oval space beneath the arena. The solution to which the architect had recourse was to truncate the outermost ring of galleries by means of a wall that closely followed the contours of the arena-wall above it (see Figure

Plate 3.14 Anfiteatro Campano, Capua: one arcade of the façade. Note the applied Tuscan half-column and sculpted keystone block. Photograph by D.L. Bomgardner.

3.7). The substructures display bilateral symmetry, i.e., they are symmetrical along both the major and minor axes of the arena.

The construction technique employed in these subterranean galleries is homogeneous throughout: cut-stone foundations with brickwork (*opus testaceum*) used for the upper portions of walls (see Plate 3.15). An enormous central bay (see Figures 3.6 and 3.7, labelled 'A', and Plate 3.16), covered by a wooden plank flooring at the arena level, formed the dominant feature along the major axis. Indeed the major axis formed the central organising focus for the layout of these substructures. Flanking each side of this grand central bay lay a series of linear vaulted galleries that held machinery to hoist thirty cages (fifteen in each row) up into the arena (see Plate 3.15). Moving further outward towards the periphery of the arena, another passageway (see Figure 3.7, labelled 'B') flanked each of these vaulted galleries; like the central bay these were covered with a timber flooring (see Plate 3.12). Then, a double row of annular vaulted galleries (supplied with trap doors through the concrete vaulting) bracketed the central zone of substructures. These galleries contained machinery to hoist thirty-two cages into the arena above, including six especially large trap doors. Finally an oval-shaped passageway (see Figure 3.7, labelled 'C') covered in timber (at the level of the arena) enclosed this area in a ring. Outside this ring-corridor lay a series of forty vaulted chambers (*posticae*). These provided storage space for stage props and temporary accommodation for the beasts prior to their exhibition in the arena. Four stairways, situated on either side of the minor axis (see Figure 3.6, labelled 'd' and Figure 3.7, labelled 'b'), led from a chamber beneath the podium down into one of these chambers. These stairs enabled arena service personnel to move between the service areas under the arena and under the podium.

Thus, if one were to slice the arena in half along the minor axis, one would have a nine-fold sequence of bays, corridors and galleries.[94] Similarly, if one were to slice the arena in half along the major axis, one would have a twenty-one-fold series of corridors and bays.[95] It is not difficult to see how easy circulation would be in these subterranean galleries: three long corridors parallel to the major axis, nine corridors parallel to the minor axis and a ring-corridor enclosing the whole assemblage.

Once again the proximity of this city to the vital sea route between Rome and the southern and eastern Mediterranean was of crucial importance in the design of its subterranean substructures.

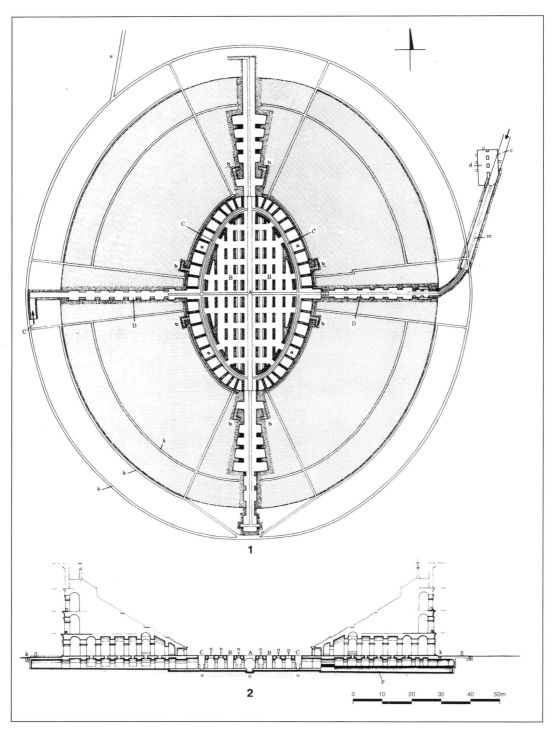

Figure 3.7 Anfiteatro Campano, Capua. Ground plan of the subterranean structures and cross-section of the amphitheatre.
Source: Golvin, Planche XLI. Copyright J.-Cl. Golvin.

The provision of ample storage space, a copious water supply for both consumption and sanitation, ready access for supplies, stage props and cages of beasts as well as a sophisticated system of machinery for the co-ordinated transport of cage-loads of wild beasts into the arena could only have been possible in a location where a steady supply of imported beasts by ships from abroad was secure. The enormous additional expense needed to provide such subterranean facilities is a clear indication of the essential importance of wild beast fights (*venationes*) in the programmes of spectacles held in this amphitheatre.

The sculptural decoration

Gennaro Pesce first published a detailed study of the sculptural reliefs from this amphitheatre in the early 1940s.[96] Although other examples have been found more recently,[97] this monograph remains of fundamental importance as the first such study of the sculptural programme of an amphitheatre.

The sculpted keystones

As mentioned above, a series of sculpted keystone bosses adorned the arches of the façade arcades (see Plate 3.14). These keystones bore detailed sculpted busts of deities, e.g., Mithras, Juno, Isis, Diana, Demeter, Jupiter, Volturnus, Mercury and Minerva. These sculptures of deities adorned the lower two storeys

Plate 3.15 Anfiteatro Campano, Capua: the subterranean structures of the arena looking down one of the long galleries parallel to the major axis of the arena. Note the construction technique employed: stone footings with brickwork above.
Photograph by D.L. Bomgardner.

of the façade, while the upper had more mundane thematic material, such as tragic masks or satyrs.[98] The bottom arcade bore the representations of Diana (see Plate 3.17),[99] Juno or Demeter (see Plate 3.18),[100] a river god, probably the local Volturnus,[101] Jupiter,[102] perhaps a Silvanus (executed in the Antinous iconography of the Hadrianic era),[103] Mercury[104] and Minerva.[105] The middle arcade sported the following ornamented keystones: a tragic mask,[106] Apollo the Archer,[107] a drunken satyr,[108] Pan,[109] the head of a drunken male figure,[110] and Diana the Huntress.[111] The smallest scale of protomes included the following: the head of a bearded satyr[112] and two unidentified male busts.[113]

Pesce identifies more than one hand at work in these carvings as well as a mixture of purely Classical and local artistic influences. This leads him to conclude that local artisans worked on this sculptural programme.[114] Pesce also argues for a Hadrianic date on the basis of the style of these representations.[115]

Plate 3.16 Anfiteatro Campano, Capua: the central bay of the substructures in the arena.
Photograph by D.L. Bomgardner.

The artistic origins of such a decorative scheme seem almost certainly Etruscan.[116] This fact is entirely consistent with the local history of Capua, once the chief centre of Etruscan Campania. Originally such decoration was probably intended to lend supernatural protection to the city gates, the most vulnerable points in the circuit of walls surrounding a settlement. Also, perhaps, these heads were designed to ward off evil influences that might enter the city through its portals. Such an apotropaic function is common in the ancient world where superstitious awe and dread predominated. However, with the passage of time, such intentions may have been submerged in more purely decorative considerations. Here at Capua, such sculptural decoration may have carried a cultural, as well as a religious, connotation: a reminder of the proud Etruscan heritage of this once mighty city.

In addition, it is clear that here spectators used this series of individual carved reliefs to help them to find the shortest route to their seats (see above p. 91). Elsewhere, as in the Colosseum, they used Roman numerals for the same purpose.

This programme of exterior sculptural adornment proved popular and at least two other major amphitheatres, both in North Africa at Carthage and El Jem, later copied this decorative system.

Plate 3.17 Anfiteatro Campano, Capua: the sculpted bust of the goddess Diana on the keystone of an arch of the ground floor of the exterior façade.
Photograph by D.L. Bomgardner.

Plate 3.18 Anfiteatro Campano, Capua: the sculpted bust of the goddess Juno (or perhaps Demeter) on the keystone of an arch of the ground floor of the exterior façade.
Photograph by D.L. Bomgardner.

The *plutei*

Spectators would pass from beneath the myriad corridors, stairways and passageways out into the open-air seating area through a series of arched exits (known as *vomitoria*). However, since the seating itself was steeply banked, there was the danger of spectators falling from above or either side into the *vomitorium*. In order to counteract this risk, each *vomitorium* was protected, on the top and both sides, by a barrier constructed of stone slabs, like a balustrade, called a *pluteus*.[117] In the Capua amphitheatre, these *plutei* were made of either marble or travertine and each was decorated with elaborate sculptured reliefs. They consisted of two distinct types. The most elaborate reliefs adorned the top face of the barrier, so that a spectator leaving the arena and glancing up as he passed through the *vomitorium* would see the relief decoration overhead. The second type of adornment consisted of sculpting the hand-rails, on either side of the *vomitorium*, into nearly in-the-round reliefs of zoomorphic forms. The study of these reliefs forms a major part of Pesce's monograph (see Figure 3.1).

The central reliefs

The backing panels of the *plutei* were rough parallelepipeds (67cm high, 164cm long and 14cm thick). The bottom and sides were straight-edged, but the top surface was carved into an elegant undulating border consisting of three peaks and four troughs. They contained the most ambitious artistic compositions, carved in low relief and sunk within the plain borders of the panel. Two panels in particular are of special architectural interest since they may depict the Anfiteatro Campano itself.

The first panel depicts the construction of a multi-storeyed, arcaded building, perhaps the Anfiteatro Campano itself.[118] If this identification is correct, then this relief adds valuable evidence for the reconstruction of the amphitheatre's façade. There are difficulties associated with the interpretation of any such relief purporting to represent a real architectural monument. Indeed there are some ambiguities concerning the 'reading' of this relief.

A wagon with a long pole is shown in the lower zone of the relief, presumably used to transport the building stones to the site of the construction. Two workmen, both wearing short tunics, are depicted engaged in construction work; one with a pulley, presumably raising one of the blocks of building stone into position, the other with a lever, probably easing another stone into place.[119]

The building, as depicted, consists of three elements (from bottom to top): a Corinthian portico, a Tuscan arcaded façade and an upper storey under construction. The Corinthian portico is shown only partially, being obscured to the left by the wheels of the wagon in the foreground. Pesce thinks that this is a foreshortened representation of an extension (*avancorpo*) joined to the main structure's ground-floor arcade.[120] He attributes the shallowness of part of the relief to an attempt to render it in the background behind the Corinthian portico. Above this portico there is an arcaded storey with engaged Tuscan half-columns, whose architectural details are rendered with a good deal of attention. It is possible to make out the robust individual blocks of the voussoirs and keystones of the arches as well as the Tuscan columns, bases and capitals and the complex architrave (*trabeazione*) above them. The top storey is depicted as still under construction with only the traces of an engaged half-column (of indeterminate order) visible.

Pesce's interpretation that the Corinthian portico was an early feature surrounding the edge of the piazza and replaced at some later date by the bollards still visible there seems unnecessarily convoluted. Perhaps the simplest explanation is that, like the wagon beside it, this portico forms a separate foreground context, perhaps not directly related to the amphitheatre, but merely in the immediate vicinity. Certainly the Tuscan arcaded storey, as represented, must be the ground floor of the amphitheatre itself with work just being started on the first storey. Without further contextual clues it is difficult to make sense of this fragmentary relief, much of which lacks sharp detail.

The second fragmentary relief depicts the sacrifice of three bulls in front of an amphitheatre.[121] Each bull is accompanied by its own sacrificial attendant (*victimarius*). Behind these figures in the foreground, the amphitheatre rises up in the background at a much smaller scale. Three storeys are clearly visible. Between the upraised hammer of the *victimarius* on the right and his sacrificial victim, one can see an arch with an engaged half-column, a Doric capital and an architrave composed of two elements. Above this, on the far left of the scene, one can see the vague rendering of the arcades of this storey with a column, apparently without a capital, unless it has been confused with the tripartite architrave, whose upper cornice projects prominently. Clearly visible above this, and running across the entire background, is the crowning storey of the monument, consisting of an attic storey bearing engaged pilasters without capitals that framed large expanses of wall in whose centre was inserted a single rectangular window. Also clearly visible continuing the line of the pilasters is a series of projecting elements which are obviously the masts used to support the awning (*vela*) above the arena.[122] This scene may have depicted the sacrifices that accompanied the official dedication of this monument at its inaugural ceremonies.

Once again Pesce's interpretation seems stretched. The capital of the lower storey is depicted in a very schematic way. It is difficult to discern its order. If one reads it as an Ionic capital, instead of a Doric one, the rest of the relief makes much more sense. The lower storey depicted thus becomes the first-floor Ionic arcade, while the ground-floor Tuscan arcade is hidden behind the figures in the foreground. The upper arcade becomes the Corinthian arcade (by the way consistent with the triple nature of its entablature) just below the crowning attic storey. Thus, like the Colosseum, the Anfiteatro Campano would have had four storeys: a Tuscan, Ionic and Corinthian arcade and a crowning attic storey of engaged pilasters with windows between them.

Two reliefs appear to depict scenes from the municipal life of Capua. The first shows six deities, five female, one male, each wearing a crown with turrets and standing in two ranks, four in the front, two in the rear.[123] Pesce interprets this fragmentary scene by analogy with similar more complete examples,[124] as one depicting the distribution of the emperor's largesse to a group of six cities (probably including Capua), represented here by the six turret-crowned deities (five Tyches and one Genius).

The second example (very nearly complete, but for some minor damage to the feet of the three figures on the left) is a scene depicting eight figures in formal procession making an entrance into an architectural setting.[125] The two figures at the front, by their short tunics, are clearly attendants of inferior status to the rest of the procession. The next two figures, from the evidence that they wear togas and are carrying the bundle of rods (*fasces*), are clearly two lictors, the official body-guard and ceremonial escort of Roman magistrates. They may help us to identify the figures that come next. If two lictors were the standard number assigned to municipal magistrates, then the four toga-clad figures that follow may be the two chief magistrates (*duoviri*) and their assistants (*aediles*). The first *duovir* is just beginning to climb a short flight of stairs, while the first four figures (the lictors and attendants) continue straight ahead. All of these figures seem to have entered this space by the archway portrayed on the far left of the relief. Perhaps this relief depicts that moment when, the official procession (*pompa*) having just ended, the presiding magistrates were escorted ceremoniously to their seats of honour in the 'royal box' (*pulvinar* or *tribunal*). Here we see the procession, just having entered the passageway along the minor axis of the arena that will take them to the stairway that will lead up into the *tribunal*. The ceremonial escorts peel off to take their seats in a less prestigious part of the seating, while the magistrates begin to climb the stairs that will lead to their privileged box of honour on the end of the minor axis of the arena.

A very large number of reliefs are concerned with the cycle of myths centring on the figure of Hercules. This should not be surprising in this context, since Hercules, the paragon of strength and courage, is regularly associated with both gladiators and beast-fighters. Indeed, Vitruvius says that the preferred location for a Temple of Hercules is near either the gymnasium or the amphitheatre, or failing these, the circus.[126]

Several fragmentary reliefs depict various of the labours set Hercules by Queen Omphale of the Lydians, who bought him when he was compelled to be sold as a slave to obtain purification after he had killed Iphitus, son of Eurytus. These reliefs of the labours include the Cleansing of the Augean Stables (n. 33).[127] Hercules had a strict time limit and had to accomplish this task before the sun had set. He achieved his goal by first punching holes in the end walls of the stables and then diverting the course of the local rivers through them, washing them out in record time. On the right, Hercules is shown using a digging tool to divert the course of the mighty river Alpheus through the stables of king Augeas. The stables may be represented by the highly foreshortened wickerwork-like structure at the bottom of the relief. On the left, there may be another labour represented, but it is in a very fragmentary state. It is reasonable to assume that the entire cycle of all twelve labours would have been depicted on six central reliefs.

Another relief depicted the epic wrestling bout between the Earth-born Antaeus and Hercules.[128] Every time Antaeus came into contact with his Mother Earth he regained his strength and Hercules was only able to overcome him by holding him in a bear hug off the ground and crushing him. This climactic moment is represented here. However, there is an unusual addition. The seated figure of a female Tyche is watching this contest from the left of the scene. Perhaps, this can best be explained as a symbolic representation of Capua (and by extension also her citizens) watching a re-enactment of this fight in the amphitheatre.

Queen Omphale also had Hercules perform tasks usually done by women. Following this theme of sexual inversion, Omphale is depicted on a fragmentary relief, naked except for Hercules' lion-skin, which she is wearing as a cloak over her head and shoulders.[129] An Eros is pictured to her left and she is reaching out her left hand, holding the hem of the lion's skin, towards Hercules, whose foot and club are visible. This episode may refer to the amorous affair that accompanied Hercules' servitude and led to the birth of a son, Lamus, to Omphale.

The cycle of myth surrounding Diana, commonly associated with wild beast fights (*venationes*) in the arena, is represented here by the legend of Actaeon.[130] While out hunting with his pack of hounds, the hapless Actaeon stumbled upon Diana's secret grotto, where she was bathing attended by her nymphs. While gazing raptly upon the divine form, he was observed by the goddess. Diana, in her anger, devised a cruelly ironic death: she turned Actaeon into a stag and his own hounds tore him to pieces. The two reliefs comprise the far left and right fragments of the same central relief panel. The left fragment shows Actaeon (to the left) gazing down from behind the rocky outcrop of the grotto at the half-naked figure of Diana (identified by her bow and quiver of arrows lying on the ground in the foreground), just rising out of the pool where she has been bathing and wrapping a garment around her lower torso and legs. Diana is flanked by two attendant nymphs. The right fragment shows a hound savagely attacking the left thigh of a figure within the same rocky grotto, whose sculptured outline is reminiscent of pie crust. The identical topographical context of the rocky grotto combined with an appropriate thematic element, a hound savaging a human figure, makes the identification of this rather fragmentary relief certain as part of the first scene. The figure's head is not visible, but would surely have been represented with a stag's antlers.

Another theme of divine retribution is represented by a relief depicting the punishment of Marsyas.[131] The goddess Athena had invented the flute (*aulos*, a reeded instrument actually much more like our oboe), but had discarded it because it caused her cheeks to distend ungraciously when she played it. The Phrygian satyr, Marsyas, picked up the instrument and became so proficient on it that he challenged Apollo to a music competition on his cithara, a harp-like instrument, the early forerunner of the guitar. Apollo won easily. The loser had agreed to submit to the will of the winner. So Apollo had Marsyas flayed alive for his affront. Either from his blood or from the tears of his mourners, the river Marsyas sprang. The relief is in the far left of the original panel and shows the naked Marsyas tied to a tree by the wrists, his arms extended above his head, and flanked on his left by a crouching Scythian and on his right by a standing Phrygian slave, reaching up towards the forearms of Marsyas. These attendants are obviously Apollo's henchmen, intended to do his dirty work for him. The left and central parts of the panel would probably have depicted the events leading up to this cruelly hideous denouement. The preserved fragment is obviously deeply influenced by the well-known Hellenistic statue group of 'The Hanging Marsyas', which gives full play to a detailed anatomical study of the body of Marsyas, suspended in his canonical posture from the tree.[132]

The preceding two reliefs depict deities cruelly punishing mortals for their behaviour in trying to beat the gods and thus incurring divine wrath and retribution. However, in the context of the arena, they also share another common element. As mentioned above in Chapter One, a well-known part of the spectacles staged in the arena included the execution of notorious criminals (*noxii*), often as part of a *tableau vivant*, depicting the mythical suffering of a legendary figure. It is possible that both these reliefs were intended to fulfil a dual role, as straightforward mythical narrative and as oblique reference to this process of executions carried out in the arena.[133]

Although the scenes described above had obvious parallels in the public executions in the arena and such echoes make good sense in the context of their location as part of the decorative scheme of a monumental amphitheatre, nevertheless it is difficult to prove that there was an intentional connection in the mind of the designer of the sculptural programme. Yet there may be such proof in the following relief.[134] This panel, forming over half of the left side of the original, depicts the well-known myth of the hunt for the Calydonian boar. To the right, the boar is crouching defensively inside what seems like a small cave, ready to lunge forward dangerously. One of the pack of hounds is busy worrying it, while Atalanta is just drawing an arrow from her quiver to fit to her bow. Behind her stands Meleager, in his heroic nudity, clad only in his hunting cape and holding his hunting spear at the ready in case the boar should charge. Behind him stands another huntsman, standing at his ease, right arm akimbo, left holding his upright hunting spear. He stands beneath the framework of a pilaster without base and topped by a Doric capital supporting the springing of an arch that disappears into the moulding along the undulating top of the panel. The boar hunt is set in the wilds of Arcadia, in the north-western Peloponnese. The inclusion here of architectural elements in what was a legendary rustic hunt may be evidence for this scene actually being a representation of a hunt (*venatio*) in the arena intended to re-enact the myth of the Calydonian boar hunt. Such re-enactments are well-attested in the arenas of the Roman empire.[135]

Mythical battles also appear among the themes on these reliefs. One fragmentary relief depicts two warriors duelling, one fallen to the ground defeated, while to their left gallops a horse, only the hindquarters of which remain.[136] Beneath the horse lies a large cantharus (wine vessel) tipped over on its side. On the basis of the elements preserved, particularly the wine vessel, it seems that Pesce is right in interpreting this as the battle between the Lapiths and Centaurs at the marriage feast of Pirithous, the best friend and constant companion of Theseus. Here the Centaurs, half-man, half-horse, unaccustomed to wine, became drunk and started a brawl, even trying to carry off the newlywed bride. The second extremely fragmentary relief shows a warrior Amazon mounted on horseback riding to the right, while to the left remain the legs and lower torso of a male figure dressed in a short tunic.[137] Pesce suggests this scene as an Amazonomachy, or battle between the Greeks and Amazons, familiar in many legendary contexts. But perhaps it formed part of the cycle of the Labours of Hercules, the task to get the sacred belt from Hippolyte, the Amazon queen. The Trojan War cycle is also represented among these reliefs. Paris is depicted before the battlements of Troy holding a hunting spear on one fragment.[138]

Distinctively Roman mythical themes also appear, as in the relief depicting the legend of the foundation of Rome.[139] Rhea Silvia and Mars make their first encounter, inevitably leading to the birth of Romulus and Remus and ultimately the foundation of Rome. Another example is the representation of one of the Dioscuri, the twin brothers of Helen and Clytemnestra, all four born of Leda by Zeus, when he coupled with her in the form of a swan. She laid two eggs, from each of which hatched a pair of twins. The Dioscuri are recorded in legend as coming to the aid of the Romans in their fight against the Latins at the Battle of Lake Regillus (*c.* 496 BC).

Another major source of thematic material for these reliefs comes from the realm of the worship of the gods. The worship of Bacchus, through the orgiastic rites of his Maenads, appears on two fragments.[140] Another fragment depicts a cult statue, probably Mars, dressed in armour and holding a shield and spear, in front of which appears an altar with flames atop it.[141] A sacred enclosure is depicted in another fragment.[142] A Corinthian portico surrounds a central sacred enclosure containing a large-scale statue of a warrior (a local hero cult?), two sacred trees and in front of these two circular altars. Within the portico itself a niche set into the rear wall contains a small cult statue of Athena. Two deities appear on a small fragment, which perhaps depicts Cybele and Ba'al in military outfit.[143]

The final category of thematic material consists of a series of reliefs depicting much the same scene: bearers, apparently two at each end, carrying a *ferculum*, a device, similar to a litter, intended for carrying things, especially in a procession.[144] Precisely what they are carrying is not possible to discern, since only the lower parts of their bodies and legs are preserved. However, they may have been part of the ceremonial religious procession (*pompa*) that inaugurated every series of games in the amphitheatre. On the basis of the number of bearers, whatever was being carried was quite heavy, perhaps an exotic species of animal in its cage.

One very small fragment depicts two comic actors in Phlyax costume engaged in performing a farce.[145] The locale is appropriate, for such farces were popular in southern Italy, but they would have seemed anachronistic, since they were at their peak of popularity during the fourth and third centuries BC.[146] Their presence in the decorative scheme of an amphitheatre rather than a theatre, their usual venue, is none the less surprising.

In summary these central panel reliefs draw their inspiration from a wide range of sources, all of which seem appropriate in the context of the decoration of an amphitheatre. There are scenes of the construction and dedication ceremonies of this amphitheatre, mythological themes, particularly those of deities appropriate for the arena (Hercules, Mars, Diana), scenes relating to representations of the gods or to their worship, scenes from the activities surrounding the amphitheatre spectacles (the procession, the entrance of the presiding magistrates) and even scenes portraying important civic occasions (the bestowal of imperial munificence). It is curious, however, that not a single gladiator or gladiatorial duel should be found amongst these reliefs, since they are well attested in the sculptural decoration of other amphitheatres.[147] There are a large number of mythological reliefs which, as stated above, could also embrace an additional reference to the *venationes* in the arena in addition to their straightforward 'reading' as examples of mythical narrative. That reliefs of *venationes* predominate here should not be surprising. The layout of the arena floor with its very large number of trap doors indicates an especial provision for *venationes* here. In addition Capua, like Puteoli, lay astride the major maritime trade route from the eastern and southern Mediterranean to Rome. Wild beasts could easily and economically be imported into this region via the port facility of Puteoli. Finally the important local sanctuary of Diana Tifatina, located on Mount Tifata, lay just outside Capua (see Plate 3.13 where the mountain is visible in the background). And yet Capua was traditionally the chief centre for gladiatorial excellence bar none during the republic. The construction of the four new imperial gladiatorial training barracks in Rome during the Flavian era would have led to a shift in excellence and expertise away from Capua and towards Rome, but one might still expect a lively interest in and a proper representation of gladiatorial duels at Capua. Doubtless such reliefs did exist, which goes to emphasise that this sample is not a random one, but skewed in ways which we shall never understand. Perhaps the early Christian Church particularly singled out such reliefs for destruction in the lime kilns of Campania. We shall never know.

The sculpted hand-rails of the plutei

A large number of the lateral panels of these *plutei* have survived. They depict zoomorphic forms, carved nearly in the round, of individual animals (rarely of a group, and then always of a lion atop its prey trying to bring it down) commonly associated with the beast hunts (*venationes*) of the arena. Individually they contribute little to our knowledge, except where an identification of a particular species is possible, but collectively they may supply further information about the general trends in preferences for particular species exhibited in the *venationes*.

Four individual panels have been identified according to a particular species. They include the addax (*Addax nasomaculatus*) of North Africa, Arabia and Syria,[148] the fallow deer (*Cervus dama*) of the Mediterranean basin,[149] the sable antelope (*Hippotragus*) of Africa[150] and the Asiatic buffalo.[151] Table 3.1 lists these reliefs by categories as defined by Pesce.

Although it is unsafe to base too restrictive a series of conclusions upon this evidence, nevertheless some general trends are readily observable. First of all, there is a remarkably high proportion of reliefs that depict felines (just over half of the sample), while herbivores, including the deer, bovine and other families, represent just under half of these reliefs. Among these herbivores, the deer family represents a high proportion of the total number of reliefs (just under a quarter of the total). The bovine family comes next in frequency (c. 9 per cent of the total), with reliefs depicting horses not far behind (c. 5 per cent of the total). On the other hand, elephants, bulls, tigers, wolves, gazelles and antelopes were rare among the relief sculptures decorating this amphitheatre.

The habitat of a large number of these species may be located in North Africa. This should not be surprising, since this geographical region was always associated in the minds of the Romans as

Table 3.1 Reliefs at the Anfiteatro Campano: frequency of finds by generic type

Animal	Number	Percentage
Unspecified feline	18	32
Unspecified deer family	6	11
Stag	5	9
Unspecified bovine	5	9
Lioness	4	7
Horse	3	5
Lion	3	5
Antelope	2	4
Gazelle	2	4
Lion attacking prey	2	4
Tiger	2	4
Bull	1	2
Cornucopia	1	2
Elephant	1	2
Wolf	1	2
Total	56	102[a]

a Error due to cumulative rounding of percentages to the nearest whole number.
  Roughly one in twenty of the slabs recovered was uncarved. The uncarved slabs
  have not been included in the percentages as calculated above.

the supplier of wild beasts *par excellence*. Furthermore, as noted above, Capua lay not far off the major coastal shipping trade route between North Africa and Rome. Wild beasts were probably off-loaded at Puteoli for trans-shipment to Capua. By the time that this amphitheatre was built (mid-second century AD) Puteoli's fortunes were on the decline (as described above, see p. 74) and Capua's were beginning to rise again.[152] The very low number of elephants represented may have to do with the cost of supplying them, or perhaps the fact that by this time the supply of elephants had virtually become an imperial monopoly reserved solely for *venationes* given by the emperor, mainly in Rome.[153] The very low number of bulls and the complete absence of bears and boars is remarkable in light of the evidence elsewhere, particularly the North African polychrome mosaics that commemorated specific *venationes* given by an eminent municipal grandee, which usually adorned his country mansion.[154] The rarity of tigers is not surprising given the similar scarcity even in Rome itself.[155]

The large number of felines in this sample reflects the general popularity of such beasts for the *venationes*; lions, panthers and leopards always remained the favourite species of the Roman public. The large number of deer represented here may be linked to the local cult of Diana Tifatina, Diana the Huntress, who is often represented in myth accompanied by her favourite stag with the golden antlers. Thus there are few surprises in this sample, apart from the scarcity of bulls, bears and boars which are represented elsewhere in the Roman world in such profusion among the beasts of the amphitheatre hunts.

Overview of the relief sculptures

A stylistic analysis of the keystone relief sculptures reveals three main influences at work in their creation. First there are Classical Greek influences from the fifth and fourth centuries BC,[156] which have been copied in the academic Classicising style typical of the reign of the emperor Hadrian, an intense Hellenophile.[157] And finally, native local artistic traditions are reflected in the manner in which the volumes of the face are moulded and the rather linear manner in which the anatomical articulations of the forms are carved. These keystones are certainly not of the same high standard of workmanship as sculpture produced for the emperor and his circle in Rome.[158] A local workforce of skilled artisans was at work here to produce these imposing reliefs, influenced by the major artistic currents of their time, but similarly preserving an indigenous element of their unique local culture. The subjects chosen for these reliefs may be related both to deities appropriate for representation on an amphitheatre (e.g., Diana and Apollo as Huntress and Hunter) and to local cults established at Capua (e.g., Volturnus, Diana Tifatina, etc.).

The central panels of the parapets (*plutei*) surrounding the entranceways (*vomitoria*) of the *cavea* reflect the well-established tradition of narrative relief sculpture, so typical of Roman art. However, there are echoes of fourth-century BC votive reliefs as well; this is consistent with the trends in art under the emperor Hadrian. In particular, there is a very close affinity between this series of relief sculptures and those on the secondary panels of Roman sarcophagi.[159] Pesce traces the unusual undulating profile of these reliefs to the design of altars with their cushion-like, undulating elements and of thrones (*cathedrae*) with their undulating backs. The themes chosen for representation reflect readily understandable choices for the decoration of a major civic monument dedicated to the celebration of religious spectacles.

The sculpted hand-rails at each side of these parapets give us an insight into the types of animals exhibited as part of the spectacles, including a general indication of relative frequencies of their appearance. Similar examples have been found in the Colosseum, adding yet more to the remarkable degree of similarity between these two monuments.

The free-standing statues

Unfortunately very little now survives of the free-standing marble sculptures from this amphitheatre. Only three statues remain: a Venus, an Adonis and a Psyche. Pesce gives little information concerning them, merely describing them in the academic Classicising style typical of Roman copyists of the Hadrianic era.[160] On the basis of their related iconography in the mythology of the goddess Venus, including the goddess herself, her lover Adonis, who tragically died, and the young Psyche, who fell in love with Eros, the son of Venus, these statues may have formed a single unified group. Such free-standing sculpture usually adorned the arches in the upper storeys of the façade.

Chronology

A fragmentary inscription records a reconstruction phase begun under Hadrian, but only completed and dedicated under his successor Antoninus Pius. The inscription as restored by Mazocchi describes the addition of sculptural decoration (*imagines*[161]) and columns (*columnas*) to the structure of the amphitheatre, originally built at the expense of the *colonia Iulia Felix Augusta Capua*, at an unspecified date.[162] However, more recent attempts to fill in the gaps of this inscription have preferred to restore an unspecified reconstruction of the fabric of the amphitheatre and the addition of columns begun under Hadrian, completed and dedicated under Antoninus Pius.[163] Beloch thought that this inscription probably referred to the addition of a colonnade to the top of the *cavea*, an elegant hypothesis supported by Pesce.[164]

Here follows a summary of the phases of construction and their chronology for the Anfiteatro Campano at Capua.

1 Phase I: Initial Construction.[165] The bulk of the structure, including the façade, *cavea* and subterranean structures. Conscious copying of the Colosseum and its sometimes rather rudimentary architectural schemes.

The evidence associated with the date for this construction is three-fold. First an argument based on a typological analysis and comparison with other amphitheatres would suggest that the Anfiteatro Campano is unlikely to be earlier than the Colosseum, which it closely emulates. Second, an argument based upon historical developments at Capua would suggest that a Flavian date for this construction is unlikely on the basis that it had supported Vitellius actively against Vespasian; as a consequence it suffered confiscation of territory and neglect at the hands of the Flavian emperors. The Flavian era was a period of blight for Capua, not one of confidence and dynamic growth. It is unlikely that a renewal of status and prosperity would have occurred much before the Antonine era. Finally an argument based upon a careful archaeological analysis of the building materials and techniques used indicates the probability that the building took place in the mid-second century AD.[166]

2   Phase II: Additions of the late Hadrianic/Antonine era. Perhaps the colonnade at the top of the *cavea* was added at this time.[167] The huge monolithic, granite columns still visible in the subterranean regions of the arena must surely be the remnants of this feature.
3   Phase III: Severan additions. Buttressing brickwork piers added to the subterranean galleries.[168]

The theoretical design

As discussed above (see p. 26), the recent work of Mark Wilson Jones has opened up a new area of our understanding of the principles and practices involved in the planning and actual laying-out of monumental amphitheatres.[169] We have already seen the so-called equilateral-triangle-and-inscribed-circle-scheme of design at work in the amphitheatres at Verona and Puteoli. This scheme treats the major axis of the arena as the dominant element and the length of the arena as the single most important determinant value in the laying out of the amphitheatre. It divides this axis into four equal lengths that together make up the length of the arena (the central two quarters) and the width of the *cavea* (equal to half the length of the arena and forming the outer two quarters). Amphitheatres laid out according to this principle tend to be somewhat elongated and pointed.

Here, however, a new scheme has been used to plan and lay out the structure (see Figure 1.11). Here the minor axis and the width of the arena, instead of the major axis, are the dominant elements in the planning of the monument.[170] Now, the minor axis is divided into three equal lengths: the inner third, i.e., the width of the arena, and the two outer thirds, i.e., the *cavea*, whose width is the same as that of the arena. This scheme produces well-rounded shapes of amphitheatres.

This scheme would have provided an arena and *cavea* width of 150 Roman ft., an arena length of 250 Roman ft., as well as radii and focal triangles whose sides were all simple multiples of 25 Roman ft. The overall dimensions would have been 550 by 450 Roman ft. However, this design had, in practice, to be modified by slightly widening both the arena (to 154 Roman ft.) and the width of the *cavea* (to 153 Roman ft.) so that each of the eighty arcaded bays of the façade might be as close to 20 Roman ft. wide as possible (in fact they ended up as 19⅞ Roman ft.).

Conclusion

The Anfiteatro Campano at Capua is so strikingly similar to the Colosseum in Rome that it is possible that either the same architect designed the two structures, or perhaps the same architectural designs were reused for the construction of this monument.

Imitation is the surest form of flattery. Capua, with its past history of disloyalty towards the Roman cause during the second Punic war and more recently against the Flavian dynasty in the civil wars of AD 69, needed to reassert its discredited position *vis-à-vis* the capital and the new

Plate 3.19 Anfiteatro Campano, Capua: the remains of the small amphitheatre. Note how its substructures underlay the paving slabs of the surrounding piazza of the later amphitheatre.
Photograph by D.L. Bomgardner.

imperial dynasty of the Antonines. The other dominant centre in Campania, Puteoli, was beginning to go into decline as the result of the massive investment in the Trajanic artificial harbour at the mouth of the Tiber at Portus near Ostia. The moment was now at hand for Capua both to reassert her position as the dominant city of Campania and to establish her loyalty to the new imperial dynasty. This monument may be seen as an attempt to do this. That this initiative was largely successful may be seen from the testimony of the dedicatory inscription of this arena. As described above, it indicates the bestowal of imperial beneficence by Hadrian, actually carried through by Antoninus Pius, upon Capua in the reconstruction of its amphitheatre.

Yet there were individual elements in this almost identical Colosseum. The series of key-stone reliefs on the three storeys of the arcaded façade reflect an injection of local cultural identity into this monument, perhaps an echo from the city's proud Etruscan past.

It is unfortunate that we know so very little about the first stone amphitheatre at Capua, now lying buried on the periphery of the paved piazza surrounding the Anfiteatro Campano (see Plate 3.19).[171] It must surely be an important link in the early development of this genre at a site renowned for its gladiatorial training schools from the republican era onwards.

Arles and Nîmes: a tale of two arenas[172]

Both Arles (*Arelate*) and Nîmes (*Nemausus*) formed part of the network of Roman settlements in the south of France (Gallia Narbonensis) that were founded to strengthen the land route from Italy to Spain as well as to take advantage of the advantageous trade opportunities presented here. Caesar settled a colony of retired veterans from the sixth legion at Arles (46 BC: *colonia Iulia Paterna Sextenarum Arelate*). Following the battle of Actium, Augustus probably demobbed some of Antony's Egyptian Greek troops at Nîmes (c. 27 BC). Nîmes certainly received the grant of colonial status from Augustus (*colonia Augusta Nemausus Voltinia tribu*).[173]

The archaeological record of both sites reveals dramatic interventions by Augustus and the Flavians. Antoninus Pius, whose ancestors were born at Nîmes, may have moved the site of the governor's residence here from Narbonne (Narbo Martius), following its destruction by a cataclysmic fire (AD 145).[174]

The amphitheatre at Arles lay to the west of the Caesarean colony, where, unlike the theatre, it did not align itself with the prevailing rectilinear street grid. The site chosen was a rocky outcrop forming a substantial basis for the massive structure, close to both the theatre and the main route to Marseilles (Massilia). However, the site needed to be terraced, levelled and extended to

Table 3.2 Table of comparative values for Arles and Nîmes

	Arles amphitheatre	*Nîmes amphitheatre*
Overall dimensions	136.13 × 107.62m	133.38 × 101.4m
Arena dimensions	69.86 × 39.12m	69.14 × 38.34m
Width of *cavea*	*c.* 34m	*c.* 31.5m
Area of arena	2,145m^2	2,081m^2
Area of *cavea*	9,356m^2	8,536m^2
Total area	11,501m^2	10,617m^2
Estimated perimeter[a]	382.9m	386.8m
Percentage of total area devoted to seating	81 per cent	80 per cent
Estimated seating capacity	*c.* 33,400	*c.* 30,500

[a] Golvin, Tableau 57, pp. 384–85.

accommodate the structure. It is significant that no attempt was made to use the readily available topography to support part of the *cavea* on a geological basis of sloping bedrock as is often found elsewhere.[175] This was an extremely costly decision to make. Instead of considerable economy of construction gained through using the rocky hillside to support the *cavea*, the citizens made a conscious decision to build a monument of imposing monumentality with a fully arcuated façade all round its perimeter. This façade was constructed before the end of the first century AD on the basis of the finds from stratigraphic excavations undertaken in the vicinity of this monument.[176]

Plate 3.20 Amphitheatre, Arles: an overview of the *cavea* including one of the towers in the background. Photograph by D.L. Bomgardner.

Plate 3.21 Amphitheatre, Nîmes: the façade of the amphitheatre.
Photograph by D.L. Bomgardner.

The amphitheatre at Nîmes lay over a flat, sparsely settled, largely horticultural region of the city to the south and just within the circuit of the Augustan walls, land eminently suitable for a structure requiring such a large surface area. This quarter had its own distinctive street alignment and was laid out at a later date than the earlier Augustan core of the city.[177]

Construction

Both monuments had a façade with sixty external arcades made of locally quarried cut stone. Inside the façade a covered gallery ran all around the perimeter of the monument at both the ground- and first-floor levels. The ground-floor gallery at Arles was covered by massive slabs of stone (4.45m wide: see Plate 3.23), while at Nîmes it was covered by a continuous single annular barrel vault. The first-floor gallery of both amphitheatres was vaulted in a revolutionary technique. Instead of a single annular barrel vault, here each bay had its own barrel vault perpendicular to the façade, sixty in all. Each vault acting as a kind of buttress, this method of construction dramatically reduced the outward thrust on the façade of the building. This is the first time it appeared in the construction of amphitheatres outside Rome (where it is used in the Colosseum) and represents a substantial advance in construction technique over previous arenas.

Each of the piers forming the basis for the arches of the façade had a corresponding pier on the inside of the exterior annular gallery (see Figures 3.8 and 3.9). At Arles spectators walking within the ground-floor external gallery could see a series of Roman numerals lightly incised on the inner faces of the outside piers of this annular corridor (i.e., on the right-hand side if walking in a clockwise direction).[178] Usually such numerals were boldly displayed incised into the keystones of the arches of the external façade as in the Colosseum and at Verona. Perhaps here, rather than being intended to help spectators to find their seats efficiently, they were markings to indicate the number of a pier during the course of the building's construction.

The inner piers of the external arcaded gallery formed the outer ends of a series of sixty walls. These walls were constructed from Roman concrete faced with courses of small, roughly squared cut stone alternating with levelling courses of brick (*opus vittatum*). There was only one drawback to this building technique: the concrete could not take a sharply defined moulding or edge. So, at those points where the wall was interrupted by annular corridors, the corners of the passageway had to be made out of large blocks of cut-stone work.

Plate 3.22 Amphitheatre, Arles: an overview of the façade. Photograph by D.L. Bomgardner.

The façade

Each amphitheatre had a façade consisting of two tiers of arcades and a low attic storey, although at Arles this last is now completely missing. The outside piers of the amphitheatre at Arles are notably less regular in their dimensions than those at Nîmes.[179] The façade at Arles had a ground-floor arcade with applied Tuscan pilasters (without moulded bases), and a first-floor arcade with applied Corinthian half-columns whose bases rested on projecting socles set into the façade wall (see Plate 3.22). The attic storey has not survived, but presumably would have been similar to that at Nîmes. At Nîmes the façade (see Plate 3.21) shared the same decorative scheme as at Arles. However, the first-floor arcade had engaged Tuscan columns, which projected from the wall a good two-thirds of the diameter of their shafts, each base resting on a small socle fitted into the outside wall. The attic had a regular series of small, shallow applied pilasters and between each pair there was a corbel where one mast of the awning (*velum*) would have rested in a sunken socket. Along the crowning cornice of the attic, a series of ring-consoles (brackets with circular holes set into them) corresponded to the series of

Plate 3.23 Amphitheatre, Arles: the ground-floor arcade. Note the giant stone slabs used to cover it. Photograph by D.L. Bomgardner.

Plate 3.24 Amphitheatre, Arles: the first-floor arcade. Note the cross-vaulting used to cover it. Photograph by D.L. Bomgardner.

Plate 3.25 Amphitheatre, Nîmes: the first-floor arcade. Note the cross-vaulting used to cover it. Photograph by D.L. Bomgardner.

corbels below. Between them they stabilised the masts for the awning (*velum*): the lower bracket provided the seating for the mast while the upper console stabilised the pole near the top. Only at Nîmes does evidence for these crowning cornice brackets still exist.

Both amphitheatres had an unusual feature in the design of their façades, shared only by the Flavian amphitheatre at Puteoli.[180] At the intersections between the ground and first floor and the first floor and attic, the entablatures stand proud of the façade around each column or pilaster base (see Plates 3.21 and 3.27). This creates a deeply modulated chiaroscuro effect similar to the treatment of the arcades of the first floor. Here the inner curve of each arch of the arcade was outlined by the barrel vault (set perpendicular to the façade and whose width was slightly less than that of the archway) that covered the interior gallery. Perhaps this penchant for deeply accentuated outlines and chiaroscuro effects may find a parallel in the art of this part of Provence. The sculptured bas-reliefs that adorned the Triumphal Arch at Orange (built sometime between AD 10 and 26–7) had a similar technique. Each of the figures depicted on the reliefs was carefully silhouetted by a deeply chiselled outline. Those who have studied this monument recently would identify this 'outline style' as typical of Gallic elements in this art work.[181]

The upper gallery of the façade at Nîmes had an intriguing architectural feature. The floor level of its gallery was the same as the base of the arcades. There was a potential safety hazard here: spectators could have fallen from between the arches of the façade. Stone slabs were inserted between the bases of the engaged columns of the first floor, perhaps intended as a safety barrier. Three of these survive and one carries a carving in bas-relief of a gladiatorial combat.

The principal entrances received particular decorative emphasis on the façades of both amphitheatres.

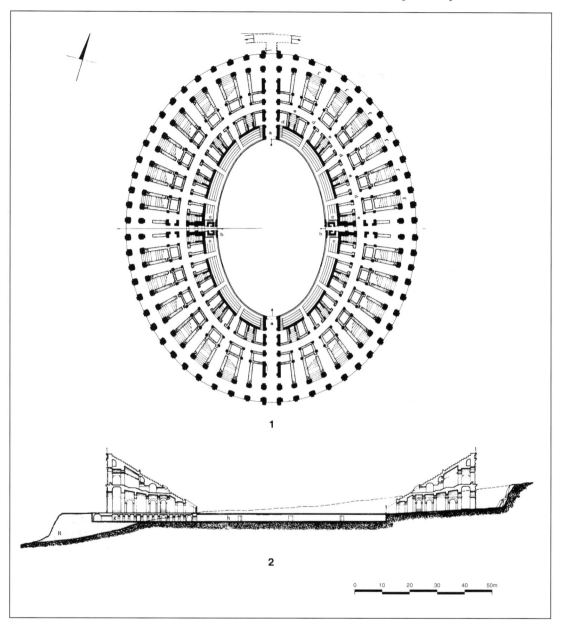

Figure 3.8 Amphitheatre, Arles. Ground plan of the structure.
Source: Golvin, Planche XXXV, 1. Copyright J.-Cl. Golvin.

At Arles both ends of the minor axis were given special prominence (see Figure 3.8). Three bays (the axial and those flanking it) formed a composite monumental entrance into the farthest recesses of the *cavea* where officials presiding at the games would have climbed up flanking stairways (see Figure 3.8, labelled 'c') into the *tribunalia* (boxes of honour). At Nîmes on the other hand only the northern end of the minor axis received a monumental treatment (see Figure 3.9). The

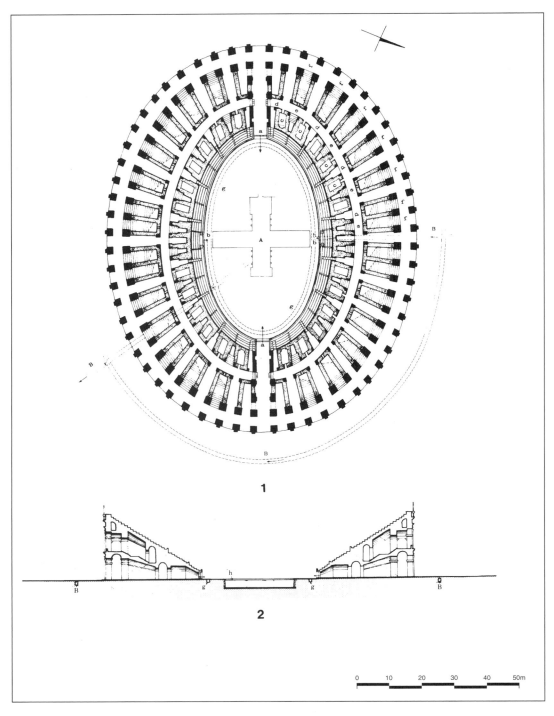

1

2

Figure 3.9 Amphitheatre, Nîmes. Ground plan of the structure.
Source: Golvin, Planche XXXIV, 1. Copyright J.-Cl. Golvin.

southern bay was ignored, perhaps because the Augustan walls lay so close to this side. Traces of a pedimented entablature containing two bull protomes still exist. In addition one of the pilasters that flanked this entrance had a carving in fairly high relief of the scene of the she-wolf suckling Romulus and Remus. Arles also had sculptural decoration, but the find spots have not been preserved. Two relief carvings survive in the archival store rooms, one depicting the same scene as at Nîmes of Romulus and Remus and the other the goddess Diana the huntress with her hounds reaching out her hand towards a small altar. The latter has obvious associations with the

Plate 3.26 Amphitheatre, Nîmes: the crowning cornice of the attic storey. Note the ring console set into the cornice to stabilise the masts of the *velum*. Photograph by D.L. Bomgardner.

wild beast hunts (*venationes*) of the amphitheatre and as such is appropriate here. The motif of the she-wolf is an obvious attempt to reinforce the *Romanitas* intrinsically associated with the amphitheatre (see above p. 42).

The seating

Both amphitheatres had a podium containing four tiers of seating divided roughly into zones by a series of cross-walls, and three *maeniana* (*imum, medium* and *summum*), each perhaps containing ten tiers of seating.[182] At both, the boxes of honour (*tribunalia*) resided on the ends of the minor axis of the arena. The officials presiding at the games entered these boxes from a series of stairways leading from beneath the *cavea* (Arles: see Figure 3.8, labelled 'c'; Nîmes: see Figure 3.9, labelled 'b').

The podium formed the last line of safety for the spectators. Both Arles and Nîmes had a vertical drop of about 3m down to the surface of the arena. Huge slabs of stone set securely on end and side by side formed the arena-wall. This wall was capped by a half-round moulding as a handrail. At Nîmes the inner face of this capstone stood proud of the front face of the arena-wall in a cyma recta moulding. These slabs were a favourite place for inscriptions, particularly at the ends of the minor axes.

Plate 3.27 Amphitheatre, Arles: a detail of the façade. Note the projecting cornice around the bases of the applied columns. Photograph by D.L. Bomgardner.

Plate 3.28 Amphitheatre, Nîmes: the *cavea*. Note the arena-wall composed of large slabs of stone set on end.
Photograph by D.L. Bomgardner.

An extremely fragmentary inscription, placed at the end of the minor axis, survives from Arles.[183] It apparently recorded that Caius Junius Priscus[184] paid for a repair to the podium (and perhaps to the portals leading into the arena at the ends of the major axis). In recognition of his generosity the town council agreed to allow him to reserve a block of seats for the *seviri Augustales* and *navicularii* (the ship owners, or perhaps boatmen [*nautae*]) of the town in the podium (the best seats in the house). The *seviri Augustales* were an association of individuals, usually, though not necessarily exclusively, freedmen, who maintained the imperial cult in their communities. This gave an outlet for individuals of low social position, but sufficient wealth, to assert their patronage and prestige in their communities.[185]

Boatmen and ship owners were an essential element in the prosperity of both Arles and Nîmes. It is not therefore surprising to find at Nîmes in the same position (at the ends of the minor axis) a series of inscriptions inscribed on the podium wall slabs.[186] One inscription in particular mentions reserved blocks of seats in the podium for the boatmen (*nautae*) of the local rivers Rhône and Saône as well as the Ardèche and Ouvèze.[187]

Gladiators

As mentioned above, a relief carving of a gladiatorial combat was found on the parapet of the first-floor arcade at Nîmes. Inscriptions have been found which reveal further evidence about gladiators in these two amphitheatres. At Arles a troupe of gladiators[188] as well as net-fighters (*retiarii*)[189] are attested.

At Nîmes, references to imperial gladiatorial troupes have been found and it has been suggested that their training barracks for the province of Gallia Narbonensis were located either at

Narbonne or Nîmes itself.[190] A free-born native Gaul, Columbus Serenianus, from the nearby tribal canton of the Aedui (modern Burgundy), fought and died as a *murmillo* in the amphitheatre where his tombstone was found.[191]

Two chariot-fighters (*essedarii*) are recorded at Nîmes. The Arabian slave Faustus ('Mr Lucky') won thirty-seven victories in the arena before he was set free during the games given by Caius Pompeius Martialis. He then turned his back on the arena, never to return. His tombstone was erected at the expense of his faithful *contubernalis*, Euche, his mate when a slave who stayed with him for the rest of his life.[192] The Greek slave Beryllus won twenty victories before he received his freedom. He settled down as a freedman and married a woman called Nomas, but died by the age of twenty-five, perhaps as a result of his many injuries suffered while fighting as a gladiator.[193]

Not every story of the arena ended so well, as attested by the sad tale of a free-born Gaul, one Lucius Pompeius, from the neighbouring town of Vienne (*Vienna*), who fought in the arena at Nîmes as a net-fighter (*retiarius*). After nine wins against his opponents (nine crowns), Pompeius died in the arena in his twenty-fifth year.[194] An even more poignant testimony comes from the young free-born Spaniard, Quintus Vettius Gracilis, who voluntarily fought in the arena here as a 'Thracian' gladiator. He was only twenty-five and had won three victories when he was killed in the arena. He was unmarried. His gladiatorial trainer (*doctor*), Lucius Sestius, paid for his funeral and tombstone – a touching episode of generosity.[195]

Venationes

There is little evidence for wild beast fights at either Arles or Nîmes. Their arenas do not seem to have been adapted for the discharge of large numbers of animals simultaneously as elsewhere, for example, the Colosseum, Capua and Puteoli.[196]

In general *venationes* seem to have been popular in only two areas. Those regions where large numbers of wild beasts were plentiful, such as North Africa, show adaptations for *venationes* in even the smallest of amphitheatres (see Chapter Four). In addition, those sites along the major supply routes from these regions (such as the Near East, Egypt and North Africa) to Italy and specifically Rome (following the Campanian coast and up to Ostia) also show adaptations for large-scale *venationes* (e.g., the Campanian amphitheatres with easy access from the port of Puteoli).

The arena

Both arenas had almost identical dimensions (see above Table 3.2). The arena at Nîmes, however, was slightly pinched on the minor axis, thus giving it a decidedly elongated appearance (see Figure 3.9 and Plate 3.28).

The arena at Arles was hewn out of the bedrock to a total depth of nearly 5.2m. A series of put-holes (roughly 12cm square) spaced evenly around the perimeter of the arena every 40cm, at a height of 2.2m above bedrock, are evidence for a continuous timber flooring at this level (3m below the level of the podium). Beneath the timber flooring machinery, hoists and apparatus must have existed to supply the arena above with the necessary equipment for the spectacles there. Now, however, it is impossible to reconstruct this zone. An annular service corridor ran behind the arena-wall (at the level of the lower level). Eight small doorways equipped with a simple single-leaf pivoting mechanism for closure gave access to the arena.

In addition there were two monumental entrances at the ends of the major axis (see Figure 3.8, labelled 'a') for access to the arena at the higher level of the timber flooring. These grand entries received a monumental treatment. A pair of herms (complete with erect phalli) with a protective grille between them provided the ornamentation at podium level. A gallery covered by stone slabs with the aid of additional internal arches led from the northern entrance down into the

Plate 3.29 Amphitheatre, Arles: a detail of the arena. Note that the modern wooden barriers are at the level of the substructures beneath the timber floor of the arena.
Photograph by D.L. Bomgardner.

subterranean structures of the arena (see Figure 3.8). The two small entrances at the ends of the minor axis (see Figure 3.8, labelled 'b') were probably the portals of Life (*porta Sanavivaria*) and Death (*porta Libitinensis*).[197] Gladiators left the arena alive through the Portal of Life. Those less fortunate were dragged out through the Portal of Death. From here the body would be taken to the *spoliarium* where it was stripped of its armour and prepared for burial.

At Nîmes the arrangements for the arena were far less complex (see Figure 3.9 and Plate 3.28; the substructures have been back-filled). A large cross-shaped trench (aligned with the axes of the arena) was dug into the subsoil of the arena.[198] During the course of excavation of these subterranean galleries an inscription was found set into one of the side walls. It commemorated the construction of these structures by Titus Crispius Reburrus, the benefactor, or the architect, or perhaps even both.[199] It is not possible to determine whether these structures were added after the initial construction of the amphitheatre or whether they represent merely a later remodelling of a pre-existing phase of construction.

The vexed question of chronology

More than any other two amphitheatres, Arles and Nîmes have received intensive study. Yet despite the intense scrutiny, the search for the date at which each was built continues unabated. The original supposition that both monuments represent part of the Augustan building programme for Narbonensis can now be shown to be most unlikely.[200] The evidence continues to accumulate for a Flavian chronology for both amphitheatres. However, there is still disagreement as to which constitutes the earlier monument.

Grenier argued for a single architect who designed both monuments, starting with Nîmes during Vespasian's reign (AD 69–79), following on with Arles within ten or twenty years.[201] Lugli, an expert on the chronology of building materials and construction techniques, launched a thorough revision by examining both monuments in detail.[202] He argued from a wide range of approaches that Arles represented the earlier structure, probably of the Neronian-Vespasianic era, while Nîmes was the later monument, probably of the Domitianic-Trajanic period. Robert Etienne also examined this problem.[203] He argued that Arles represented an early Flavian monument, while Nîmes was almost contemporaneous, but built towards the end of the Flavian era. Golvin holds essentially the same view, arguing for both monuments being built within the Flavian era, but with Nîmes representing a more advanced and technically more evolved structure and therefore somewhat later in date.[204] A recent study by a group of French archaeologists has resulted in a refinement for the proposed date of construction for the arena at Nîmes.[205] Based partly upon new stratigraphic excavations in the outer part of the southern minor axis bay of the façade and partly upon a new study of this monument by Miriam Fincker for her doctoral dissertation, the new study suggests a date between the middle and third quarter of the first century AD. In a recent study of these monuments, Mark Wilson Jones has analysed the architectural forms employed.[206] He points out that one way of viewing the construction of the amphitheatre at Nîmes is as a fundamentally flawed conception, especially in the way in which the vaulting of the first-floor arcade was covered with cross-vaults (see Plate 3.25). He sees the unorthodox system of using massive stone slabs in the vaulting of the ground-floor arcade and the treatment of the cross-vaults of the first-floor arcade at Arles as a rectification of these design flaws (see Plates 3.23 and 3.24). Thus more space was available for taller arches in both arcades, producing a more graceful façade (see Plate 3.27). In conjunction with these observations, Wilson Jones has shown that the amphitheatre at Arles had an unusually designed façade. Instead of the usual care taken to provide a well-ordered system of piers and arches in simple ratios for the façade (most usually 20 Roman ft. for each fornix), the piers are 21½ Roman ft (a unique figure among the ten major amphitheatres studied). In addition many of the piers of the ground floor at Arles are fractionally larger than those at Nîmes, as if consciously trying to outdo the latter in size.[207] All of these factors would tend to indicate that Nîmes was the earlier and Arles the later monument, although sharing essentially the same design and layout. This is a minority view, but it does have a certain internal logic that makes sense of the observations, which are otherwise hard to explain.

The arguments are bound to continue with unabated zeal, but it does look like a consensus of professional opinion for a Flavian chronology for both monuments. A better understanding of the constructional history and architectural phases of the important amphitheatre at Narbonne[208] would doubtless help to clarify this picture further. It would be very surprising indeed if all three of these sites did not have a late republican/Caesarean military amphitheatre. Other Caesarean veteran colonies in Spain (Carmo and Ucubi) had early examples of amphitheatres, and these sites in Gallia Narbonensis would seem equally likely to follow this pattern.

Design principles

Wilson Jones has studied the amphitheatre at Nîmes and has proposed a design scheme and details of its actual laying out.[209] Like Verona, Nîmes was initially planned around an 'equilateral-triangle-and-inscribed-circle' scheme (see above p. 70, for a detailed description of the laying out of such a scheme). The original arena was 250 × 144 Roman ft. (see Figure 3.10) and the *cavea* was 100 Roman ft. wide. These dimensions, however, produced a façade perimeter that was too large. Wilson Jones postulates that the arena was compressed so that a nicely regulated, sixty-bay, arcaded façade with each bay nearly 20 Roman ft. wide resulted. The arena, rather than the *cavea*, was probably compressed so that seating capacity tended to its maximum. This procedure did, however, result, as noted above, in a markedly pointed oval trace for this monument. Thus the final dimensions for the arena were 232 × 126 Roman ft. with a *cavea* width of 104 Roman ft., resulting in overall dimensions of 440 × 334 Roman ft.

Wilson Jones also speculates that a supplementary tightening of the curvature at the ends of the major axis of the arena and its entrance passageway, similar to that described above for the Colosseum (see Chapter One, p. 26), may have also been used here. The purpose of such a tightening of curvature was apparently to emphasise, by making it very nearly a right angle, the junction of the arena-wall with the major axis entrance passageway's walls.

Arles shares essentially the same design features as Nîmes. However, as mentioned above when discussing chronology, the perimeter interval between piers of the façade is unusual. It is as if two different units of measurement were being used in the same monument. A similar duality of dimensionality occurred in the construction of the El Jem amphitheatre in North Africa. Here

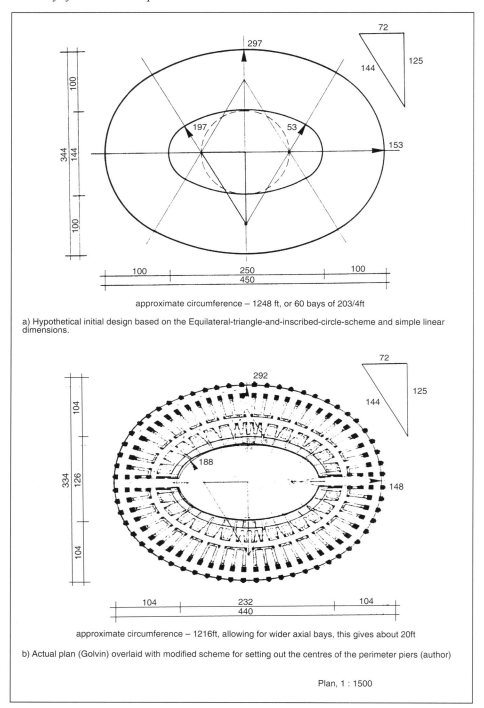

a) Hypothetical initial design based on the Equilateral-triangle-and-inscribed-circle-scheme and simple linear dimensions.

b) Actual plan (Golvin) overlaid with modified scheme for setting out the centres of the perimeter piers (author)

Plan, 1 : 1500

Figure 3.10 Amphitheatre, Nîmes. Reconstruction of layout and design by Mark Wilson Jones. *Source:* M. Wilson Jones, 'Designing Amphitheatres', *MDAI(R)* 100 (1993), 413, fig. 19. Copyright Mark Wilson Jones.

both the Roman foot and the Punic cubit were used in the same building project with interesting results (see p. 146f.).

In addition the treatment of the covering of the ground-floor arcade using massive stone slabs, as well as the gentler rake of the seating in the *cavea* and a smaller top-storey corridor, allowed additional space for the upper arcade with its cross-vaulted ceiling. The net effect of all of these design features was the creation of additional space for higher arches in both arcades of the façade. This gave the façade a much more graceful appearance.[210]

Later history, disuse and reuse

The later histories of these monuments are relatively well known and exhibit many common elements shared by other amphitheatres elsewhere. From the late third century, Arles suffered repeated depredations and sieges. In AD 275 the Alamanni pillaged the city. The fifth century saw an unremitting series of troubles. Within a hundred-year period (*c.* AD 410–508) six major sieges afflicted the town.[211]

Following upon this devastation, the Roman emperor Theoderic the Great sent money to the citizens of Arles to repair the walls and turrets of their civic defences.[212] Formigé feels that this was the time when the upper portions of the amphitheatre were torn down and reused in the repair of the walls and towers of the city.[213]

These precautions seem well founded for the succeeding decades saw numerous attacks upon Arles once again.[214] Finally in AD 735 the Saracen raider Abderaman succeeded in capturing the city and pillaging it. This was the high-water mark of the Saracen incursion in southern France. Within four years Charles Martel had not only recaptured Arles, but had also defeated the Moors in battle near Narbonne.

At this time we hear that the amphitheatre at Nîmes had already been in use as a fortification. For Charles Martel in AD 739 ordered the defences of the arena and the city gates to be burnt.[215] Formigé has interpreted this burning to indicate that wooden barriers barred the arcades of the façade thus forming a fortification. The arena suffered damage from the burning.

Formigé also thinks that it was at this time, if not from the sixth century, that the arena at Arles was turned into a fortress with the addition of four tall towers springing directly from the cross-vaulting of the first-floor arcade (see Plate 3.30). It was commonly known as the *castrum arenarum*. The towers themselves reveal numerous phases of construction and repair and in their present state probably date from the twelfth century.[216]

During the Middle Ages a dense cluster of houses and two chapels (Saint-Michel-de-l'Escale beneath the arcades on the western side and Saint-

Plate 3.30 Amphitheatre, Arles: a detail of the towers added to the top of the first storey. Note the many phases of construction and repair obvious in the fabric of the tower. Photograph by D.L. Bomgardner.

Plate 3.31 Amphitheatre, Nîmes: a detail of the *cavea*, where the vaulting and seating of the *media cavea* have been robbed out, and probably reused elsewhere, revealing an intriguing glimpse within the area normally covered over by the vaults carrying the seating. Note the excellent preservation at the level of the *summa cavea*.
Photograph by D.L. Bomgardner.

Génès-aux-Arènes in the arena) sprang up within the protection of the fabric of the Arles amphitheatre. When the monument was finally cleared of occupation between 1825 and 1830, at least 212 houses had to be demolished. The Nîmes amphitheatre had its own medieval chapel of Saint-Martin-des-Arènes and probably underwent a similar urban development.

Formigé mentions the amphitheatres at Fréjus, Périgeux, Tours, Trier, El Jem (see p. 146 for more details about this amphitheatre) and the *amphitheatrum castrense* in Rome as comparable examples of a late phase of fortification after the spectacles of the arena fell into disuse. The ultimate fate of the gladiatorial spectacles and *venationes* as well as their arenas will be treated in Chapter Five. In the next chapter we shall look in some detail at a representative collection of amphitheatres from North Africa, including small and medium-sized examples.

Chapter Four

The North African amphitheatres

This chapter will present a case study of the Roman amphitheatres of the North African provinces.[1] Two amphitheatres Carthage and El Jem,[2] will be presented in some detail, while the others will form part of a broader survey looking at wider trends and implications rather than individual monuments. This study aims to understand these monuments both within the framework of their provincial setting as well as within that of the wider context of the Roman empire and its mechanisms for the dissemination of architectural styles and knowledge.

THE NORTH AFRICAN PROVINCES: A HISTORICAL SKETCH

Stretching from the Pillars of Hercules (Straits of Gibraltar) to the burning sands of the western deserts of Egypt, the North African provinces occupied the mountainous zone between the Mediterranean Sea and the Sahara Desert to the south. Today this region is not particularly renowned for its fertility, except perhaps for its famous dates. However, in antiquity, the fertile plains stretching northward from the Atlas and Aurès mountain ranges towards the coast formed the most fertile zone for cereal agriculture in the Roman world, comparable to the great plains of the North American corn belt today. Ancient authorities on agriculture praised the legendary fertility of its rich soils, yielding up to a hundred-fold harvest on the seed corn sown.[3]

Out of the ashes of the Carthaginian empire (see p. 130f. for a brief account of the Punic Wars) and the utter destruction of Carthage itself arose the Roman province of Africa (146 BC). It consisted of the immediate territory of Carthage and its possessions in its hinterland governed by a praetor from its capital, Utica.[4] An early amphitheatre of this period has been proposed for Utica, as the provincial capital; however, the site lies beneath the later circus.[5] Following increasing tensions with the client-kingdom of Numidia (bordering the Roman province to the west and south) and after the defeat of the Pompeian forces supported by the Numidian king, Juba I, Julius Caesar finally added Numidia to the empire as the province of Africa Nova. The original province based on Carthage now became Africa Vetus.

Caesarean policy

Under Julius Caesar, an intense phase of settlement of both veteran soldiers[6] and Italian landless peasants[7] followed in the new provinces. Caesar did not live long enough to implement all his plans and it was left to his adopted son, the emperor Augustus, to set about reorganising the Roman empire including the African provinces.[8]

Augustus's reorganisation

Augustus joined the two former provinces into a single new province, Africa Proconsularis, governed by a proconsul now at Carthage, once more the capital.[9] Unusually, the governor also commanded the single legion (*legio III Augusta*) garrisoning the province and stationed at Ammaedara (Haidra). The hinterland of Carthage was also reorganised into the *pertica Carthaginiensium*, within which formerly independent settlements of Roman citizens (*oppida civium Romanorum*) were now placed under the jurisdiction of Carthage, or a nearby Roman colony, or else themselves elevated in status to municipal or colonial status. He also reorganised Mauretania, the widespread kingdom of the Moors in the west, under the pro-Roman client-king, Bocchus. The earliest phase of the Carthage amphitheatre should belong roughly in this period at the time when the new provincial capital was being laid out.[10]

Following the establishment of peace under Augustus after the long years of civil war, tens of thousands of legionary soldiers needed to be demobbed and supplied with land to guarantee peaceful conditions. Augustus established a ring of veteran colonies around the *pertica Carthaginiensium* at Maxula, Uthina and Thuburbo Minus.[11] He established a series of colonies at strategic sites in the interior of the former Numidian kingdom. He planted colonies at Sicca Veneria, an important Numidian town and ancient cult centre for the worship of Venus, at Simitthu, the quarry site for the highly prized Numidian marble, at Thabraca, the port for this marble production, and perhaps also at Assuras. The old Caesarean colonisation of the area around Cirta had a new colony of veterans added to it under Augustus in 26 BC.[12] When king Bocchus died, Augustus, fearful of potential disruptions during the interregnum, planted six maritime veteran colonies on pre-existing native sites (Igilgili, Saldae, Rusazus, Rusguniae, Gunugu and Cartennae) along the coastline of the client-kingdom of Mauretania and three more in the interior (Tubusuptu, Aquae Calidae and Zucchabar). Each of these sites was important strategically or economically. Mauretania was eventually split into an eastern half, governed by the pro-Roman king, Juba II, and a western zone ruled by king Bogud. Augustus shrewdly planted three further veteran colonies in king Bogud's territory at Zilis, Babba and Banasa, to cement his loyalty to Rome.[13]

The earliest phase of the amphitheatre at Iol Caesarea perhaps dates from the era of king Juba's reign (25 BC–*c*. AD 23), an era of intense urbanisation and Hellenisation of his kingdom.[14]

Julio-Claudian policy

During the reign of Tiberius (14–37), an important highway was built linking Carthage with the port of Hippo Regius. Under Caligula (37–41) an important reorganisation of the province of Africa Proconsularis took place. Following the catastrophic bungling of the campaign against the Numidian deserter Tacfarinas (17–24) by the Senate, the emperors had to intervene through their own legates. Caligula made this state of affairs a permanent fixture. No longer would the senatorial proconsular governor also command the legion stationed at Ammaedara. From now on this legion would be split away from the powers of the governor and placed under an imperial legate chosen by the emperor. He also started events which eventually led to the annexation of Mauretania as a province. He had Ptolemy, the son of king Juba II, killed. This event started a rebellion among the native tribes. Caligula's assassination (41) brought Claudius (41–54) to the throne. Claudius successfully ended the revolt and annexed Mauretania as two provinces (*c*. 44): Mauretania Caesariensis (in the east) with its capital at Caesarea (Cherchel) and Mauretania Tingitana (in the west) governed from Tingis; both provinces had an equestrian procurator as governor. In line with the liberal policy of Claudius in extending Roman and Latin rights to provincials, Caesarea, Lixus and Tingis each received the status of a colony under Claudius, while a veteran colony was planted at Oppidum Novum. Volubilis was given the status of a municipium and Rusuccuru and Tipasa the Latin right.[15]

During Nero's reign, in AD 56, the amphitheatre at Lepcis Magna was dug into the sandstone hill just beyond the city to the east.[16]

The Flavians and municipal reform

During the reign of the Flavian emperors, several significant changes occurred. The first military campaign against one of the principal tribes of the Sahara took place. A local conflict between the Tripolitanian cities of Oea and Lepcis escalated when, in a search for allies, the Oeans negotiated an agreement for help from the Garamantes. Under siege the Lepcitans received help from the legate Valerius Festus who led a mixed force against the Garamantes, pursuing them far into the desert. Later Domitian launched a campaign against the Nasamones in this region who tried to abrogate their tribute-paying status. This region was pacified and the route along the coast to Alexandria secured. The stabilisation of the south-eastern approaches to the *pertica Carthaginiensium* allowed the transfer (AD 75) of the *legio III Augusta* from Ammaedara to the south-west at Theveste (Tébessa). Accompanying this shift a new highway was built from Theveste to Hippo Regius.

The earliest amphitheatre at Theveste has been assigned a date at this time to coincide with the arrival of the legion.[17] The intense military activity in the south-eastern approaches to Carthaginian territory perhaps resulted in the establishment of a military camp at Sufetula and the construction of its amphitheatre at this time.[18] After these successful military campaigns and the ensuing enhanced security, the city of Thysdrus probably constructed the first phase of the smaller amphitheatre there.[19]

By the reign of Titus a vexillation of this legion had established a camp at Lambaesis (after AD 81), deep within the Numidian heartland, at a strategically important site controlling key access points in the region. This was part of a plan to lay out a military cordon of forts, observation posts and a military road north of the Aurès Mountains.[20]

The Antonines

Nerva (AD 97) built a highway from Tacapae to Lepcis Magna through the now peaceful Tripolitanian Great Syrtis. Three new veteran colonies (Sitifis, Cuicul and Mopth[. . .?]) at this time secured the north-western approaches to the High Plains of Numidia, which were coming into agricultural productivity.[21]

Trajanic reorganisation (AD 98–117)

The rapid development of this region of Numidia allowed the final transfer of the legion to Lambaesis, perhaps from the first years of Trajan's reign,[22] but certainly from AD 129.[23] Accompanying this move Trajan built two new highways, one from Thamugadi to Mascula, the second from Theveste to Thelepte. Both Thelepte and Thamugadi (Timgad: AD 100) received veteran colonies under Trajan. Meanwhile Theveste, Hadrumetum and Lepcis Magna received the titular status of *colonia* from Trajan. The south-eastern frontier of the African province now began to see an organised frontier (*limes*) with the construction of the military road from Tacapae (Gabès) to Turris Tamalleni on the shores of the great salt lake, the Chott el Djerid (*Lacus Tritonis*), while a similar frontier was being implemented to the south of the Aurès Mountains under Trajan's legate, L. Minicius Natalis. Increasingly the Moorish tribes of the west felt a pincer-like pressure on their annual migratory and transhumance routes from lowland grazing in winter to highland pasturage in summer. They were blocked to the north by the Romans and increasingly troubled from the south by their brethren of the far south-eastern zone, who could no longer freely roam on to high pasture in summer in their own regions. As we shall see, this area would provide the flashpoint for future conflicts in North Africa.[24]

Hadrianic policy (AD 117–38)

Hadrian was the first emperor to travel extensively throughout the provinces of the empire, visiting Africa in the summer of AD 128. He landed at Carthage and proceeded via Avitta Bibba, Lares, Theveste and Thamugadi to Lambaesis where he reviewed the troops stationed there, then on to the Saharan border to inspect an auxiliary outpost at Zarai. Perhaps he returned to Italy via Cirta to the port of Rusicade.[25] Many cities in Africa recorded benefactions at this time, doubtless some during his personal visit; neighbouring communities, who were able to send ambassadors requesting boons, also gained benefits. Hadrian was passionately interested in architecture, designing many buildings himself including some at his own villa in Tivoli. It would make sense that Hadrian should encourage building projects during his tour. The amphitheatres at Carthage and the neighbouring Utica, which received the coveted title of *colonia* from Hadrian, and the more distant Thysdrus (El Jem) and Lepcis Magna, all had important extensions added at about this time. The communities of Carpis (on Cap Bon), Uthina, Bulla Regia, Simitthu, Sicca Veneria, Thibari, Djebel Moraba, Upenna, Agbia, Seressi, Thuburbo Minus (in the heartland of the *pertica Carthaginiensium*), Acholla, Thaenae, Thapsus, Ulisippira, Leptiminus (in the south-eastern zone of the Sahel), Lambaesis, Gemellae, Mesarfelta (military sites on or near the Numidian frontier zone [*limes*]) and Rusicade (the port from which Hadrian may have left Africa), all these built an amphitheatre at about this time. The Tripolitanian cities of Lepcis Magna (addition) and Sabratha also either had major extensions added or else an amphitheatre built in this era. It is naive to assume that all these amphitheatres may be attributed to the visit of Hadrian to Africa in AD 128. However, it is probable that a few communities, almost certainly Carthage, Utica, Lambaesis and Lepcis Magna, and perhaps Uthina, Bulla Regia, Thaenae, Acholla and Rusicade too, built or renewed their amphitheatres at or near this time, thus encouraging other communities in their areas to copy their example as the second century progressed.

Hadrian encouraged the cultivation of marginal scrubland in vineyards and olive plantations by a scheme which combined security of tenure with built-in tax exemptions during the initial start-up phase (the first five years for grape production and ten years for olive trees). This land, which had not been planted in large agri-business farms, the imperial *saltus* of North Africa, producing corn for export to Rome, had previously been overlooked for cultivation. The south-eastern zone of Tunisia, the Sahel, in the rain shadow of the mountains of the Haut Tell, took up this incentive scheme avidly and the agricultural prosperity of this region dates from this period.[26]

Hadrian actively promoted the advancement of indigenous communities of Africa, particularly in the wealthy corn-producing regions of the lower and middle Medjerda valley (Utica and Bulla Regia, titular colonies; Thuburbo Maius, a *municipium*), as well as the region of the Tunisian 'Haut Tell' (Zama Regia and Lares, and Thaenae, on the coast, titular colonies; Althiburos, a *municipium*). Tipasa in Mauretania also became a *colonia*.[27]

The Moorish campaigns of Antoninus Pius (AD 138–61)

Between 144 and 152 a major series of military campaigns using troops brought into Mauretania from a widespread area finally resulted in the re-establishment of order in this province. The amphitheatre at the military camp of Tigava Castra doubtless dates from these campaigns.[28] At about the same time, the amphitheatre at Lepcis Magna underwent a major modification (*c.* AD 162) in conjunction with work in the adjacent circus.[29] At Sufetula the amphitheatre had an extension of seating added. And in this same region, the Sabratha amphitheatre had a band of seating added around its periphery at about this time. The end of the military campaigns of AD 170–76 in Mauretania Tingitana under Marcus Aurelius marks a period of intense remodelling for the amphitheatres of the Numidian *limes*. The amphitheatres at Lambaesis (AD 176/77–180) and Mesarfelta (AD 177–80) were both repaired in the period immediately after the cessation of conflict.

Commodus (AD 180–92)

After further military action against Moorish tribes (*c.* AD 182), Commodus turned his attention to upgrading a cordon of forts along the edge of the Aurès Mountains and building a road from Lambaesis to Vescera. He then turned his attention eastwards, upgrading a line of forts from Tacapae to Lepcis Magna, along the future *limes Tripolitanus*. He reorganised the transport of corn from Carthage to Rome, establishing a new fleet at the former city, the *classis africana Commodiana*. He continued to grant civic privileges, awarding titular colonial status to Thuburbo Maius and Pupput, and fusing the double community of Lambaesis into a single *municipium*.[30] It was perhaps at this time, following its elevation in civic status, that Thuburbo Maius first built its amphitheatre.

Severan policy (AD 193–235)

Septimius Severus (AD 193–211), a native of Lepcis Magna with Punic ancestry, created a new province by separating Numidia from Africa Proconsularis. The legate (*praeses provinciae Numidiae*) of the *legio III Augusta* governed the province from Lambaesis, its new capital. From January to September, AD 194, the third Augustan legion rebuilt and ornamented the fabric of the amphitheatre at Lambaesis as would befit a new provincial capital.[31]

The security needs of Tripolitania were obviously well known to Severus and he established the definitive frontier zone (*limes*) here by establishing forts garrisoned by detachments from the *legio III Augusta* and auxiliary regiments, e.g., at Bou Njem and Bezereos.[32] A similar arrangement guarded the southern approaches of the Numidian province with the establishment of the new fort of Castellum Dimmidi and a line of 'early warning' stations along this frontier. So too in Mauretania a new security zone (*nova praetentura*) encircling the Ouarsenis and Frenda mountain ranges added valuable land for cultivation, while a system of winter camps for cavalry units to patrol and control the transhumance migrations of nomadic tribes in the spring added further security to the south-western corner of Numidia where it adjoined Mauretania Caesariensis.[33]

By the end of Severus's reign, the two provinces of Mauretania Caesariensis and Tingitana had coalesced into a single province governed by one procurator at Caesarea. The expansion here of the amphitheatre's *cavea* by the addition of 5m of seating may date from this period or perhaps later, from the brief reign of Macrinus (AD 217), a native of Caesarea.[34]

Severus worked hard to help North African agriculture prosper, particularly encouraging the occupation of marginal farmland by small freehold farmers (under the long-standing provisions of the *lex Manciana*) and the production of oil for export to Rome.[35] Even the most modest of communities in the rich cornlands of the north and in the rich oil-producing regions of the south and south-east were becoming very wealthy, each one reproducing nearly a full range of Roman civic monuments.

Severus encouraged the municipal aspirations of native communities and honoured mature North African cities as well. The highly prized privilege of the *ius Italicum* (the right to be considered as part of Italy not a province) was granted to the metropolises of Carthage, Utica and Lepcis Magna, Severus's home town. Full colonial status came to Auzia, Lambaesis, the new provincial capital, and Vaga. Many small native communities in the rich agricultural lands of Africa Proconsularis received the grant of municipal status: Thugga, Thignica, Thysdrus, etc. The amphitheatre at the small community of Thignica may perhaps date to this period of civic advancement to celebrate its newly won status.[36] Perhaps the community of Thysdrus expanded its amphitheatre in line with its expanding political status.[37] The prosperity of this era is also reflected in the construction of amphitheatres at Mactaris[38] (late second/early third century) and perhaps at Ptolemais also.[39]

Christian persecutions

The Christian faith had taken deep root in the provinces of North Africa, making rapid progress over a wide area. The numerous Christian texts of Tertullian (AD 160–*c*. 225), a native of Carthage, inform us about many aspects of the new faith in the African provinces.

In the last decades of the second century AD, persecution of Christians came to North Africa. In AD 180, twelve Christians from Scillium (a small community somewhere within the jurisdiction of the governor of Carthage), after a brief trial before the proconsul P. Vigellius Saturninus on 17 July, suffered martyrdom by beheading in Carthage.[40] They are the first attested North African martyrs. They probably came to the notice of the governor through the process of denunciation by an informer. At this stage of persecution, denunciations often followed some misfortune, such as drought, famine, plague or similar catastrophe, seen as the result of divine anger. Christians received the blame for rousing the pagan gods to anger through their impious attitudes and practices, refusing steadfastly to sacrifice or take part in any of the long-established and cherished Roman traditions (*mores Romanorum*) for averting or appeasing the wrath of the gods. As Robin Lane Fox has written:

> Coercion to 'Roman *mores*' was something more general, a wish to oblige a return to Roman 'discipline,' the inherited way of behaviour. The form of the governors' trials puts the moral slanders [against the Christians' misunderstood behaviour] in perspective. If a Christian suspect honoured the gods, he went free. No suspicion of past immorality was held against him, because immorality was irrelevant to the essential grounds of the trial. Bygones, therefore, were allowed to be bygones.[41]

A more general period of persecution took place under the reign of Septimius Severus, perhaps the result of a rescript of AD 202.[42] From this time magistrates and governors were urged to be proactive, rather than merely responding to denunciations as in the past, in countering Jewish proselytism and Christian worship (still deeply interlinked at this period).[43] To this era of intensified persecution belongs the poignant account of the trial and martyrdom in the amphitheatre at Carthage of Saints Perpetua and Felicitas (AD 203). This episode will be treated in detail below under a discussion of the Carthage amphitheatre. From this time Christian martyrs would suffer and die in the amphitheatres of North Africa. It is tempting to see the Christian burial in the apsed vaulted chamber beneath the seating of the amphitheatre at Thuburbo Maius as connected with a martyrdom in the arena, with the later establishment of a martyr's grave within the disused monument under a Christian emperor.[44]

The next century would be swept by ever more frenzied waves of persecution of Christians, including those of Decius (AD 249–51) and the Great Persecution of Diocletian and Maximian (AD 303–05). Far from eradicating the nascent faith, persecution drove it underground. There it became better organised under a system of bishops and communal charity to the poor and needy. Persecution also stiffened the resolve of the faithful through the valiant testimonials and faithful deaths of the martyrs and those who had suffered but not died for their faith, the *confessores*. In North Africa particularly the cult of the martyrs became one of the dominant themes of Christianity.

Indeed the treatment of lapsed Christians, *traditores*, those who had yielded to torture to betray their faith by handing over precious hand-copied manuscripts of the Scriptures during the Great

Persecution (AD 303–05), would sow the seeds of division. The rise of the Donatists (fourth and early fifth century), uncompromising in their implacable opposition to the reinstatement of lapsed Christians, pitted the more forgiving Catholics against Donatists throughout much of North Africa, leading to much violence, loss of life and destruction of property.[45] Ultimately the Church, weakened by long, bitter dissension and further persecuted by the interregnum of the Arian Vandals (AD 429–533), eventually succumbed to the onslaught of the new faith of Islam from the seventh century AD onwards.

The revolt of the Gordians and the Colosseum at Thysdrus

By the third century, the North African provinces could boast an unrivalled agricultural prosperity and over six hundred towns and cities dotted across its fertile landscapes. However, a series of political chances and Machiavellian intrigues centred upon the community of Thysdrus (El Jem) in the fertile olive plains of the south-eastern Sahel would bring ruin on a whole generation of the guilty as well as the innocent, all of whom happened to be in the way of the steamroller of imperial power politics.

The years following the last of the Severans, Alexander Severus (AD 222–35), ushered in nearly half a century of political chaos (AD 238–85) in which the ambitious, the envious, the powerful and the cunning fought with one another for control of parts the empire and ultimately the imperial throne of Rome, like ravenous dogs over a much-chewed bone.

The early years of these struggles affected North Africa, particularly the homeland of Carthage. The Thracian shepherd Maximinus who rose through the ranks to be eventually hailed emperor by his troops quickly became unpopular. Maximinus's brutal fiscal measures, including increasingly common exiles and confiscations of private property under the charge of informers (*delatores*), to pay for his campaigns and the frequent donatives to maintain the loyalty of his troops, quickly earned him enemies among all the propertied classes of the empire, who felt the sting of his exactions. For in March, AD 238, Maximinus's *procurator fisci* was at Thysdrus trying to demand just such a payment from the local burghers. They chose to resist, arming their slaves and peasants, killing the procurator and hailing the octogenarian Roman aristocrat, M. Antonius Gordianus Sempronianus, senatorial governor of Africa Proconsularis, as emperor in opposition to the detested military dictator Maximinus Thrax. At his side Gordianus appointed his son (with the same name) as his co-regent (*Augustus*) and proclaimed himself the emperor Gordian I alongside his son as Gordian II. They based their enterprise at Carthage, but suffered from a critical lack of trained troops. Quickly, by the beginning of April, the Senate hailed the Gordians as rightful emperors, turning against Maximinus. However, Maximinus played his trump card with devastating speed. He dispatched word to his loyal military governor of neighbouring Numidia, Capellianus, who quickly led the third Augustan legion and the auxiliary regiments under his command towards Carthage. Here a pitched battle was fought between the seasoned troops of Capellianus and the militia levies of the Gordians; the outcome was never in doubt. Gordian II was killed outright, the army slaughtered and Carthage sacked by the victorious troops of Capellianus, and Gordian I committed suicide (20 April). The unsuccessful revolt of Gordian I and II had lasted some twenty days.[46] A terrible revenge was wrought throughout the province. All who had resisted were killed and the cities that had joined the rebellion were pillaged and sacked.[47] Traces of burning have been uncovered in various houses at Thysdrus, which have been attributed to this phase of vengeance upon the site of the origins of the revolt.[48] It is tempting to assume that the small amphitheatre which lay on the south-eastern side of the city was damaged in these reprisals.

The re-emergence of the Gordian line came about through the adoption later in 238 of the young grandson of Gordian I as Caesar by Pupienus and Balbinus, the senatorial rebel emperors who rose against Maximinus, who was murdered by his own troops in the spring. Thus the Gordian line once again entered the mainstream of imperial politics. The Praetorian Guard in Rome assassinated Pupienus and Balbinus, then declared the 13-year-old Gordian III emperor. He reigned for nearly six years (AD 238–44).

The phenomenon of lavish imperial beneficence towards one's birthplace is well attested in the Roman empire, e.g., the lavish building programme at Lepcis Magna (Lebda) under Septimius Severus, and the imperial monuments erected at Philippopolis (Shebda), Philip the Arab's home town. In much the same vein, it is very tempting to see the 'Colosseum' at Thysdrus as an attempt on the part of the young Gordian III to honour the memory of his grandfather and uncle as well as to compensate the citizens of Thysdrus for the losses suffered under Capellianus due to their loyalty to the Gordian cause. Indeed, despite the absence of any published dating evidence for the other monumental structures at Thysdrus, such as the circus (550 × 95m), the bath complex (*c.* 2,400m²), and the 'palatial' residence that lay between the amphitheatre and the forum,[49] it is tempting to see this as an imperial complex in the city where his grandfather rose to the purple, albeit briefly. Thus the large amphitheatre at Thysdrus may be seen to be in some ways a dynastic monument to the Gordians, an *amphitheatrum Gordianum*.

Gordian III's reign of nearly six years would have provided a good start towards the construction of this monument. One imagines that with Gordian's death in AD 244, funds would have been diverted towards the new building projects of the new emperor, Philip the Arab, at Philippopolis (Shebda). Indeed, observers as early as Pellissier have noted that the amphitheatre appears to have been left unfinished.[50] Perhaps, as with Lepcis Magna and its Severan building programme, Thysdrus could not sustain such a brief and intense outburst of imperial building munificence. As Louis Foucher has pointed out, Sufetula and Thaenae eventually superseded Thysdrus as the most important distribution centres for olive oil in the southern Sahel.[51]

Golvin sees the grandiose, apparently unfinished, scheme for the amphitheatre at Bararus, some 12 km south of Thysdrus, as a conscious imitation of the Colosseum there. Presumably it was initiated soon after the start of the Colosseum at Thysdrus and halted by the same factors that affected the work there.[52]

These were the last attested amphitheatres that were built in the provinces of North Africa. With them the sequence that began in the Caesarean military colonies and flourished throughout the years of the Flavian and Antonine eras came to an abrupt, spasmodic end. Our knowledge of these monuments is scanty, piecemeal, hard won by intensive survey and much in need of further stratigraphic excavation.

We shall begin our investigation of these monuments by a close look at the most important metropolis of North Africa and second city of the western empire, Carthage.

The Carthage amphitheatre (Golvin #95 and #174)

The Carthage amphitheatre was the most important amphitheatre in North Africa in antiquity, yet paradoxically it is also the least known. It shared the fate of the other major monuments and buildings of Roman Carthage. The builders of medieval Tunis systematically searched for ancient building materials just across the Lac de Tunis at the site of ancient Carthage. They especially prized the bronze crampons and lead sealings used in monumental cut-stone masonry such as the façade of the Carthage amphitheatre. As medieval Tunis rose, ancient Carthage disappeared stone by stone.

When the monument was finally unearthed by the Pères Blancs (the 'White Fathers', a French Augustinian order of monks so-called from the white habits they wore) in the years bracketing the turn of the nineteenth to twentieth century, few records were kept and quite substantial alterations were made to the fabric of the arena, including the construction of a chapel to Saints Perpetua and

Felicitas (see Plate 4.1 and 4.2), who were mistakenly believed to have been martyred in this amphitheatre.[53] We are, therefore, forced to rely heavily upon the surviving descriptions of this monument to be found in the accounts of medieval Arab chroniclers and geographers. Al-Idrisi, the twelfth-century Arab geographer, wrote a most accurate geographical treatise, commissioned by his patron, King Roger of Sicily. Based partly upon his own wide travels and partly upon the first-hand accounts of his informants, this treatise described many Roman monuments in Spain and North Africa, including the so-called 'Thiater' at Carthage.[54]

It is ironic that due to modern suburban development pressures from Tunis (Carthage is now a fashionable seaside suburb of the capital), Roman and Punic Carthage have, phoenix-like, risen again from their ashes, uncovered by the patient excavation efforts of a large number of international teams. This 'Projet de Sauvegarde du Site de Carthage', an intensive campaign of international excavations under the sponsorship of the United Nations (UNESCO), has vastly enriched our knowledge of this, the most important ancient metropolis of North Africa.

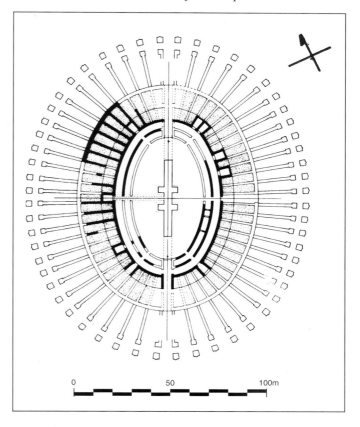

Figure 4.1 Amphitheatre, Carthage (Phase II), Golvin #174. Ground plan of the amphitheatre.
Source: Golvin, Planche XXI, 5. Copyright J.-Cl. Golvin.

Historical background

During the late Bronze Age, Phoenician traders from the mighty trading emporia of the eastern shores of the Mediterranean, Tyre, Sidon and Byblos, sent out vessels laden with manufactured goods towards the rich mineral resources of southern Spain, the fabled land of Tartessos. Successful trading links were soon forged and the settlement of Gades (modern Cádiz) founded. To facilitate this trade a series of smaller or larger settlements was established along the southern fringe of the Mediterranean, the North African littoral.[55] In general these sites were located a day's sailing apart and most were little more than caches of emergency supplies and provisions in case of trouble at sea. However, some grew into towns and prospered, such as Lepcis Magna, Hadrumetum and Utica, but none more so than Carthage.

Following the fall of the mother cities of Phoenicia to the Assyrian onslaught of the seventh century BC, Carthage took over the hegemony of this sea-borne trading empire. Under the leadership of the city, the fertile plains of the African hinterland were explored, settled and brought under cultivation (an area roughly the size of modern Tunisia), and alliances were struck with local African kingdoms, notably the war-like tribes of the future Roman provinces of Numidia and

Plate 4.1 Amphitheatre, Carthage: an overall view of the surviving remains looking north. Photograph by D.L. Bomgardner.

Plate 4.2 Amphitheatre, Carthage: an overall view of the surviving remains looking south. Note the chapel to SS. Perpetua and Felicitas in the foreground surmounted by the column with spiral fluting. Photograph by D.L. Bomgardner.

Mauretania. Carthaginian influence spread overseas to include the islands of Sardinia, Corsica, the Balearics, Malta and the western parts of Sicily, while the south-eastern part of the Iberian peninsula became an important asset of this trading empire, both for its gold, tin and silver as well as for its rugged warriors who swelled the ranks of the Carthaginian armies as mercenaries.

The Punic Wars

By the middle of the third century BC, such expansion brought Carthage into conflict with the Greeks of eastern Sicily and their allies, the Romans. Whoever controlled Sicily effectively controlled the east–west trade routes in the

Mediterranean itself. The city of Messina, on the north-eastern tip of Sicily, and a band of rene-gade south Italian mercenaries who styled themselves the Mamertines, or 'Sons of Mars', provided the fuse that ignited the conflict between the two greatest powers in the Mediterranean when they seized this city, an act which eventually led to Roman conflict with Carthage here.

The First Punic War (264–241 BC) was the struggle for naval supremacy between Rome and Carthage. Although the Romans had no tradition of naval warfare, they managed to salvage virtually intact a Carthaginian warship which had been lost at sea and washed ashore in Italy. Then with the help of their southern Italian Greek allies, the inhabitants of the cities of Magna Graecia, the residue of considerable Greek colonisations along the coasts of southern Italy, they set about taking the vessel apart and building a fleet based on this pattern, pre-fabricating all the individual pieces for rapid assembly later: possibly the earliest recorded instance of an 'assembly line' to create a mass-produced fleet.

The Greeks helped to captain, man and train new crews for this fleet. In addition, the Romans had a 'high-tech' secret weapon up their sleeves, the *corvus* (literally, 'the crow'). This device consisted of a long gang-plank, which was mounted on a swivel pivot attached to the mast in such a way that it could be lowered with great force on to the deck of an enemy vessel. A large spike (obviously similar to the profile of a crow's beak) protruded from below its end; this secured the plank to the enemy vessel. When the *corvus* was securely in place, a boarding party of Roman marines would dash across the plank and overpower the enemy crew, thus capturing the vessel. In this way the Romans turned a sea battle virtually into a land battle, a form of warfare in which they had supreme confidence.

The traditional way of engaging in naval warfare, by ramming opponents' ships, resulted in the destruction of a fleet. The Roman method had the advantage of both depriving the enemy of a ship, while adding it to one's own fleet, possibly a more important consideration than hereto-fore appreciated at this early stage of the conflict. There were, however, drawbacks. The *corvus* apparently raised the centre of gravity of the Roman ships, which were liable to capsize more easily, especially in a squall. And the Romans lost several fleets to storms in this war. However, they persevered and finally wore the Carthaginians down, ending the war with a stunning victory off the Aegates Islands near Sicily. Carthage was fined a huge war indemnity, lost control of Sicily and was restricted to a navy of not more than twenty vessels. Rome took advantage of Carthage's continuing discomfiture to seize both Sardinia and Corsica.

The Carthaginians under the generalship of Hamilcar Barca, the father of Hannibal, now turned to Spain in an attempt to turn this area into a new source of resources and troops. The Romans, ever fearful of a resurgent Carthage, intervened in an effort to limit Carthaginian expansion. They made the Ebro river the unofficial border between the two spheres of interest in Spain and placed all territory north of it under Roman protection.

Utilising Hamilcar Barca's conquests in south-eastern Spain and having trained and equipped a new land army, Hannibal set about putting a daring plan into effect. He would lead his army out of Spain, evade the Roman armies of the provinces on that side of the Alps and cross the Alps themselves early in the spring, when the passes were still heavily laden with ice and snow. His plan succeeded brilliantly and he found himself in Italy itself. He had succeeded in bringing the war to the Roman heartland. During the Second Punic War (218–202 BC), for twelve years he roamed almost at will across the Italian peninsula, inflicting terrible losses whenever a Roman army engaged in a pitched battle.

Fabius 'Cunctator' (the 'Delayer') proved the salvation of his country through his wise counsel to wear down Hannibal's forces slowly through natural attrition and to avoid disastrous set-piece battles. Eventually Hannibal was forced to return to Africa to defend Carthage against a Roman invasion led by P. Cornelius Scipio. At the battle of Zama (202), Scipio turned the tables on

Hannibal. With the aid of the native Numidian cavalry, Scipio had overwhelming superiority in this arm of battle and was able to trap Hannibal's army in a 'double encirclement' pincer movement, as Hannibal had done to the Romans at the battle of Cannae (216), and to inflict such a crushing defeat that Carthage sought peace immediately.

Hannibal, one of the most brilliant generals who ever lived, had to flee for asylum to a series of Hellenistic monarchs in the eastern Mediterranean, where he finally took poison (183 BC) rather than face extradition to Rome. Carthage was left crippled by war indemnities, hamstrung militarily and stripped of her overseas possessions.

Two worthy opponents faced one another in this conflict that dragged on for over a century. One must admire the pertinacity of the Carthaginian civilisation. After each defeat it salvaged the best that could be gleaned from the wreckage. Turning to its own hinterland, all that was left of its once extensive empire, Carthage nurtured it so attentively and cultivated it so intensively that it became a veritable garden and a source of renewed agricultural prosperity.

The final chapter in the history of Punic Carthage came with the protracted siege of the city itself (149–146 BC), the so-called Third Punic War. The citizens defended themselves heroically and for a time the Romans found it difficult to make headway. When a new commander, P. Cornelius Scipio Aemilianus, the son of one great general Aemilius Paullus, and the grandson by adoption of another, Scipio Africanus,[56] was appointed, he seemed well endowed by birth as the best choice. Through sheer drive and persistence, Scipio Aemilianus finally succeeded in reducing the once proud capital of Punic North Africa to a smouldering pile of ruins. Its buildings and walls were razed to the ground and the very site itself was solemnly and ritually cursed so that never again should there be another Carthage (146 BC).

The rebirth of Roman Carthage

The story of Carthage might have ended there had it not been for the foresight of Julius Caesar.[57] The destroyed cities of Carthage and Corinth (both sacked in 146 BC) were both refounded as part of the scheme for Julius Caesar's reorganisation of the Roman empire. The motives for the foundation of these colonies were related to his desire to stimulate the economic activity of the empire and two such exemplary sites for commercial development could not be overlooked.

The new colony quickly prospered and, by the reign of Claudius, Carthage could be described by the geographer Pomponius Mela as having regained its former prosperity.[58] A sure index of success is the date at which a native son of a provincial city finally succeeds in achieving the consulship in Rome. Already by the end of the first century AD, under Domitian, one Senecio Memmius Afer, a native of Carthage, had been appointed consul for the year AD 99 (*consul suffectus*).[59] The enormous potential of the corn-growing plains of northern Tunisia was soon realised and organised to feed the ever-increasing urban proletariat of Rome. Carthage became the chief focal point for the trans-shipment of this corn to feed the Roman populace, supplying two-thirds of the annual requirement, while Egypt supplied only half as much. The emperor Commodus established a fleet of transport vessels at Carthage (*classis africana Commodiana*) to safeguard the vital corn shipments upon which the stability of the Roman government depended, when it seemed as if the Egyptian supply might be interrupted.[60] In addition, the stationing of such an important fleet at Carthage attests a well-developed complex of docks, warehouses and harbour facilities by the late second century, if not before. By the Severan era (late second to early third century AD), Carthage had become the most important centre in North Africa for the political, religious, cultural and intellectual life of the empire. This great metropolis boasted a complete set of urban imperial monuments: extensive public baths (the Antonine Baths), a large theatre, an odeon (a covered theatre for recitals, public recitations and musical competitions), a vast hippodrome for chariot racing and a monumental amphitheatre.[61]

The amphitheatre: phase I

At this point, it is perhaps best to quote in full the twelfth-century description of this monument by the Arab geographer al-Idrisi:[62]

> . . . and there [*scilicet* Carthage] still are the famous buildings, among them for instance the theatre, which has no match among the buildings of the earth as regards worth and power [probably , 'beyond today's wealth and ability to build']. That is because this theatre was built in circular form (lit., in a circle), and is about fifty arches (lit., anything bow-shaped) standing in the air, as to width, each arch is more than thirty spans,[63] and between each arch and its sister (is) a column, and the greatness and the width of the column and the two pilasters (are) four spans and a half. There are standing on each arch of these arcades five arches, arch on arch, of a similar kind and similar construction, (made) from kadhdhan rock which is unmatched for quality. Above each of these arches (is) a circular boss (lit., sea) and there are depicted on the circular boss on the lowest arcades (various) kinds of pictures and impressions of wonderful images in the rock in the likeness of people and craftsmen and animals and ships fashioned with great skill. The rest of the upper part of the building (is) smooth with nothing on it. And it was said that this 'building' was a place for games and assemblies at fixed seasons of the year.

It is obvious that this description is quite detailed. Most of the observations noted are in harmony with known parallels from other amphitheatres, such as the multi-storeyed façade of arches with engaged columns. Even the description of the sculpted bosses above the arches of the ground floor has a well-known parallel in those on the Anfiteatro Campano at Capua (described in Chapter Three).

Two aspects of this description, however, are problematical. First there is the statement that five superposed storeys of arcades rose above those on the ground floor, which is a design without precedent: the largest number of storeys attested rests at four in total, and this on the largest amphitheatre known, the Colosseum. It is, therefore, unlikely that this statement can be taken at face value. By the time that al-Idrisi visited the site of ancient Carthage, medieval Tunis would have been almost two centuries old. Such a prominent monument, with a massive cut-stone façade offering not only ready building blocks but, far more importantly, the bronze metal crampons and lead sealings used to affix them into their positions, one presumes would have been quarried to a large extent. It is unlikely that much, if any, of the material of the upper storeys of the façade would have existed then: logically the dismantling of the façade would take place from the top down. It is perhaps best to treat this statement as information that was provided by informants who confused the original, now long disappeared, number of upper storeys. The second statement at variance with comparable monuments is that regarding the extreme narrowness of the piers on the façade: piers of little more than a metre with arch spans of just under 6 metres.[64] One feature that might partly explain such proportions is the use of 'Kedel' stone in the façade. This extremely durable form of limestone was quarried on Cap Bon; most of the early monuments at Carthage were constructed of the rather friable sandstone found in abundance locally. Such high-quality, durable stone would allow more slender pier proportions than normal. However, it is unwise to place too much emphasis upon these proportions.

Al-Idrisi's description remains tantalising in its apparently precise details, yet elusive in its obviously erroneous statements as well.

Golvin's reconstruction

Due partly to the extremely fragmentary state of its preservation and partly to the substantial reconstructions of the original remnants by the Pères Blancs, it is not surprising that different conclusions may be drawn from two studies of the same monument.

Golvin sees the original monument as an Augustan, but possibly Julio-Claudian, creation. It is characterised by the widespread use of Roman concrete faced with small, regular pyramidal cubes of cut stone laid with precise regularity on the diagonal in a pattern that imitates the lines of a net (*opus reticulatum*: see Plate 4.3 for a detail of this construction here). Hazel Dodge[65] has stressed the very special nature of this type of construction technique. It is particularly associated with Rome and buildings that are either deeply influenced by, or else are consciously imitating, Roman models. Many such monuments were built by Roman veteran colonists, including a large number of Italian amphitheatres.[66] Such construction in *opus reticulatum* occurs most commonly in North Africa during the Augustan and Julio-Claudian eras, tending to die out during the Flavian era.[67]

Plate 4.3 Amphitheatre, Carthage: a detail of the construction technique known as *opus reticulatum* ('net-work'). Photograph by D.L. Bomgardner.

Golvin reconstructs the first phase of this monument as follows (see Figure 4.1, where the earlier phase is shaded). The arena (64.66 × 36.7m) was bordered by three concentric walls. Along the inside of the first wall ran a series of put-holes (0.3 × 0.2m in section and interspersed at 2.86m intervals) designed to hold the vertical poles for a defensive net erected in front of the arena-wall. The first two walls (see Plate 4.4), built of massive Cap Bon sandstone blocks laid dry and with a decorative V-shaped drafting along the vertical joints (anathyrosis),[68] formed the arena-wall and were interconnected by a series of transverse cross-walls to form a series of small cells, perhaps *carceres* (beast-pens) with perhaps a small chapel (*sacellum*) at one of the ends of the minor axis.[69] The flat podium rose above these two walls (rising *c.* 2.5m high above the arena floor and extending *c.* 2.9m in width) and accommodated the folding seats of honour, *subsellia*, of the VIPs who were seated here. A continuous barrel-vaulted *ambulacrum*[70] (see Plate 4.5) ran between the second and third walls, giving internal access to the seating of the *ima* and *media cavea* and leading ultimately to the major entrances

Plate 4.4 Amphitheatre, Carthage: the remains of the earliest phase of the amphitheatre. Note the anathyrosis on the blocks of *opus quadratum* in the foreground. Photograph by D.L. Bomgardner.

into the arena. Behind this *ambulacrum* a series of radial walls fanned out to form a network of fifty-four caissons. Each caisson consisted of two earth-filled radial walls (built of massive masonry below, while the top consisted of *opus reticulatum*) spanned by a sloping barrel vault in concrete and truncated by a massive plain façade also in *opus reticulatum*. The exterior façade was a plain expanse of *opus reticulatum*, except at ground level, where individual arches pierced the façade into galleries that led to the internal *ambulacrum*. In all the *cavea* attained no more than 28m in width. A vaulted gallery along the eastern branch of the minor axis gave access from the arena to either the internal *ambulacrum* mentioned above or else to the exterior of the monument through an archway in the façade (see Figure 4.1).

The initial monument is thus not a truly monumental amphitheatre, but a medium-sized provincial arena of about 22,000 seating capacity. What is remarkable is the unusually early date of its construction outside Italy and the fact that its design and construction reflect

Plate 4.5 Amphitheatre, Carthage: the remains of the earliest phase of the amphitheatre. Note all three of the inner walls are visible and how poorly preserved the inner two are.
Photograph by D.L. Bomgardner.

purely mainstream Roman principles; nothing, apart from the use of local building materials, reflects indigenous influences. It is only in the second phase that a much expanded *cavea* and a monumental multi-storeyed façade give this monument its imperial form.

The amphitheatre: phase II

Golvin assigns a date in the second century AD to the second major phase of this monument. At that time the *cavea* roughly doubled in capacity, a programme of sumptuous decoration began, a monumental, multi-storeyed arcaded façade in Kedel cut stone arose and a series of subterranean galleries and chambers were added beneath the arena floor.

The Arab geographer al-Bakri, writing in the later eleventh century AD, gives us a further account of the 'theatre' at Carthage.[71] He described the upper storeys as being like the ground-floor arcade, adorned with engaged half-columns. He also described the individual pieces of sculpture above the arches of the façade, but added that they were executed in marble and that they depicted many species of animal and many diverse types of craftsmen, specifically mentioning a series depicting The Winds, and, in particular, the East Wind represented as smiling, while the West Wind bore a gloomy countenance. On the basis of al-Bakri's and al-Idrisi's descriptions, it is possible to reconstruct the façade.

The ground-floor arches bore sculpted protomes on their keystones representing 'people and craftsmen and animals and ships'. The ground floor and each of the upper storeys, probably two in all with an attic storey like the Colosseum, were adorned with engaged columns and entablatures, probably in alternating orders as was common on other such monumental amphitheatres.[72]

Alexandre Lézine's attempts at a chronological framework

The French architect Alexandre Lézine, who studied the Roman monuments of North Africa, especially Tunisia, first proposed that the addition of a monumental façade built of Kedel limestone was a separate, later expansion phase for this monument.[73] The figure traditionally given for the width of the new *cavea* (45.65m) and thus the overall dimensions of the later amphitheatre were also supplied by Lézine, presumably based upon 'sondages' undertaken at that time, but never published.

The interior of the amphitheatre was completely transformed by a sweeping series of adornments. Marble slabs adorned the arena-wall, marble chancel screens trimmed windows, marble sculptural decoration ornamented the architectural elements of the *cavea*, such as the fragments of dolphins that embellished the sides of the *vomitoria* of the *cavea*, marble columns and capitals bedecked the colonnade that crowned the top of the seating, marble statues and statuettes of the gods and of members of the imperial house garnished the architectural niches of the structure.[74] Marble everywhere, everywhere the eye wandered.

The subterranean structures of the arena

Golvin also assigns the construction of the subterranean galleries and chambers beneath the arena to this phase of the monument's history. A long rectangular central gallery ran the length of the centre of the major axis of the arena. Symmetrically along both sides of the centre of this gallery were added a series of chambers which contained the hoists and machinery necessary for conveying stage props and cages of beasts into the arena above through trap doors in the arena floor. Smaller barrel-vaulted tunnels extended beyond the ends of this central gallery and ran on beneath the major axis entranceways of the *cavea*. The outer limits of these tunnels are no longer visible since they were blocked off by late accretions of masonry near their junction with the arena-wall. A secondary gallery, aligned with the western branch of the minor axis of the arena, led to a small cross-vaulted chamber (see Plate 4.7) beneath the seating. The outer wall of this chamber, now blocked up with masonry clearly added long after the last phase of construction of the amphitheatre, probably originally continued by tunnel and ran under the *cavea* and perhaps emerged beyond the periphery of the structure.

Several details of these subterranean structures are of interest. First the central gallery was revetted internally with neatly dressed ashlars. Its void was spanned by means of split-log wooden floors: the individual semicircular, stone brackets for supporting this flooring still exist in places along the sides of the gallery. Both of these details of construction are strongly reminiscent of the substructures of the Italica amphitheatre in Spain. The small, cross-vaulted chamber on the western end of the minor axis of the arena should, I think, be identified as the *spoliarium*, the room where the bodies of dead gladiators were prepared for burial. The presence on each side of this chamber of low benches that are long enough to lay out a corpse and the existence of two large cemeteries on this western side of the amphitheatre, just a few hundreds metres beyond the perimeter of the monument, seem to support this conjecture.

Plate 4.6 Amphitheatre, Carthage: the remains of the subterranean galleries and chambers beneath the arena.
Photograph by D.L. Bomgardner.

In every gladiatorial contest the hinge of fate turned during the fighting in this mortal combat: life or death, or reprieve (*missio*), if one had fought well enough to impress by one's courage, skill and bravery, after defeat at the hands of one's opponent. Luck played a vital part here. It is no wonder that so many chapels dedicated to Nemesis, the goddess of one's fate for good or ill, have been found in or immediately adjacent to amphitheatres. Gladiators and beast fighters (*venatores*) offered sacrifice to this dread goddess before each performance in the arena. It is not, therefore, surprising that a fragmentary inscription dedicated to Nemesis was found here at Carthage, perhaps from the small chamber that nestled beneath the podium and *ima cavea* at the eastern end of the minor axis of the arena, which Golvin has tentatively identified as a chapel (*sacellum*).

The *porta Sanavivaria* and the *porta Libitinensis*

The layout and architecture of the arena itself reflected this duality between the alternative outcomes of life or death. Two portals known respectively as the *porta Sanavivaria* and the *porta Libitinensis* opened on to the arena from beneath the podium and its galleries and chambers.

The *porta Sanavivaria* was the 'Gate of Life' through which the victorious or spared gladiator strode in triumph and glory out of the arena, having defeated death itself, if only for a time. The

Plate 4.7 Amphitheatre, Carthage: the subterranean cross-vaulted chamber beneath the *cavea*, probably the *spoliarium*, where the bodies of dead gladiators were prepared for burial. Photograph by D.L. Bomgardner.

porta Libitinensis, so named from the Roman goddess of funerals, Libitina, was the 'Gate of Death'. Through this gateway a figure dressed as Charun, the Etruscan demon of death and a traditional attendant of the gladiatorial combats, dragged the lifeless corpse of the luckless opponent. Charun had the job to test whether a gladiator was feigning death and to dispatch him with the large mallet that he carried, if necessary.

The best seats in the arena were at the ends of the minor axis and the most privileged reserved seating was found there. Given the primary architectural importance of the minor axis of the arena, it is logical to assume that the *porta Sanavivaria* and the *porta Libitinensis* should lie at opposite ends of this axis of life and death. At Carthage it is perhaps possible to identify them: the *porta Sanavivaria* lay at the eastern end of the minor axis, the *porta Libitinensis* lay at the western end, near the cross-vaulted chamber, the *spoliarium*, where the corpses of gladiators were taken before burial, and also near the cemeteries on this side of the monument.

The inscriptions and sculptures

A very large number of fragments of inscriptions and sculptures were found during the excavations of the late nineteenth/early twentieth centuries. Although many of these fragments have been published as part of the *corpus* of the contents of the Musée Lavigerie at Carthage, there has never been an intensive study of the sculptures in their own right in order to shed light upon the architectural decoration of the Carthage amphitheatre. The inscriptions were published together in a nineteenth-century study,[75] but largely due to the extremely fragmentary state of the majority of them, little was added to our knowledge of the sociological context of this monument.

The epigraphical evidence can be separated into two categories: first, inscriptions commemorating the beneficence of individual donors (*editores munerum*), and second, those which deal with the performers themselves. Quintus Voltedius Optatus, as *duovir quinquennalis*, the chief municipal magistracy at Carthage, gave a magnificent four-day series of games in the amphitheatre, including *munera gladiatorum* and *venationes*, that cost more than 200,000 *sesterces* to celebrate his election victory (*c.* AD 133–39).[76] Similarly an aedile gave a *munus gladiatorum* to commemorate his election at Carthage.[77]

The second category of evidence consists of lead curse tablets (*tabellae defixionum*) and *ex voto* inscriptions found during the clearance of the arena in the late nineteenth century. Where the performers are named, the majority were *venatores*, like Cn. Lurius Abascantianus, a member of the *familia Taelegeniorum* (*sic*), the well-known itinerant troupe of professional wild beast hunters. Lead curse tablets were prayers scratched on to strips of lead, then usually folded up and buried in a cemetery, or sometimes a circus or arena. They carried prayers to the infernal deities for an eagerly sought outcome: the punishment of a thief who had not been caught; the jinx on a charioteer or gladiator or *venator*, where betting might take place on the outcome. Among the fifty-five lead curse tablets uncovered in the Carthage arena, the names of ten beast hunters and two gladiators are discernible.[78] This proportion should reflect the relative frequency of such performances in the Carthage amphitheatre. Where animals are mentioned specifically in connection with *venationes*, bears, bulls, boars and lions are recorded.[79]

A brief discussion of the small finds discovered in and around the amphitheatre will help to reconstruct its appearance. The white marble sculptures included a female bust, the torso of a statuette of Diana the Huntress, the torso of a youthful Bacchus (based upon a well-known Praxitelian type), a loricate (perhaps imperial) torso, a head of Hercules, a lion's-head table leg and a bas-relief of a seated god, perhaps Neptune.[80] In addition, numerous fragments of white, grey, bluish and shell-filled marbles were found. Although not found in the vicinity of the amphitheatre, a terracotta figurine of a musician playing the hydraulic organ (*organum hydraulicum*) has a good parallel on the border zone of the 'Gladiator Mosaic' from the Roman villa at Zliten (Dar Buc Ammera) as providing musical accompaniment in the arena.[81] A series of Roman, Jewish and Christian lamps were also unearthed in the clearance of the arena, including one which bore a decoration of the goddess Caelestis seated on a lion, doubtless a personification of Carthage.[82] Four rectangular marble plaques found in the arena consisted of a pair of bronze insoles set into the imprint of a pair of feet in the plaque. A single pair of these bronze insoles was recovered, of which the right foot bore the name, T. Modius Felix.[83] An *ex voto* marble plaque dedicated to the deity, Bonus Eventus, was also found in the Carthage arena.[84] As mentioned above, fifty-five lead curse tablets were found in an unspecified 'fosse carrée' in the arena, on which a variety of chthonic deities and demons were represented or invoked (e.g., Mercury, Typhon-Seth, etc.).[85] A gaming table (*tabula lusoria*) was also found in the amphitheatre.[86] Finally a series of coins found by Père Delattre in the excavation of the arena, but never catalogued, were assigned dates ranging from the mid-third to the mid-fourth century AD.[87]

From the finds one may draw several conclusions about the religious context of the amphitheatre. In addition to those deities usually associated with the arena, such as Diana and Hercules, other deities of local importance or associated function are also found: Mercury as 'psychopompos', chthonic demons and deities (on the lead curse tablets); Bonus Eventus, a logical deity to be placated in the lucky or unlucky outcome of the *munus* or *venatio*; and probably Caelestis and Saturn on the *ex voto* plaques. Generally *ex voto* plaques are a necessary though not always a sufficient condition for the conclusion that a *sacellum* (chapel) to the specified deity occurred there. Possible corroboration for the presence of such chapels here may be provided by the small size of the statuary recovered, e.g., Diana and Bacchus. At least life-size or even larger figures would be needed for architectural adornment, e.g., between the arcades of the façade. Both Diana and Bacchus have known roles as the patrons of *venationes* in North Africa and so one should expect to find chapels with small niches for these statues here.[88] On the evidence of the other *ex voto* dedications, shrines to Bonus Eventus, Caelestis and Saturn may also have been located in this amphitheatre. In addition the Carthage amphitheatre should also have possessed an impressive shrine dedicated to the imperial cult for which games were given by the *sacerdos provinciae Africae* (provincial priest of Africa).[89]

The professional guilds of wild beast hunters

Among the inscriptions was found a votive plaque that recorded the performance here of a well-attested and obviously widely travelled troupe of professional North African beast hunters (*venatores*), the Telegenii. The Telegenii are most commonly represented on figured polychrome mosaic pavements and inscriptions from the Sahel region of Tunisia (the south-eastern coastal plain), particularly Hadrumetum (Sousse) and Thysdrus (El Jem). They are representative of a large number of such professional, travelling troupes of beast hunters.[90]

Each such guild had its own patron deity, its own unique iconographical symbol, doubtless possessed of magical properties/associations, and even its own special 'lucky number'. The Telegenii, for example, especially worshipped the god Bacchus, regarded the millet plant stalk as their sacred totem and believed that the Roman numeral 'III' was particularly lucky for them. This last was often found as part of a compound symbol representing both the numeral III and the end of a crescent-shaped hunting spear peculiar to this guild. They travelled around from amphitheatre to amphitheatre and contracted to perform in the arenas against wild beasts.

One famous mosaic from a maritime villa at Smirat was probably commissioned by the benefactor of a series of *venationes* probably held at nearby Hadrumetum (Sousse) to commemorate his well-received munificence in his own private seaside residence.[91] The mosaic depicts four individually named *venatores* of the Telegenii fighting against four individually named leopards. The mosaic also records a lengthy inscription that includes a sort of 'business contract' under which the Telegenii fought. This contract consists of the speech made to the audience by the herald of the guild in which he asks them for the sum of 500 *denarii* for each of the four leopards. The mosaic also records the bountiful generosity of the benefactor of the games, a certain Magerius, who paid in the end double the going rate for this exhibition, 1,000 *denarii*. The guild of the Telegenii is easily recognisable by the iconographical attributes on the mosaic, which has been assigned a date to the middle of the third century AD.

The question of where these professional travelling troupes got their wild beasts remains unanswered. Furthermore their precise role in the complex chain of trapping, transport and supply that ultimately supplied the amphitheatres of Italy and especially Rome needs investigation. There is some evidence to indicate that these guilds engaged in commercial enterprises between the Sahel and Rome, e.g. the export of olive oil.[92] In light of this perhaps they should also be considered intermediaries in the chain of supply for wild beasts to the amphitheatres of North Africa and Italy.

The annual games given by the provincial priest of the imperial cult

As the capital of one of the richest provinces in the empire, Carthage naturally played host to the annual convocations of the provincial assembly (*concilium provinciae*). Provincial assemblies seem to have served two main purposes: first, to report the views on important contemporary issues of the main provincial cities and large landed estates to the governor of the province, and second, to perform a unifying act of loyalty and homage to Rome through annual sacrifices and public games in honour of the emperor.

From the reign of Vespasian (AD 69–79) the imperial cult became established in North Africa. The practice of paying divine honours to a living human being seems to have originated in the interactions between the tradition of god-kings in the Middle East and the influence of the Stoic philosophers and their teachings in the west. The belief was held that the offering of sacrifices to the genius of the emperor made his guardian spirit stronger and perhaps even helped to promote the vigour and longevity of the princeps himself. As well as being part of the sacrifices, the offering of public games for the emperor's well-being (the phrase *pro salute Imperatoris* is frequently found in dedicatory inscriptions recording such spectacles) further enhanced the prestige and popularity of the sole ruler of the empire.

Each province in which the imperial cult took place had a high priest (*flamen*), who was elected annually by the provincial council (*concilium provinciae*) and was in charge of the proper administration of these religious duties. He also, doubtless, made a considerable contribution towards the expenses for the annual games in honour of the emperor held during the convocations of the provincial assembly.[93] This arrangement was reflected throughout the empire, for example at Lyons, where the Council of the Gauls met annually in the amphitheatre adjacent to the Altar of the imperial Cult there, and at Pergamon, where the Asiarch of the *koinon* of the Greek Asiatic cities held annual games in the amphitheatre.[94]

These spectacles would have been among the most elaborate of the annual cycle of games at Carthage, forming the apogee of the personal career of the high priest (*sacerdos provinciae Africae*).[95] He would have spared no expense to try to impress his colleagues and fellow provincials by the magnificence of his spectacles. There were, however, external checks on his benefaction. Probably since the time of Augustus, the number of pairs of gladiators that were permitted to appear in non-imperial spectacles was strictly regulated both within Italy and in the provinces. A direct and successful petition to the emperor himself was needed to exceed this number. Furthermore additional performances beyond the statutory regulation needed the express permission of the emperor to take place.[96] However, from the surviving mosaic evidence, it is quite clear that the wild beast hunts (*venationes*) were always the most popular features of the games, and perhaps only the numbers of lions that could be exhibited were regulated in this area of the contests. Thus the high priest could indulge his fancy to provide a more lavish spectacle in this regard.

We can get some idea of the types of spectacles that took place in the Carthage amphitheatre from the testimony of figured mosaics found in the Carthage region. North Africa abounded in polychrome figured mosaics and the Musée du Bardo possesses some of the finest examples of this art form in the world. A most interesting type of mosaic pavement that Katherine Dunbabin has christened the 'catalogue mosaic' presents the spectator with a review of the events of a series of spectacles in the amphitheatre in schematic form. One such later third-century mosaic from Carthage, known as the 'Beasts of the Amphitheatre' mosaic,[97] depicts three groups of animals on a largely plain background, arranged roughly into three vertical zones surrounded by a fairly standard geometrical border. The central band shows six leopards grouped into three pairs, one above the other. Between the top pair of leopards are the words 'MEL QUAESTURA'.[98] To the left and separated from the leopards by three stalks of millet, the totem and magic number of the Telegenii, is another zone of animals consisting of a bull, a bear, an ostrich, a boar, a moufflon, two antelopes and a deer. To the right of the leopards are a boar, a bear, an ostrich, a moufflon and a stag. Inscriptions are emblazoned on the haunches of some of the animals: on the right side, the bear (~N XL), the ostrich (~N XXV) and the moufflon (~N X); on the left side, the bear (~N XXX), the moufflon (~N VI) and the antelope (~N XV) bear such markings. Dunbabin interprets the whole ensemble as the commemoration of a series of *venationes* that formed part of a privately funded series of games. The inscriptions on the animals represented Roman numerals which indicated the numbers involved of each kind; the duplication of some species might suggest that at least two separate days of events are here depicted and perhaps three, if the leopards in the central zone are separated from the others. The iconography of the triple millet stalks clearly indicates that the Telegenii were the troupe responsible for supplying the *venatores*, if not the animals themselves.

From such mosaics we find that boars, bears, bulls, herbivores and felines are represented. Interestingly only big cats and bears are depicted with individual names. What this implies about the relationship of the viewing public to these species is hard to reconstruct. However, it is possible that some form of betting took place on the outcome, and individual names certainly indicate a certain 'star quality' associated with these beasts. One is reminded of a parallel from the circus spectacles, where heavy betting took place on the outcome of the races: chariot horses are depicted on mosaics bearing individual names.

The execution of condemned criminals in the arena (datio ad bestias*)*

A discussion of the Carthage amphitheatre is the ideal place to introduce the topic of the public execution of condemned criminals in the arenas of the Roman empire (*datio ad bestias*) for two reasons. First there is excellent contemporary evidence for this practice in the account of the martyrdom of Saints Perpetua and Felicitas at Carthage.[99] Second, the cult of the martyrs, who died professing their faith, was a central feature of North African Christianity. The reconstruction of a modern chapel to Saints Perpetua and Felicitas in the substructures of the Carthage arena that commemorated the 1700th anniversary of their martyrdom is cogent testimony of the importance of this event both for North Africa and the Church (see Plate 4.2).

Criminals who had been convicted of especially heinous crimes, such as poisoning or parricide, or those whom the Romans wished to make the target of especially brutal punishment or suppression with the aim of deterring others from pursuing a similar course, were set aside to be executed in public by wild beasts, usually in an amphitheatre or a theatre specially adapted for such a purpose. Only non-Roman citizens were normally treated in this fashion; Romans were reserved the relatively quick and more humane execution by beheading. To the Romans the Christian sect was doubly dangerous both because it was a secret cult, which prejudice and misinformation said indulged in infant sacrifice and cannibalism (the Eucharist), and because members refused to worship any other deity, including the genius of the emperor, and thus were guilty of treason in the eyes of the Romans.[100] Doubtless the chief purpose of such a savage punishment was to deter the spread of this new religion and to encourage renunciation of the faith. Often Christians brought before magistrates in public, in the hope of achieving martyrdom, tried to provoke both the officials and the public into violently repressive punishments by their flagrant behaviour.[101]

From at least the time of Trajan, the normal procedure for bringing a Christian to trial before a Roman magistrate was to issue a formal denunciation before the magistrate. He was then bound by law to investigate the charges and, if there was substance in them, to bring the case to trial. However, during the reign of Septimius Severus, a rescript (probably of *c.* AD 202) allowed magistrates to prosecute both Jewish prosletism and the Christians (still closely linked with each other at this date) directly without the need of a formal charge from an accuser.[102] Its aim was clearly to prevent the spread of these faiths, not to persecute those who already were practising believers. Both the recent converts and those who had led them into conversion were liable to be punished with the full measure of the Roman law's severity. Free-born foreigners could expect death, slaves to be thrown to the beasts in the arena, Roman citizens to be exiled or decapitated.

Clearly the onus was upon the magistrate, who, if he were zealous in his convictions, was given ample scope to work his ends.

Such a magistrate was Hilarianus, the imperial procurator of Africa, who temporarily fulfilled the role of provincial governor following the death of the proconsul Minucius Timinianus.[103] Unlike those that would follow later in the third century AD, the persecution of AD 202 was not launched by a general edict denouncing all practising Christians. None the less it is clear that from as early as AD 197, persecution of Christians had taken place in North Africa.[104]

The martyrdom of Saints Perpetua and Felicitas

The account of the martyrdom of Saints Perpetua and Felicitas (*Passio SS. Perpetuae et Felicitatis*), written in the style of the circle of the third-century African Christian apologist Tertullian, and perhaps even by himself, claims to be an authentic, first-hand account of the martyrdom of a group of Christians from Thuburbo Minus in an *amphitheatrum castrense* in Carthage, probably commemorating the *dies natalis* of Geta in AD 203.[105] Two individual accounts, those of Vibia Perpetua and her companion Saturus, were combined with a linking commentary into a single document that recounted in graphic detail the fate that befell Perpetua and her companions in the arena at Carthage where they suffered public execution by wild beasts. Whether this martyrdom took place in the military or civilian amphitheatre at Carthage, this account provides invaluable data about the terminology, apparatus and personnel of the arena, the actual detailed procedures involved in executions *ad bestias* and the role of the crowd in affecting the outcome of the events in the arena at Carthage.

The account of the martyrdom may be summarised briefly as follows. As part of the preliminaries of the trial, the men were forced to wear the robes appropriate to a priest of Saturn and the women, those of the goddess Ceres. Some have tried to interpret this action as evidence to support the theory that such public executions of criminals were, at least in North Africa, deeply linked with the once common practice of human sacrifice to the native Punic deities of Carthage, Ba'al and Tanit.[106] By altering the viewpoint to the worship of the Roman gods Saturn, a syncretism with Ba'al, and Ceres, another Roman equivalent for Tanit, and by performing these practices in an amphitheatre rather than in a *tophet*, or sanctuary to the Punic gods, such executions were in effect an 'underground' continuation of this practice under the Romans, who officially banned all human sacrifice, but perhaps turned a blind eye to such practices when performed in an amphitheatre.

This account of the *datio ad bestias* reveals a great deal about the procedure, personnel and apparatus used at Carthage in the context of the amphitheatre during the early third century. Three distinct phases of the execution can be identified.

The first phase entailed the preparation and the exhibition of the prisoners – the preliminaries before the execution (§18.4–9 in Musurillo's text). The second phase included the exposure of first the men (§19.3–6) and then the women (§20.1–7) to the beasts in the arena. Finally, those martyrs who had survived this second phase were exposed to a different type of animal or dispatched by a gladiator in the final phase of the spectacle (§21.1–2).

Several important details concerning the procedures of the arena can be extracted from this account. First, the women were segregated from the men: two separate *venationes* (§19.3–6 and §20.1–7) were held. Second, the use of restraining devices on the condemned (*noxii*) was a necessary, though sometimes ineffective, measure during such an execution. The *reticulum* (§20.2), the rope or chain used to tether Saturus to a boar (§19.5), and some forms of elevated platform, the *pulpitum* (§19.3) and the *pons* (§19.6), are mentioned in this context.[107] Third, the personnel of the arena are referred to by the terms *venatores* and *gladiatores* only. The *venatores* formed the line which beat the prisoners with *flagella* (§18.9). One of these bound Saturus to a boar, and the *venator* himself suffered an injury, proving subsequently fatal, in doing so (§19.5).

The *gladiatores* – net-fighters (*retiarii*) according to Louis Robert[108] – performed the public executions, either by beheading or by slitting the jugular artery with a dagger, at the close of the spectacle (§21.8–10). Fourth, the remarkable ability of the crowd (*populus*) to alter the course of events in the arena at will must have been one reason why these spectacles were so popular. The emotions of the crowd are reflected in a wide variety of demands: outraged hostility towards the martyrs (§18.9), common decency and modesty (§20.2–3), compassion or, perhaps more accurately, boredom (§20.7), and vicious cruelty (§21.7).

An alternative architectural interpretation[109]

Any attempt to interpret the extant remains of the amphitheatre must begin with an assessment of the restorations undertaken by the Pères Blancs. At the turn of the nineteenth to twentieth century during the course of the clearance of the arena under the supervision of Père Delattre, significant alterations were made to many of the structural elements of the arena. In particular, the arena-wall and two concentric annular walls behind it (see figure 4.2) were reconstructed: the

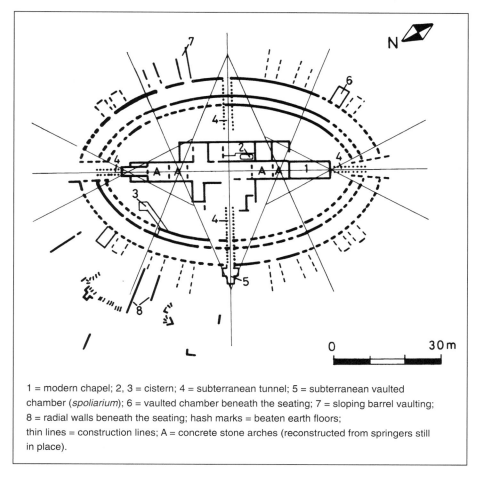

1 = modern chapel; 2, 3 = cistern; 4 = subterranean tunnel; 5 = subterranean vaulted chamber (*spoliarium*); 6 = vaulted chamber beneath the seating; 7 = sloping barrel vaulting; 8 = radial walls beneath the seating; hash marks = beaten earth floors; thin lines = construction lines; A = concrete stone arches (reconstructed from springers still in place).

Figure 4.2 Amphitheatre, Carthage (Phase II), Golvin #174. Ground plan of the extant remains of the amphitheatre with a proposed design layout.
Source: D.L. Bomgardner, 'The Carthage Amphitheatre: A Reappraisal', *AJA* 93 (1989), 87, fig. 1. Copyright D.L. Bomgardner.

arena-wall and its nearest neighbour in part, the outermost annular wall completely. The materials chosen for this purpose were the blocks of sandstone *opus quadratum* which lay tumbled about the arena for the inner two walls, and concrete for the outermost ring with some blocks of sandstone incorporated as well. The existence in some spots of the original masonry *in situ* in the lowest courses of these walls indicates that these reconstructions are reasonably faithful so far as their positioning is concerned (see Plate 4.4). There is, however, no extant evidence for the details of this reconstruction, particularly that of the third (outermost) annular wall. In addition the southern end of the main subterranean gallery has been substantially altered by the construction there of a chapel to Saints Perpetua and Felicitas (see Plate 4.3). Furthermore, concrete steps have been added in the north-eastern sector of this gallery to provide access to this chapel. Other details of construction such as arches in concrete have also been added to the substructures.[110] Two cisterns (unconnected with these alterations) were installed in the arena, presumably after it had gone out of use and become a defended nucleus for secure settlement in uncertain times (Plate 4.6 and Figure 4.2, labelled '2' and '3').

Those portions of the amphitheatre which remain unaltered include the collapsed barrel vaulting of the *cavea* constructed of *opus caementicium* faced with *reticulatum* (Plate 4.3); no trace of the blocks that formed the seating now remains.[111] The so-called 'primitive arena' of Père Lapeyre (the area immediately inside the outermost annular wall: see Figure 4.1) cannot have served such a function. It is most unlikely that barrel vaulting from the exterior of an amphitheatre should lead directly into the arena; almost all such constructions lead to an intermediate annular gallery beneath the seating. As Figure 4.1 demonstrates, all the vaulting which survives around the periphery of this outermost annular wall leads directly to this wall. Thus this third (outermost) wall must form the outer face of an annular covered gallery (*ambulacrum*), some 3.85m wide, with its inner face being the second wall. At an unknown date some of these barrel vaults were converted into small chambers by blocking them off near the arena (see Plate 4.8). A covered service corridor (2.9m wide) ran beneath the podium of the arena.

In general Cap Bon sandstone is used for the major annular and radial walls (*opus quadratum*), the revetment of the vaulting in *opus reticulatum* and the 'petit appareil' facing the walls of the subterranean structures. Kedel limestone was used for the façade and perhaps elsewhere. Where the vaulting survives, the *caementa* are laid on end as if they are voussoirs in an arch (see Plate 4.8). The architect did not place much confidence in the load-bearing capabilities of this concrete because, in the subterranean vaults, wherever a wall line passes above a vault, additional internal arches in cut stone have been added to support the

Plate 4.8 Amphitheatre, Carthage: the barrel vaulting surviving outside the third, outermost annular wall of the arena, later blocked off.
Photograph by D.L. Bomgardner.

structure.[112] The conscious choice to use *opus reticulatum* reflects a commitment to the *Romanitas* of this monument.

The French architect Alexandre Lézine studied the Roman monuments and their building materials and construction techniques.[113] He assigned approximate dates for both materials and techniques. He concluded that the Cap Bon sandstone quarries were used early in the history of the Augustan *colonia*, whereas the Kedel limestone (a very hard, rose-tinted stone found at Fondouk near Hammam Lif on Cap Bon) quarries were exploited later.[114]

By comparing the *opus quadratum* in the amphitheatre with that in the Antonine Baths, Lézine concluded that the technique used in the amphitheatre (V-shaped drafting around the joints of the stones) represented the earlier construction technique. The Baths are dated by their dedicatory inscription to the mid-second century AD.[115] By a similar comparative process he concluded that the mortars used in the vaulted substructures of the amphitheatre were roughly contemporaneous with those used in the Baths. Finally, since Kedel limestone was not used in the Baths, but first appears in the fabric of the Odeon, he assigned those phases in Kedel limestone in the amphitheatre's façade to roughly the early third century AD.[116]

In order to make this tripartite scheme work, Lézine had to postulate an initial first-century construction phase, then a mid-second-century expansion and finally, an early third-century revetment of the façade in Kedel limestone. Objections must be raised. First, such a revetment of a monument at a later date is completely unparalleled elsewhere. The fragments of limestone found around the periphery of the monument do not constitute proof for such a building phase. Also Lézine's chronology is based upon too few dated monuments. There is no necessity for the Odeon to have been the first monument at Carthage to have used Kedel limestone in its construction.

It is possible to clarify the chronology of the amphitheatre through the use of epigraphical evidence. On the basis of an inscription found at Carthage that records that *munera* were held *in amphitheatro*, the amphitheatre must have been completed before AD 133–39.[117] In addition, Delattre discovered a fragmentary white marble monumental inscription (letter height, 23cm) in the amphitheatre, which was probably a dedicatory inscription, bearing imperial titulature on two fragments ('a' and 'b').[118] If one accepts that this monumental inscription commemorated the dedication of a construction in the Carthage arena, then two possibilities exist: the construction was either the original work or a later reconstruction, repair or ornamentation phase. Fragment 'c' of this inscription bears the Roman numeral XX; the letters to both left and right have been effaced. This number must be at least equal to twenty. In general such iterations indicate imperial assumptions of the *tribunicia potestas* or the consulship, or acclamations as *imperator*.[119] By referring to standard epigraphical reference works, it is possible to find out which emperors held each of these titles at least twenty times. Wilmanns (*CIL* 8.24551) presumably went through a similar procedure and expressed his opinion that this inscription pertained to the reigns of M. Aurelius and L. Verus (after 10 December AD 165, when M. Aurelius held the *tribunicia potestas* for the twentieth time and before January/February AD 169, when L. Verus died).[120] Since the amphitheatre must have been in existence by AD 133–39, this inscription should commemorate another building phase soon after AD 165.

Golvin has assigned an early chronology of the Augustan era for the first amphitheatre at Carthage on this site.[121] This is consistent with a construction date before AD 133–39 from the epigraphical evidence discussed above.[122] The reconstruction phase in the amphitheatre (shortly after AD 165) might represent one of the first uses of Kedel limestone in a public monument at Carthage. Indeed a fire is recorded during the reign of Antoninus Pius, which damaged the forum at Carthage, and perhaps did far greater damage in the city.[123] The Kedel limestone quarries may have first been tapped in response to this conflagration to provide a more fire-resistant material than the friable sandstone in use.

Little evidence for the later phases of the amphitheatre has survived. The inscriptions re-carved on the seats of the cavea and those engraved on the balustrade of the arena-wall demonstrate the frequent appearance in the genitive case of individual *nomina* and *cognomina* with qualifiers such as *c(larissimi) v(iri)*. If a similar development from 'block seating' reservations to reserved places for individuals occurred at Carthage, as is documented to have taken place in the Colosseum in Rome, then these individual *loca* should be no earlier than the Constantinian era (early fourth century) and perhaps as late as the fifth century.[124] A late fourth-century pedestal base dedicated to the emperor Valens (364–78) by the proconsul Iulius Festus Hymetius was found in the western zone of the amphitheatre.[125] The testimony of the epigrams of Luxorius, the court poet to the Vandalic kings of Carthage (439–533), attests the continuing vigour of spectacles in the amphitheatre throughout this period.[126] The troubled years of the Byzantine exarchate in Carthage are perhaps the best period in which to look for the final hiatus of activities in the amphitheatre. Certainly the Arab conquest would have spelled the end of spectacles here.

Evidence for later, undated occupation within the arena suggests that during the troubled last years of the city people sought a form of security by retreating within the easily fortifiable walls of the amphitheatre to live.

The greatest amphitheatre in the whole of North Africa thus died, not with a bang, but with the continuing whimpers of those huddled within its crumbling shelter for safety in times of peril.

The amphitheatre at El Jem (Thysdrus) [Golvin #186][127]

The ancient town of Thysdrus (modern El Jem) was in a central position in the region of Tunisia known as the Sahel. It formed the key junction in the road network connecting the interior with the coastal ports where the agricultural products of the hinterland were exported. During the late second and third century, the Sahel's agricultural prosperity developed into a substantial market share of the export trade in olive oil. This success was largely due to earlier widespread efforts to implement olive tree plantations here from the reign of Hadrian onwards.

The civic history of Thysdrus remains unclear. Italian merchants (*negotiatores Italici*) resided alongside an indigenous settlement (*civitas*) from as early as the period of the Civil Wars (later first century BC).[128] Either during the last years of Julius Caesar, or perhaps early in the reign of Augustus, a substantial influx of Romans, quite likely veterans, settled here. This politically advantaged community probably kept the local community under its thumb until the reign of the emperor Septimius Severus, a native of North Africa himself, 'freed' the local town, giving it the title of *municipium Septimia libera Thysdritana*.[129]

This scenario also makes sense of the existence here of a second, earlier and smaller amphitheatre (the so-called *amphitheatrum minus*,[130] built perhaps early in the second century AD and with an estimated capacity of about 9,000 spectators). The existence of two amphitheatres in one city is rare, except for very large cosmopolitan cities, such as Rome, Puteoli or Capua, or else in cities where there is a duality of civic status, such as the legionary forts and associated civilian settlements along the Rhine/Danube frontiers, e.g. Carnuntum and Aquincum. If the earlier amphitheatre was the product of the municipal construction projects of the Roman veteran colony, then this later monument might represent the fruits of the liberality of either a united community or, perhaps, the now-dominant native *municipium*.

A wide range of polychrome-figured mosaics and inscriptions (mainly from the third century) leaves no doubt that Thysdrus played a crucial role in the organisation and distribution of the beasts (from the interior) and the professional hunters for the amphitheatres of a very wide territory within Africa Proconsularis. Recent research by Beschaouch into the nature of these guilds of professional hunters in Africa Proconsularis (modern Tunisia) has shown their remarkable degree of organisation.[131] Individual guilds (*sodalitates venatorum*) supplied professional hunters (*venatores*) and probably their own beasts, travelled widely within their 'circuits' and had their own religious associations, including totemic symbols and numerals, which appear on inscriptions and mosaics, thus helping to identify them.

The larger amphitheatre at El Jem is important for its good state of preservation as well as the detailed history of its reuse and the architectural innovations incorporated into its fabric. Next to the circus-amphitheatre complex at Lepcis Magna, the 'Colosseum' at El Jem is among the best-preserved amphitheatres in the Roman world. In terms of architectural influences, the El Jem 'Colosseum' was a direct lineal descendant of the Campanian tradition of amphitheatre construction. The monumental amphitheatre at Capua, the Carthage amphitheatre and the El Jem arena all share an unusual design feature: massive sculpted protomes of Greco-Roman deities adorning the spandrels between the arches of their façades.

The romantic legend of al-Kahina, the Berber queen of the Jarawa tribe of the eastern Aurès Mountains, who led the local tribes of the Sahel in their resistance to the Arab conquest of the late seventh century AD, lends an air of historical drama to this monument. Complex elements of folklore, legend, magic, superstition and historical fact intertwine to make up the fabulous tale of how al-Kahina successfully opposed several attempts to subdue this corner of Tunisia, including the use of magical powers to frustrate her attackers.

The historical events surrounding the probable origins of this amphitheatre have been discussed above (p. 127). The small amphitheatre (see Figure 4.3) at Thysdrus had served the city for a hundred years and may have been damaged in the violence of Maximinus's vengeance upon

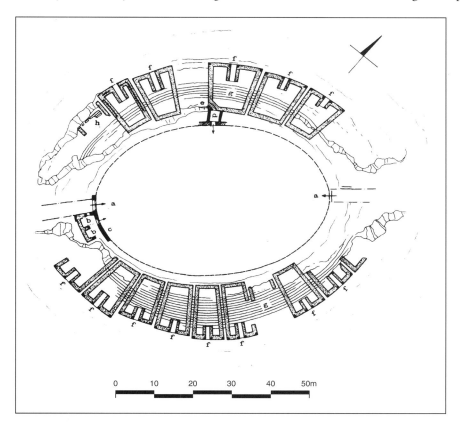

Figure 4.3 Small amphitheatre (*amphitheatrum minus*) (Phase II), Thysdrus (El Jem) (Golvin #25). Ground plan of the amphitheatre: later phase overlying earlier phase.
Source: Golvin, Planche XLIV, 1. Copyright J.-Cl. Golvin.

Plate 4.9 Amphitheatre, Thysdrus (El Jem): the façade. Note the massive piers and heavy proportions of the upper entablatures. Photograph by D.L. Bomgardner.

the seat of the rebellion against him under the Gordians.[132]

The Colosseum at Thysdrus preserves some remarkable evidence. Two different units of measurement are detectable in its architecture, both the Roman foot and the Punic cubit,[133] firm evidence of the persistence of native influences in this hinterland entrepôt strongly imbued with Punic cultural traditions. Second, there is a remarkably rigid standardisation in the proportions and the architectural decoration of the façade resulting in an extremely heavy appearance. This was partly because of lack of confidence in the extremely friable local dune sandstone, each upper storey of the façade being set back to lessen the thickness of the upper walls, thus diminishing the loading on the structures below.[134] The façade was never finished and construction was abandoned before the finer detailing could be added, such as the sculpting of the keystones. Third, sophisticated architectural advances are found in its construction. Cross-vaulting is used to cover the external arcaded galleries of the structure, thus providing a very effective counterpoise to the pressures trying to push the façade away from the rest of the monument. The steeper pitch of the seating allowed the incorporation of four *maeniana* plus a crowning colonnade into its *cavea*, whereas the Colosseum in Rome had only three *maeniana*. The steeper pitch of the seating also reduced the 'blind zone' immediately in front of the arena-wall not visible from the seating to less than 5m wide (compare the 5–7m width of the same region in the Colosseum).[135] The system of subterranean galleries and chambers beneath the arena includes complex vaulted geometric chambers (see Figure 4.4, labelled 'b').

Design principles

The initial design scheme and the subsequent modifications, as it was actually laid out, have been studied by Wilson Jones.[136] He notes the extreme similarity to the Colosseum, almost as if it had been shrunk to fit and reused here. Two major differences, however, distinguish the two monuments. First, whereas the Colosseum used an eight-centred polycentric curve for the trace of its monument, the amphitheatre at El Jem uses a simpler, four-centred curvature to obtain the trace of its arena and façade. Second, the Colosseum had eighty bays in its exterior arcaded façade, but only sixty-four bays occur in El Jem's frontage.

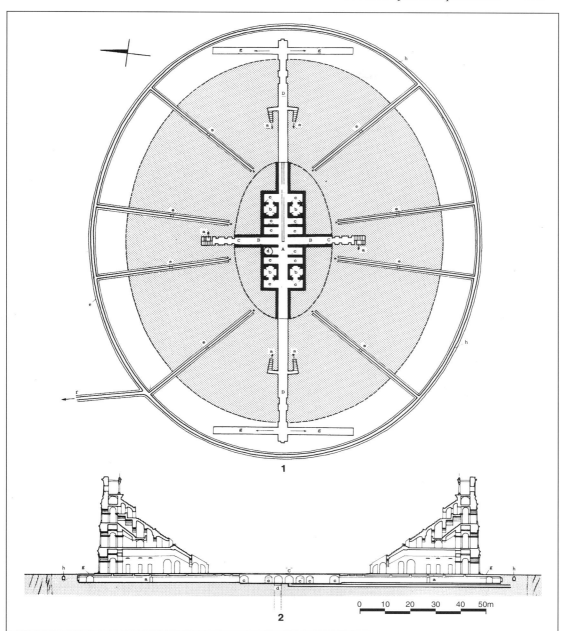

Figure 4.4 Amphitheatre, Thysdrus (El Jem) (Golvin #186). Ground plan of the substructures beneath the arena and cross-section of the amphitheatre.
Source: Golvin, Planche XLVI, 1 and 2. Copyright J.-Cl. Golvin.

Like the Colosseum, the trace of the amphitheatre relies upon a 'Pythagorean-triangle-and-inscribed-circle' initial design scheme (see above, p. 26, for a detailed description of how such a scheme worked). However, here, unlike the 28 Roman ft. module used for the Colosseum, a module of 22 Roman ft. provided the unifying linear dimension for the plan.[137] The initial scheme envisaged an arena whose dimensions were 220 by 132 Roman ft. (or 10 by 6 modules), with a *cavea* 132 Roman ft. wide (6 modules) and an overall size of 484 by 396 Roman ft. (22 by 18 modules). In order to achieve a perimeter whose individual bays had intercolumniations that were nearly 20 Roman ft. each, sixty-four bays were adopted for the arcaded façade. In addition a slight increase in the width of the *cavea* (from 132 to 141 Roman ft.) as originally specified in the initial design scheme was implemented in the actual construction of the monument. This resulted in no changes in the size of the arena, but an overall increase in size to 502 by 414 Roman ft.

Later history and reuse

Perhaps the most interesting feature of this amphitheatre is the remarkably detailed history of its later reuse as a centre of armed rebellion in this region against the Arab invaders of the seventh century. The amphitheatre was abandoned and converted into a military redoubt by the Byzantine era (before AD 648), if not earlier.[138] The widely known legend of the Berber queen, al-Kahina, and her heroic struggle for freedom against the Arab invaders at the end of the seventh century from her base inside the fortified amphitheatre here is considered to be largely apocryphal by modern Islamic scholars.[139] However, only the embroidered details are considered fictitious; the use of this amphitheatre at such a time for such a purpose is not disputed. Local resistance to centralised authority has always found the amphitheatre an easily defensible refuge. Indeed, in the mid-eighteenth century (1756–59), three arcades of its façade (at the western end of the major axis) were blown up so that it could not be used as such against the authority of Muhammed Bey in Tunis.[140] It seems reasonable to believe the local accounts of this structure being used for the manufacture of saltpetre (for gunpowder) during the later eighteenth and early nineteenth

Plate 4.10 Amphitheatre, Thysdrus (El Jem): a breach in the western façade, looking east across the arena. Photograph by D.L. Bomgardner.

century.[141] Under the authoritarian ruler of Tunis, Ahmed Bey, the original three-arcade breach was widened to some 30m to end the use of this structure as a defensive refuge against the assertion of central authority's control (*c.* 1850). Thereafter the saltpetre manufactory became a state monopoly.[142] Nineteenth-century travellers recorded that the arcades of the façade were being used for shops, the storage of grain and forage, and dwellings.[143]

Iol Caesarea (Cherchel) (Golvin #81)[144]

The medium-sized amphitheatre of Iol Caesarea, which eventually could accommodate some 16,000 spectators, is uniquely important among stone structures of this type. For it is quite possible that within its weird geometry lie clues to the very origins of the building-type of the amphitheatre. The arena consists of a central rectangle (57 × 44 m) with a semicircle attached to each end (each semicircle has a radius of 22m). Thus a lozenge-shaped area emerges.

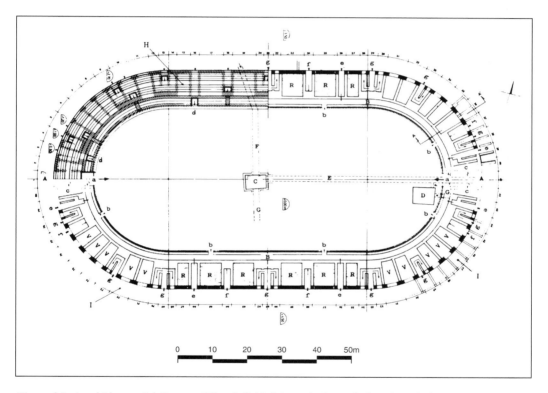

Figure 4.5 Amphitheatre, Iol Caesarea (Cherchel) (Golvin #81). Ground plan of amphitheatre.
Source: Golvin, Planche XXIX, 1. Copyright J.-Cl. Golvin.

It was probably built initially during the reign of the polymath, pro-Roman Mauretanian king, Juba II (25 BC–*c.* AD 23). He had been held hostage at Rome during his childhood and would have witnessed the earliest stages of the development of the monument there in temporary wood prototypes in the fora of Rome. The latest theory concerning the origins of the type anticipates this shape in order to fit best in the space available within an elongated rectangular forum.[145] Thus, the weird geometry of this arena probably holds the key to understanding the origins of the building-type in Rome during the late republican era.

Plate 4.11 Amphitheatre, Iol Caesarea (Cherchel): overview of the amphitheatre looking north towards the sea.
Photograph by D.L. Bomgardner.

Lambaesis (Golvin #60 and #111)[146]

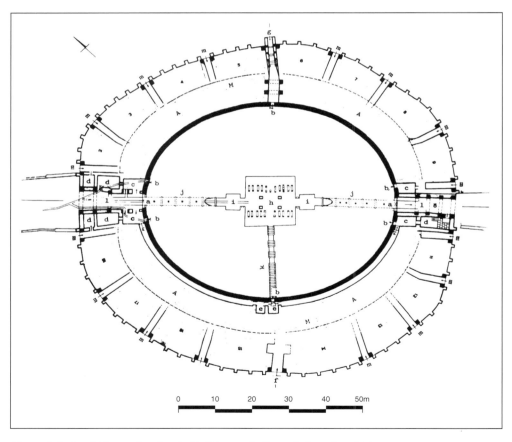

Figure 4.6 Amphitheatre, Lambaesis (Golvin #111). Ground plan of amphitheatre.
Source: Golvin, Planche XLIV, 2. Copyright J.-Cl. Golvin.

Plate 4.12 Amphitheatre, Lambaesis: overview of the amphitheatre looking north. Photograph by D.L. Bomgardner.

The story of this amphitheatre is the story of the third Augustan legion (*legio III Augusta*), stationed here probably from early in the reign of Trajan, but certainly by AD 128. The first amphitheatre (Golvin #60) was certainly for the use of the military stationed here with a seating capacity of about 7,200 spectators – about the size of a full-strength legion (*c.* 5,500) with attached auxiliary regiments (1,500–2,000). The arena (*c.* 2,937 m²) took up more than half (*c.* 57 per cent) of the entire surface area of this monument. Such a disproportionately large

Plate 4.13 Amphitheatre, Lambaesis: the vaulting carrying seating over the western major axial entrance into the arena.
Photograph by D.L. Bomgardner.

Plate 4.14 Amphitheatre, Lambaesis: the beast-pen (*carcer*) on the north-eastern side of the western major axial entrance into the arena. Photograph by D.L. Bomgardner.

Plate 4.15 Amphitheatre, Lambaesis: the central chamber of the arena's substructures. Note the stone sockets into which wooden uprights would have slotted for hoisting machinery. Photograph by D.L. Bomgardner.

percentage of space devoted to the arena as opposed to seating is typical of a military-type amphitheatre, for many of the functions of such an arena would require the accommodation of large formations of troops. Also the seating would be relatively restricted since at this stage the *canabae* (civilian settlement) which inevitably grew up outside the gates of a legionary camp would have been still of modest size. A series of phases of repair and adornment, well documented by inscriptions, took place in the course of the later second century AD (AD 169, 176–180).

Later, in AD 194, the troops of the legion built an extension to the initial 10m wide seating bank, expanding it to nearly twice this size (*c.* 19.5m) by the addition of a ring of massive hollow, wedge-shaped compartments filled with debris that formed the basis for the seating extension (see Plate 4.12). The new amphitheatre now had more of the trappings of a prestigious civic monument and it could seat some 15,400 people as befitted Septimius Severus's new provincial capital of Numidia. Vaulting carried the seating over the main axial entrances (see Plate 4.13). Four beast pens, one on each flank of both major entrances into the arena, would release animals into the arena for the *venationes* that took place there (see Figure 4.6, labelled 'c', and also Plate 4.14). The well-preserved substructures of the arena still contain the holes in stones that would have held the wooden machinery for hoisting equipment and cages of animals into the arena (see Plate 4.15).

The outline of the monument is extremely irregular, each caisson bearing little relation to the next, indicating an *ad hoc* construction technique. Here, on the western fringes of the civilised world, the exterior of such a monument mattered little. The arena and the seating took pride of place in the frontier capital of the Numidian military zone and its frontier.

Other second-century military amphitheatres, similar to the first earth embankment-style amphitheatre here at Lambaesis, were also found nearer the frontier at Gemellae (Golvin #44: *c.* AD 132–33) and Mesarfelta (Golvin #45: early second century).[147] Another embankment-type military amphitheatre was found along the Mauretanian coast at Tigava Castra (Golvin #46).[148] It was probably constructed by units brought in for Antoninus Pius's major campaign here against the Moorish tribes. All of them share a simplified embankment-type *cavea* with an unusually large proportion (above 50 per cent) of the surface area of the monument devoted to the arena and a modest seating capacity (2,000–3,000).

Tipasa (Golvin #130)[149]

Far and away the weirdest geometry can be found in this amphitheatre, built in the late second or early third century AD at this strategic port site on the Mauretanian coast which became a mid- to late second-century *colonia*. Obviously influenced by the neighbouring amphitheatre at Iol Caesarea, Tipasa is an ellipse inscribed within a rectangle with extremely irregular exterior contour. The arena and seating were the dominant features here.

Just off a radial corridor, in the south-western sector of the *cavea*, there is a well-preserved chamber (*c.* 3 × 3m) which contained a low bench around three sides and three niches in the wall opposite the doorway (see Plate 4.17). Such *sacella* are rarely this well preserved and a triad of deities were probably propitiated by the combatants prior to their bouts in the arena.

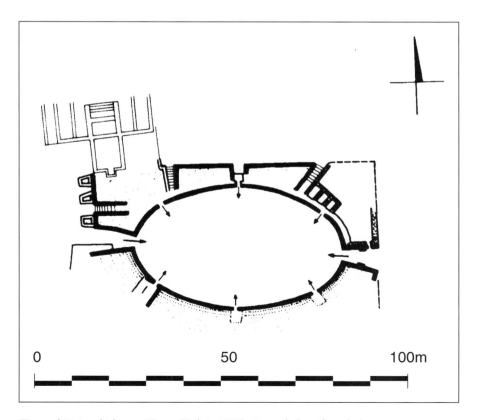

| 0 | 50 | 100m |

Figure 4.7 Amphitheatre, Tipasa (Golvin #130). Ground plan of amphitheatre.
Source: Golvin, Planche XX, c. Copyright J.-Cl. Golvin.

This amphitheatre may have been turned into a fortified redoubt by the construction of a triple circuit wall in its later history. It was certainly abandoned to sporadic stone-robbing and squatters from the end of the fourth or perhaps the beginning of the fifth century AD, when a potter's kiln was built into one of the gateways to the *cavea*.

Plate 4.16 Amphitheatre, Tipasa: overview of the amphitheatre. Photograph by D.L. Bomgardner.

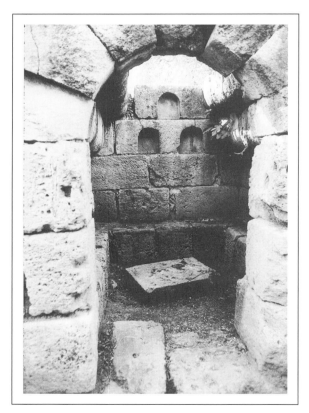

Plate 4.17 Amphitheatre, Tipasa: the *sacellum* with niches for cult statues near the arena. Photograph by D.L. Bomgardner.

A CATALOGUE OF NORTH AFRICAN AMPHITHEATRES

Acholla (Hr. Ras Botria): Golvin #118[150]

Municipal history: Hadrianic *municipium* (*CIL* 6.1684).

Comments: Amphitheatre possibly sited near the local Punic *tophet*. Sited in a depression: lower part of *cavea* supported by soil, upper by debris-filled compartments. Second phase: addition of *c.* 4m of seating to outside of *cavea*. Guérin saw a buttressed façade here.[151] The technique of *petit appareil* used here closely matches that of the local Trajanic Baths. Rake of middle *cavea* was 21 degrees.

Dimensions:[a]

Overall:	*c.* 90 × 86m	*c.* 6,080m²	Bomgardner's dimensions
Arena:	*c.* 58 × 54m	*c.* 2,460m² (*c.* 40 per cent)	
Cavea:	*c.* 16m wide	*c.* 3,620m² (*c.* 60 per cent)	
Seating estimate:	*c.* 11,600		
Overall:	*c.* 72 × 56m	*c.* 3,167m²	Golvin's dimensions
Arena:	*c.* 48 × 32m?	*c.* 1,206m² (*c.* 38 per cent)	
Cavea:	*c.* 12m wide	*c.* 1,961m² (*c.* 62 per cent)	
Seating estimate:	*c.* 6,300		

[a] For all the amphitheatres detailed, the first column indicates the linear dimensions, the second the area (sometimes including percentage of total surface area – oval area = pi × a × b, where a = semi-major axis and b = semi-minor axis). The third column gives further information, such as sources, where appropriate. Amphitheatres are catalogued by geographical area.

Agbia (Hr. Ain-Hadja): Golvin # 64[152]

Municipal history: Possible Severan *municipium*.[153]

Comments: This site lies about 3km from Dougga, on an elevated point about 300m south of the Byzantine citadel. Lachaux postulates that citizens of Dougga may have used this amphitheatre since none was located there. However, the small seating capacity (*c.* 3,000) would argue against this. Sunken arena with seating on embanked upcast stabilised by annular walls. *Petit appareil* wall construction and barrel-vaulted *vomitoria*.

Dimensions:

Overall:	*c.* 57 × 42m	*c.* 1,880 m²	Golvin, p. 94: major axis less than 60m
Arena:	*c.* 43 × 28m	*c.* 946m² (*c.* 50 per cent)	
Cavea:	*c.* 14m wide	*c.* 934m² (*c.* 50 per cent)	
Seating estimate:	*c.* 3,000		

Bararus (Hr. Rougga): Golvin #187[154]

Comments: Located some 12km south of El Jem. On a flat site, with a sunken arena, seating on radial barrel vaulting. Arena-wall (3m high × 1.25m thick) lacks a parapet and is thickly coated with plaster. Barrel-vaulted service corridor behind it opens on to arena via fourteen doorways (1.5m wide). Main entrance (W) into arena (4.3m wide). Golvin thinks the monument was begun in rivalry to the Thysdrus 'Colosseum' but left unfinished after AD 238, when region collapsed economically.

Dimensions:

Overall:	*c.* 98 × 73.5m	*c.* 5,657 m²
Arena:	*c.* 63.75 × 37.5m	*c.* 1,878m² (*c.* 33 per cent)
Cavea:	*c.* 17–18m wide	*c.* 3,779m² (*c.* 67 per cent)
Seating estimate:	*c.* 12,100	

Bulla Regia (Hammam Darradji): Golvin #117[155]

Municipal history: Hadrianic *colonia* (*CIL* 8.25522). Augustine in the first quarter of the fifth century commends the residents of Simitthu for having abandoned their spectacles, while castigating those of Bulla Regia for their continuing hedonism.[156]

Plate 4.18 Amphitheatre, Bulla Regia: overview of the amphitheatre looking uphill towards quarries above. Photograph by D.L. Bomgardner.

Plate 4.19 Amphitheatre, Bulla Regia: overview of the amphitheatre looking across the hillslope. Photograph by D.L. Bomgardner.

Plate 4.20 Amphitheatre, Bulla Regia: a detail of construction. Note that the vaulting on the left was made using fictile vaulting tubes (later), while that on the right used a wooden armature (earlier), thus indicating two phases of construction. Photograph by D.L. Bomgardner.

Comments: Sited in extramural quarry to north-east of the city; theatre lay 750m to the south-west and a probable necropolis lay further uphill to the north. The north and east parts of the *cavea* supported on a re-cut hillside, the south and west on vaulted substructures (see Plate 4.19) incorporating both wooden armature and fictile vaulting tubes (not usually found before the second half of second century[157]) in vaulting – two phases of construction (see Plate 4.20). Traces of frescoes depicting green foliage reported on ceiling of *vomitorium*.[158]

Dimensions:

Overall:	*c.* 73.6+ × 66+ m	*c.* 3,815+ m²
Arena:	*c.* 33.6 × 30m	*c.* 792m² (*c.* 21 per cent)
Cavea:	*c.* 18+ m wide	*c.* 3,023+ m² (*c.* 79 per cent)
Seating estimate:	*c.* 9,700	

Carthago Phase I (Carthage): Golvin #95[159]

(Plates 4.1–8 and Figures 4.1–2)
Municipal history: Augustan *colonia*.

Dimensions:

Overall:	*c.* 120 × 93m	*c.* 8,765m²
Arena:	64.66 × 36.7m	1,860m² (*c.* 21 per cent)
Cavea:	*c.* 27m wide	*c.* 6,905m² (*c.* 79 per cent)
Seating estimate:	*c.* 22,200	

Carthago Phase II (Carthage): Golvin #174

Dimensions:

Overall:	156 × 128m	15,680m²
Arena:	64.66 × 36.7m	1,860m² (*c.* 12 per cent)
Cavea:	46m wide	13,820m² (*c.* 88 per cent)
Seating estimate:	*c.* 44,400	

(See detailed discussion earlier in this chapter.)

Lepcis Magna (Lebda): Golvin #24[160]
(See Figures 4.8–4.9)

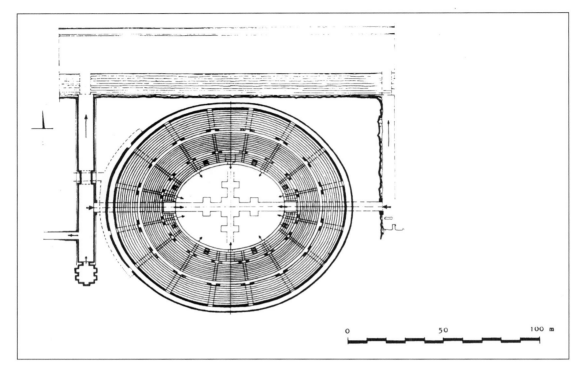

Figure 4.8 Amphitheatre, Lepcis Magna (Golvin #24). Ground plan of amphitheatre.
Source: Golvin, Planche XIII, 1. Copyright J.-Cl. Golvin.

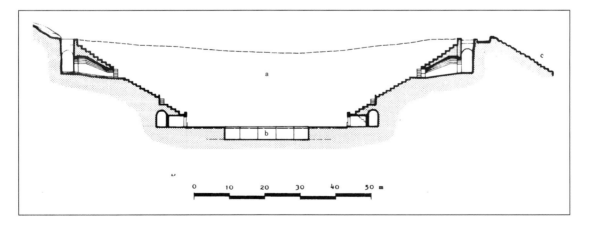

Figure 4.9 Amphitheatre, Lepcis Magna (Golvin #24). Cross-section of amphitheatre, including south *cavea* of associated hippodrome.
Source: Golvin, Planche XLVII, 2. Copyright J.-Cl. Golvin.

Municipal history: Flavian *municipium* (*IRT* 342) and Trajanic *colonia* (*IRT* 284).

Comments: Part of a unique amphitheatre-circus architectural complex – circus to north along shore; both monuments interconnected. Amphitheatre dug into soft sandstone at the top of Sidi Barcu hill. Relatively unpublished, although nearly perfectly preserved by drifting sands and precisely dated by an inscription to Nero's reign (AD 56).[161]

Remarkably well-preserved series of service rooms, storage areas, entrance galleries and viaduct. Arena-wall (2.85m high) was originally revetted in Proconnesian marble and had a protective net assembly overhanging the edge of the arena; it was later covered with plaster rendering, painted to imitate marble. Well-preserved *carceres* set into podium for release of wild beasts into arena (NB slits at the back of chambers allowed burning straw to be thrown into chambers thus forcing animals out of the cages). Continuous service corridor behind arena-wall with ten entries into the arena.

Cavea: Three *maeniana* with sixteen *cunei* in each. Elaborated cross-shaped subterranean galleries and chambers in arena probably part of a second-century phase (see Figure 4.8). Small shrine to Ephesian Diana located in *summa cavea*. Stele dedicated to Nemesis found; also votive reliefs to Mars, Diana and Victory. Epigraphical evidence for reserved block seating for merchants from the eastern Mediterranean.

Dimensions:

Overall:	*c*. 100 × 90m	*c*. 7,069 m^2
Arena:	*c*. 57 × 47m	
	(= 110 × 90 Punic cubits)	*c*. 2,104m^2 (*c*. 30 per cent)
Cavea:	*c*. 21.5m wide	*c*. 4,965m^2 (*c*. 70 per cent)
Seating estimate:	*c*. 16,000	

Leptiminus (Lemta): Golvin #114[162]

Municipal history: Trajanic *colonia*.[163] Important port for central Sahel with road links to Thysdrus.

Comments: Located on extreme west of the site on rising ground. Lower *cavea* supported by sub-soil, upper portions by debris-filled compartments with *vomitoria* between. *Gradus* (40 × 70 cm). Five *cunei* in eastern half, six in western half of *cavea*. Major entry on western end of minor axis opposite the city. Vaulting carried seating over at least the south-eastern major axis entranceway to arena.

Dimensions:

Overall:	*c*. 85.84 × 65.12m	*c*. 4,390 m^2
	290 × 220 Roman ft.	
Arena:	*c*. 56.24 × 35.52m	*c*. 1,569m^2 (*c*. 36 per cent)
	190 × 120 Roman ft.	
Cavea:	*c*. 14.8m	*c*. 2,821m^2 (*c*. 64 per cent)
	50 Roman ft.	
Seating estimate:	*c*. 9,100	

Mactaris (Maktar): Golvin #119[164]

(See Figure 4.10 and Plates 4.21–23)

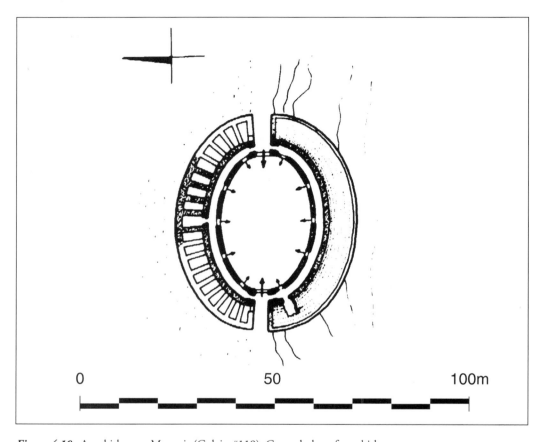

Figure 4.10 Amphitheatre, Mactaris (Golvin #119). Ground plan of amphitheatre.
Source: Golvin, Planche XVI, 8. Copyright J.-Cl. Golvin.

Plate 4.21
Amphitheatre, Mactaris:
overview of the
amphitheatre.
Photograph by D.L.
Bomgardner.

Plate 4.22 Amphitheatre, Mactaris: a detail of the system of doorway and *carcer* in the arena-wall.
Photograph by D.L. Bomgardner.

Plate 4.23 Amphitheatre, Mactaris: a detailed view of the *carcer*.
Photograph by D.L. Bomgardner.

Municipal history: Perhaps a *municipium* under Hadrian,[165] an important administrative centre for its region under Trajan,[166] a *colonia* of M. Aurelius and Commodus (*CIL* 8.11801); probably a double community, i.e. a native and a Roman settlement in close proximity.[167]

Comments: Strikingly similar in construction technique and materials to the Great Baths dated epigraphically to AD 199[168] and therefore roughly contemporaneous: end second century/third century AD. Located on the north-west edge of this city near a triumphal arch and important spring bordering the road from Sicca Veneria. An extensive *tophet* and sanctuary to Ba'al/Saturn were adjacent to the arch.[169] Arena-wall (preserved to a height of 2m and 1.35m thick) covered with plaster; service corridor behind, with ten doorways equipped with wooden doors that opened into the arena (see Plate 4.22). North-west doorway well preserved (1m wide × 1.8m high) and beside it there is a *carcer* (65 cm high × 50 cm wide) equipped with a shutter at the front (see Plate 4.23) and evidence for two wooden bars (vertically) to close the cage at the rear: two other similar *carceres*. One small chamber beneath the south-west *cavea*, perhaps a *sacellum*.

Dimensions:

Overall:	63.2 × 49.6m	2,46 m²
Arena:	38.4 × 24.8m	*c.* 12.4m wide
Cavea:	*c.* 12.4m wide	*c.* 1,714m² (*c.* 70 per cent)
Seating estimate:	*c.* 5,500	

Pupput (Souk el Abiod)[170]

Municipal history: A titular *colonia* under Commodus (*CIL* 8.24094).

Dimensions:

Overall:	—	—
Arena:	*c.* 45 × 36m	*c.* 1,272m²
Cavea:	—	—
Seating estimate:	—	

Sabratha: Golvin #120[171]

(See Plates 4.24–26)
Municipal history: A *colonia* before AD 175–80 (*IRT* 23).

Comments: Perhaps second century AD. Sited in a quarry on the eastern edge of the city. North entrance gave access from the coast road. Phase I: *cavea* supported upon re-cut quarry sides; Phase II: *summum maenianum* supported on debris-filled compartments (south side only – north rested on bedrock) added to periphery. Well-preserved main subterranean gallery (major axis), including hoisting mechanisms (see Plate 4.26) with a small cross gallery (minor axis), arena service corridor with ten doorways into the arena, storage chambers and *carceres* hewn into bedrock flanking major entrances to the arena, and sunken ambulatory between *media/summa cavea*. Late phase of fortification (not dated).

Dimensions:

Overall:	*c.* 104 × 90m.	*c.* 7,350m²	Ward's dimensions[172]
Arena:	65 × 49m	2,500m² (*c.* 34 per cent)	
Cavea:	*c.* 20m wide	*c.* 4,850m² (*c.* 66 per cent)	
Seating estimate:	*c.* 15,600		
Overall:	*c.* 115 × 99m	*c.* 8,942m²	Golvin's dimensions
Arena:	65 × 49m	*c.* 2,500m² (*c.* 28 per cent)	
Cavea:	*c.* 25m wide	*c.* 6,442m² (*c.* 72 per cent)	
Seating estimate:	*c.* 20,700		

Plate 4.24 Amphitheatre, Sabratha: overview of the northern *cavea* of the amphitheatre.
Photograph by D.L. Bomgardner.

Plate 4.25 Amphitheatre, Sabratha: a detail of the southern *cavea* with its
later added seating to left of gallery.
Photograph by D.L. Bomgardner.

Plate 4.26 Amphitheatre, Sabratha: a detail of the hoisting mechanisms in the subterranean structures of the arena. Photograph by D.L. Bomgardner.

Seressi (Hr. Oum el Abouab): Golvin #66[173]
(Plate 4.27)

Plate 4.27 Amphitheatre, Seressi: a detail of the exterior of the *cavea*. Note the orthostates used in *opus africanum* construction. Photograph by D.L. Bomgardner.

Municipal history: A *municipium*, probably not before the Hadrianic era.[174]

Comments: Dug into a hilltop on the southern edge of the site near a triumphal arch; seating supported on upcast spoil stabilised between annular terrace walls in *petit appareil*. Evidence of orthostates suggesting *opus africanum* also used. Perhaps mid- to late second century AD.[175]

Dimensions:

Overall:	76 × 65.2m	3,892m^2	Bomgardner's dimensions
Arena:	51.5 × 40.7m	1,646m^2 (*c.* 42 per cent)	
Cavea:	12.25m wide	2,246m^2 (*c.* 58 per cent)	
Seating estimate:	*c.* 7,200		
Overall:	*c.* 69 × 54m	*c.* 2,926m^2	Golvin's dimensions, p. 95
Arena:	*c.* 41 × 26m	*c.* 837m^2 (*c.* 29 per cent)	
Cavea:	*c.* 14m wide	*c.* 2,089m^2 (*c.* 71 per cent)	
Seating estimate:	*c.* 6,700		

Sicca Veneria (Le Kef): Golvin #183[176]

Municipal history: Augustan veteran *colonia* (*CIL* 8.15858).

Comments: Located to the north, just beyond the city walls, near the second theatre. Golvin compares it with Thapsus (Golvin #185).

Dimensions:

Overall:	*c.* 100 × 80m	*c.* 6,280m^2
Arena:	*c.* 70 × 50m	*c.* 2,750m^2 (*c.* 44 per cent)
Cavea:	*c.* 15m wide	*c.* 3,530m^2 (*c.* 56 per cent)
Seating estimate:	*c.* 11,300	

Simmithu (Chemtou): Golvin #67[177]

(Plate 4.28)

Municipal history: Augustan *colonia* (*CIL* 8.14612) alongside the opening of the Numidian marble quarries here as an imperial monopoly (*CIL* 8.14578–79, 14583).

Comments: Poorly preserved apart from sections of the arena and immediately adjacent areas. Augustine, in the first quarter of the fifth century, commends the residents of Simmithu for having abandoned their spectacles, while castigating those of Bulla Regia for their continuing hedonism.[178] The amphitheatre lay on the south-eastern edge of the site, beyond the mound of marble chips and the Roman necropolis. Marble *gradus* came from the nearby quarry. There is an important Punic, and later Roman, sanctuary (atop Djebel Chemtou) dedicated to Ba'al/Saturn towards which the axis of the amphitheatre points. Possible cultic significance. Leglay has surveyed the links between human sacrifice in arenas of North Africa and the cult of Saturn.[179]

Dimensions:

Overall:	61 × *c.* 52.2?m	*c.* 2,500m^2?	Dimension for overall length certain, but width obtained by comparison with Thibaris and Uchi Maius.
Arena:	*c.* 30? × 21.5m	*c.* 510m^2? (*c.* 20 per cent?)	Dimension for width of arena is certain; its length obtained as above.
Cavea:	*c.* 15.5m wide	*c.* 1,990m^2? (*c.* 80 per cent?)	
Seating estimate:	*c.* 6,500?		

Plate 4.28 Amphitheatre, Simmithu: overview of the amphitheatre taken from the summit of Djebel Chemtou.
Photograph by D.L. Bomgardner.

Sufetula (Sbeitla): Golvin #113[180]
(Figure 4.11 and Plate 4.29)

Plate 4.29 Amphitheatre, Sufetula: a detail of a *vomitorium*. Note the construction in *opus incertum*. Photograph by D.L. Bomgardner.

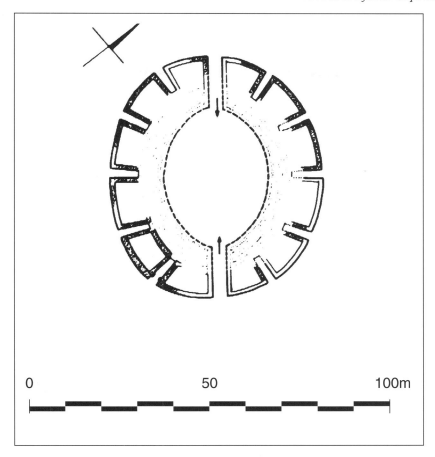

Figure 4.11 Amphitheatre, Sufetula (Golvin #113). Ground plan of amphitheatre.
Source: Golvin, Planche XVI, 1. Copyright J.-Cl. Golvin.

Municipal history: A *colonia* perhaps by the end of the second century AD.

Comments: Site *c.* 100m north-west of the Arch of the Severi (AD 209–11) that spanned the road to Theveste. A Christian necropolis lay to the south-west of the amphitheatre. The arena was dug into the crest of a hillock and the upcast was consolidated into hollow masonry caissons as the basis for the seating; *vomitoria* were placed between caissons (see Plate 4.29). Façade constructed in *opus africanum* (orthostates: 20 × 53 cm in section spaced about 2.4m apart), *vomitoria* in *opus incertum*. Late antique redoubt, perhaps by late fourth century. Material from arena robbed to build Byzantine temenos walls around Capitolium precinct (sixth century).[181] E. Kirsten dates this monument to *c.* AD 160 along with the local baths.[182]

Dimensions:

Overall:	*c.* 72 (± 2) × 60 (± 2)m	*c.* 3,400 (± 200)m²
Arena:	*c.* 47 (± 1) × 37 (± 1)m	*c.* 1,370 (± 60)m² (*c.* 40 per cent)
Cavea:	*c.* 12m wide	*c.* 2,030 (± 200)m² (*c.* 60 per cent)
Seating estimate:	*c.* 6,500	

Thaenae (Henchir Thina): Golvin #71[183]

Municipal history: Hadrianic titular *colonia* (*CIL* 8.1685).

Comments: Perhaps second century, Hadrianic? Site lies *c.* 500m to north-north-west of the Tacapae Gate, probably along the road to Tacapae. Dug into the summit of a large hill. Vaulting carried seating over both major axis entrances to arena. At least three *vomitoria* still visible in each half of the *cavea*.

Dimensions:

Overall:	*c.* 90 × (61?)m	*c.* 4,310m²	Golvin, p. 96: 66 × 54m
Arena:	*c.* (62?) × 33m	*c.* 1,610m²	Golvin, p. 96: 42 × 30m
		(*c.* 37 per cent)	
Cavea:	*c.* 14m wide	*c.* 2,700m²	
		(*c.* 63 per cent)	
Seating estimate:	*c.* 8,700?		

Thapsus (Hr. Ras Dimas): Golvin #185[184]

Comments: Sited on the southern edge of the settlement, *c.* 750m south-west of the harbour mole. Lower seating on geologic basis, upper seating on barrel-vaulted substructures. Traces of arena-wall in massive *opus quadratum*; continuous service corridor with doorways into arena (only those on minor axis visible).

Dimensions:

Overall:	73.2 × 61m	3,510m²	Temple's dimensions[185]
Arena:	45.7 × 33.5m	1,200m² (*c.* 34 per cent)	
Cavea:	13.75m wide	2,310m² (c. 66 per cent)	
Seating estimate:	*c.* 7,400		
Overall:	80 × 58m	3,640m²	Golvin's dimensions
Arena:	67 × 43m	2,260m² (62 per cent)	
Cavea:		1,380m² (38 per cent)	
Seating estimate:	*c.* 4,440		

Thibaris (Hr. Thibar): Golvin #62[186]

Municipal history: Perhaps a Severan *municipium*.

Comments: Sited in the south-western sector of the city not far beyond its ramparts; near the circus, Byzantine citadel and 'Chateau d'eau' of the Djebel Goraa aqueduct. Arena-wall 3m high; podium had four tiers (49 × 80 cm) of seating; *primum maenianum* had twelve tiers (6.5m wide: each *gradus* 47 × 47 cm); *secundum maenianum* had perhaps nine tiers (6.2m wide). Major entries into arena: major axial: 2.2 wide × 2m wide; minor axial: 1.2m wide × 2m high. Traces of a balustrade (53 cm thick × 39 cm high) bordering podium. Arena dug into soil upcast consolidated for lower seating, upper on vaulted substructures.

Dimensions:

Overall:	61.2 × 51.5m	2,475m²
Arena:	30.8 × 21m	508m² (*c.* 21 per cent)
Cavea:	*c.* 15.2m wide	1,967m² (*c.* 79 per cent)
Seating estimate:	*c.* 6,300	

Thignica (Ain Tounga): Golvin #116[187]
(Plates 4.30–32)

Plate 4.30 Amphitheatre, Thignica: overview of the amphitheatre taken from outside the monument. Photograph by D.L. Bomgardner.

Plate 4.31 Amphitheatre, Thignica: a detail of the construction of the chamber at the end of the short axis of the arena. Note the use of fictile vaulting tubes.
Photograph by D.L. Bomgardner.

Plate 4.32 Amphitheatre, Thignica: details of the service corridor and chamber flanking the arena entrance (*carcer?*).
Photograph by D.L. Bomgardner.

Municipal history: A double community (*CIL* 8.15212); advanced to a combined *municipium* perhaps as early as Septimius Severus (*CIL* 8.1406).[188]

Comments: Major building phase, post mid-second century (fictile vaulting tubes usually only found in second half of the second century and later: cf. Bulla Regia). Major structural alterations in north-eastern sector of *cavea* and entranceways, either vaulted or re-vaulted to carry seating (fourth century?). Amphitheatre out of use by Byzantine era (sixth century). Situated on northern edge of site, separated from urban centre by a necropolis to the south. Localised outcrops of limestone have been used to support parts of the *cavea*. Extensive use of *opus africanum* and fictile vaulting tubes in construction. Traces of fresco on arena-wall; a well-preserved series of vaulted chambers beneath seats and their associated service corridors, stairways tangential to façade, stone-lined drain beneath southern branch of minor axis in arena.

Dimensions:

Overall:	65.2 × 52m	2,663m²	
Arena:	40.4 × 27.2m	863m² (*c.* 32 per cent)	
Cavea:	*c.* 12.4m wide	1,800m² (*c.* 68 per cent)	
Seating estimate:	*c.* 5,800		
Overall:	56 × 46m	*c.* 2,023m²	Golvin's dimensions
Arena:	39 × 26.5m	812m² (*c.* 40 per cent)	(p. 133)
Cavea:		*c.* 1,210m² (*c.* 60 per cent)	
Seating estimate:	*c.* 3,900		

Thimisua (Sidi bou Argoub)[189]

Comments: Situated on the southern periphery of the site, about 500m south of the Byzantine citadel. Built near the crest of a shell-laden limestone escarpment (cf. circus at Thugga) overlooking the nearby oued (seasonally dry river bed). Half the seating rests on the upper slopes of the escarpment, the rest probably upon fill inside masonry caissons with *vomitoria* between (a common technique in this region, cf. Thuburbo Maius). Local *opus quadratum* plus *opus africanum* in arena-wall (60 cm thick) and in side-walls of main entranceways into arena (north entry: 3.5m wide at arena).

Dimensions:

Overall:	*c.* 54.7 × 39.8m	*c.* 1,710m^2
Arena:	38.3 × 23.4m	704m^2 (*c.* 41 per cent)
Cavea:	*c.* 8.2m wide	*c.* 1,006m^2 (*c.* 59 per cent)
Seating estimate:	*c.* 3,200	

Thuburbo Maius (Hr. el Kasbat): Golvin #121[190]
(Figure 4.12 and Plate 4.33)

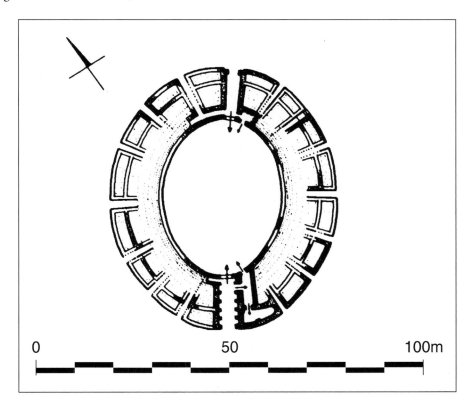

Figure 4.12 Amphitheatre, Thuburbo Maius (Golvin #121). Ground plan of amphitheatre. *Source:* Golvin, Planche XVI, 10. Copyright J.-Cl. Golvin.

Municipal history: Either a native *civitas* raised first to the status of a *municipium* under Hadrian, then to a *colonia* under Commodus[191] or a double community (*civitas* and *pagus civium Romanorum*), with *civitas* achieving *municipium* status under Hadrian, and both communities uniting to form the Commodan *colonia*.[192]

Comments:

Phase I: Original construction – *opus incertum*: late second/early third century.[193]

Phase II: Addition of a 4m wide band of seating to the periphery of the *cavea* – reddish-orange shale ashlar revetment: perhaps mid-fourth century.[194]

Phase III: Reconstruction of south-west entry to arena and parts of *cavea* adjoining – rubble work and reused inscription: perhaps late fourth century.[195]

Amphitheatre was built into a hilltop (second highest point, only the Temple of Saturn is higher) on south-south-eastern edge of the city. Major axis points towards the forecourt of the Temple of Saturn. Large cistern complex adjacent to the west. Arena (very irregular contour) dug into the ground with service corridor behind arena-wall (western side of *cavea* only). Lower seating rested upon bedrock while upper rested upon fill inside *opus incertum* masonry caissons with *vomitoria* between (cf. Sufetula). Four trapezoidal inhumation burials (at least one Christian) in apsed chamber beneath seating, possibly a *martyrium* for an unrecorded Christian martyrdom in the arena. Apsed chamber, probably a *sacellum*, possibly a *Nemeseum*.

Golvin's phasing: Phase I: second century; Phase II: early third century.

Plate 4.33 Amphitheatre, Thuburbo Maius: details of the apsed chamber and associated service corridor and chamber (*carcer*?) flanking the entrance to the arena.
Photograph by D.L. Bomgardner.

Dimensions:

Overall:	*c.* 73.6 × 61m	*c.* 3,526m²	
Arena:	45.6 × 33m	1,182m² (*c.* 34 per cent)	
Cavea:	*c.* 14m wide	*c.* 2,344m² (*c.* 66 per cent)	
Seating estimate:	*c.* 7,500		
Overall:	77 × 62.5m	3,780m²	Golvin's dimensions
Arena:	45 × 32.5m	1,149m² (*c.* 30 per cent)	
Cavea:	*c.* 11m wide	2,631m² (*c.* 70 per cent)	
Seating estimate:	*c.* 8,500		

Thysdrus 'Colosseum' (El Jem): Golvin #186[196]

Municipal history: Dual community joined in a common *municipium* under Severus.
Comments: See detailed discussion above, p. 150.

Dimensions:

Overall:	147.9 × 122.2m	14,195m²
Arena:	64.5 × 38.8m	1,966m² (*c.* 14 per cent)
Cavea:	*c.* 41.7m wide	12,229m² (*c.* 86 per cent)
Seating estimate:	*c.* 39,300	

Thysdrus, *amphitheatrum minus,* Phase I (El Jem): Golvin #25[197]

Comments: Poorly known, rock-cut, asymmetrical *cavea*: more seating on south-eastern side than on the north-west. First century AD.

Dimensions:

Overall:	*c.* 79 × 70m	*c.* 4,343m²
Arena:	*c.* 49 × 40m	*c.* 1,539m² (*c.* 35 per cent)
Cavea:	*c.* 15m wide (variable)	*c.* 2,804m² (*c.* 65 per cent)
Seating estimate:	*c.* 9,000	

Thysdrus, *amphitheatrum minus,* Phase II (El Jem): Golvin #112[198]

Comments: Built over the earlier *cavea*: hollow, wedge-shaped masonry coffers filled up with debris as basis of seating. Well-preserved *carceres* (see Figure 4.3, labelled 'b').

Dimensions:

Overall:	*c.* 92 × 72m	*c.* 5,202m²
Arena:	*c.* 60 × 40m	*c.* 1,885m² (*c.* 36 per cent)
Cavea:	*c.* 16m wide	*c.* 3,317m² (*c.* 64 per cent)
Seating estimate:	*c.* 10,700	

Uthina (Oudna): Golvin #115[199]

(Figure 4.13 and Plates 4.34–35)

Plate 4.34 Amphitheatre, Uthina: overview of the *cavea* with the summit of Djebel Zaghouan in the distance.
Photograph by D.L. Bomgardner.

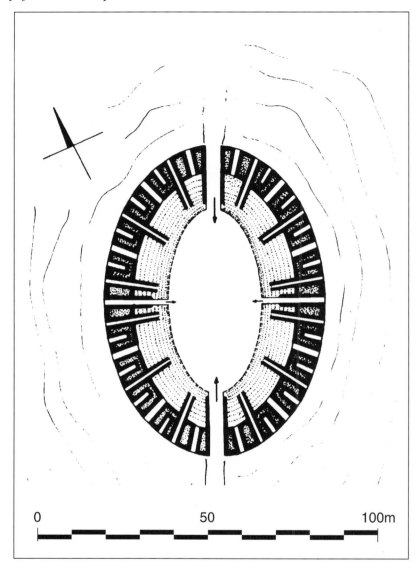

Figure 4.13 Amphitheatre, Uthina (Golvin #115). Ground plan of amphitheatre.
Source: Golvin, Planche XI, 8. Copyright J.-Cl. Golvin.

Municipal history: Octavian *colonia* and unspecified Hadrianic benefits (*indulgentia*) (*ILS* 6874, 6789).

Comments: Sited in a disused quarry (cf. Sabratha): lower *cavea* supported upon hillside, upper upon a structure of adjacent masonry compartments between which *vomitoria* to the seating were placed; *caementa* of vaulting laid radially in mortar, as if they were voussoirs, typical of early second century AD.

Plate 4.35 Amphitheatre, Uthina: overview of the *cavea* with the highly symmetrical elements of its construction.
Photograph by D.L. Bomgardner.

Dimensions:

Overall:	*c.* 96 × 81m	*c.* 6,107m^2
Arena:	*c.* 52.5 × 37.5m	*c.* 1,546m^2 (*c.* 25 per cent)
Cavea:	*c.* 21.75m wide	*c.* 4,561m^2 (*c.* 75 per cent)
Seating estimate:	*c.* 14,700	

Utica (Hr. bou Chateur): Golvin #61[200]

Municipal history: First capital of *Africa vetus*; Octavian *municipium*; Hadrianic titular *colonia*; *ius Italicum* (equivalent to Italian soil, i.e., non-provincial status) granted under Severus and Caracalla.

Comments: Amphitheatre was placed into a natural ravine; seating rested on hillsides stabilised by annular terrace walls; very simple conception, and thus perhaps initially as early as the late first century BC when Utica was the provincial capital. Later expansion, perhaps under Hadrian. Unusual grille or balustrade atop arena-wall inserted between black marble columns. Early observers claimed to have seen underground beast cages in arena. Dunant estimated the seating capacity at about 20,000 spectators.[201]

On the basis of aerial photographs, Lézine[202] proposed a second, small republican amphitheatre, whose site is beneath the later imperial circus at Utica and thus unexplored.

Dimensions:

Overall:	*c.* 118 × 98m	*c.* 9,082m^2	
Arena:	*c.* 80 × 60m	*c.* 3,770m^2 (*c.* 42 per cent)	This unusually large arena is probably the result of topographical constraints.
Cavea:	*c.* 19m wide	*c.* 5,312m^2 (*c.* 58 per cent)	
Seating estimate:	*c.* 17,100		

Ulissipira (Hr. Zembra): Golvin #70[203]

Comments: Hedi Slim has identified the site of Henchir Zembra with the ancient Ulissipira (disputed and various attributions proposed[204]) and given the following details about the amphitheatre there.

Dimensions:

Overall:	*c.* 69 × 53m	*c.* 2,872m²
Arena:	*c.* 48 × 32m	*c.* 1,206m² (*c.* 42 per cent)
Cavea:	*c.* 10.5m wide	*c.* 1,666m² (*c.* 58 per cent)
Seating estimate:	*c.* 5,400	

Ptolemais (Tolmeita): Golvin #76[205]

Municipal history: Considerable growth and prosperity during the first century and first half the second century AD.[206]

Comments: Sited in an old quarry (cf. Sabratha); rock-cut *cavea* (cf. Lepcis Magna); *gradus* well preserved (40 × 60 cm). A gladiatorial *ludus* existed in the south-western quarter of the city (undated).[207]

Dimensions:

Overall:	*c.* 89 × 86m	*c.* 6,011m²
Arena:	47.5 × 44.5m	1,660m² (*c.* 28 per cent)
Cavea:	*c.* 20.75m wide	*c.* 4,351m² (*c.* 72 per cent)
Seating estimate:	*c.* 16,300	

Each *locus* here would be 40cm wide and 60cm deep, thus 0.24m² per spectator here.

Iol Caesarea, Phase I (Chercel): Golvin #81[208]
(Figure 4.5 and Plate 4.11)

Municipal history: Capital of Mauretania Caesariensis; Claudian veteran colony (Pliny, *Historia Naturalis* 5.2.20) first century AD, probably under King Juba II, 25 BC–*c.* AD 23.[209]

Comments: Idiosyncratic lozenge shape; arena-wall 3.8m high; service corridor behind it. Subterranean structures in arena: central chamber (6.5 × 4.4 × 2.4m) served by two vaulted galleries along the major and minor axes (see Figure 4.5, labelled 'C', 'E' and 'F') with another chamber (6.2 × 5.0 × 2.4m [labelled 'D' on Figure 4.5]) in south-eastern area of the arena. Lowest *gradus* of *cavea* (43 × 73 cm).

Dimensions:

Overall:	124 × 67m	7,328m²
Arena:	101 × 44m	4,029m² (*c.* 55 per cent)
Cavea:	11.45m wide	3,299m² (*c.* 45 per cent)
Seating estimate:	*c.* 10,600	

Unusual geometry of arena: central rectangle (57 × 44m) with semicircular ends (radius 22m)

Iol Caesarea, Phase II (Chercel): Golvin #81

Comments: Addition of an outer ring of vaulting supported on radial walls 5m wide to augment *cavea*. Façade of ends of vaulting in arches of *opus quadratum*.

Dimensions:

Overall:	134 × 77m	9,028m²	
Arena:	101 × 44m	4,029m² (*c.* 45 per cent)	Unusual geometry of arena: central rectangle (57 × 44m) with semicircular ends (radius 22m)
Cavea:	16.45m wide	4,999m² (*c.* 55 per cent)	
Seating estimate:	*c.* 16,100		

Tipasa: Golvin #130[210]
(Figure 4.7 and Plates 4.16–17)

Municipal history: Claudian *municipium* with Latin rights; Hadrian or Antoninus Pius gave it the status of a *colonia*.

Comments: Late construction impinging upon earlier monuments nearby; after *c.* AD 145, possible chapel for a triad of deities in south-western sector (see Plate 4.17);[211] subterranean gallery with machinery for hoisting props into arena,[212] fortified redoubt in late antiquity; abandoned for stone-robbing and sporadic occupation (end of fourth/beginning of fifth century).[213]

Dimensions:

Overall:	*c.* 77 × 55m	*c.* 4,235m²	Extremely irregular exterior façade; elliptical arena inserted into a rectangular *cavea*.
Arena:	*c.* 57 × 37m	*c.* 1,656m² (*c.* 39 per cent)	
Cavea:	*c.* 10m wide	*c.* 2,579m² (*c.* 61 per cent)	
Seating estimate:	*c.* 8,300		

Gemellae (El Kasbate): Golvin #44[214]

Municipal history: Hadrianic camp of AD 132–33 with *canabae*[215] raised to the status of a *municipium* with Latin rights before AD 183–85 (*CIL* 8.18247); headquarters of the *praepositus limitis Gemellensis* during fourth century.[216]

Comments: Dug into rocky soil; baked mud brick *gradus* (50 × 120 cm) coated thickly with plaster rendering; contemporary with military camp of AD 132–33. Baradez estimated the seating capacity at about 1,600–2,500 spectators.[217]

Dimensions:

Overall:	*c.* 72 × 52m	*c.* 2,941m²	Total dimensions of monument = 84 × 64m, but this includes the external berm, 6m wide.
Arena:	52 × 32m	1,307m² (*c.* 44 per cent)	

| *Cavea*: | *c.* 10m wide | *c.* 1,634m² (*c.* 56 per cent) | |
| Seating estimate: | *c.* 3,100 | | Based upon an allocation of 40 cm of width per spectator and a *gradus* breadth of 1.2m = 0.4m² per spectator. |

Tigava Castra (Bel Abbès): Golvin #46[218]

Site history: A vexillation of an unknown legion garrisoned here under the command of the procurator of Mauretania in AD 167.[219]

Comments: Another arena was found (55 × 30m) 300m to the south-east, surrounded by a border of stones (6–8m wide), interpreted by Leveau as a possible practice arena.[220]

Dimensions:

Overall:	*c.* 56 × 37m	*c.* 1,627m²	
Arena:	*c.* 44 × 26m	*c.* 898m² (*c.* 55 per cent)	This large percentage of the total surface area given over to the arena is characteristic of a military amphitheatre.
Cavea:	*c.* 6m wide	*c.* 729m² (*c.* 45 per cent)	
Seating estimate:	*c.* 2,300		

Lambaesis, Phase I (Lambèse): Golvin #60[221]

Site history: A vexillation of the *legio III Augusta* stationed here by AD 81; by AD 128, if not before, the legion had moved here;[222] the *canabae* grew and prospered becoming a *municipium* in its own right before AD 183–85, probably under M. Aurelius;[223] capital of Severan province of Numidia (by AD 198/99) and seat of the *concilium provinciae*;[224] titular *colonia* under Philip the Arab.[225]

Comments: Probably contemporary with the Trajanic camp. Arena dug into the ground and the spoil stabilised within terrace walls to form the basis for the seating.

Dimensions:

Overall:	*c.* 88 × 75m	*c.* 5,184m²
Arena:	*c.* 68 × 55m	*c.* 2,937m² (*c.* 57 per cent)
Cavea:	*c.* 10m wide	*c.* 2,247m² (*c.* 43 per cent)
Seating estimate:	*c.* 7,200	

Lambaesis, Phase II (Lambèse): Golvin #111[226]
(Figure 4.6 and Plates 4.12–15)

Comments: Inscriptions of AD 169, 176–80 and 194 indicate repairs done to this structure.[227] A series of hollow, wedge-shaped compartments filled with debris formed the basis for the seating of the outside ring extension (see Figure 4.6). Well-preserved T-shaped subterranean galleries (minor axis gallery = 1.4m wide; major axis gallery = 2.3m wide; central chamber = 14.3 × 14.37m) containing clear traces of four hoisting mechanisms; exterior entrances through façade via arches in cut stone (cf. Uthina); major entrance on south-west side and thus *tribunal* probably on this side of the short axis; *sacellum* beneath podium here; stairway down into substructures of arena from here; arena-wall (2.5–3m high × 1.2m thick); service corridor behind it (1.4m wide).

Inscriptions mention reserved seating for five *curiae* of Lambaesis (*CIL* 8.3293).[228]

Dimensions:

Overall:	104.6 × 94m	7,722m²	
Arena:	68 × 55m	2,937m² (*c.* 38 per cent)	
Cavea:	*c.* 19.5m wide	*c.* 4,785m² (*c.* 62 per cent)	The western side of the *cavea* is larger than the eastern (see Figure 4.6).
Seating estimate:	*c.* 15,400		

Rusicade (Skikda, Philippeville): Golvin #72[229]

Municipal history: It received an early colony of veterans under P. Sittius; later became one of the four Cirtan *coloniae*.[230]

Comments: Sited in the valley of an *oued*, whose sides were used as the basis for the seating stabilised by a series of annular terrace walls (cf. Utica). *Gradus* average 42 × 65 cm; however, those of *summa cavea* are 40 × 80 cm; arena-wall (3.8m high); service corridor behind it (1.8m wide). A fragmentary inscription (*ILAlg* II.34) mentions 30,000 *sesterces* paid towards the building of the amphitheatre: [*ad opus*] ampitheatri (*sic*). *CIL* 8.7969 (of AD 187) shows amphitheatre built before this date. Perhaps Hadrianic like the theatre here.[231]

Féraud estimated the seating capacity at about 7,000–8,000 spectators, while Vars arrived at a figure of about 8,000.[232]

Dimensions:

Overall:	*c.* 77.3 × 58.8m	*c.* 3,570m²
Arena:	*c.* 57 × 38.5m	*c.* 1,724m² (*c.* 48 per cent)
Cavea:	*c.* 10m wide	*c.* 1,846m² (*c.* 52 per cent)
Seating estimate:	*c.* 5,900	

Theveste, Phase I (Tébessa): Golvin #30[233]

(Figure 4.14)

Municipal history: Headquarters of *legio III Augusta* between AD 74 and 79,[234] Trajanic veteran[235] or titular[236] *colonia* when legion transferred to Lambaesis (*CIL* 8.16530).

Comments: Contemporary with the legionary camp. Western *cavea* on hillside, eastern side embanked spoil stabilised by annular retaining walls (cf. Gemellae).

Dimensions:

Overall:	*c.* 83 × 70m	*c.* 4,563m²
Arena:	52.8 × 39.5m	1,638m² (*c.* 34 per cent)
Cavea:	*c.* 15m wide	*c.* 2,925m² (*c.* 64 per cent)
Seating estimate:	*c.* 9,400	

Theveste, Phase II (Tébessa): Golvin #30

Comments: Outer ring of seating and fine cut-stone façade added after AD 270 (coin of Claudius II found in fills beneath this phase), i.e. late third/early fourth century AD. Arena-wall (3–3.4m high) of *opus quadratum* covered with plaster and painted white and red; carried inscriptions reserving blocks of seating for VIPs of the town; service corridor behind it with six doorways into arena. Main entrances consist of a triple-bay arrangement along ends of major axis. *Gradus* 40 × 60 cm.

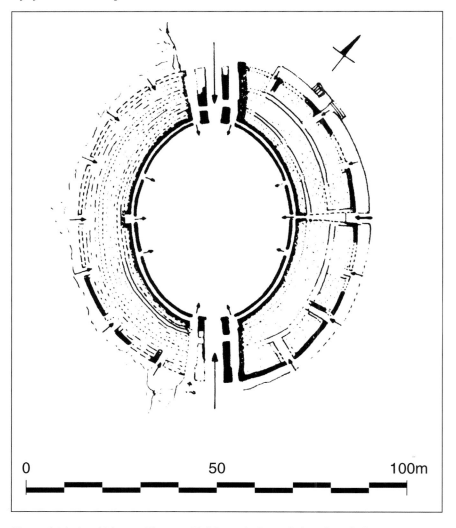

Figure 4.14 Amphitheatre, Theveste (Golvin #30). Ground plan of amphitheatre.
Source: Golvin, Planche XIV, 3. Copyright J.-Cl. Golvin.

Fortification and occupation of arena, perhaps in Byzantine era; abandonment and destruction by fire (C[14] date *c.* AD 900); then continuous occupation levels building up in the arena until they reached the level of the podium, then on to parts of the *cavea* itself, particularly in south-western sector.

Dimensions:

Overall:	*c.* 94.8 × 81.5m	*c.* 6,068m²
Arena:	52.8 × 39.5m	1,638m² (*c.* 27 per cent)
Cavea:	*c.* 21m wide	*c.* 4,430m² (*c.* 73 per cent)
Seating estimate:	*c.* 14,200	

CHRONOLOGY

Table 4.1 Chronology of first-century AD North African amphitheatres

Amphitheatre	Golvin number	Date according to Golvin	Date according to Bomgardner
Carthage Phase I	#95	Phase I: Augustan (27 BC – AD 14)	Before end of first century: *opus reticulatum.*[a]
Caesarea Phase I	#81	Phase I: beginning of first century AD	Perhaps Julio-Claudian[b]
Lepcis Magna Phase I	#24	Phase I: AD 56 (epigr.)	Idem
Theveste Phase I	#30	Phase I: *c.* AD 74–79	Idem
Thysdrus, minus Phase I	#25	—	Flavian *c.* AD 80[c]
Sufetula Phase I	#113	—	Perhaps Flavian[d]
Utica, Phase I?	#61	(Earlier amphitheatre suspected beneath circus site)[e]	

a Lézine, *Architecture romaine*, 60–64.
b Bomgardner, 'North African Amphitheatres', 379–84: an urban cohort perhaps here from the reign of Juba II (M. Speidel, *AntAfr* 14 [1979], 121 f.) and a Claudian veteran colony.
c Foucher, *Découvertes archéologiques*, 63; Foucher, *La maison de la procession*, 101 f.; Foucher, *Hadrumetum*, 314 and n. 1299.
d Bomgardner, 'North African Amphitheatres', 304–09: the amphitheatre is aligned with the orthogonal grid system of the original town centre and not with that of the third-century suburb in which it lies; thus it was probably built in close temporal connection with the original settlement, probably Flavian (Broughton, *op. cit.*, 206).
e Lézine, *Utique*, 66.

Table 4.2 Chronology of second-century AD North African amphitheatres

Amphitheatre	Golvin number	Date according to Golvin	Date according to Bomgardner
Sicca Veneria	#183	Perhaps second century	Perhaps end of first century[a]
Thysdrus, minus Phase I	#25	Probably beginning of second century	—
Uthina Phase I	#115	Probably second century	Probably early second century[b]
Thysdrus minus Phase II	#112	Later phase: probably second century	Beginning of the second century[c]
Lambaesis Phase I	#60	Phase I: c. AD 128 (probably correct)	Phase I: AD 169[d]
Acholla	#118	Probably Hadrianic	Perhaps Trajanic: very similar to Trajanic Baths technique[e]
Mesarfelta Phase I	#45	Phase I: beginning of the second century	Trajanic[f]
Leptiminus	#114	Probably second century	Perhaps first half of the second century[g]
Lepcis Magna Phase II	#24	Later phases: refurbishments second century	Reconstruction phase: Hadrianic, perhaps later.
Sabratha Phase I	#120	Second century	Two phases: perhaps second century and late second century (Antonine)[h]
Utica, Phase II	#61	Extension during the Hadrianic era (117–38)	t.p.q. AD 1–20[i]
Lepcis Magna Phase III	#24	—	Modification phase: c. AD 162
Gemellae	#44	c. AD 132–33	Later second century[j]
Rusicade	#72	Second century (by comparison with Lambaesis Phase I)	Perhaps Hadrianic[k]
Bulla Regia	#117	Perhaps Hadrianic (post-128)	t.p.q. second half of the second century[l]
Seressi	#66	Second century (by comparison with Lambaesis Phase I)	Mid-second century or later[m]
Simitthu	#67	Second century (by comparison with Lambaesis Phase I)	c. mid-second century[n]

Site/Phase	No.	Description	Dating
Sufetula Phase II	#113	Probably second century	c. AD 160[o]
Carthage Phase II	#174	Second-century extension	Second century[p]
Sabratha Phase II	#120	Second century	Perhaps late second century (Antonine)[q]
Lambaesis Phase II	#111	Later phases: restorations AD 169, 176–80, 194 with extension of the *cavea*	Phase II: AD 176/7–80[r]
Mesarfelta Phase II	#45	Phase II: repair AD 177–80	c. AD 177–80[s]
Cyrene	#75	Theatre transformed into an amphitheatre: second century	Second half of the second century or perhaps Severan[t]
Lambaesis Phase III	#111	—	Phase III: AD 194[u]
Caesarea Phase II	#81	Phase II: probably second-century extension	Perhaps late second or early third century[v]
Mactaris	#119	Probably second century	Late second or early third century[w]
Thignica Phase I	#116	Probably second century	Late second century or perhaps early third century[x]
Thuburbo Maius Phase I	#121	Phase I: probably second century	Perhaps late second century or early third century[y]
Ptolemais	#76	Second century or third century	Third century or Severan[z]
Tigava Castra	#46	Probably second century	—
Thibari	#62	Second century (by comparison with Lambaesis Phase I)	Similar in design to Simitthu
Djebel Moraba	#63	Second century (by comparison with Lambaesis Phase I)	—
Agbia	#64	Second century (by comparison with Lambaesis Phase I)	—
Carpis	#65	Second century (by comparison with Lambaesis Phase I)	—

continued

Table 4.2 continued

Amphitheatre	Golvin number	Date according to Golvin	Date according to Bomgardner
Upenna	#68	Second century (by comparison with Lambaesis Phase I)	—
Thuburbo Minus	#69	Second century (by comparison with Lambaesis Phase I)	Perhaps *t.a.q.* AD 143[aa]
Ulisippira	#70	Second century (by comparison with Lambaesis Phase I)	—
Thaenae	#71	Second century (by comparison with Lambaesis Phase I)	—
Thapsus	#185	Probably second century	—

a Bomgardner 1985, 297–98. No archaeological evidence bears directly upon the date of the monument. However, the importance of this strategic cross-roads and the early Augustan veteran colony here suggest a possible military amphitheatre by the end of the first century AD, at the latest.

b *Ibid.*, 353–57: use of aggregate laid radially (as if voussoirs in an arch) in the concrete structures should indicate a date near the beginning of the second century. J.B. Ward-Perkins, *Roman Architecture* (New York 1977), 152.

c Foucher, *Découvertes archéologiques*, 63.

d Leschi 1954, *op. cit.*, 171–80; *AE* (1955), 134.

e Bomgardner 1985, 238–40.

f Baradez, *op. cit.*, 65 ff.

g Bomgardner 1985, 278–80.

h D.E.L. Haynes, *An Archaeological and Historical Guide to the pre-Islamic Antiquities of Tripolitania* (Tripoli 1957), 128 f.

i Bomgardner 1985, 360–61: *terminus ante quem* provided by archaeological materials uncovered by Abbé Moulard, *BAC* (1926), 230, including small, round Roman lamps without handles or beaks dated by Dr David Soren to the period AD 1–20.

j *Ibid.*, 400: the large seating capacity should indicate a monument built after a period of urban growth of the *canabae* outside the military camp, perhaps in the later second century.

k *Ibid.*, 409–11: *CIL* 8.7969 (of AD 187) indicates that a *munus legitimum* took place; thus we may assume the amphitheatre was in existence by this date. The theatre here is dated to the Hadrianic era on the basis of a coin of Hadrian's wife, Sabina, found in the concrete matrix of its construction. J. Roger, *RAfr* 60 (1865), 391 f. The amphitheatre may also date to this era.

l *Ibid.*, 245–47: fictile vaulting tubes used in construction, perhaps mid-second century.

m *Ibid.*, 295–96: based upon Broughton, *op. cit.*, 82 n. 205, and his analysis of the pace of Romanisation in this strongly indigenous region, only beginning to respond to outside forces by the Hadrianic era.

n   *Ibid.*, 299–303: the use of aggregate laid radially in its concrete matrix should indicate an earlier, rather than a later date, perhaps early second century. J.B. Ward-Perkins, *Roman Architecture*, 152.

o   *Ibid.*, 304–09: fabric of theatre closely resembles that of amphitheatre, both dated to *c.* AD 160 by Kirsten, *op. cit.*, 77.

p   Lézine, *Architecture romaine*, 60–64, based on architectural comparisons at Carthage.

q   Haynes, *op. cit.*

r   Leschi 1954, *op. cit.*, 181–85; *AE* (1955), 135: Leschi thinks that only the northern half of the seating was restored.

s   Baradez, *op. cit.*, 65 ff.; *CIL* 8.2488: the amphitheatre *vetustate corruptum* required a complete restoration by the sixth Commagenian cohort under M. Aurelius and Commodus (AD 177–80).

t   S. Stucchi, *Architettura cirenaica*, Monografie de Archeologia libica IX (Rome 1975), 287 ff.; L. Crema, *L'architettura romana* (Turin 1959), 541.

u   Leschi 1954, *op. cit.*, 185 f.; *AE* (1955) 137: this inscription was found in the west entrance to the arena.

v   Perhaps under the emperor Macrinus (AD 217), traditionally born at Iol Caesarea. Recent excavations of the forum area indicate archaeological restorations that may also date to his reign. N. Benseddik and T.W. Potter, *Fouilles du forum de Cherchel* (Algiers 1992).

w   The construction technique and materials employed in the Great Baths at Mactaris, dated by their dedicatory inscription to AD 199 (Picard *CRA* [1974] 14), are very close in style and materials to those used in the amphitheatre.

x   Fictile vaulting tubes are used in the construction of the concrete barrel-vaulted chambers beneath the seating. P. Romanelli, *Storia delle provincie romana dell'Africa* (Rome 1959), Ch. 5, places their use after the first half of the second century.

y   Chronology based on the general development of civic monuments at Thuburbo Maius. See *PECS s.v.* 'Thuburbo Maius' by A. Ennabli, 916–17 and A. Lézine, *Thuburbo Maius* (Tunis: S.T.D. 1968), 28.

z   Rock-cut monuments are notoriously difficult to assign dates of construction. Stucchi, *op. cit.*, 294, and Crema, *op. cit.*, 550, who have studied the architectural traditions of this part of Cyrenaica intensively, think that it is a late creation of the third century or the Severan era respectively. The date is certainly unlikely to be prior to the second century, the period of the city's greatest prosperity and development (Kraeling, *op. cit.*, 95 f.).

aa Dureau de la Malle, ed. Peysonnel and Desfontaines. *Voyages dans les Régences de Tunis et d'Alger* (2 vols, Paris 1838), I, 99 f. Peysonnel found an inscription near a barrage dam supposedly made from the material of the amphitheatre at Thuburbo Minus. The inscription should probably be dated between AD 138 and *c.* 143. If it is indeed the dedicatory inscription for this monument, then valuable chronological evidence has survived. However, this all remains problematical.

Table 4.3 Chronology of third-century AD North African amphitheatres and phases of earlier amphitheatres

Amphitheatre	Golvin number	Date according to Golvin	Date according to Bomgardner
Lepcis Magna Phase IV	#24	Later phases: refurbishments beginning of the third century	Reconstruction phase: Severan[a]
Thysdrus maius	#186	Beginning of third century between AD 230 and 238	*Idem*[b]
Bararus	#187	Perhaps second century or beginning third century	—
Tipasa Phase I	#130	Probably third century	Late second century or third century: *t.p.q. c.* AD 145[c]
Theveste Phase II	#30	Last phase: third century	Modification phase: *t.p.q.* AD 270/late third century or early fourth century[d]
Thysdrus minus Phase III	#112	—	Undated second expansion phase[e]
Thignica Phase 2	#116	—	Expansion phase/undated[f]

a A. di Vita, *Supplements to Libya Antiqua*, 'Lepcis Magna, anfiteatro-circo, relazione preliminare', II (1966), 85.

b D.L. Bomgardner, 'The Revolt of the Gordians and the Amphitheatre at Thysdrus (El Djem)', in A.C. King and M. Henig, eds., *The Roman West in the Third Century. Contributions from Archaeology to History*, BAR International Series 109 (Oxford 1981), 211–14.

c St. Gsell, *Promenade archéologique aux environs d'Alger* (Alger 1926), 97 f., proposes a date of the late second or early third century on the basis of the construction technique. Excavation has provided confirmation of this date through the discovery of sarcophagi, reused in the *cavea*, which provide a *terminus post quem* of *c.* AD 145 on stylistic grounds (*Libyca* [1957] 133–35).

d Lequément, *op. cit.*, 196 f., 239 f. The *terminus post quem* was provided by a coin of Claudius II (AD 270) found during excavation.

e J. Kolendo, *Archeologia* (1973), 76.

f Field notes of 8 July 1977. At an unknown date (perhaps fourth century), major structural alterations occurred in the north-eastern sector of the *cavea* and in the entranceways to the arena, which were either re-vaulted or vaulted for the first time to carry seating over them.

Table 4.4 Chronology of fourth-century AD phases of earlier North African amphitheatres

Amphitheatre	Golvin number	Date according to Golvin	Date according to Bomgardner
Tipasa Phase II	#130	—	Restoration phase early fourth century[a]
Thuburbo Maius Phase II	#121	—	Phase II: beginning of the third century, perhaps mid-fourth century[b]
Theveste Phase III	#30	—	Reconstruction phase: fourth century[c]
Thuburbo Maius Phase III	#121	—	Reconstruction phase in reused inscriptions: *t.p.q.* AD 177–80, probably late fourth century[d]

a *Libyca* (1954), 277 f.
b Date by comparison with the repairs to the Baths of the Labyrinth here, both using a revetment of reddish-orange shale ashlars.
c Lequément, *op. cit.*, 196 f., 239 f.
d *Terminus post quem* provided by a series of inscriptions reused in the fabric of the arena and its entranceway. *ILT* #720–21, 723–29.

Table 4.5 Typology of North African amphitheatres: simple embankment type (*cavea* stabilised by annular terrace walls)

Amphitheatre	Golvin number	Amphitheatre	Golvin number
Lepcis Magna	24	Djebel Moraba	63
Thysdrus, minus Phase I	25	Agbia	64
Theveste Phase I	30	Carpis	65
Theveste Phase II	30	Seressi	66
Theveste Phase III	30	Simitthu	67
Gemellae	44	Upenna	68
Mesarfelta Phase I	45	Thuburbo Minus	69
Mesarfelta Phase II	45	Ulisippira	70
Tigava Castra	46	Thaenae	71
Lambaesis Phase I	60	Rusicade	72
Utica	61	Cyrene (rock cut)	75
Thibari	62	Ptolemais (rock cut)	76

Table 4.6 Typology of North African amphitheatres: simple embankment type – sizes and seating capacities

Amphitheatre	Full size (m²)	Arena (m²)	Seating
Utica	9,082	3,770	17,100
Ptolemais	6,011	1,660	16,300
Lepcis Magna	7,069	2,104	16,000
Theveste Phase II	6,068	1,638	14,200
Theveste Phase I	4,563	1,638	9,400
Thysdrus, minus Phase I	4,343	1,539	9,000
Thaenae	4,310	1,610	8,700
Seressi	3,892	1,646	7,200
Lambaesis Phase I	5,184	2,937	7,200
Thibaris	2,475	508	6,300
Rusicade	3,570	1,724	5,900
Ulissipira	2,872	1,206	5,400
Gemellae	2,941	1,307	3,100
Agbia	1,880	946	3,000
Tigava Castra	1,627	898	2,300
Averages	4,392	1,675	8,740

Source: Data taken from catalogue entries.

Table 4.7 Typology of North African amphitheatres: compartmentalised fill type (*cavea* supported by hollow, masonry caissons filled with geologic fill)

Amphitheatre	Golvin number	Amphitheatre	Golvin number
Caesarea	81	Thignica Phase I	116
Caesarea Phase II	81	Thignica Phase II	116
Carthage Phase I	95	Bulla Regia	117
Lambaesis Phase II	111	Acholla	118
Lambaesis Phase III	111	Mactaris	119
Thysdrus minus Phase II	112	Sabratha	120
Thysdrus minus Phase III	112	Thuburbo Maius Phase I	121
Sufetula Phase I	113	Thuburbo Maius Phase II	121
Sufetula Phase II	113	Thuburbo Maius Phase III	121
Leptiminus	114	Tipasa Phase I	130
Uthina	115	Tipasa Phase II	130

Table 4.8 Typology of North African amphitheatres: compartmentalised fill type – sizes and seating capacities

Amphitheatre	Full size (m²)	Arena (m²)	Seating
Carthage Phase I	8,765	1,860	22,200
Sabratha (G)	8,942	2,500	20,700
Caesarea Phase II	9,028	4,029	16,100
Lambaesis Phase II	7,722	2,937	15,400
Uthina	6,107	1,546	14,700
Thysdrus, minus Phase II	5,202	1,885	10,700
Caesarea Phase I	7,328	4,029	10,600
Leptiminus	4,390	1,569	9,100
Thuburbo Maius (G)	3,780	1,149	8,500
Tipasa	4,235	1,656	8,300
Sufetula	3,300	1,350	6,600
Thignica	2,663	863	5,800
Mactaris	2,462	748	5,500
Thimisua	1,710	704	3,200
Averages	5,402	1,916	11,243

Source: Data taken from catalogue entries; (G) denotes Golvin's dimensions were used, where these differ from my own.

Table 4.9 Typology of North African amphitheatres: vaulted substructure amphitheatres (*cavea* supported by concrete barrel vaulting)

Amphitheatre	Golvin number
Carthage Phase II	174
Sicca Veneria	183
Thapsus	185
Thysdrus, 'Colosseum'	186
Bararus	187

Table 4.10 Typology of North African amphitheatres: vaulted substructure amphitheatres – sizes and seating capacities

Amphitheatre	Full size (m²)	Arena (m²)	Seating
Carthage, Phase II	15,680	1,860	44,400
Thysdrus, 'Colosseum'	14,195	1,966	39,300
Bararus	5,657	1,878	12,100
Averages	11,844	1,901	31,933

CONCLUSIONS

The distribution of amphitheatres in the Roman empire

The vast majority of Roman amphitheatres are found in the Latin-speaking western half of the empire. Louis Robert has convincingly demonstrated that the small number in the east does not represent a lack of enthusiasm for such spectacles, but a tendency to stage them in another venue, such as specially adapted theatres or stadia.[237]

In the west the chief factors in the construction of amphitheatres included the attempt to promote Romanisation by providing a provincial focus for the imperial cult (e.g., at Lugdunum [Lyons]), the result of private beneficence (e.g., the bequest of Ummidia Quadratilla to Casinum for the construction of an amphitheatre there), the desire for civic status and prestige (e.g., the Flavian amphitheatre by the *colonia* of Puteoli), and the fact that the amphitheatre was seen as appropriate for cities possessing sufficient Roman municipal status (particularly colonies and provincial capitals). Other factors would include the local demand for such a monument as well as a competitive desire to provide one's own city with an arena because a local rival was planning one or already had one.[238] Practical constraints of economics could intervene, especially when the most costly form of amphitheatres was considered, for only bath complexes and circuses would be more expensive in a community's budget. The wealthiest communities could always find money from municipal magistrates' fees (*summae honorariae*) and other sources both private and public. Locals who made good in the wider world often shared their good fortunes with their home towns. For less wealthy cities the options were limited to, first, using another venue, e.g., a forum or a converted theatre, for spectacles; second, using an amphitheatre at a wealthier neighbouring town; or third, building a modest monument at home. A large number of modest arenas were developed and these are well represented in North Africa.

The distribution of North African amphitheatres

Many amphitheatres are found in the fertile Mediterranean littoral at major ports and in their immediate hinterland. At the two extremities, Cyrenaica (eastern Libya) and Mauretania Tingitana (Morocco), amphitheatres are almost always found on or near the coast. These two regions had distinctively different cultural backgrounds compared with the rest of Roman North Africa. Cyrenaica had long-established Greek and Egyptian cultural links, while Tingitana retained strong Punic and Berber traditions with important cross-contacts with the Iberian cultures of southern Spain.

In the central provinces of Numidia (central and eastern Algeria) and Africa Proconsularis (northern Tunisia), however, amphitheatres are found in the major coastal settlements but also elsewhere. The fertile Bagradas and Miliana river valleys (*oueds*) had a large number of settlements with amphitheatres. This area accounts for over one-third of the total number in North Africa. Alternatively, settlements which formed either part of the military frontiers (*limites*), such as at Gemellae, Mesarfelta and Lambaesis, or one of the headquarters for the third Augustan legion (*legio III Augusta*), such as Theveste and Lambaesis, often had an amphitheatre. There the amphitheatre formed part of a military installation or the military authorities supervised its construction using troops, as occurred at each of these examples. These amphitheatres all share an unusually large arena in comparison to the size of the *cavea*. On the other hand, inland cities which exercised a powerful administrative role in their regions, such as Mactaris, Sufetula, Cirta and Sitifis[239] (the last two of which eventually became provincial capitals in the later empire), also tended to have amphitheatres.

Wealth, political status, the presence of the Roman military and geographical location were the principal factors at work in determining what type(s) of entertainment structures a city would possess. The influence of Carthage upon her territory is responsible for the concentration there of amphitheatres either alone or also in conjunction with a theatre. The general absence of amphitheatres in Numidia, an area apparently teeming with wildlife suitable for *venationes*, is surprising.[240] In general, amphitheatres are found in Numidia either at cities which had the highest fees for their magistracies (*summae honorariae*),[241] e.g., Cirta, Rusicade, Lambaesis, or else at sites where the military was probably responsible for their construction, e.g., Theveste, Lambaesis, Gemellae, Mesarfelta.

Chronology

Since there are so few well-dated, well-published amphitheatres in North Africa, it is not possible to discuss the chronological developments of its amphitheatres in detail. Due to a lack of data, neither the drainage systems nor the façades can be studied in detail. However, it is possible to comment on the circulation of spectators and the arrangement of the substructures for the *cavea*. In general, the earliest examples of amphitheatres relied upon external systems of circulation similar to those in the Pompeii amphitheatre. Like Pompeii the number of *ambulacra* and internal passageways were limited due to the geologic basis of the *cavea*. Sophisticated systems of vaulted concrete substructures and complex systems of circulation similar to those in the largest imperial amphitheatres elsewhere did not appear in North Africa before the second century AD, as in the enlargement of the Carthage amphitheatre at this date.

Subterranean structures beneath the arena (probably not an original feature of the earliest monuments in North Africa) were apparently first added during the course of the second century AD and then only to the most important arenas, such as Carthage, Thysdrus, Caesarea, Lambaesis, Sabratha, Lepcis Magna, and perhaps Utica. Instead of elaborate galleries and chambers beneath the arena, most North African arenas had relatively simple beast pens built into the fabric of the arena-wall. These pens (known as *postica*, as *caveae* or *carceres*) were loaded with animals from the arena's service corridor at the rear. Then, by means of a portcullis mechanism the beasts were released into the arena (see Plates 4.22–4.23 at Mactaris).[242] The usual position for these seems to have been flanking both sides of the major axial entrances to the arena. Mactaris is unusual in its asymmetrical triple arrangement of doorways flanked by *carceres*. Perhaps this may be accounted for by an association with the triple deities worshipped locally in North Africa.

Our knowledge of the defensive mechanisms for the arena-wall is limited apart from the arrangement of a low balustrade at Carthage, Theveste and Lepcis Magna (with protective net assembly overhanging the edge of the arena), and the unusual grille or balustrade atop the arena-wall inserted between black marble columns at Utica. The revetment of the arena-wall with marble slabs was ornamentally ostentatious. Only the most prestigious monuments had this feature, such as Carthage, Lepcis Magna, and Lambaesis after it became a provincial capital. It may also have helped to make the arena-wall more slippery and less easy to climb, thus enhancing its safety features. In general arena-walls were thickly plastered and painted, often to resemble marble revetment, as at Thignica.

If one compares the development of the amphitheatre in both Italy and North Africa several features emerge. In North Africa the development of the amphitheatre lagged behind that in Italy by more than a century. During the latter half of the first century AD, when sophisticated amphitheatres were built in Italy (e.g., Puteoli, Syracuse, the Colosseum in Rome), those in North Africa resembled the earliest generation of arenas in southern Italy. However, after the technology of Roman concrete was introduced into North Africa (widespread by the second century), the gap between North African and Italian amphitheatres began to close rapidly. From this time the mainstream of amphitheatre production shifted from Italy to North Africa and other provincial areas.[243] This trend culminated in the mid-third century with the advances in design and construction in the 'Colosseum' at Thysdrus (El Jem).

Typology

Since few amphitheatres are readily visible, lying buried, scattered and eroded across the austere North African landscape, the study of the typology of their construction remains tentative. Doubtless, with future excavation, study and publication, the situation will be clarified. Golvin's proposed typology is the best framework currently available. However, as the details of these monuments emerge, there should be a greater appreciation that a large number of hybrid forms exist: embankment-vaulting; embankment-compartmentalised fill, etc.

The vast majority of monuments are based upon either the technique of cut-and-fill, or that of contouring existing hillsides. The use of hollow masonry compartments filled with rubble seems to be a feature common to the western provincial amphitheatres of Gaul, Spain and North Africa, perhaps originating in Spain where its earliest use would seem to be in the Augustan amphitheatre at Emerita (Golvin #77; of 8 BC). Vaulted substructures occurred only in the most prestigious monuments such as in the provincial capitals.

Regardless of their typology, the size of the arena in North African amphitheatres is fairly constant over a wide range of monuments, ranging from 1,600 to 1,900 square metres. There may be a distinctive subgroup here in which the arena is distinctly smaller than the above dimensions, ranging from 500 to 1,000 square metres (Agbia = 946; Tigava Castra = 898; Thignica = 863; Seressi = 837; Mactaris = 748; Thimisua = 704; Simitthu = 510; Thibaris = 508; and perhaps Bulla Regia = 792?). This group of arenas clusters in the fertile cornlands of central Tunisia and has arenas which are about 30 per cent of the total area of the monuments and seating capacities of approximately 6,000 spectators. Tigava Castra is a spurious member of the group, since it is certainly a military amphitheatre far removed from the region where all the rest occur. The close resemblance of the amphitheatre at Agbia to Tigava indicates that it too may have a military origin.

The three typological groups distinguished by Golvin may usefully be further classified into three large groupings. The first group consists of those amphitheatres which have embankment or compartmentalised-fill as the basis for their seating. They have an average size of 4,000–5,000m² overall and they also have arenas that average from 1,700 to 1,900m² and a seating capacity of about 9,000 to 11,000 spectators. The embankment-type amphitheatres fall on the low side of these ranges, while the compartmentalised-fill-type monuments usually reach higher figures (see Tables 4.5–4.8). The second group is the monumental imperial monuments with vaulted substructures that have an average size of nearly 12,000m² overall, with arenas of roughly 1,900m² and a seating capacity of roughly 30,000 spectators (see Tables 4.9–4.10). The central Tunisian cornlands with small arenas and moderate size and seating capacity form the third grouping, distinctive from the others.

Regional trends

Is it possible to identify regional groupings? Two obvious groups at either end of the North African littoral are immediately apparent. The amphitheatres of the coast of Mauretania Caesariensis (Tipasa, Caesarea) share many anomalous features unlike any others. Similarly, the rock-cut structures of Tripolitania and Cyrenaica (Lepcis Magna, Sabratha, Ptolemais) share a regional identity centred about the early amphitheatre at Lepcis Magna. Another grouping may be found in the heartland of the Bagradas and Miliana valleys among those amphitheatres which are of the embankment type, discussed in the previous section. The settlements here tended to become *municipia* or *colonia* at a late date, indicating native communities (*civitates*) promoted in status or coalesced with older Roman communities (so-called 'double communities') into a single polity. The various headquarters of the third Augustan legion (Theveste, Lambaesis) as well as the Numidian military zone around Gemellae and Mesarfelta provide another regional group.

These monuments share excavated arenas and the use of hillsides and embankments for the *cavea*. By analogy with its later headquarters and their amphitheatres, it would be most surprising if the original garrison of this legion at Ammaedara did not also have an amphitheatre. That at Lambaesis forms the exception to this group for it later became an important civic monument when Lambaesis became the capital of Numidia under Septimius Severus. Finally, there are the imperial amphitheatres of Carthage and Thysdrus with their mainstream Italian influences from the Colosseum and the Anfiteatro Campano in Capua. Carthage and Thysdrus had sculptured keystones on their façades, an obvious echo from the Capuan amphitheatre. As seen above (p. 148), Mark Wilson Jones has linked Thysdrus to the Colosseum as almost a 'carbon copy', slightly reduced in scale. For most other monuments such a pedigree is not yet possible.

Cultural influences

In his study of early provincial architecture in the west, Ward-Perkins has identified Campania and Sicily as the chief areas of architectural influence upon North Africa.[244] For the most part this analysis of architectural influences on monuments other than amphitheatres is also valid for the amphitheatres of North Africa, especially the geologic-based examples. In particular Sicily was key in the transmission of ideas in that it formed a natural stepping stone for shipping to and from Italy.[245] It is also probable that northern and central Italy and Sardinia were also in contact culturally with North Africa. Gaulish amphitheatres also share many traits in common with their North African cousins, but the cultural links are more difficult to discern. Certainly one point of contact occurred during the reign of Vespasian when the *cohors I urbana* stationed at Lugdunum changed places with the *cohors XIII urbana* at Carthage.[246]

The role of the military in architectural transmission and design

The Roman army provided the dominant architectural input for construction projects throughout the military zone of North Africa as well as Mauretania.[247] Although local auxiliary troops provided much of the muscle for local construction, technical expertise resided with the third Augustan legion. One example will provide a useful illustration of this point. Nonnius Datus was a surveyor (*librator*) attached to this legion at Lambaesis. He was sent to survey the course of an aqueduct through a mountainside at Saldae (Bougie) on the coast. He came, he surveyed, he initiated the project with the muscle power of fleet auxiliaries (*milites classici*, probably seconded from their home port at nearby Caesarea) and Celtic auxiliary light infantry spearmen from the Rhône valley (*gaesates*). Datus returned to Lambaesis. Word reached his superiors that he was needed again. The tunnelling, starting from both ends and working towards the middle, had gone off line, either one gallery or both diverging from true, and missed the survey's projected juncture. The survey would have to be undertaken again. On his way back, Datus was set upon by brigands and left for dead. He recovered, did his duty, returned to base and was mentioned in dispatches for his troubles.[248] The point is that the legionary headquarters, over 400 miles away, was the nearest point for such architectural and civil engineering expertise within the entire area.

Further evidence for the concentration of such expertise in the legionary forces can be found in an examination of the attested *architecti* and *libratores* (surveyors) in North Africa. One *architectus* (*CIL* 8.2580) and two *libratores* (*CIL* 8.2728 [= Datus] and 2934) are attested, all three of whom served in the third Augustan legion. Evidently this situation was not unique, for Pliny, when he had appealed to Trajan (early second century AD) to send a surveyor (*librator*) to Bithynia to establish the feasibility of a canal project, was told to apply to the governor of Lower Moesia, the nearest province where legionary troops were garrisoned.[249] In addition to this legion, the governor of Africa Proconsularis may have had a cohort of the Praetorian Guard stationed at Carthage (perhaps the *cohors VI praetoria*) available for detached service where needed.[250] The

Praetorian cohorts became a prime repository of technical expertise including architectural skills.[251]

Non-military architectural expertise in North Africa

The proconsular governor of Africa Proconsularis had a truly formidable bevy of bureaucrats assigned to his permanent staff.[252] Perhaps those architects who were civil servants, i.e., non-military personnel, were organised under the *praefectus fabrum* attached to his staff. Land surveyors (*agrimensores*) were regularly attached to the emperor's procurators for the Carthage territories (*procurator Augusti provinciae Africae tractus Karthaginiensis*) as part of their staff.[253]

Human sacrifice to Saturn in the arenas of North Africa?

In those areas of recalcitrant indigenous influences where the practice of human sacrifice to Ba'al (later syncretised with the Roman deity Saturn) and Tanit (later syncretised with the Roman deity Juno Caelestis) had taken deep root in the psyche and worship of the natives, Roman rule came as a heavy blow. For the Romans did not allow human sacrifice under their laws. The execution of prisoners condemned to be thrown to beasts in the arena (*ad bestias*) has been linked to a continuation of these practices under the subterfuge of amphitheatral spectacles.[254] Such a continuation of ritual under the disguise of a spectacle, acceptable in the eyes of the Romans, might explain the close association between sanctuaries of Saturn (*tophets*) and the amphitheatres at Thuburnica, Thuburbo Maius, Simitthu and Mactaris (*tophet* of Bab el-Aïn adjacent).[255] Such connections between provincial amphitheatres and native cults have also been demonstrated elsewhere, such as the connection between gladiatorial combats (*trincii*) in Gaul and the Celtic cult of the severed head.[256] The cult of the goddess Nemesis, perhaps accompanied by human sacrifice, was especially predominant among the amphitheatres of the Danubian provinces.[257] In its uncompromising cruelty the arena provided an appropriate outlet for this darker side of cult behaviour in the provinces.

Gladiators or beast hunts?

There is a remarkable lack of iconographical references to gladiatorial themes on the mosaic pavements of North Africa compared with the abundant material exhibiting representations of *venationes* here.[258] In general this situation is consistent for the literary, epigraphical and other types of archaeological evidence for North Africa, such as figured representations on African Red Slip ware vessels of so-called El-Aouja type.[259] As discussed above, the evidence from the lead curse tablets found inside the Carthage arena bears this out. Whether the preponderance of *venationes* exercised a recognisable influence on the geometry and proportions of the arenas of North Africa remains to be investigated. Certainly the readily available supplies of wild beasts would have made *venationes* economically more feasible. As we shall see in Chapter Five, it may be possible that such active culling of wild beasts was proactively encouraged by the central authorities as part of an overall programme to maximise agricultural productivity here.

The final act

Ultimately the cost of financing the games, the increasingly acute problems of procuring wild beasts and the Christian reaction to the human slaughter took their cumulative toll and irrevocably changed the appearance of the spectacles. Having begun as a heartlessly cruel exhibition where humans and animals were maimed and killed at each session, the spectacles gradually evolved into exhibitions of trained animal acts and bear-baiting as well as performances of gymnasts and clowns, the forerunners of the modern itinerant circus.[260]

Chapter Five

Endings and new beginnings

OVERVIEW

In this chapter we shall first investigate the latest of the amphitheatres in the declining tradition of their construction. In these last, waning monuments we shall see the fruits of technical innovation and experimentation in their use and structural components.

Then we shall look into the question of the end of the gladiatorial *munera* and the *venationes*. We shall examine to what extent the pressures from the new religion, Christianity, the changing role of the system of patronage for the games, the altered political and economic realities of the late antique world, and perhaps a world-wide catastrophe in AD 535 contributed to the ultimate extinction of the long tradition of amphitheatre spectacles.

After the spectacles had waned, the amphitheatre could no longer fulfil its major role and a variety of new uses were found for the now disused arenas of the Roman world. Such uses included places for public punishments, fortified emplacements in the insecure atmosphere of barbarian invasion or internecine civic strife, nuclei for settlements (often fortified), and the sites for Christian shrines, churches or *martyria*.

We finally suggest a programme for future investigation to chart the influences of the amphitheatre and its spectacles upon the succeeding generations of western Europe down to the present day.

THE LAST AMPHITHEATRES

The Salona amphitheatre (Golvin #181)

Dimensions:
Overall: 124.75 × 100.65m
Arena: 64.30 × 40.20m
Seating estimate: *c.* 13,380[1] or *c.* 25,172[2]
Initial construction: *c.* AD 170[3]
Major renovation: third century AD – including the addition of a colonnade atop the *cavea*.
Late antique phase: Still in use during the persecutions of Diocletian (early fourth century AD).[4]
Disuse and dilapidation: Survived virtually intact into the thirteenth century.[5]

Salona was the most important city and port of the Dalmatian coast and the capital of this province. It was an early Caesarean titular *colonia* (the so-called *urbs vetus*), complete with its own walls, and a later Augustan settlement was appended to its eastern side (the so-called *urbs nova*).

This later site received its walls during the Marcomannic crisis of the AD 170s – the manpower and expertise being supplied by the legions II Pia and III Concordia (later known as II and III Italica respectively).[6] The emperor Diocletian was born near Salona and built himself an extensive palace nearby. He retired here when he voluntarily gave up power – a unique example in the history of the Principate. In the late antique period Salona retained its significance into the sixth century AD, forming one of the most important centres for Christianity in the province.

The amphitheatre,[7] probably dating to the era around AD 170 when the city was at its zenith, lay in the north-western angle of the walls of the *urbs vetus*. This position is strikingly reminiscent of the way in which the city walls of Pompeii were used to provide buttressing for the *cavea* of the amphitheatre. Partly for this reason and partly on the basis of historical probabilities, it is possible that Salona may well have had an amphitheatre from perhaps as early as its Caesarean colony. Tucked into the same corner of the circuit walls, the later monument may have largely obliterated its traces.

The amphitheatre was like many others and in itself does not merit special attention. One aspect of note is the way in which the lower portions of the northern sector of the *cavea* were supported upon the rising ground in this quarter. The rest of the *cavea* rested upon the usual barrel vaulting laid upon the radial network of piers and walls of the foundations. The façade consisted of sixty-eight bays comprising two superimposed arcades and an attic storey complete with its array of masts for the awning (*velum*). An altar to Nemesis attests the existence of a chapel to this deity and in the palaeo-Christian era, numerous chapels were inserted beneath the bays of the ground-floor arcaded façade.

One possible innovation incorporated into this late amphitheatre may have been the degree of complexity of its design and laying out. Einar Dyggve studied this monument and published his results in a monograph.[8] In this study he postulates that a twelve-centred system of circular segments comprised the contours of the arena and surrounding annular walls of the foundations and façade. If this hypothesis is correct, Salona provides evidence for an increasing level of sophistication in the laying out of the perimeters of oval arenas.

The El Jem amphitheatre (Thysdrus *amphitheatrum maius*) (Golvin #186)
This monument has been discussed in detail in Chapter Four (see p. 146). The use of cross-vaulting to cover the arcaded gallery of its façade, the steeper rake of its *cavea* allowing four *maeniana* to be inserted instead of the usual three, and the reduced area of the 'blind zone' in its arena all represent technical advances.

The so-called 'Palais Gallien', Bordeaux (Golvin #188): early third century AD[9]

Dimensions:
Overall: 132.3 × 110.6m
Arena: 69.8 × 46.7m
Seating estimate: *c.* 28,700
Initial construction: Early third century AD based upon historical probabilities – other monumental architectural projects at Bordeaux during Severan era, particularly prosperous here. It is probable that this monument replaced an earlier amphitheatre, as yet undiscovered, at this important Aquitanian site. Other comparable cities in this region, e.g. Saintes, had an amphitheatre already from the first century AD.
Destruction: Thick layer of ash found during excavations – destruction by fire.
Terminus ante quem: AD 276, the date of the Germanic incursions into Aquitania with attendant destruction.

New technological innovations

Unlike other amphitheatres, where the seating is normally supported upon barrel vaulting laid upon segments of walls disposed radially around focal points of curvature, here we now see a new conception (see Figure 5.1) – an integrated utilisation of stone foundations and wooden superstructure. Here a sequence of seven concentric stone segments of ovals acts as the basis for the wooden superstructure tied into the stone walls. The reasons for this use of wooden elements for the superstructure are unclear, but perhaps it reflected the widespread earlier use of turf-and-timber construction throughout the north-western provinces of the empire.

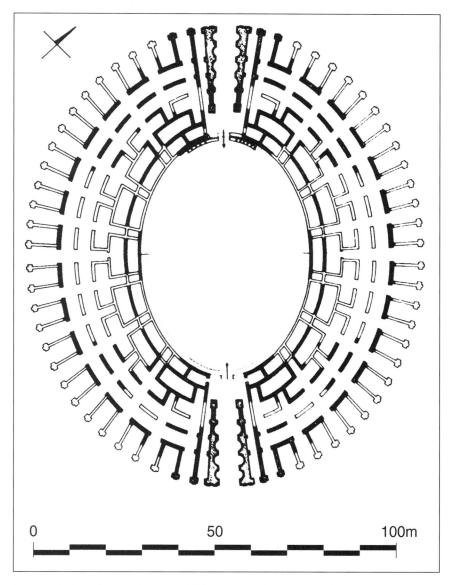

0   50   100m

Figure 5.1 Amphitheatre, Bordeaux (Golvin #188). Ground plan of amphitheatre.
Source: Golvin, Planche XXI, 9. Copyright J.-Cl. Golvin.

Anfiteatro Castrense, Rome (G #189): AD 218–222[10]

Dimensions:

Overall:	88 × 75.8m
Arena:	indeterminate
Seating estimate:	*c.* 7,000 (?)[11]

Initial construction: Originally this structure formed part of the larger imperial villa-palace complex known as the *Sessorium* or *Palatium Sessorianum*, built during the reign of Elagabalus (218–22). It lay in the fifth region of Rome and is first mentioned in the Regionaries as the *Amphitheatrum Castrense*. By late antiquity the term *castrensis* had gained in addition to its purely military connotations an additional layer of meaning, applied in connection with the personal world of the emperor and his entourage. Hence this was not a military or camp amphitheatre, but part of the private palace of the emperor in Rome. The emperor Constantine took possession of the complex in the early fourth century and the arena was used for spectacles staged strictly for the private enjoyment of the emperor and his select audience of personally invited guests. This was an even more exclusive audience than in the Colosseum – a members-only private club.

Abandonment: Unknown, but this monument became part of the circuit of the Aurelian Walls (270–80/1). At this time the square apertures between engaged brick columns on the façade were blocked up.

Reuse: Until the mid-sixteenth century, the exterior of this monument stood relatively unscathed. However, after this date, only the ground floor of the façade remained. It now became a fortified redoubt.

Plate 5.1 *Amphitheatrum castrense*, Rome: details of the all-brick construction of the façade.
Photograph by D.L. Bomgardner.

Innovations

This structure formed part of the transition between the old style of imperial architecture and the new conceptions of late antiquity. The use of brick for all major parts of the monument, including elements for columns and decorative mouldings, reflects an increasingly dominant trend in Roman construction.

This amphitheatre formed part of the tradition of imperial palaces on an increasingly lavish and grandiose scale. There was even a full-size hippodrome in addition to an amphitheatre attached to this complex – an early example of the predominant mode of expression of imperial majesty in the later empire, the ubiquitous palace-circus complexes of the imperial residences of the emperors.

Castra Albana (Golvin #190): second phase – Severan era, post-AD 212[12]

Dimensions:
Overall: 116.5 × 94m
Arena: 67.5 × 45m
Seating estimate: *c.* 20,000
Initial construction (Golvin #25bis): This earlier phase may have formed part of an imperial villa complex belonging to Domitian in this region.
Overall dimensions: 91.5 × 69m Arena: same as later phase.
Expansion phase: An expansion of an earlier, perhaps Domitianic, phase of this structure. Almost certainly prompted by the billeting in the immediate vicinity of the *legio II Parthica*, transferred here by Septimius Severus, in the early third century AD.

Until the Severan era, the only large-scale military presence in the immediate vicinity of Rome had been the barracks for the Praetorian Guard, on the north-eastern outskirts of the city. The Severi relied more and more upon the support of the military to maintain their rule. A logical extension of this policy was the transferral of the *legio II Parthica* to a permanent garrison in Italy only a short distance along the *via Appia* south of Rome, in the picturesque Alban hills. Now the emperor could call upon a legion, stationed locally, instead of having to await reinforcements from the distant frontier garrisons. This force could be useful either in a civil war or to suppress discontent in the capital itself. Camp amphitheatres were almost an integral part of every legionary fortress throughout the empire.

THE END OF THE SPECTACLES

By the middle of the fifth century AD, there is good evidence that combats between gladiators had ceased, even at Rome.[13] At a much earlier date, by the end of the third century AD in the western Roman empire, the evidence for gladiatorial *munera* had dried up.[14] The reasons for this situation are complex. They lie in the crucial period from the military anarchy of the third century AD to the mid-fifth century, the time of the eventual domination of the empire by Christian emperors following the conversion of Constantine the Great. The political, religious and economic history of this age will reveal the profound changes within Roman society that eventually ended the slaughter of human beings in the gladiatorial games.

It is interesting that, throughout the empire, long after the gladiatorial *munera* had ended, beasts continued to perform in amphitheatres. Alongside *venationes* where *venatores* (beast fighters) hunted animals to the death in the arena, a new type of spectacle developed. For a variety of reasons which will be investigated later, the format of these *venationes* had changed. Now the human performers themselves, usually unarmed, faced the gravest dangers in the arenas. The beasts themselves were now spared and reused. Thus we can see an evolution from a spectacle, where the death of the beasts that took part was certain, to an event, where the *venatores* tried to elude the claws and jaws of the beasts. However, by the middle of the sixth century AD, references to *venationes* come to an end, at both Rome and Constantinople.[15]

The end of the gladiatorial *munera*

Philosophical opposition

Even before the official spokesmen for the newly-organised Christian Church had begun to denounce these spectacles, there had been denunciation from the philosophical elite, e.g., Stoics such as Seneca and Cicero.[16] While there were important differences in the objections that each of these groups raised, there were also important similarities in their criticisms. A recent analysis of such opposition clearly demonstrates that the prime concern, among both the philosophical sects and the Christians, was not that human beings were suffering cruelly in the arena, but that the spectators were being adversely affected by what they witnessed.[17] In the traditional view of Roman 'society', the blood shed in the arena was worthless, the dregs of society, for whom no pity or compassion need be wasted. Rather, at the core of the objections raised was the belief that watching such bloodshed and cruelty would adversely affect the spectators, whether pagan or Christian. Each viewpoint had an agenda differing in details, but both shared this common belief.

Ultimately, such a conviction derived from the philosophical conception of the pagan nature of divinity.[18] The world contained a continuum of 'being': animals, humans, gods. Imagine the world of 'being' as a stairway made up of three steps. On the lowest step, the animals, on the second, humans, and the gods occupied the top step. In this view, the 'divine' became in one sense simply 'superhuman'. A human being, lying thus between the irrational passions of the animal world and the divine rationality of the gods, could move in either direction: upwards, ultimately to become a 'sage', or downwards towards 'gross carnal sensuality', i.e., 'bestiality'. The philosophical sects objected to the upper classes of Roman society watching gladiatorial combats simply because these spectacles appealed to the baser emotions and passions. They brought about the debasement of the spectator down towards the level of the irrational and bloodthirsty animal world. In much the same sense, the beating of a slave in a fit of rage was roundly condemned: not so much on the grounds that it was an act of inhumanity, but rather because such an outburst represented a collapse of the harmonious image of the self of the well-born man; it had caused him to behave in an uncontrolled manner, no better than a slave might be expected to act.[19]

An analysis of the seating composition of the Colosseum shows that the vast majority of the seating was intended to accommodate solid Roman citizens.[20] Thus the spectators at the gladiatorial combats, far from being the rabble of the urban mob, as has often been assumed in popular accounts, were the epitome of Roman society, assembled in formal attire at solemn civic ceremonies carried out with proper religious rituals and sacrifices. We can now easily see why the philosophers worried about the effects of the spectacles upon the 'worthy' of Roman society.

The Christian reaction

In common with the pagan philosophical opposition to the spectacles, patristic critics voiced their profound concerns about the effects watching gladiators had upon their Christian brethren.[21] For example, both Tertullian, the third-century Christian apologist from Carthage, and St Augustine, the late fourth-century bishop of Hippo Regius (modern Bône, Algeria), sound this same note of concern. In his pamphlet, *De spectaculis*, about a proper Christian response to the spectacles, Tertullian condemns all spectacles as places of pollution, since they are places where pagan sacrifices and religious rites and rituals are practised. The amphitheatres were the special precinct of the deities Mars (for the gladiatorial combats) and Diana (for the hunting of beasts). He also called the arena the 'temple of all demons' (*templum pandaemonium*), who were drawn by the blood shed there. He warns of the dangers of pollution by contact with pagan religious festivals and sacrifices and the dire peril in which they are placing their immortal souls by the momentary gratification of their senses. Having once been a Manichaean, Tertullian saw the world as the battleground between the forces of good and evil: God and his angels vs. Satan and his demons.

St Augustine, like Tertullian himself also a former follower of Manichaeism, vividly described the personal tensions that a new convert felt when faced with his former life style. In his account of his conversion to Christianity, the *Confessiones*, Augustine describes how a friend of his, a young convert named Alypius, was dragged unwillingly to the amphitheatre by his friends in Rome in the 360s AD. He was determined to resist the temptation to watch and so put both hands over his eyes. However, when he heard a tremendous outcry by the crowd, his curiosity got the better of him and he looked at the scene in the arena below him.

When he saw the blood, it was as though he had drunk a deep draught of savage passion. Instead of turning away, he fixed his eyes upon the scene and drank in all its frenzy, unaware of what he was doing. He revelled in the wickedness of the fighting and became intoxicated with the fascination of the bloodshed. . . . He watched and cheered and grew hot with excitement, and when he left the arena, he carried away with him a diseased mind which would leave him no peace until he came back again, no longer simply together with the friends who had first dragged him there, but at their head, leading new sheep to the slaughter.[22]

Jewish tradition and holy law unconditionally abhorred and condemned the shedding of human blood in the arena. The Ten Commandments expressly forbade the killing of human beings. Clearly Christians, sharing these beliefs, would also object to the gladiatorial combats on these grounds.[23]

In addition Christians believed that the gladiatorial games were a waste of money that should more properly be put to charitable uses. The giving of gifts, spectacles, public buildings, public banquets and other such acts of beneficence by the grandees of the ancient city-state were an expression of their generosity (*liberalitas*). Such munificence presented their fellow citizens with enjoyment, but it also elicited gratitude towards the donor and enhanced the donor's status.[24] Such lavish expenditures were the unquestioned obligation of high status and high office in the municipalities of the Roman empire. St Ambrose, the bishop of Milan, who inspired Augustine's conversion, writing in the fourth century AD, attacked such gifts of spectacles. He claimed that such gifts were nothing less than hedonistic trifles and as such were examples, not of generosity (*liberalitas*), but of a profligate waste of resources (*prodiga effusio*) ultimately leading to bankruptcy and a squandering of all their wealth (*patrimonium*). True generosity lay, he argued, in 'receiving guests hospitably, clothing the naked, and ransoming captives, who did not have the wealth to ransom themselves'.[25] This is an intriguing argument since it has its roots in similar denunciations by Cicero. He wrote to his son that the giving of public banquets to the voters or the ransoming of captives from brigands or pirates was more properly the realm of an educated man's liberality, rather than bankrupting himself for the transitory and morally questionable pleasures of the giving of games: 'This sort of amusement gives pleasure to children, silly women, slaves and free persons with the characters of slaves; but an intelligent man who weighs such matters with sound judgement cannot possibly approve of them.'[26] What is interesting in the examples of Christian criticisms cited above is that the language of their denunciations is firmly rooted in the philosophical and literary traditions of classical culture.

Such diatribes against the spectacles by the Christians would have had limited impact had it had not been for the single most significant event in the history of the new religion, the conversion of a Roman emperor to the new faith. The imperial persecutions, begun as early as the reign of Nero, following the Great Fire at Rome of AD 64, and continued intermittently through-out the second and third centuries with greater or lesser vigour, depending upon both the temperament of the times and the ruling emperor, finally ceased.[27] Constantine, on the eve of the Battle of the Milvian Bridge against Maxentius in AD 312, had a vision in which he saw the symbol of the 'Chrism' (the Greek letters 'chi' [c] and 'rho' [r] intertwined) in the heavens.[28] Constantine had his soldiers emblazon this Christian 'logo' on their shields, convinced that, with the help of the Christian god, he would be victorious over Maxentius and his forces. His victory the next day consolidated his belief that the god of the Christians had been decisive in his triumph over Maxentius. During the course of his reign, Constantine recognised Christianity as an 'officially accepted' religion of the empire and his mother, Helena, a devout believer, went on pilgrimage to the Holy Lands, causing monumental basilical churches to be built there at the most sacred sites of the life, death and resurrection of Christ.

Henceforth an intriguing symbiosis between the imperial power of the Caesars and the other-worldly preoccupations of the Christian Church began. Both sides were altered irrevocably by their interventions in the affairs of the other. From this time, Constantine began to try to walk the tightrope between his new-found faith and the still pre-eminent beliefs of the pagan aristocracy of Rome and the soldiers of the Roman army. From now on, the Christian emperors of Rome attempted to influence the pagan world they ruled. Over the course of the next century, the Christian Church, under the patronage of Christian emperors, the earthly 'vicars of Christ', became the dominant new force in the empire.

Imperial actions against gladiatorial munera

From as early as the reign of Augustus, Roman emperors had issued laws intended to limit and control the gladiatorial *munera*.[29] Augustus himself, in 22 BC, decreed that the praetors responsible for organising and funding the annual combats at Rome should spend an equal amount (from their own resources), thus seeking to control the spiral of competitive spending to elicit popular support. In addition, the praetors had first to seek permission from the Senate and were limited to a maximum of two displays in any year of not more than 120 gladiators each.[30] Tiberius acted decisively to eliminate the role of the popular assemblies in the election of praetors, thus undermining the motivation for lavish spending by the aediles in order to court popular support when later they would stand for election as praetors.[31]

The emperor was keen to acquire the status of being the unrivalled source of supply for gladiators. Competition in this area among prominent political leaders of the republic had been an important ingredient in the run-up to the civil wars of the first century BC. By rigorously controlling the privilege of giving gladiatorial combats, the emperors also sought to minimise competition from potential political rivals. The emperor must be seen to be the chief patron from whom all benefits ultimately flowed downwards into the ranks of Roman society.

Nero, in AD 57, forbade provincial governors or the imperial procurators in their provinces from giving gladiatorial *munera*, *venationes* or theatrical performances in the provinces.[32] Later Marcus Aurelius and Lucius Commodus, as co-rulers in AD 176–77, proposed a law to limit the cost of gladiators hired by private individuals or magistrates.[33] We shall examine this legislation in greater detail below. Apparently, the original framework of its regulations remained in force throughout the Roman empire until the pressure from the Christians forced further radical alterations and ultimately the abolition of the *munera*.

Constantine was the first emperor to embrace Christianity. In a legal document (rescript) concerning Beirut (Berytus), dated 1 October 325, he first published his intention to abolish the practice of sentencing criminals to the arena as gladiators.[34] This rescript states that henceforth criminals condemned to the arena, rather than being sent to a gladiatorial barracks (*ludus*) to be trained as gladiators, should have their sentences commuted to working in the mines instead. While the former punishment was not necessarily a sentence of death, because a gladiator who survived for five years would be set free, to all intents and purposes it was tantamount to it, as this more favourable outcome rarely occurred.

We need to place this decree in context. First of all, it was a rescript, a personal reply from the emperor to another letter asking for guidance in a specific incident. It was not a general decree or edict. Second, as Wiedemann has pointed out, the episode to which this rescript responded was probably the sentencing of Christians to work in the mines of the eastern empire under Licinius.[35] Constantine had just completed the conquest of the eastern empire from Licinius in the previous year and the main thrust of this rescript was probably the need to replace the Christians, who were presumably freed by Constantine, by criminal labour in the mines. Whether we see this rescript as a genuine expression of Constantine's convictions, or merely as a rhetorical argument to justify its later stipulations, as Wiedemann suggests, is irrelevant to the reality of Constantine's situation. Whatever his intentions, Constantine was unable to act as he wished regarding the 'Christianisation' of the empire. The pagan opposition was still too widespread and too entrenched in powerful governmental and military positions to be seriously threatened at this early date. The fact that he eventually gave up his attempts to 'Christianise' Rome and turned afresh to his new capital, Constantinople, to establish a 'Christian capital of the empire' is eloquent testimony to the harsh realities of Constantine's position.[36] There is no evidence that gladiators ever fought in Constantinople, unlike numerous examples of *munera* elsewhere, after this decree, such as at Antioch a mere three years later.

A generation later, there is evidence that Valentinian (5 January, AD 363) issued a rescript to Symmachus, the Urban Prefect of Rome, threatening a heavy fine for any judge who sentenced a Christian 'to the arena'.[37] Whether this rescript would have seriously affected the future supply of manpower for the gladiatorial schools is difficult to gauge. Admittedly, the world of late antique Rome was becoming more Christianised, if only outwardly, at all levels of society, but particularly among the lowest classes of society. This could eventually have had an effect upon the number of non-Christian criminals available for sentencing 'to the arena'. But it is hard to quantify this issue.

If Constantine's rescript, some forty years earlier, was intended to have universal effect throughout the empire, there should have been no need for Valentinian's enactment. If, however, Constantine's decision was intended solely for the eastern part of the empire, and if Valentinian's decision was primarily concerned with the situation in Italy and Rome itself, then both rescripts would be in concord rather than at odds.

From the end of the third century AD, gladiatorial combats apparently ceased in the western empire, apart from Rome and certain parts of Italy. They still continued in the eastern empire, except Constantinople, where they apparently never took place.[38] As late as the third quarter of the fourth century, judges, at least in Rome if not elsewhere, were passing sentences condemning criminals of sufficiently low social status to the gladiatorial barracks (*ad ludos*).

There is a difference of opinion as to exactly when the imperial gladiatorial training barracks at Rome were shut down, but one interpretation is that they were closed in AD 399.[39] Even if we cannot be precise about this date, the last explicit reference to them was in AD 397,[40] and they closed down some time thereafter, probably sooner rather than later.

We saw in Chapter One how the emperors organised the supply of beasts, hunters and gladiators for their spectacles through a system of imperial training schools, both in Rome and in the provinces. We have also investigated the way in which the emperor rigorously controlled the giving of private and public *munera*, exercising a very tight rein upon every aspect of this potentially politically sensitive area. It follows, therefore, that with the emperors supplying their own spectacles and perhaps also supplying private individuals and magistrates for their games, there should be little demand for the private entrepreneurs, the *lanistae*, who ran private training schools, and who were once so numerous under the Republic. Thus, one might reasonably assume that this branch of the private sector had withered away to an insignificant level during the late empire, particularly during the troubled times of the third century AD. We have already seen how the early Christian emperors began to act forcefully in law towards the ultimate abolition of gladiatorial combats. It makes sense that, as part of this long-term programme, they should at some point no longer fund or support the imperial training schools for gladiators and beast hunters in Rome. It is reasonable to assume that the other imperial sources of gladiators, the provincial imperial gladiatorial troupes (*familiae gladiatorum*), each under the control of an imperial procurator, would also have closed down, probably even before the training barracks in Rome. Whenever these sources of imperially-supplied gladiators came to an end, probably at some time during the first quarter or half of the fifth century AD, there was by then no effective alternative supplier in the private sector.

By the mid-fourth century AD, as is seen in the Chronograph of AD 354 (also known as the Calendar of Furius Dionysius Philocalus), among the 177 days of festivals in the annual games, there were only 10 days (all in December, around the festival of the Saturnalia) devoted regularly each year to gladiatorial combats. A clear indication of the future of such spectacles at Rome is provided by the emperor Theodosius the Great. In AD 389 he abolished all pagan festivals and instituted a new Christian calendar, in which the Christian 'Sabbath' and other such Christian holy days and festivals alone were celebrated. In fact, many of the games, for example chariot racing, continued much as before, even taking place on the same days of the year, simply under different names.[41]

However, it is clear that gladiatorial contests continued unabated, at least in some parts of the empire. At Apamea in Syria, the local bishop, Marcellus, fired with Christian zeal, set out to destroy as many of the local temples as possible. Meeting with equally spirited resistance from the local pagans, he enlisted the aid of hired gladiators and Roman troops to quell this opposition. Thus large numbers of gladiators were still available to fight as mercenaries in the last quarter of the fourth century AD. It is not clear whether they were available as mercenaries because of a recent cessation of *munera gladiatorum* or not. None the less, their very existence attests to quite recent training of new gladiatorial recruits in large numbers in gladiatorial barracks in this region.[42] It is interesting that a Christian bishop should have no qualms about using 'demonic' forces, hired gladiators, in his fight against paganism: fighting fire with fire, so to speak. In the same region, Libanius writes with some dismay of the roving bands of militant monks who roamed the countryside at will destroying rural pagan shrines in the countryside around Antioch.[43] This theme of militant persecution of paganism by Christian monks may have had a decisive effect upon the gladiatorial spectacles.

An event that aroused great public outrage among the Christian community and perhaps fostered sympathy among the pagans for the Christian opposition towards gladiatorial combats occurred in AD 404. During a gladiatorial combat in Rome, doubtless in the Colosseum, a Christian monk, named Telemachus, tried to make the embattled pair stop their fighting. The pagan crowd were so enraged at this attempt at violent intervention that they tore the monk to pieces in their frenzy. The Christian emperor Honorius was so disgusted by this that he is said to have banned the gladiatorial combats. Yet, as Wiedemann has pointed out, this cannot have been a universal ban, merely a local punishment along the lines of for example Nero's ten-year prohibition on *munera* at Pompeii, for gladiatorial combats are still well attested after this event.[44] Ville, in his seminal study of the end of gladiatorial spectacles under the Christian empire, is doubtless correct that this episode did not in itself bring about the end of gladiatorial *munera*, but he is none the less unwise to discount the effects of this episode entirely.[45] It is surely significant that an account traditionally linked in the minds of the people of late antique Rome with the ending of gladiatorial combats should have as its central figure a militant monk. As seen above at Antioch, in addition to zealous bishops, the religious fervour of the monks of the empire could have bitter consequences for pagans who got in the way of their 'reforming and cleansing frenzy'. The role of the militant agitation by the monks of Rome against the gladiatorial spectacles would repay investigation as the basis for a future study.

As we have seen, from the latter half of the fourth century, the Christian emperors began actively to persecute pagan temples as well as public acts of worship and sacrifice.[46] Gladiatorial combats persisted until perhaps AD 439/40.[47] By this time the Christian Church's influence in the Roman world, particularly in the person of the emperor, the 'vicar of Christ' on earth, was pre-eminent and may have been pivotal in dealing the final blow to the *munera*.[48] When Christians in the late fifth century continue to denounce the pernicious influence of the pagan spectacles, they still rail against the chariot races, theatrical displays and beast hunts, but they no longer mention the gladiatorial *munera*.[49]

The role of Christianity in the abolition of gladiatorial combats has been both overestimated and underestimated. It is clear that the preaching of the Christian Church against the spectacles and particularly against the duels to the death of gladiators alone would not have been enough to bring about the end of this form of spectacle. However, emperors and their relations, converted to Christianity, directing their administrative and legal staffs and acting under the guidance of such Christian precepts, and either actively encouraging, or merely turning a blind eye to, the militant persecution of paganism through bishops and monks, ultimately provided the necessary compulsion to effect, in the course of just over a century from the reign of Constantine to the mid-fifth century, the abolition of gladiatorial combats.

Yet the games were already under severe pressures from the sheer expense involved in mounting grandiose spectacles on such a lavish scale. Christian opposition alone, even with the whole-hearted support of converted emperors, does not offer a complete explanation for the end of the *munera*. We shall now investigate the role of the economic factors involved in bringing about the end of gladiators.

The harsh economics of the new world order of late antiquity

Changing patterns of beneficence in late antiquity

Peter Brown has convincingly painted a picture of the changes in patterns of gift-giving in late antiquity. The former pattern of the so-called '*homo civicus*', the citizen who gave benefits to his fellow citizens so that in return he might reap the rewards of status and public honour (*gloria*), gave way to a totally different pattern. Under the impact of Christian teaching and practice, a new type of citizen emerged, the so-called '*homo interior*'. This 'new man' no longer looked for his rewards in the immediacy of public adulation and recognition by his fellow citizens; he rather looked forward to a divine reward in heaven. His beneficence took the form of charity to the poor, the sick, the needy (and also to his local bishop towards these same ends), so that their prayers might sanctify his life and death in the sight of God. Thus a profound change in patterns of giving occurred, turning wealth away from the cities and their monuments and internal structures, and towards a new world order of Christian charity and almsgiving.[50]

As has been demonstrated elsewhere, gladiatorial spectacles played only a minor role in the official Roman festivals and games each year. A mere ten days of *munera* were held during December, around the time of the Saturnalia.[51] The exhibition of gladiators was normally a private show, linked to a special reason for such celebrations with great pomp and ceremony. In the municipalities of the Roman empire the most common reasons for the giving of gladiatorial games were either to commemorate a magistrate's election to high civic office (e.g., the aedileship or the duovirate) or as part of his duties as one of the provincial priests of the imperial cult to provide gladiatorial games for the emperor's genius each year at the provincial assembly. In Rome, the emperors gave such games either to commemorate a great occasion, such as a successful military campaign or the inauguration of a great public building, or else to celebrate a significant anniversary of their reign, such as the fifth and tenth anniversaries of their accession. Private individuals were strictly limited as to what they were allowed to present to the Roman public in the form of gladiatorial spectacles. By the later third century, election to the consulship was the chief reason for the giving of gladiatorial spectacles at Rome by a private individual, during January at the start of his career. The costs involved in the production of such displays could be crippling, leading to actual bankruptcy in some cases.

Nero in AD 57 published a decree banning any form of gladiatorial display, beast hunts or any other spectacle by provincial officials in the provinces. Tacitus (*Annals* 13.31) says that this ban was intended to protect provincials from having to bear the burden of funding such displays.[52] This decree was obviously only a temporary measure, very likely rescinded following Nero's death and official censure by the Senate (*damnatio memoriae*). The problem, however, did not abate.

The *senatus consultum de pretiis gladiatorum minuendis* (AD 177–80)

During the joint reign of Marcus Aurelius and Lucius Verus, these emperors made a serious attempt to control the prices paid by *editores* for gladiators who performed in their spectacles. The Senate passed a law (*senatus consultum*) sponsored by the emperors.[53]

This law imposed a detailed set of regulations concerning the precise composition of each gladiatorial show, according to a rigorous grading into categories by quality of performer, as well as a complete pricing policy that regulated the maximum price that could be charged for each of these grades of quality. There are difficulties regarding some of the provisions detailed in this law, but the main thrust of it is crystal clear: to institute a precise regulatory control upon the pricing structure and the organisation of the gladiatorial *munera*.

At this time, privately-funded performances primarily designed to raise money for their organisers (the so-called *munera assiforana*) were very small beer indeed. They form the bottom rank of the classification scheme, *munera* costing less than a total of 30,000 *sesterces* (perhaps about £200,000).[54] Perhaps because of their small scale nature, or perhaps because of the difficulties involved in attempting to regulate such a decentralised, *laissez-faire* enterprise, such *munera* remained unregulated by the emperors.

Four classes of *munera*, where control was to operate, were outlined in this law:

- Class IV: *munera* costing 30,000–60,000 *sesterces* (perhaps £200,000–£400,000).
- Class III: *munera* costing 60,000–100,000 *sesterces* (perhaps £400,000–£650,000).
- Class II: *munera* costing 100,000–150,000 *sesterces* (perhaps £650,000–£1,000,000).
- Class I: *munera* costing 150,000–200,000 *sesterces* and above (perhaps £1,000,000–£1,250,000).

In each of these categories, at least half of the total number of gladiators in each display had to be from among those who did not fight individually in pairs, but rather in groups (*gregarii*). This class of gladiator ranged in price from 1,000 *sesterces* (perhaps £6,500), for those of a lower standard of skill, to 2,000 *sesterces* (perhaps £13,000), for the more experienced members.

The fourth class of *munera* (from 30,000 to 60,000 *sesterces*) contained three categories of more experienced gladiators (first, second and third class) in addition to the *gregarii*. First-class gladiators had a maximum price of 5,000 *sesterces* (perhaps £32,500) each, second-class, 4,000 *sesterces* (perhaps £26,000) each, and third-class, 3,000 *sesterces* (perhaps £19,500) each. If one applies these prices and combines them with the rule that at least half of the total number of gladiators had to be *gregarii*, you can calculate how many gladiators would perform within this band. There are two possible combinations. Either one pair of each class of gladiators fought, one pair after another, and in addition a mêlée of up to twelve *gregarii* did battle in the arena, or else two pairs of each class fought, one pair after another, with a mêlée of six *gregarii* (a total of either twelve or twenty-four gladiators, but at the same average price of approximately 2,750 *sesterces* [perhaps £18,000] per man). (See Table A, p. 230 for detailed calculations.)

The third class of *munera* (from 60,000 to 100,000 *sesterces*) had the same number of categories as the fourth. Here, however, the top grade of gladiator fetched not more than 8,000 *sesterces* (perhaps £52,000) each, the next lower grade, 6,000 *sesterces* (perhaps £39,000) each, and the bottom grade, 5,000 *sesterces* (perhaps £32,500) each. Only one combination is possible for this band: four gladiators from each of the three grades fought one pair at a time and in addition a mêlée of twelve *gregarii* took place (twenty-four gladiators in all at an average price of some 3,917 *sesterces* [perhaps £25,400] per man).

The second class of *munera* (from 100,000 to 150,000 *sesterces*) had five grades of gladiators within it. The top-quality gladiators would cost no more than 12,000 *sesterces* (perhaps £78,000) apiece, the second grade, 10,000 *sesterces* (perhaps £65,000) apiece, the third grade, 8,000 *sesterces* (perhaps £52,000) apiece, the fourth grade, 6,000 *sesterces* (perhaps £39,000) apiece and the lowest grade, 5,000 *sesterces* (perhaps £32,500) apiece. Again only one combination is possible within this price band. Two gladiators from each of the five grades would fight in pairs and a mêlée of ten *gregarii* would engage in combat (a total of twenty gladiators at an average price of 4,850 *sesterces* [perhaps £32,000] per man).

The top class of *munera* (from 150,000 to 200,000 *sesterces* and above) had the same number of quality bands as the second class. A top-grade gladiator here would cost no more than 15,000 *sesterces* (perhaps £97,500) apiece, the second grade, 12,000 *sesterces* (perhaps £78,000) apiece, the third grade, 9,000 *sesterces* (perhaps £58,500) apiece, the fourth grade, 7,000 *sesterces* (perhaps £45,500) apiece, and the lowest grade, 6,000 *sesterces* (perhaps £39,000) apiece. Five possible combinations are possible within this price band, with each one yielding the same average price per man of 5,850 *sesterces* (perhaps £38,000). Four, six, eight, ten or twelve pairs of each of the five grades of gladiator would fight in matched pairs and in addition some combination of the *gregarii* (either twenty, thirty, forty, fifty or sixty in total respectively) would engage in mêlée combat.[55]

It seems quite clear from looking at this legislation in this way that each price band was structured to preserve the same average price per gladiator within its band (it is perhaps best to round these figures off so that the average price of a gladiator for the fourth class would be approximately 3,000 *sesterces* (perhaps £19,500) apiece, 4,000 *sesterces* (perhaps £26,000) apiece for the third class, 5,000 *sesterces* (perhaps £32,500) apiece for the second class and 6,000 *sesterces* (perhaps £39,000) apiece for the top price band.

The law mentions that the imperial treasury (the *fiscus*) directly benefited in an unspecified manner from the gladiatorial displays by receiving revenue ranging from 25 per cent to 33 per cent of the total spent, amounting to 20 to 30 million *sesterces* (perhaps £125 million to £190 million) annually. Some have thought that this was a reference to a tax on the hiring of gladiators, like VAT at 25–33 per cent.

Fergus Millar argues that the sums mentioned in the law may not represent a loss of direct taxes to the *fiscus* through the enactment of this law at all.[56] He argues rather that they represented a general loss of revenues to the *fiscus* resulting from the general lowering and stabilisation of prices decreed in this law. If, as he posits, the provincial 'schools' maintained by the emperor (and attested in Rome, in Italy, in the grouped provincial area of Gaul, Britain, Spain, Germany and Rhaetia, in the area of the Pannonias and Dalmatia, in Asia Minor and Cyprus and at Alexandria in Egypt[57]) sold gladiators to civic magistrates and provincial high priests of the imperial cult, then a lowering of prices by 25–33 per cent would affect not just the private sector suppliers, but also the revenues coming into the imperial treasury as well. Whatever the precise meaning of these provisions, this is nevertheless striking testimony of the amounts of money being spent annually at this time on the provision of gladiatorial *munera* throughout the empire. The total estimated expenditure (or revenue to the *fiscus*) would have been at least 60 to 120 million *sesterces* annually (roughly £375 million to £750 million).[58] The legislation was designed to save the *editores* of gladiatorial displays between 20 and 30 million *sesterces* annually. These represent staggering amounts of money. It is not surprising that imperial legislation should attempt to lessen the burden upon provincials for giving mandatory *munera*, part of their normal civic or priestly responsibilities.[59]

It is clear that these regulations would not be applicable everywhere, but they were intended for major cities and their displays. Special provisions were made for isolated provincial areas or small-scale private games, where the prices would not approach the high levels cited in the legislation. Here provincial governors were enjoined to fix prices at reasonable levels on the basis of the costs of the past ten years of displays.

In addition, special religious ceremonies unique to particular provincial areas were also dealt with. Criminals who had been condemned to be thrown to the beasts (*damnati ad bestias*) were available for purchase to be executed in private displays at a cost of 600 *sesterces* (roughly £3,750) apiece. There is some evidence to suggest that in the remoter areas of the North African hinterland, where the Punic language was still spoken and where Punic religious practices still continued, such criminals were executed in the arenas as a continuation of the practice of offering human sacrifices to the Punic deities, Ba'al and Tanit.[60] In Gaul, a special class of sacrificial victims, the so-called *trinquii*, were made available as a substitute for gladiators at a cost of 2,000 *sesterces* (roughly £13,000) apiece.[61] Perhaps here too we may see a continuation of a tradition of human sacrifice in a guise 'officially tolerable' to Roman sensibilities; officially such practices were strictly forbidden.

The Edict of Maximum Prices by Diocletian (AD 301)

Imperial attempts to regulate soaring inflation and rising prices reached their apogee in the detailed series of enactments issued by Diocletian in AD 301 and known familiarly as the Edict of Maximum Prices.[62] Large numbers of fragments of this decree have turned up in various places around the Mediterranean describing maximum pricing policy for goods and services of all kinds. However, none of the existing fragments bears any witness to attempts to regulate the price of gladiators for displays. None the less, the fact that reference is made to a maximum price structure for lions intended for the arena (see p. 211) should indicate that such provisions existed, but that they have not yet been discovered.

Conclusion

Thus, we can see a picture of continuing attempts by the emperors of the second and third centuries to intervene in the economics of their era through a policy of control of pricing as well as salaries and wages. In particular, the exorbitant fees that were being demanded to supply gladiators to the public for displays provoked a series of enactments in which efforts were made to regulate this area and to drive prices down. It is clear that the soaring prices of gladiators in an era of economic recession made a significant contribution to the eventual abolition of gladiatorial combats.

The *venationes*

Although the hunting of beasts in the arena had always been included among the spectacles openly criticised by the Christians, it is clear that this did not this spring from any concern for the welfare of these animals or about the cruelty of what was taking place in the arena. The Christian reaction was always based upon deep concerns about the effects of the events upon their fellow Christians who were spectators. Their concerns were two-fold. First, they were concerned that religious pollution would occur when a Christian came into contact with pagan sacrifices and religious ceremonies, where demons of all sorts were to be found. Second, they lamented the debasement of the Christian spectators that would follow upon their watching events that appealed to the passions rather than to the intellect, events that distracted their attention away from their sole aim, the deeper contemplation of God.

It is, therefore, interesting that the *venationes* should have carried on for so long, being among the last of the spectacles to cease, alongside chariot racing. Long after gladiators had been officially banned by Christian emperors, beast hunts and execution of criminals by being thrown to the beasts in the arena continued. 'Christian Rome and Byzantium found no difficulties in suppressing any pagan associations of chariot races and wild-beast shows and integrating these activities into a Christian polity.'[63] Indeed, the destruction of wild beasts could be given a Christian interpretation. The beasts dispatched were the sins of the flesh that every Christian had to overcome in order to contemplate more perfectly the Godhead – an allegory of Christian virtue over carnal/animal vice. It is fascinating how the beast hunts of the arena changed over the course of their history and we must now turn to look at some of the aspects of those changes.

The supply of beasts for the arena

The costs

There is relatively little surviving evidence for the prices of wild beasts for the arena. However, an early third-century polychrome figured mosaic, the so-called 'Magerius Mosaic' from a villa near the major city of Hadrumetum (Sousse), is a rare example. It contained an inscription in which are stated the price for animals intended for the *venationes*.[64] This pavement probably decorated the suburban or seaside villa of the Magerius mentioned in its inscriptions. The mosaic depicted an amphitheatre scene in which four hunters confront four leopards (all participants, men and animals, are identified by individual names) in the arena. To one side a herald addresses the spectators; his words are provided by an inscription. Magerius himself is shown and so is his declamation to the audience. The crowd's enthusiastic response (*acclamatio*) to Magerius's generosity is also supplied. Among the precious details provided by this most interesting artefact is the price paid by the *editor*, Magerius, for each of the leopards exhibited: 1,000 *denarii* (4,000 *sesterces* or perhaps about £25,000) each. This figure is double the agreed contractual figure and is a further reflection of the unstinting nature of Magerius's beneficence and his pleasure in the magnificence of the spectacles. Magerius thus spent a total of 4,000 *denarii* (16,000 *sesterces* or perhaps about £100,000) for the leopards alone; presumably this also covered the fees for the hunters – a package deal. Given the ephemeral nature of such expenditure, literally over in a single day, it is not surprising that Magerius may have wished to have a more enduring memorial to his vast expenditure and civic beneficence. Katherine Dunbabin has identified a whole genre of figured polychrome mosaics from North Africa that presumably fulfilled this role. Incorporated into their luxurious villas, such pavements would both adorn the building and provide a constant reminder of the benefactor's moment of triumph before his fellow citizens, the zenith of his municipal career.

By the end of the century, the situation was vastly different. In his Edict of Maximum Prices (AD 301; see p. 210), the emperor Diocletian laid down a detailed list of regulated prices for all kinds of goods and services. These prices were intended to provide a safeguard for the government itself, not individual consumers. Among the goods listed are the prices for lions for the arena.[65] A top-quality African lion now costs a maximum of 600,000 *sesterces* (nearly £4 million today), considered a fair price! A second-class African lioness now costs 400,000 *sesterces* (about £2.5 million). Although we are not entirely comparing like with like, in that the prices of leopards in North Africa are being compared with the prices of lions presumably in Rome, nevertheless there is evidently an enormous inflation in costs, nearly a thousand-fold increase in the course of one century.

In spite of these enormous rises in the price of animals, the correspondence of Symmachus, Urban Prefect of Rome in the late fourth century AD, makes it abundantly clear that even when money was no object, sufficient animals could not be had, no matter what the bidding price offered. It is quite clear from these references that money is not the limiting factor here, but rather the scarcity of satisfactory supplies within readily transportable distances from any of the major ports of the Mediterranean. This would also go a long way towards explaining the skyrocketing prices, even as early as the previous century.

The complex network supporting the supply of animals to the arena

From as early as the second century BC, the acquisition of beasts for the arena had been a high priority for ambitious politicians in Rome. During the Jugurthine War in North Africa, the young Sulla's reputation was immensely aided by his 'special relationship' with the king of Mauretania, Bocchus. He handed over the rebel insurgent Jugurtha, by then a defeated, political exile seeking asylum at Bocchus's court, as a prisoner to Sulla, rather than to Marius, the commander-in-chief of operations. In addition, he later supplied Sulla with a magnificent assemblage of lions for his games back in Rome, which became the talk of the town. Such a large number of lions had never before been seen in Rome at a *venatio*. Sulla's future political career was launched by this series of brilliant manoeuvres.

From the time of Julius Caesar, every major political figure strove to secure a reliable supply of top-class animals for the *venationes* that he would one day stage at Rome as part of his political career. The Roman emperors, as part of their policy to pre-empt potential political rivals from getting too much of the limelight at Rome or in the provinces, had passed laws limiting the size of games given by those other than the emperor.[66] The emperor remained a law unto himself: he organised and presented as many gladiators and animals as he was able to muster, thus eclipsing all potential rivals.

As we have seen earlier in Chapter One, the early Julio-Claudian emperors brought under their own control the means of supplying such gladiators and animals. A series of gladiatorial 'training schools', initially in the Capua area, but later under Domitian also in Rome itself, were either purchased or purpose-built. Similarly, a series of special imperial menageries were established in Italy and Rome to assemble, train, accommodate and breed animals for the arena. At Laurentum there was an imperial compound for elephants. In Rome a large walled area lay just outside the *porta Praenestina*. It was known as the *vivarium* in the Regionary Catalogues and was the main holding area for animals immediately prior to their exhibition at Rome as well as being a long-term storage facility for those species that would breed well in captivity, such as lions. All of these specialised facilities became part of the legacy handed down from one emperor to his successor.

In addition to these facilities, the emperors had access to a vast network of imperial manpower. At the cutting edge of this process were the special units of soldiers on permanent detached service, whose job it was to capture animals alive and to ship them back to Rome. On the German and Danube frontiers, such units, known as *ursarii*, are attested as having been in charge of supplying bears for the emperor.[67] On one inscription found at Cologne, a centurion from the *legio I Minervia* boasts that in six months he has captured fifty bears.[68]

In addition to such full-time Roman legionary soldiers on detached duty to supply animals for the emperor's menageries and games, it is tempting to presume that a large, more or less formally-organised network of native trappers and traders must have existed certainly beyond, if not within, the frontiers of the empire. At the end of the fourth century AD, Symmachus, the Urban Prefect of Rome, in his attempts to provide wild beasts for his son's quaestorian and praetorian games (AD 393 and 401 respectively), makes reference to professional dealers in wild bears (*negotiatores ursorum*).[69] In North Africa there were numerous guilds of itinerant hunters, the so-called *sodalitates venatorum*, such as the Telegenii, who both supplied their own animals and probably also were middlemen in the transport of rarer, more exotic feline species bound for major arenas elsewhere, especially Italy and Rome.[70]

The animals would travel to collection centres where the vast logistical machinery of the empire's heavy goods transport system, the *cursus clabularis*, a sub-division of the imperial post, the *cursus publicus*, would transport these animals on ox wagons (bearing 1,200 to 1,500 pounds each) to the nearest seaport bound for their final destinations, such as Italy, especially the Bay of Naples area and Rome itself. Diocletian's Edict specifies the cost for transport by ox wagon as 20 *denarii* (roughly £500) per mile.[71] This is extremely expensive when compared with comparable costs for transport by inland waterways or by sea.[72]

There is a plausible explanation for the rapidly soaring prices for beasts that relates to transport costs. When one bears in mind the high cost of transport by ox wagon overland, once supplies that were within easy striking distance from the major seaports of North Africa or from the Bagradas river valley (a navigable system around which the majority of the high-yield corn lands of northern Tunisia clustered) dwindled, longer and longer road transport costs would accrue in order to supply fresh stock. These very areas would by nature be prime agricultural land since it has been calculated that it was uneconomical to transport corn more than about 50 miles to a navigable river/canal or to a seaport.[73] In the sections that follow we shall see that such prime agricultural land was especially subject to destruction of natural breeding habitat for indigenous species and probably also culling to maximise productivity. As the numbers of cities with their inevitable adjacent agricultural lands increased in North Africa, so the territory where wild animals flourished was pushed farther and farther into the hinterlands of the provinces. This in turn would necessitate larger and larger transport costs to Italy.

Maintenance costs for these animals in transit, as well as the train of officials, the military escort and the other attendants necessary, were partly borne by the government (from provincial taxes for the upkeep of the posting stations, *mansiones* and *mutationes*, including their staffing) and partly by the cities (direct taxes in kind, especially the supply of livestock and fodder) through which these caravans passed. A legal document from AD 417 shows that such costs could be a heavy imposition upon the municipalities.[74] In it the civil officials of Hierapolis (Euphrates province) wrote an official petition to the emperor Theodosius II complaining that the military governor's department (*officium*) had contravened the normal protocol for official missions. Their transport caravan of animals had stayed in the city for the last three or four months, not the prescribed seven or eight days. Their insolence even went so far as to demand the provision of cages (*caveae*), an unprecedented and unlawful demand. Such considerable maintenance costs were a heavy burden on the citizens. The emperor decreed that all such caravans of wild beasts from a military governor of a frontier district bound for the department of the *comes domesticorum* in Rome (the commander of the *protectores*, a corps of officer cadets in training) must stay no longer than seven days in any one municipality. Here we have further confirmation of the continuing role of the military in the collection of wild beasts for the emperor; the military governors of the frontier zones are in the first instance charged with the capture and assemblage of wild beasts into transport caravans, presumably also including military escort during the journey.

It is clear that some species, such as crocodiles, did not travel in captivity at all well and that the attrition rate for them was considerable. Careful professional handling in transport was essential to ensure that as many animals as possible reached their destinations in good condition.

Once the animals had arrived, another network kicked into action. Skilled professional handlers, trainers and veterinarians were needed to bring the untrained animals to their peak before they were ready to be exhibited in the arena. Many of these professionals came from

Alexandria in Egypt, which had been the undisputed centre of excellence in such matters ever since the days of the Ptolemies with their extensive zoological gardens and menageries. Proper care, feeding and training all added further to the total price of each animal displayed.

When viewed in this context, one sees how dependent the emperors and others who wished to give *venationes* were upon the vast interlocking systems of supply, transport, care and training of these animals. By the end of the fourth century AD, if not earlier, there are clear indications of long delays in transport of wild beasts, at least for non-imperial clients of the *cursus publicus*.[75]

Diminishing numbers

From the second century AD, efforts were made to bring marginal land, especially in North Africa, into productive use through a scheme of incentives to farmers. The much debated *Lex Hadriana* offered free, stable tenancy to anyone who would reside permanently upon marginal land and put it under full-time cultivation, either in vineyards or olive tree plantations. In addition, as an incentive, taxes were waived during the initial establishment phase of cultivation (five years' exemption for vines, ten for the olive) until the plot began to make a profit. The proof that this policy was a success lies in the rapid agricultural development of such areas as the Sahel (roughly the south-eastern zone of modern Tunisia), a semi-arid climatic zone lying in the rain shadow of the Aurès Mountains to the north-west. By the third century this region had become an extremely wealthy agricultural territory and was developing an urban infrastructure of market towns (e.g., Municipium Bararus), key nodal distribution centres (e.g., Thysdrus/El Jem) and ports (e.g., Leptiminus, Sfax and Hadrumetum).

The high plains of Algeria such as the areas around Djemila and Sitifis also witnessed their apogee of prosperity during this period. Here, in this wetter climatic zone, the intensification of agricultural exploitation and urban development was fuelled by olive and vine plantations as well as the cultivation of corn. Doubtless, too, the improvements under the Severan dynasty, early in the third century AD, to the security of the southern frontier along the fringes of the Sahara and along the mountain passes of the southern Aurès range enhanced the economic prospects of these areas.

A similar story can be told in the Tripolitanian hinterland areas where recent survey work has revealed a boom in farming settlements and population through careful management and employing dry farming techniques to harness and capture the brief torrential rains that would normally run off uselessly.[76] An intricate system of barrage dams across wadis (dry river channels) interconnected to massive storage reservoirs and irrigation canals utilised the meagre rainfall to its utmost potential.

On the negative side this widespread intensification of agricultural development was accompanied by the destruction of vast tracts of natural habitat, so vital for the survival of the indigenous wildlife. It is not without significance that from this era, herbivore species, such as moufflon, gazelles and antelopes, begin to supplement the traditional favourites of the arena: lions, leopards, bulls, bears, boars. We have already described above the inflation in the cost of supplying big cats for the arena during the course of the third century.

We have learned to our own cost the devastating toll on indigenous wildlife species that accompanies large-scale clearance of natural habitat for agriculture or grazing. Surely such widespread destruction of habitat in North Africa must have made a significant impact on the numbers of animals and the variety of species living there.

The transition from big cats towards a greater diversity of herbivores in the arenas of the empire during the later second and third centuries AD may perhaps be partially explained on the basis of this system of organisation. The Roman government was extremely reluctant to employ middlemen in the supply of its needs.[77] If one assumes that big cat species were no longer readily available within the empire by means of these detached legionary 'hunter-trappers', then it would make sense to utilise them to supply alternative kinds of species that were ready to hand where legionary units were stationed. By the time of Symmachus, the Urban Prefect of Rome during the early fifth century AD, even these alternative species were apparently no longer readily available to his agents and contacts in the provinces.

A further factor in the decline of animal numbers may have been excessive hunting and trapping. At the beginning of the principate, the emperor Augustus recorded in the official commentary he published of his own reign, the so-called *Res Gestae Divi Augusti*, 'Twenty-six times I provided for the people, in my own name or in the names of my sons or grandsons, hunting spectacles of African wild beasts in the circus or in the Forum or in the amphitheatres; in these exhibitions about 3,500 animals were killed.'[78] Roughly 135 African lions appeared in each of these *venationes*.[79]

In the lavish series of games that accompanied the solemn ritual of dedication of the Colosseum (AD 80), the emperor Titus exhibited 9,000 wild beasts in a hundred days of spectacles.[80] Not to be outdone, the emperor Trajan, to celebrate his Dacian triumph in AD 107, exhibited 11,000 animals over the course of 123 days.[81] There is in all of this a consistent one-upmanship, an attempt to establish a new baseline for extravagance in imperial beneficence with each succeeding reign. With Trajan, however, the Roman empire reached its zenith. From the troubled times of the later second century AD onwards, there began an inexorable decline in its fortunes.

By the third century AD, animals were already becoming hard to obtain in such large numbers. At the games to celebrate the millennium of Rome in AD 248, the emperor Philip the Arab could muster only 32 elephants, 10 elks, 10 tigers, 60 tame lions, 30 tame leopards, 10 hyenas, 6 hippopotami, 1 rhinoceros, 10 wild lions, 10 giraffes, 20 wild asses and 40 wild horses. The account is notable in two essentials. First, it is unusually discursive in listing both the numbers and the species involved; previously the totals alone were enough to induce a sense of awe in the reader. Obviously, times had changed: now the animals are counted in their tens, rather than in their hundreds. Now it is perhaps the novelty of exhibiting rare species, not seen in Rome since the reigns of the Julio-Claudian emperors, that is intended to arouse a sense of awe among the spectators. There was no fundamental change of attitude towards *venationes* by the spectators or the emperors; harsh reality dictated the scale of the games. Second, the emperor now includes a large number of herbivores; the crowd's favourites, the big cats, now amount to less than a total of 100 animals, hardly worthy of mention for an imperial spectacle of the early empire. Indeed, there is a consistent trend among the evidence for numbers and kinds of animals exhibited during the later empire. More bears, boars, bulls and other herbivore species appear more frequently in *venationes*, while fewer and fewer big cats appear.[82]

The reasons behind this steady decline are complex and reflect systematic changes in both the structure and the organisation of the Roman empire. As described above, by the late third century AD the attempts at a more intensive agricultural exploitation in general and in particular the reclamation of marginal land for the cultivation of the vine and the olive had met with remarkable success in North Africa.

Combined with this destruction of natural habitat for agriculture, from the second century AD in North Africa a large number of amphitheatres sprang up. Even the smallest of the numerous cities, such as Agbia, Thuburbo Minus and Seressi, in the rich corn-producing region of northern Tunisia, had one, and each one was specially equipped for *venationes* (see Chapter Four).

In addition the age-old tradition of hunting flourished among the landed aristocracies of the empire. It is difficult to gauge the extent to which this practice prospered, Indeed, it is probable that there was a certain ebb and flow of fashion following the tastes of the reigning emperor – emperors such as Trajan aggressively broadcast their taste for such sport. None the less hunting always had been and remained one of the favourite activities of the royal house, the nobility and the landed gentry. Yet it is hard to judge the amount of damage to wildlife populations caused by it. Suffice it to say that it was a contributing factor in the overall decline of numbers and species.

The destruction of habitat for agricultural exploitation, the widespread performance of *venationes* in the amphitheatres of North Africa, the export of animals for the arenas of the empire and the organised hunting of animals by the aristocracy all contributed to the shortages of supply that began to make themselves felt by the late third century AD. The price of big cats, as revealed in Diocletian's Maximum Price Edict (discussed above), was astronomical by the end of the third century AD, with top-quality animals costing up to 600,000 *sesterces* apiece (nearly £4 million today).

A policy of systematic exploitation of agriculture at the expense of wildlife?

Such dramatic reductions in the number of animals may have occurred simply through the natural working out of a series of trends, such as those detailed in the previous section. However, there does seem to be discernible in the workings of the Roman administration of North Africa a consistent aim to maximise the productivity of this vitally important agricultural region of the empire.

As early as the reign of Augustus, Strabo, the Greek geographer, notes that Numidian agriculture has improved through the widespread hunting of wild beasts for the arena.[83] This widely read source convinces us that there was a conscious linkage in the minds of the Romans between a reduction in the numbers of wild beasts in an area and an increase in its agricultural productivity.

By the later second century AD, the African cornlands provided two-thirds of the domestic supply to the city of Rome each year, or about 27 million *modii* (6.75 million bushels) of corn annually.[84] After the establishment of Constantinople as the capital of the eastern Roman empire in the fourth century AD, the Egyptian corn was diverted and now supplied the needs of the new capital. Rome became totally dependent upon sources of supply in the western Mediterranean and particularly the African cornlands for her needs. The efficient exploitation, organisation and transport of this corn was an imperative consideration of all emperors if hunger and famine, alongside their attendant political consequences, were to be avoided in Rome itself. Towards the end of the second century AD, the emperor Commodus organised the *classis africana Commodiana*, the special fleet of super-tanker supply ships (with a capacity of 250–400 tonnes each) that plied between Carthage and Rome carrying the corn.[85]

In Rome, along the banks of the Tiber at the foot of the Aventine Hill and near the warehouses and docks of the city, a mound of broken and discarded pottery vessels, the so-called Monte Testaccio, nearly a kilometre in circumference, rises some 50m into the sky. The evidence of the shattered amphorae from this mound, where imported cargo containers were discarded, perhaps to be eventually recycled into waterproof concrete (*opus signinum*) to line water channels, drains and aqueducts, indicates the rise of North African exports of oil in the later empire.[86]

The presence of large numbers of wild animals in the North African countryside produced a doubly negative impact upon attempts to maximise agricultural production. First herbivores, such as antelopes and wild boar, would wreak havoc among the tender shoots of newly sprouted crops. Wild boars have even been known to kill small domestic herd animals, such as lambs.[87] Second the presence of carnivores posed a potential, if not actual, threat both to herds and to humans working in the fields. It would be beneficial from both points of view to curtail dramatically the wildlife in such agricultural regions. It is impossible to say whether this was a local reaction arising as an *ad hoc* solution to promote maximum productivity in individual locations or whether it arose from a higher level of bureaucratic administration over wider areas.

Such an end, to maximise productivity, would be well served both by the culling of wild animals through systematic export abroad and by their destruction in the arenas of North Africa. It is difficult to say whether the special adaptation of the arenas of North Africa for *venationes* was as a response to the readily available local supply of wildlife or as an attempt to regulate the levels of such.

There is, however, evidence that there was a readily perceived connection in the Romans' view of their world between the killing of animals in the arenas and the agricultural productivity of North Africa.

Luxorius, the official Latin poet at the court of the Vandalic kings of Carthage, composed a series of epigrams in the style of those written by Martial for the Flavian emperors of Rome and covering many of the same topics. Amphitheatre spectacles and chariot racing were among his favourite sources of inspiration. One epigram describes a seaside villa with its own private amphitheatre (*amphitheatrum maritimum*) and combines novelty with the love of the spectacles.

> The countryside marvels at the triumphs of the amphitheatre and the forest notices that strange wild beasts are there. The many farmers look at new struggles while ploughing and the sailor sees varied entertainments from the sea. The fertile land loses nothing, the plants grow in greater abundance while all the wild beasts fear their fates here.[88]

The apparent paradox of increased agricultural production in spite of devoting useful farmland to the construction of an amphitheatre is resolved by the solution that the decrease in the numbers of wild animals would be beneficial in the long term to the farmer in the ways described above. This is the clearest indication I have found of an acknowledgement of the link between control of natural wild animal populations and peak agricultural efficiency.

It is characteristic of Roman civilisation that it utilised and adopted practical wisdom in the management of its resources. Reportedly the only Punic literary work translated into Latin following Rome's ultimate defeat of Carthage and her empire was the agricultural treatise by Mago the Carthaginian. It is hard to imagine that such an obvious practical consideration as the limitation of animal depredation on growing crops would not have been an official priority in Rome's attempts to encourage the utmost production of grain from the North African provinces.

Changes in the venationes

During the course of the fourth to early sixth centuries, a gradual shift in the nature of the *venationes* began to take place. During the reign of the eastern emperor Anastasius (AD 498), an imperial decree banned the slaughter of beasts henceforth in the *venationes* (see p. 219). Thus, at least in the eastern empire, from this time alternative, 'tame' (*mites*) *venationes* took place. The situation is not so clear cut for the western half of the empire, but there too, as the evidence indicates, a similar evolution occurred. The chief evidence for this mutation lies in the series of ivory diptychs (souvenirs of consular games given to senators as a proud memento of the spectacles)[89] and the detailed account of the historian Cassiodorus (*Variae* 5.42).

Originally, the *venationes* presented the certain death of either the wild beasts or their hunters in the arena, ending in tragedy of one sort or another. Perhaps because of the soaring costs of replenishing the supplies of animals for the arenas, the slaughter in the arena was mitigated and tamed. In its place, a series of comic turns occurred. Now the object was not the death of the animal, but successful escape from its teeth and claws by the performers involved. In effect, the tables were turned and now the potential mutilation or death of the humans became the element that titillated the crowds. Remarkable skill and agility in evading the lunges and pursuits of the animals now took the breath away from the eager spectators. Both condemned criminals (identifiable by their lack of clothing except for a loincloth) as well as trained professionals (wearing long tunics with apotropaic emblems prominently displayed on their chests, and various types of defensive armour) took part in these 'tame' *venationes*.

All manner of special effects and apparatus formed part of these new spectacles. In their simplest form the performers first provoked the beast to charge at them and then ran away from, jumped, leapt or somersaulted over their pursuers, sometimes with the aid of a long pole to vault over the beast and out of harm's way. Other variations included a device similar to a set of parallel bars that provided a climbing frame. The taunting hunter nimbly climbed up on to this frame and, after the pursuing bear had lumbered up after him, he leapt down on to the soft sand of the arena to safety.

Another variation of the apparatus took the form of a series of door-like grilles. The actor first baited the beast, then fled behind the nearest grating; through this the taunter could be seen by his pursuer, but it could not reach through and harm him. A kind of hide-and-seek took place when a device much like a modern revolving door was used, with individual panels (varying from three to four in number and made not of transparent glass, but of an opaque material, such as wood) revolving about a vertical axis. This was called in Latin, *cochlea*, from its resemblance to a type of chambered shell. Thus, again the hunter first provoked his pursuer, then darted nimbly into one of the compartments of the revolving contraption, becoming temporarily invisible to his pursuer. Tantalising glimpses, followed by strategic retreats, would further enrage the beast and amuse the spectators.

Another device like an elevated carousel consisted of a series of large baskets suspended from a circular rigging stuck atop a long central pole. The hunters would taunt their animals, then nimbly retire to their elevated perches, which whirled about overhead just out of reach of their frustrated pursuers. A contraption similar to the giant cage-like, hollow balls used in the television series *Gladiators* provided effective protection as well as unrestricted mobility for the enclosed taunter. Obviously the elements of the beast's ineffectual pursuit of its taunter and the frustration at being able to see him without being able to harm him formed the crowd's cruel amusement.

When the hunters dared to taunt bulls in the arena, another device provided an element of protection for them. Following a successful attempt to get the bull to charge, at the last moment, attendants would throw straw dummies dressed up to resemble gladiators into the path of the charging beast. The distracted beast would toss the dummy about the arena while the performer made good his escape.

The descriptions of these 'tame' *venationes* share much in common with later performances, such as the itinerant circuses of the Middle Ages and beyond, and the modern American rodeo, in particular, the Brahma bull-riding competitions. Here we observe many similarities both in the devices and in their uses. The rodeo clowns who distract the attention of the bull away from the fallen rider by throwing a straw dummy dressed like the rider into its rampaging path, remind one of the nimble acrobats of the amphitheatre with their gladiatorial mannequins. Alternatively, the clown running wildly around the arena to draw the bull away, perhaps jumping into an oil drum which the bull will proceed to toss about the ring, echoes the events of the Roman arena of late antiquity. Yet, here there is a crucial difference – there is no overt cruelty for its own sake. Here the taunts and distractions of the bull, amusing as they may be, are of a life-saving variety.

The 'tame' *venationes* were still cruel spectacles, engaging agile performers to provoke, enrage and frustrate repeatedly the animals captive in the arena. The impotent rage of the animals in face of the technological superiority of mankind or else the physical suffering of the maladroit or unlucky performers now formed the basis of the crowd's enjoyment: variations on a theme of bear-baiting. Indeed Cassiodorus records that the tame beast displays were hardly less dangerous to the human performers than the old-fashioned, full-blooded variety had been to their hunters.[90]

The last official venationes

The evidence for *venationes* for the period after the late third century AD is very scrappy,[91] consisting mainly of the odd reference, usually from the late codifications of the Roman law or else Christian literary sources, and supplementing this, the important archaeological evidence of monuments.

The eastern empire and Constantinople

Several late sources refer to a ban on *venationes* in the east by the emperor Anastasius (AD 498).[92] This act is consistent with the many important fiscal reforms that characterise Anastasius's reign. In the sources this ban is linked with his abolition of Constantine the Great's institution, the *chrysargyron*, or *collatio lustralis*, a four- or five-yearly tax on traders (in the widest possible sense of the word, anyone who bought or sold goods) of a fixed quantity of silver and gold – by the fifth/sixth century, only in gold.[93] The linkage of this ban on *venationes* with a fiscal reform leads one to suspect that it was motivated largely by financial pressures to economise on these tremendously expensive arena spectacles, rather than arising principally from moral or theological objections. Chastagnol, artfully uncovering historical evidence previously overlooked, has discovered that only 'lethal' *venationes* were banned by this decree.[94] From this time, the only *venationes* that took place were 'tame' (*mites*), i.e. not entailing the slaughter of the beasts involved. Such an enlightened strain of the *venationes* had been developing since the fourth century AD. The apparent 'crowd pleasing' features were two-fold: first, admiration for the remarkable skill and agility of the humans who dodged, weaved and leapt out of harm's way as the beasts tried to catch them; and second, the suspense felt by the spectators as they watched the events unfolding before them, knowing that one false move or one slip might lead to serious harm or even death for the performers. It is difficult to say to what extent these changes were brought about either by the increasingly costly provision of wild beasts for such spectacles or by the pressures of the Christian Church upon the emperors to mollify the savagery of the 'full-blooded' hunts of the past. Doubtless, both factors were at work to varying degrees.

That this ban was not final is aptly attested by *venationes* that occurred after this time and by the evidence of ivory diptychs (see p. 217). The last mention of a *venatio* in the amphitheatre at Constantinople (the 'Kynegion') took place in Justinian's reign on 1 January AD 537 during the consular games of that year.[95] By this time, the practice of giving *venationes* was only a regular part of the games given by the new consuls at the beginning of each January. It is probable that, when Justinian suppressed the ordinary consulship in the thirteenth year of his reign (AD 541),[96] the giving of *venationes*, too, ceased – perhaps never to be resuscitated, or perhaps only infrequently in the inaugural year of each new monarch's accession.

At Constantinople, the all-powerful chariot-racing factions of the Blues and Greens seem also to have been responsible for the supply and training of the wild beasts intended for use in the amphitheatre there. This is a unique piece of evidence for a circus organisation extending into the world of the amphitheatre spectacles, and perhaps only applicable here at Constantinople.[97]

The western empire: Italy and Rome

At Rome there is surprising epigraphic evidence for a final flurry of activity during the mid-fifth to early sixth century AD. As related above, the serious earthquake of AD 429 badly damaged the Colosseum, making it unfit for use for almost a decade. The decision to repair it under Valentinian III (*c.* 439) reflects the continuing vitality of the spectacles there. Even under the Ostrogoths, the Colosseum remained an important venue. An important series of inscriptions come from the two lowest banks of seating (those reserved for senators on the podium), where individual senators had their names carved upon the space reserved for their seat. This series falls within the reign of the first German king of Rome, Odoacer (476–93). It is remarkable that the amphitheatre spectacles, now limited to *venationes*, should continue with enough vigour to warrant the redecoration of the podium of the Colosseum even under a barbarian king. It is notable that under the next Ostrogothic king of Rome, Theoderic (493–526), senators no longer felt it worthwhile to engrave their names upon their reserved seating – a possible sign of the tailing off of the spectacles.

The last record of a *venatio* at Rome occurred on 1 January AD 523.[98] A Roman aristocrat, Maximus, wrote to king Theoderic asking for special permission to provide a *venatio* for his inaugural consular games.[99] The special attention given to the description of this spectacle by Cassiodorus has led Chastagnol to propose that it is an 'archaeological exercise in reconstruction' of a tradition all but dead within this era. It is indicative of the resilience of Rome and her universal prestige that, in spite of the many hardships, plagues, sacks and destructions during the preceding century, the Roman aristocracy were still able to muster the vast resources needed to stage such a display.

Theoderic's high regard for Roman civilisation, including maintaining intact most Roman civil offices and administrative procedures, as well as his unremitting attempts to inculcate more civilised behaviour in his Ostrogothic subjects, are well attested.[100] The epigraphic evidence from the Colosseum clearly indicates that the reign of Odoacer marks the end of the long series of inscriptions reserving seats on the podium for the distinguished senatorial order of Rome. Theoderic, whatever his reasons may have been, whether religious or economic, apparently did not consider the spectacles of the amphitheatre as an essential element of his programme of Romanisation by which he attempted to instil more civilised behaviour into his Gothic kinsmen. Theoderic's successors were less enthusiastic Romanophiles and it is not surprising that with his passing (AD 526) the institutions of the Roman state, including the holding of the annual ordinary consulship and the *venationes* regularly associated with it, should thereafter dwindle away. In addition the impoverishment of the Italian senatorial aristocracy under the Ostrogothic kingdom is well attested and should also be considered as a contributory factor in the final lapse of the *venationes*. With the fall of Italy to the barbarians, the widespread communications and trade network links of the empire withered and died. It was no longer possible to muster the services and expertise of the imperial post and the widespread network of trappers and suppliers of wild beasts for the games.

It is not surprising that *venationes* had come to an end at Rome at a somewhat earlier date than Constantinople. In each capital there is a link between the end of *venationes* and the date when a regular succession of annual ordinary consuls came to an end. The last attested *venatio* at Rome occurred in AD 523, while the last recorded such spectacle happened in Constantinople in AD 536. The eastern half of the empire was richer and better organised, and it took slightly longer for the *venationes* to come to an end there.

The global climatic crisis of AD 535

Over the past five years, David Keys has been researching a problem he first encountered in dealing with dendrochronological (tree-ring) dating.[101] He began to discover that in every area of the world where such evidence was available, tree rings had suffered terrible perturbations due to a climatic crisis of world-wide proportions in AD 535 and succeeding years. His research led to the startling conclusion that a volcanic eruption of gargantuan proportions, probably of Krakatoa in modern-day Indonesia, had spewed enormous quantities of debris high into the atmosphere where it spread over the entire globe within months and caused a 'nuclear winter' effect lasting for several years. He has traced the repercussions of this world-wide disaster, including the great outbreaks of plague caused by the lowering of the temperature in Ethiopia and the transport of rats carrying plague-infected fleas from here to Constantinople together with the vast quantities of ivory that were imported by ship.[102] From Constantinople's docks the plague spread across Europe. Widespread crop failures and disruption of feeding and breeding patterns for animals were also predicted and apparently observable in the downfall at this time of the horse-dependent Avar empire in central Asia, replaced by the more cattle-dependent Mongols. The horse processes its feed less efficiently than cattle and is more susceptible to perturbations in foraging patterns. Is it not possible that the end of the *venationes* is also linked to this global climatic catastrophe? More research into this question is needed to establish the validity of this theory.

THE IMPLICATIONS FOR AMPHITHEATRES AND THEIR USE

As we have seen above, both the gladiatorial combats and the exhibition of wild beasts in the arena had come to an end by the middle of the sixth century AD. From this time, even the premier monument for such spectacles, the Colosseum in Rome, began to fall into disuse and disrepair.[103]

As late as the early sixth century we have evidence for the continued repair of amphitheatres in Italy. The Colosseum received a substantial renovation to the marble seating in the podium area reserved for senators; the inscriptions engraved on these seats (AD 510–11) are attested by Cassiodorus.[104] Theoderic was still giving games in the Colosseum in AD 523.[105]

The increasingly important fortified military centre of Pavia (Ticinum), at the upper limit of navigability in the Po valley, eventually became the capital of the Lombard kingdom. Alongside other imperial benefactions including a palace complex, it received the gift of a new amphitheatre under Theoderic in AD 523.[106] To the best of my knowledge, this is the latest construction or rebuilding of an amphitheatre, including even those that were in a central position in one of the major urban centres of the late empire, such as the Tetrarchic capitals or major military centres. It attests the increasing importance that barbarian rulers came to place in this heavily fortified city.

The gradual reuse of amphitheatres

The gradual cessation of *venationes* during the mid-sixth century AD had serious implications for the future use of amphitheatres. The final eclipse of *venationes*, the last major spectacle still performed in amphitheatres, meant that there was no longer any reason to build new monuments. At the same time the uncertainties of the political and economic situation of Italy as well as of the empire meant that there was little surplus funding for such monuments or such spectacles.

Places for public execution

Only one function now remained for these monuments that had at one time seen gladiatorial combats and beast fights. The public execution of condemned criminals still took place in their traditional venue, the amphitheatre. Now, however, the elaborate spectacle that had once surrounded these 'fatal charades' was gone. Public executions of criminals had once provided the opportunity for lavish re-enactments of mythical scenes involving the death of the protagonist, such as Icarus flying too near the sun with his wax wings and falling to his doom or the rather twisted humour of Orpheus this time failing to tame the savagery of the wild beasts with his lyre playing and singing.

In the period of decline, disrepair and disuse of the amphitheatres, simple public punishments without the elaboration of former salad days took place here. The Colosseum, long after it fell into disuse and disrepair, when Stephen III was Pope (768–72), was used for the public punishment of a criminal who had his tongue and eyes ripped out.[107] In a similar fashion public punishments occurred in the Hippodrome and the abandoned amphitheatre (the 'Kynegion') of Constantinople.[108] Eventually even this function that still remained for the amphitheatres dwindled into oblivion. It is recorded that after the Colosseum had fallen into disrepair its open spaces were the site for markets and fairs.

Fortified outposts

In a climate of deteriorating stability, the later empire witnessed a dramatic transformation in the use of its amphitheatres. At Lepcis Magna and Sabratha in North Africa, the amphitheatres, sunk deeply into hilltop sites, became fortified small-scale settlements. The inhabitants blocked off the entranceways, thus transforming the monument into a relatively secure haven in an increasingly unstable world. The citizens of Arles, an important administrative centre and the site of an important imperial palace complex, probably from the sixth century, blocked up the lower arcades of the amphitheatre's façade and added a series of tall towers around its periphery to transform it into a strong fortress. At Pola in Istria, similar changes transformed the monumental arena there into a fortified redoubt.

The best studied example of such a transformation is that of the Colosseum in Rome. As discussed in detail in Chapter One, by AD 1130 at the latest, during the internecine warfare of the High Middle Ages, the Frangipani had fortified the Colosseum, but the vaults of the ground level still belonged to the church of Sta. Maria Nova to lease as workshops and dwellings (until *c.* 1180).[109] By 1240 the Annibaldi shared half of this structure with the Frangipani and within a generation they had total control of the Colosseum.[110] Control of the Colosseum by the Frangipani/Annibaldi meant that they controlled the western and northern approaches to the pope's residence. They could either defend a 'friendly' pope in the Lateran Palace or else besiege an 'enemy' as circumstances dictated.[111]

Theveste: a case study

At Theveste, in North Africa, excavations have revealed the fascinating story of the later use of the amphitheatre there. Following its reconstruction during the fourth century AD, the monument became a fortified settlement, perhaps during the Byzantine era, by blocking up its entranceways. This fortress met with a violent end. A blackened layer of soil indicates abandonment and destruction. With the aid of radiocarbon dating techniques, this episode has been assigned a date of *c.* AD 900. Inside the arena at some later date, locals set up their simple dwellings with dry-stone walls and simple beaten earth floors during the medieval Arab period. Generation upon generation of apparently continuous occupation occurred. These dwellings gradually built up the level of the arena until it finally reached the top of the arena-wall and the level of the podium itself.

This monument forms an almost unique example of the sequence of continued use of an amphitheatre into recent times, long after it had ceased to be an entertainment structure. It is rare for such care to be taken in the elucidation of the later levels of occupation and we owe a debt of gratitude to the excavators for this insight.

Reuse as a site for Christian worship

It must never be forgotten that amphitheatres formed part of the religious apparatus of the ancient Roman world as well as temples and shrines. The spectacles staged in the arena were framed in a context of religious ritual, albeit increasingly secularised as time passed. It was the pagan religious context of the spectacles as much as the content that so offended the early Christians, such as Tertullian.

The new religion often sought to soften or obliterate earlier memories of pagan ritual and of sacred places through the construction of churches, *martyria* or sacred shrines on the sites of former pagan worship. In much the same way, some arenas were re-consecrated to a Christian purpose. We have seen above in Chapter Three how both Arles and Nîmes received Christian churches into their structures. At Tarragona, the provincial capital of Hispania Tarraconensis, the Visigothic conquerors built a church into the substructures of the amphitheatre's arena during their hegemony (sixth/seventh century AD). Salona, an important seaport on the Illyrian coastline and the site of the emperor Diocletian's palace complex (third century AD), had a series of palaeo-Christian chapels installed beneath the bays of the amphitheatre's façade.[112] Under pope Benedict XIV (1740–58) even the Colosseum itself finally came under the protection of the Church, and eventually it became a shrine to the Christian martyrs slain there.[113]

CONCLUSION

Thus we have seen how, when amphitheatres ceased to be used for gladiatorial contests and beast fights, they continued for a time as places of public execution, but without the elaboration of former days. No longer were there criminal executions in the guise of lavish re-enactments of myths and legends; in hard times, the simple deed now sufficed.

As amphitheatres crumbled and fell into disrepair, some were taken over and renovated as fortified redoubts during the troubled times that followed the breakdown of the Roman empire. Some continued in such use well into the internecine warfare of the early medieval period, and some, like the Colosseum, became small-scale local communities when former large-scale urban complexes, like Rome, began to break up in the harsh realities of the Middle Ages. Others were plundered for pre-fabricated building materials, for iron and lead metallic building crampons, and for marble, which was rendered down into quicklime for making concrete. Others, particularly those sunk into high ground, with few exterior arcades in the façade, were reused as small-scale protected settlements. Still others were converted into Christian shrines and churches in order to commemorate the martyrdoms of Christians in the arenas, or else to purify and efface the pagan associations of such monuments. The saints martyred in the arena were powerful intercessors for the prayers of penitents who flocked to these shrines. The ultimate survival of these monuments relied upon enlightened civic authorities, such as those at Verona, or else the patronage of the Church, for example the protection of the Colosseum in the eighteenth century under pope Benedict XIV. Most were left to decay more or less slowly, prey to plundering builders and vandals. Their structures suffered the silting up of the arena by erosion and flooding, and increasing decrepitude. Today the forlorn remnants of many of the smaller examples are rarely clearly visible. The relentless tides of time have effaced all trace of others, often buried beneath more modern structures. The rare exceptions that still survive, standing proud and magnificent, and more than a little melancholic, are monuments to the stern disciplines of *Romanitas*, the military and manly virtues of courage and skill at arms and disciplined obedience. And ultimately they are derelicts of the decadence and cruelty of the once mighty Roman empire.

EPILOGUE: RIPPLES IN THE FABRIC OF TIME

It is beyond the scope of this work to do more than to pose some questions about possible residual influences that the amphitheatre and its spectacles may have had upon succeeding ages and cultures. It will be left to others better qualified to take up the search either to vindicate these educated 'shots in the dark' or to refute them.

Medieval imitations

As we have seen above, both the gladiatorial combats and even the so-called 'mild' *venationes* (in which the animals tried to catch humans who either fled before their charge or else escaped into some form of elaborate stage-prop contraption, and then, after recapture, returned many times to the arena) had died out by the later sixth century AD. It would be fascinating to learn how much influence the North African amphitheatres, particularly Carthage, may have had upon this process with their expertise in the exhibition of *venationes*.

Itinerant circus troupes

Is it possible that the multifarious itinerant circuses of the early Middle Ages, with their combination of trained animal acts and overt cruelty, such as bear-baiting, had their origins in the latest phase of the 'mild' *venationes*? It would be interesting to trace how far these similarities extend and to try to ascertain how much these troupes owe to the last days of the amphitheatre spectacles. I suspect that the corporate associations of performers in the amphitheatre gradually evolved into the bands of roving entertainers in the circus troupes. Many of the same skills and training techniques would have had to be applied in both areas.

Venationes on the fringes of civilisation

There are tantalising scraps of information recorded in the accounts of the medieval Arab historians and geographers about the continuation of the baiting of animals, particularly lions, in a manner that strikingly resembles that of the arena.

At the early sixteenth-century court of the Sultan of Fez, Leo Africanus, an Arab captured by Christians and forced to convert, in his treatise about Africa, described the baiting of a lion by *venatores*, the fight of a bull and a lion, and the eventual slaughter of the lion by the *venatores*, who received payment for their pains.

> In a large field, there are certaine little cels made, being so high, that a man may stand upright in them: each one of these cels is shut fast with a little doore; and containe within every of them an armed man, who opening the doore presents himselfe to the view of the lyon: then the lyon seeing the doores open, comes running toward them with great furie, but the doores being shut againe, he waxeth more furious than before . . .[114]

This account clearly shares much in common with the depictions of the late forms of the 'mild' *venationes*, combining beast-baiting with potential danger to the performers. Here, however, the lion is slain by the huntsmen as in earlier times in the arena.

Tantalisingly this is the only reference that I have found about the continuation of spectacles resembling *venationes* in the later eras of North African history. This may be an isolated phenomenon, but it clearly bears the hallmarks of Roman influences continuing long after the eclipse of Roman contacts in North Africa, which fell under the sway first of the Vandals and finally of the Arabic armies of Islam.

Renaissance reawakenings and beyond

Renaissance 'pageants'

During the florescence of creativity and self-confidence known to us as the Renaissance, Italy witnessed a remarkable fountain of artistic and literary talent and productivity. Amid the wealthy, powerful and cultured Renaissance princes of the city-states of Italy, the Medici of Florence held an unrivalled position through their patronage and lavish spending. Leonardo da Vinci was perhaps the best known of the illustrious artists who obtained the patronage of the Medici. Among his many commissions for them, he designed and executed the elaborate stage-props for their formal courtly spectacles known as 'pageants'. These pageants, involving song, dance, Classical legends, elaborate costumes, drama and impressive special effects, combined many of the elements previously seen in the epic spectacles in the amphitheatres. Such performances involved elaborate stage-props (*pegmata*) that often appeared dramatically from beneath the floor of the arena by means of mechanical hoists and trap doors as part of a dramatic presentation or else as part of an execution or *venatio*. While there were also theatrical traditions that incorporated many of these same elements, it seems to me that in their desire to impress by the novelty, apparent impossibility and extravagance of their special effects, the pageants have more in common with the spectacles of the amphitheatre. Only an engineering genius, such as da Vinci, could achieve the extraordinary special effects that the Medici were looking for.

It is highly fitting that, during this period when the Classical tradition was 'reborn' in the area, dramatic spectacles of the Classical era should re-emerge in 'new clothes' in the city-states of an Italy once more self-assured and confident of her place at the centre of European history.

Renaissance dramatic masques and early modern reproductions

That most precocious of Renaissance princes, Henry VIII, king of England and Defender of the Faith, took a fancy to the Italian art of spectacular dramatic performances and imported them into his own kingdom. There they came to be known as courtly 'masques'.

This tradition of courtly masques was to endure with much vigour into the era of the Stuarts in England. Their most accomplished creator was the talented dramatist and *bon vivant*, Ben Jonson (1572–1637). In collaboration with Inigo Jones, he wrote numerous masques for performance at court. Like the spectacular special-effects extravaganzas of the arena, these performances were a tangible expression of the sovereign's power and wealth. Doubtless, there were strong influences from the Classical dramatic tradition as well, but the most direct linkages may perhaps be seen in the Renaissance tradition of royal 'pageants' (described above).

Only the austere Puritanism of the Commonwealth brought about a cessation of these gay courtly spectacles. They were re-introduced under Charles II, but then lapsed forever with the passing of the Stuarts into history.

The Royal Fireworks

Under the Hanoverians royal patronage once more prompted large-scale spectacular entertainments, such as the well-known Royal Fireworks display given by king George II in 1749. This spectacle teamed one of the most famous producers of fireworks, one of the Ruggieri brothers from Bologna, with one of Europe's premier composers, George Frideric Handel. The Ruggieri brothers had produced spectacles on an unprecedented scale for king Louis XIV at his palace of Versailles. George II was literally trying to 'steal his thunder' when he commissioned one of them to produce an unparalleled display in Green Park in London to commemorate the peace of Aix-la-Chapelle (1748). Handel composed a series of eight suites, 'Music for the Royal Fireworks', to accompany these magnificent pyrotechnics. Regrettably even the best-laid plans can misfire. The grand spectacle almost degenerated into slapstick when a mock-up of a Greek temple caught fire and burnt down during the performance, leading the Producer to brandish a sword and chase the Master of Ceremonies who was responsible for the stage properties and their proper functioning. This scene is highly reminiscent of the emperor Claudius's punishment of his less than successful technicians mentioned in Chapter One.

Once again the tone and the intention of these displays mirror those of the spectacles of the arenas of ancient Rome. Music accompanied the spectacles of the amphitheatre, adding atmosphere to the lavish displays presented.

The Spanish corrida: a modern venatio

Undoubtedly, the closest modern equivalent and direct lineal descendant of the Roman amphitheatre spectacles is the bullfight (*corrida de toros*) as practised in the Spanish-speaking world. There is an almost complete conjunction of both form and function between the *venationes* of the arenas of ancient Rome and the bullfights in the modern ring (*plaza de toros*). All the aspects of the bullfight follow closely what we know about the ancient *venationes*. The stylised procession at the start of the festival, the band of musicians accompanying every phase of the spectacle, the religious shrines in the vicinity of the arena at which the *matadors* make their final prayers and vows before their entrance into the ring, the details of the construction of the ring, the pens and the seating: all these closely parallel those in the ancient arena.

It is beyond the scope of this work to describe the origins, early history and stages of development of the modern bullfight.[115] It would form an interesting study of the survival of Roman spectacles into the modern world almost intact.

REPRISE

In his introduction to an article about 'corruption' for the third edition of the *Oxford Classical Dictionary*, Christopher Kelly has remarked that, 'beyond underlining the difference between classical societies and our own, the imposition of expectations or prescriptions derived from contemporary ideals does little to advance our understanding of the past'.[116] He concludes:

> when dealing with highly emotive or unashamedly moralising terms, they indicate the importance of viewing the classical world in its own context. Sweeping condemnations . . . should be resisted. If we insist on judging the ancient world against contemporary standards, we will not achieve much – other than a misplaced smugness as to our own superiority.

The same sentiments are equally applicable to the subject of this book. The philosopher Spinoza wrote that the purpose of the historian was to attempt to understand the past on its own terms of reference. The historian's task is to seek to understand a historical phenomenon in the light of its own contemporary moral, philosophical and religious traditions.

Bullfights and the spectacles of the amphitheatre easily generate strong, visceral, emotional responses. The cruelty seems mindless, senseless, without justification. However, in its own terms, it is understandable as one facet of a complete society: not an attractive society, nor a society that one wishes to see re-created today. Nevertheless, in its own frame of reference it is intelligible; it makes sense in its own time and place.

It is hoped that this book has been able to elucidate some of the elements that constituted the essentials of the arena spectacles: the religious origins of the spectacles as homage to the spirits of the illustrious dead of the Roman nobility (the *patres*); the physical embodiment of the social hierarchy of Roman society that was the amphitheatre's seating plan; the critical zone of interaction between emperor and his subjects that the spectacles provided; the incarnation of the martial virtues of courage, discipline and highly trained professional skill that the gladiatorial combats provided; the architectural symbol of the martial virtues of *Romanitas* that the arena itself represented; the deterrent against anti-social behaviour that the arena provided in its public executions – all of these were important aspects of understanding what the arena and its spectacles meant to the Romans themselves. Ultimately, the arena and its practices were an integral part of the fabric of Roman society. They were immensely popular, costing enormous sums of money for their provision. In one sense they offered tangible proof with every 'technological miracle' performed in the arena that the emperor was able to accomplish whatever he wished – no matter how seemingly impossible or far-fetched.

Pagan philosophers and Christians both believed that watching such carnage regularly ultimately degraded the 'humanity' of the spectators, dulling their sensibilities, making them accustomed to the sight of blood. In one sense, this was exactly what they were designed to accomplish. The toughness, skill and disciplined tactics of Rome's military manpower were the *sine qua non* for her continuing empire.

As seen on p. 202, St Augustine described how his friend Alypius, initially reluctant, came to become addicted to watching gladiators. Augustine likens Alypius's condition to a 'sickness of the soul'; he suffered damage to his soul by watching the butchery of others. He became a 'junky', hooked on the quick 'fix' of gladiatorial action, which offered temporary titillation, but not long-term satisfaction or pleasure. Not only did he attend regularly himself but he even dragged others unwillingly into the amphitheatre to witness the spectacles.[117] This account reveals as much about Alypius and his personality as it does about the gladiatorial spectacles. It also presents the 'other side of the coin' to the intentions set out above.

This is certainly not an accurate picture of the average spectator, as a kind of drug-crazed 'junky'. For Augustine's commentary is highly biased – clearly he has a personal agenda here to deter fellow Christians from ever attending the amphitheatre through the fear that they might end up like Alypius. Yet it does express a certain worldliness concerning the potential frailty of the human will to resist temptation: one view of what could happen to an impressionable, easily-led youth with the right kind of temperament to become a 'fanatical fan'.

Oscar Wilde wrote: 'The truth is rarely plain and never simple.' As much as we might wish the world we live in to be plain and simple truth, inevitably it is far more complex with no quick fixes or easy answers.

Appendix

THE DECREE OF THE EMPERORS MARCUS AURELIUS AND LUCIUS VERUS LIMITING THE PRICE OF GLADIATORS (*Senatus consultum de pretiis gladiatorum minuendis*)

The *Senatus Consultum de pretiis gladiatorum minuendis* regulating the prices of gladiators sold to organisers of games (AD 177–80)

Interpretations

Oliver and Palmer interpret this text as the minutes of an actual meeting of the Senate in Rome and the *sententia prima* of the senior ranking senator present at the debate.[1] They also associate the excesses of the martyrdom of the Christians at Lyons in AD 177 with the way in which this legislation was applied locally.

Millar thinks that this decree may reflect an attempt to lower prices generally by controlling those from a major source of supply, namely, the imperial training schools in the provinces.[2] In any case, this decree reflects the rising trend in prices and enough concern on the part of the emperors M. Aurelius and L. Verus and the Senate to try to regulate and stabilise prices through some form of official action. Many public officials in the ruling classes throughout the empire came close to bankruptcy to outfit as lavish a series of spectacles as possible during their municipal magistracies and priesthoods of the imperial cult.[3]

Wiedemann interprets this inscription as the minutes of a debate held at Lyons in AD 177, 'profusely thanking the emperor M. Aurelius for a senatorial decree the previous year'.[4] He links this legislation not only to M. Aurelius' well-known humanitarian values, but also to much-needed financial retrenchment in face of the fiscal crisis brought about by the compound tragedies of the plague of the 160s and the barbarian incursions on the Danube frontier of the 170s.

Perhaps this text contains evidence for both the cancellation of an imperial tax (*vectigal*) on the sale of gladiators (at a variable rate from 33 per cent to 25 per cent, probably depending upon the sums of money involved and the type of *munus*) and legislation to regulate and lower prices in general.

Provisions

- Repeal of an imperial tax (25–33 per cent) on the sale of gladiators.
- The establishment of a legal framework regulating maximum prices for gladiators.
- Five categories of *munera* (graded according to the total expenditure).

1 *Munera assiforana* (small-scale, local entrepreneurial spectacles for profit) < 30,000 *sesterces* – no intervention, too small a scale (?) to require action.
2 *Munera* costing 30,000–60,000 *sesterces* (see Table A for details).
3 *Munera* costing 60,000–100,000 *sesterces* (see Table A for details).
4 *Munera* costing 100,000–150,000 *sesterces* (see Table A for details).
5 *Munera* costing 150,000–200,000 *sesterces* and above (see Table A for details).

- At least half of the total number of gladiators must be *gregarii* (those who did not fight singly, but in a group) at a cost of 1,000–2,000 *sesterces*.
- *Damnati ad bestias* were available at a cost of 600 *sesterces*.
- Special Celtic sacrificial victims (so-called *trinquii*) were available as substitutes for gladiators at 2,000 *sesterces*. Oliver and Palmer[5] argue that these were a type of *bestiarius*.

Implications

The estimated loss of revenue to the imperial treasury (*fiscus*) was some 20 million to 30 million *sesterces*. Thus, the total expenditure, upon which this tax would accrue, was between 60 million and 120 million *sesterces* annually.

Table A Calculations of numbers of gladiators according to the *senatus consultum de pretiis gladiatorum minuendis* (= CIL 2.6278) (see pp. 208ff. for a more detailed discussion)

	Number of gladiators[a]	Price	Price
Munera costing 30–60,000 sesterces			
First class (<5,000 *sesterces*)	2	10,000	10,000
Second class <4,000 *sesterces*)	2	8,000	8,000
Third class (<3,000 *sesterces*)	2	6,000	6,000
Sub-total	6	24,000	24,000
Gregarii (1,000–2,000 *sesterces*)	6	6,000	12,000
Total	12	30,000	36,000
Average price per head (*sesterces*)		2,750	
First class (<5,000 *sesterces*)	4	20,000	
Second class (<4,000 *sesterces*)	4	16,000	
Third class (<3,000 *sesterces*)	4	12,000	
Sub-total	12	48,000	
Gregarii (1,000–2,000 *sesterces*)	12	12,000	
Total	24	60,000	
Average price per head (*sesterces*)		2,750	
Munera costing 60–100,000 sesterces			
First class (<8,000 *sesterces*)	4	32,000	32,000
Second class (<60,000 *sesterces*)	4	24,000	24,000
Third class (<5,000 *sesterces*)	4	20,000	20,000
Sub-total	12	76,000	76,000
Gregarii	12	12,000	24,000
Total	24	88,000	100,000
Average price per head (*sesterces*)		3,917	
Munera costing 100–150,000 sesterces			
First class (<12,000 *sesterces*)	2		24,000
Second class (<10,000 *sesterces*)	2		20,000
Third class (<8,000 *sesterces*)	2		16,000
Fourth class (<6,000 *sesterces*)	2		12,000
Fifth class (<5,000 *sesterces*)	2		10,000
Sub-total	10		82,000
Gregarii	10		20,000
Total	20		102,000
Average price per head (*sesterces*)		4,850	
Munera costing 150–200,000 sesterces+			
First class (<15,000 *sesterces*)	4	60,000	60,000
Second class (<12,000 *sesterces*)	4	48,000	48,000
Third class (<9,000 *sesterces*)	4	36,000	36,000
Fourth class (<7,000 *sesterces*)	4	28,000	28,000
Fifth class (<6,000 *sesterces*)	4	24,000	24,000
Sub-total	20	196,000	196,000
Gregarii	20	20,000	40,000
Total	40	216,000	236,000
Average price per head (*sesterces*)		5,650	

Table A Calculations of numbers of gladiators according to the *senatus consultum de pretiis glad. minuendis* (= CIL 2.6278)

	Number of gladiators[a]	Price	Price
First class (<15,000 *sesterces*)	6	90,000	90,000
Second class (<12,000 *sesterces*)	6	72,000	72,000
Third class (<9,000 *sesterces*)	6	54,000	54,000
Fourth class (<7,000 *sesterces*)	6	42,000	42,000
Fifth class (<6,000 *sesterces*)	6	36,000	36,000
Sub-total	30	294,000	294,000
Gregarii	30	30,000	60,000
Total	60	324,000	354,000
Average price per head (*sesterces*)		5,650	
First class (<15,000 *sesterces*)	8	120,000	120,000
Second class (<12,000 *sesterces*)	8	96,000	96,000
Third class (<9,000 *sesterces*)	8	72,000	72,000
Fourth class (<7,000 *sesterces*)	8	56,000	56,000
Fifth class (<6,000 *sesterces*)	8	48,000	48,000
Sub-total	40	392,000	392,000
Gregarii	40	40,000	80,000
Total	80	432,000	472,000
Average price per head (*sesterces*)		5,650	
First class (<15,000 *sesterces*)	10	150,000	150,000
Second class (<12,000 *sesterces*)	10	120,000	120,000
Third class (<9,000 *sesterces*)	10	90,000	90,000
Fourth class (<7,000 *sesterces*)	10	70,000	70,000
Fifth class (<6,000 *sesterces*)	10	60,000	60,000
Sub-total	50	490,000	490,000
Gregarii	50	50,000	100,000
Total	100	540,000	590,000
Average price per head (*sesterces*)		5,650	
First class (<15,000 *sesterces*)	12	180,000	180,000
Second class (<12,000 *sesterces*)	12	144,000	144,000
Third class (<9,000 *sesterces*)	12	108,000	108,000
Fourth class (<7,000 *sesterces*)	12	84,000	84,000
Fifth class (<6,000 *sesterces*)	12	72,000	72,000
Sub-total	60	588,000	588,000
Gregarii	60	60,000	120,000
Total	120	648,000	708,000
Average price per head (*sesterces*)		5,650	
Damnati ad bestias		600	
Trinquii		2,000	

[a] There was a limit of a maximum number of 60 pairs of gladiators on shows not given by the emperor(s) and not more than twice a year (Cassius Dio 54.2.4).

Notes

PREFACE

1 J.-Cl. Golvin, *L'amphithéâtre romain* (Paris 1988).

CHAPTER ONE   THE COLOSSEUM

1 A good short, recent survey may be found in A. Claridge et al., *Rome. An Oxford Archaeological Guide* (Oxford 1998), 276–81. Recent research into the architectural history of the Colosseum has largely focused upon the substructures of the arena. Among the most recent research papers are: R. Rea et al., 'Gli ipogei dell'Anfiteatro Flavio nell'analisi delle strutture murarie: L'impianto dell' éta flavia', *MNIR* 50 (1991), 169–235; H.-J. Beste, 'Relazione sulle indagini in corso nei sotteranei i cosidetti ipogei', *MDAI(R)* 105 (1998), 106–18; L.C. Lancaster, 'Reconstructing the restorations of the Colosseum after the fire of 217', *JRA* 11 (1998), 146–74. I thank Peter Connolly, who is undertaking research into this zone of the Colosseum for a doctoral thesis in progress, for bringing these references to my attention.

2 Bede, *Collectanea*, 1.iii: *quamdiu stabit coliseus, stabit et Roma; quando cadet coliseus, cadet et Roma; quando cadet Roma, cadet et mundus.*

3 Suetonius (*Divus Vespasianus*) informs us that, by this time, Vespasian had aroused the enmity of the emperor Nero and so his appointment here may have been one that prevailing 'political wisdom' states denotes those on the way up, or on the way out. Even if Vespasian succeeded in his post, his origins were not sufficiently high that he should have posed a serious threat to the emperor.

4 K. Welch, 'The Roman Arena in Late-Republican Italy: A New Interpretation', *JRA* 7 (1994), 59–80. Among the earliest examples of amphitheatres in Campania are specifically those communities that had particularly close ties with Rome, either as Roman veteran colonies, such as Pompeii, or as old Latin and maritime colonies, such as Liternum.

5 They may also have been used as sturdy anchor points for the ropes that secured and controlled the awning (or *velarium*). The awning protected spectators from the blazing sun and the rain. A group of marines, permanently stationed in Rome, manned the rigging and manoeuvred the awning of the Colosseum.

6 A. Boëthius, *Etruscan and Early Roman Architecture* (Harmondsworth 1978), 93–94, 151, 155–56.

7 F. Sear, *Roman Architecture* (London 1982), 19–28.

8 Golvin, Pl. XXXVII, 1.

9 Cf. *Martial Epigrammata* 5.8.

10 For a good recent treatment of the topic of reserved seating see J. Kolendo, 'La répartition des places aux spectacles et la stratification sociale dans l'Empire Romain', *Ktema* 6 (1981), 301–15.

   Senators were the most prestigious social class in the empire: a body of extremely wealthy politicians (a minimum property qualification of one million *sesterces* was mandatory) who entered the Senate for life either upon successful election to the quaestorship, a post of financial responsibility in the Treasury, or by personal selection of the emperor acting as censor.

11 *Equites*: the second most prestigious class, wealthy men (a minimum property qualification of 250,000 *sesterces* was mandatory), often businessmen, appointed to this honorific order by the emperor.

12 Perhaps under the term *pullati*, 'the darkened ones', i.e. those not entitled to wear the brilliantly white *toga* (one of the visible marks of honour of a Roman citizen) or those citizens too poor to afford this garment.

13 Suetonius, *Divus Augustus* 44.

14 The bays of the façade that corresponded to these stairways are as follows: Group Number 1: 5, 9, (19), (20), 30, 34; Group Number 2: 43, 47, (57), (58), 68, 72 (bracketed bays required a minor deviation to reach the innermost *ambulacrum*).

15 The exact identification of the bays is as follows: 1, 2, 4, *5, 8, *9, 12, 13, 15, 17, west entrance, 22, 24, 26, 27, *30, 31, *34, 35, 37, 38, south entrance, 39, 40, 42, *43, 46, *47, 50, 51, 53, 55, east entrance, 60, 62, 64, 65, *68, 69, *72, 73, 75, 76, north entrance (bays leading directly to stairways up to the podium are indicated by an asterisk).

16 Corresponding to the following bay numbers: north-west quadrant (3, 7, 11, 16); south-west quadrant (23, 28, 32, 36); south-east quadrant (41, 45, 49, 54); north-east quadrant (61, 66, 70, 74).

17 Originally this was probably a regular subvention to pay for the care and feeding of a cavalry mount, but later, an honorific position.

18 *Decoctores*, literally 'those who had been boiled down': J. Crook, *Law and Life of Rome* (Ithaca, NY 1967), 176 n. 189 referring to Cicero, *Philippicae* 2.44.

19 The measurements of vertical height are taken from Golvin, Planche LX (see Figure 1.8). The gallery lying between the first and second floors was +19.5m above ground level; the first floor was +12m and the second +24m above ground level.

20 Some +27.5m above ground level.

21 Some +27.5m above ground level.

22 Some +31.4m above ground level.

23 Some +37.2m above ground level.

24 This hypothesis is attributable to Sear, *op. cit.*, 138.

25 For example, Plautus, *Poenulus* 19; Ulpian, *Digesta* 3.2.4.1; Martial, Epigrammata 5.8.11–12 (by extension).

26 The precise dimensions of the podium are problematic due to the poorly preserved traces of it that remain. See M. Wilson Jones, 'Designing Amphitheatres', *MDAI(R)* 100 (1993), 418 and note 59.

27 This estimate does not take into account the area of the imperial box and the *editoris tribunal* opposite it. However, the amount of seating space within these boxes should have been similar to that for the senatorial order, but on a more regal scale. The *tribunalia* were approximately 12m wide (Golvin, 361: Tableau 45). Thus, if one subtracts the area of these *tribunalia* from that of the platform, one obtains seating capacities of approximately 220 (for a single row) and 440 (for a double row of *subsellia*).

28 If one assumes that only an average amount of space (0.4 m) was given to each individual, then some 3,500 individuals could have sat in this section. This assumption, however, is unlikely. These seats were by nature honorific and therefore, almost certainly, allocated the double portion of space appropriate to the *subsellium*. If one assumes that the *tribunalia* extended from front to back of the podium, then an adjustment to the area of the seating must be made. Such an adjustment results in figures of some 1,630 (for a double allocation per person) and some 3,270 spectators (for a single allocation).

29 Sear, *op. cit.*, 138.

30 These fourteen rows of seating would comprise the entire *ima cavea* of the theatre. Senators sat in the *orchestra* on *subsellia*. The Theatre of Marcellus in Rome may be used to calculate the approximate seating capacity of this part of the *cavea*. Allowing a double allocation of space per person (0.8 m) produces an estimate of about 3,380 spectators, while a single width allocation (0.4 m) produces about 6,760 onlookers.

31 *OCD*[3], s.v. 'Senate' by C.P. Burton, 1385–87.

32 Golvin, 400: Tableaux 62 and 63.

33 P. Garnsey and R. Saller, *The Roman empire. Economy, Society and Culture* (London 1987), 20–26.

34 Terence, *Hecyra*, prologue 33–42.

35 There is of course a problem with this interpretation. The various sectors of the seating are described as if they all existed at the same time. But, as has been pointed out, at least the podium and probably so too the *summum maenianum in ligneis* had been rebuilt at a later date. We know of lightning strikes damaging this structure and the highest point would surely have borne the full fury of such a catastrophe, perhaps setting the wooden seating ablaze. The precise chronology of the uppermost portions of the Colosseum is still debated. See, for example, the article by A. von Gerkan, 'Das Obergeschoss des flavischen Amphitheaters', *MDAI(R)* 40 (1925), 11–50.

36 The so-called *Loca in amphitheatro adsignata fratribus Arvalibus: ILS* 5049 = *CIL* 6.32363. See now J. Schied, *Les Fréres Arvales. Recrutement et origine sous les empereurs Julio-Claudiens* (Paris 1975).

37 The tiers of seating behind the platform on the podium had only seven rows of seats. Thus a reservation of eight tiers of seating is impossible in this sector.

38 Five *pedes* and five *digitus*. The *pes* was the Roman foot consisting of 16 *digitus*: 1 *pes* = 296 mm; 1 *digitus* = 18.5 mm. Thus the total distance on each seating tier was 1.5725 m.

39 The problem probably arises from parts of the text being recopied, but in the wrong position. Portions of four tiers of marble seats in the sixth *cuneus* of the second *maenianum* are mentioned as well as the amount of reserved space: 22 *pedes* and 8 *digitus* (= 6.66 m).

40 Throughout this book the following method for calculating seating capacity estimates will be used unless otherwise stated. A working average for the depth of an individual seating tread (*gradus*) is about 0.70 m, based on the evidence as preserved over a wide area and range of amphitheatres (Golvin, 380–81). A working average for the width of seating space allocated per seated spectator is about 0.4. Thus each spectator would occupy an area of roughly 0.28 m.[2] The space allotted to seating in the *cavea* was never 100 per cent. Stairways (*scalae*) and radial circulation aisles (*praecinctiones*) took up some of the space. I have assumed that about 90 per cent of the total surface area of the *cavea* would have been taken up with seating. Thus, dividing the surface area of the *cavea* devoted to seating (assumed to be 90 per cent of the total area) by the amount of space allotted per seated spectator (0.28 m²), gives a quick and consistent estimation of the seating capacity of any monument.

41 G. Jennison, *Animals for Show and Pleasure in Ancient Rome* (Manchester 1937), 158–61.

42 Gilbert Hallier, dactylography of his review notes of Golvin. There are difficulties associated with trying to pin down one particular method of design or layout for an amphitheatre; from my, admittedly limited, experience in attempting to do this, sometimes several alternative solutions appear equally appropriate and equally probable for a given architectural ground plan.

43 Suetonius, *Divus Claudius* 34. Obviously this did not happen in the Colosseum, which had not yet been built, but probably at the Saepta Iulia, none the less typical of the genre as a whole.

44 *Venationes* were performed in the mornings, when a combined gladiatorial and wild beast spectacle was planned. Thus the 'Morning School' was an appropriate name.

45 In 49 BC according to Cicero, in a letter he wrote to his friend Atticus: Cicero, *Epistulae ad Atticum* 3.14.

46 *CIL* 6.8583 = *ILS* 1578.

47 *ILS* 5160: *a veste gladiat(oria)*.

48 *ILS* 1762: *a veste venatoria*, a freedman.

49 *EAOR* 1.12–20: imperial freedmen.

50 *ILS* 1771: *adiutores proc(uratoris) rationis ornamentorum*.

51 *ILS* 5159: *p(rae)p(ositus) herbariorum*.

52 *EAOR* 1.10: *adiutor ad feras*

53 *EAOR* 1.11: *venatores immunes*.

54 By the Severan era (late second/early third century AD), this post was certainly paid at the rate of 200,000 *sesterces* a year (*procurator ducenarius*). *EAOR* 1, 127–29.

55 The *procurator Ludi Matutini* was initially paid at the annual rate of 60,000 *sesterces* (*sexagenarius*). At an unknown later date, but probably at the same time as the increase in the salary of the *procurator Ludi Magni*, this post was paid at the increased rate of 100,000 *sesterces* (*centenarius*). *EAOR* 1, 127–29.

56 That part of the inscription containing his name has been lost: *EAOR* 1.22.

57 *EAOR* 1.21. *procurator familiarum gladiatoriarum per Italiam*. This post was a *sexagenarius* (60,000 *sesterces* annually) procuratorship.

58 Examples of provincial equestrian procurators of *familiae gladiatoriae Augusti* include *Gallia Transpadana*: *ILS* 1412; *Galliae, Britannia, Hispaniae, Germania et Rhaetia*: *ILS* 1396; *Asia, Bithynia, Galatia, Cappadocia, Lycia, Pamphylia, Cilicia, Cyprus, Pontus, et Paphlagonia*: *ILS* 1396; *Alexandria ad Aegyptum*: *ILS* 1397.

59 Postulated by Einar Dyggve for the Salona amphitheatre; exceedingly complex and one wonders whether such complicated designs would have been actually used 'on the ground'.

60 M. Wilson Jones, 'Desigining Amphitheatres', *MDAI(R)* 100 (1993), 391–442, esp. 418–20 and Figure 22 (foldout).

61 The major and minor axes are extended from the two perpendicular sides of the original construction right triangle (see Figure 1.11). This triangle is then reflected in the major and minor axes so that four

identical, congruent (touching) triangles now occupy each of the four quadrants of the intersecting axes of the arena. By projecting the outer sides of these triangles, the four segmental arcs and their corresponding vertices are produced for the construction of the trace of the arena and *cavea*. Next a circle is inscribed, whose centre is the intersection of the major and minor axes, so that its circumference passes through both vertices lying on the major axis. Whereas many amphitheatres that follow this scheme would proceed to construct the trace of the arena and the outer façade of the *cavea* based upon the four-centred arc segments thus constructed, the Colosseum, perhaps to achieve a smoother trace on such a large monument, adopted a further refinement. Four additional arc segments based on four additional focal centres (located near the edge of the arena and on the sides of the original haunch segments) were added to the original four, thus making a total of eight focal points and segments of arc used in the construction of the trace of the arena and façade of the *cavea* (see Figure 1.12).

62 This effect was produced by interposing a stake between the focal point and the trace of the arena. See Wilson Jones, *op. cit.*, Figure 22d.

63 Thus the Pythagorean focal triangle now became 84:112:140 Roman ft. The radii of the haunch segments became 196 Roman ft. and the end segments, 56 Roman ft.

64 G. Hallier, 'La géométrie des amphithéâtres militaires sur les limes du Rhin et du Danube', in *Akten des 14. Internationalen Limeskongresses in Carnuntum* (Vienna 1990), 71–82.

65 The *summa cavea* itself had to wait until the upper parts of the façade were completed. In *The Colosseum: The Flavian Amphitheatre* (Rome 1971), G. Cozzo has pointed out the need for both external and internal scaffolding for the third level of arcades and the crowning storey of the Colosseum.

66 Sear, *op. cit.*, 1982, 140 citing Frontinus, *de aquis urbis Romae* 123, in which it is stated that repairs to aqueducts were only possible during the period 1 April and 1 November each year. An alternative interpretation of this passage might be that frozen water itself in the aqueducts might prevent repairs.

67 See above n. 2 for references. I thank Peter Connolly for discussions about this region of the arena and its complexities.

68 See among others, C. Moccheggiani Carpano and R. Luciano, 'I restauri dell'Anfiteatro Flavio', *RIA* 4 (1981), 9–69; R. Rea, 'Le antiche raffigurazioni dell'anfiteatro', in *Anfiteatro Flavio. Immagine, Testimonianze, Spettacoli* (Rome 1988), 23–46.

69 Moccheggiani Carpano and Luciano, *op. cit.*; Rea, *op. cit.*; F. Garello, *MNIR* 50 (1991), 173–95.

CHAPTER TWO THE ORIGINS AND EARLY DEVELOPMENT OF THE AMPHITHEATRE

1 G. Ville, *La gladiature en Occident des origines à la mort de Domitien* (BEFAR #245) (Rome 1981), 1–8.

2 Valerius Maximus 2.4.7.

3 Nicolaus of Damascus (a Greco-Syrian historian of the Augustan era) cited in Athenaeus 4.153f, credits the importation of such practices from the Etruscans. M. Grant, *Gladiators* (Harmondsworth 1971), 14–15.

4 Compare the scenes in Book Eleven of *The Odyssey* where Odysseus descends to the Underworld to consult the dead seer Teiresias and meets many other shades, including his own mother. He first sacrifices some sheep, carefully collecting their blood in a trough dug for this purpose. The shades must drink of this blood before they are able to remember and converse with Odysseus. There are similar scenes described in Book Six of Virgil's *Aeneid*: Aeneas descends into the Underworld, first having made sacrifice of black sheep and carrying the magical Golden Bough, the passport into the dark realm of the shades.

5 Polybius 7.53.

6 Cicero, *Pro Sestio* 133.

7 Ville, *op. cit.*, 81–84.

8 P. Sabbatini Tumolesi, *Gladiatorum paria. Annunci di spettacoli gladiatorii à Pompei* (Rome 1980), 147–49: Cicero, *Epistulae ad Atticum* VII.14.

9 Ville, *op. cit.*, 68–71. Caesar, during his curule aedileship in 65 BC, had already so honoured his dead father with 320 pairs of gladiators. *Ibid.*, 60: Pliny, *Historia Naturalis* 33.16.40, Dio Cassius 37.8.1, Plutarch, *Vitae Parallelae. Caesar* 6.5 and 10.3.

10 Pliny, *Historia Naturalis* 8.20–21.

11 Throughout this section extensive use has been made of the following: J.P.V.D. Balsdon, *Life and*

Leisure in Ancient Rome (London 1974), 302 ff.; G. Jennison, *Animals for Show and Pleasure in Ancient Rome* (Manchester 1937), *passim*; Ville, *op. cit.*, 51–56.

12 Ville, *op. cit.*, 53–56. Ville points out that these rituals continued quite distinct from the *venationes* in the amphitheatre and that they were never amalgamated into these spectacles.

13 Jennison, *op. cit.*, 28–41.

14 Pliny, *NH* 8.6.17.

15 Plautus, *Persa* 199. Cf. Ville, *op. cit.*, 52.

16 Livy 39.22.2. Cf. Ville, *op. cit.*, 52–53.

17 Although it is not specifically recorded where these animals came from it is perhaps most appropriate if they came from the region where Fulvius had triumphed, Greece and/or Asia Minor. Jennison, *op. cit.*, 23–24, but also 184.

18 Hippopotamus and crocodiles (58 BC) formed part of the games celebrating the dedication of Pompey's theatre: Pliny, *Historia Naturalis* 8.70f. The giraffe (46 BC), perhaps a present from Cleopatra, was part of Caesar's magnificent quadruple triumphal games in Rome: Pliny, *Historia Naturalis* 8.69.

19 Ville, *op. cit.*, 53–54.

20 Livy 44.18.8: the curule aediles were Scipio Nasica and Cornelius Lentulus.

21 Valerius Maximus 2.7.13; Livy, *Periochae* 51.

22 Valerius Maximus 2.7.14; Polybius 30.25.1; Livy 45.32.8–11 and 33.5.

23 Pliny, *Historia Naturalis* 8.16.53: during Scaevola's games – the probable reason for Pliny's noting this occurrence is that it was the first time that multiple hunts had occurred simultaneously.

24 Seneca *De brevitate vitae* 13.6: *ad conficiendos missis a rege Boccho jaculatoribus.*

25 Pliny, *Historia Naturalis* 36.15.116–20; see also the valuable discussions in Ville, *op. cit.*, 67–68 and Golvin, 30–32, particularly the clever reconstruction of the arrangement of the twin theatres/amphitheatre (see Figure 2.1).

26 Ville, *op. cit.*, 67–68.

27 Cicero, *Epistulae ad familiares* VIII.2.1.

28 See Robert Etienne, 'La naissance de l'amphithéâtre, le mot et la chose', *REL* 43 (1965), 213–20, for the early development of the nomenclature of the amphitheatre.

29 See K. Welch 'The Roman Arena in Late-Republican Italy: A New Interpretation', *JRA* 7 (1994), 59–80, where the tradition of holding gladiatorial spectacles in the *fora* of Rome is investigated in particular.

30 C.K. Williams II and Pamela Russell, 'Corinth: Excavations of 1980', *Hesperia* 50/1 (1981), 15–19. Williams does not think that this was the Greek agora of Corinth, merely the site of the later Roman forum. An apparently similar complex, consisting of a racecourse, shrines and a roughly circular area surrounded by a moat for athletics called the 'Platanistas', existed at Sparta when Pausanias visited it in the second century AD (Pausanias, *Periegesis Hellados* 3.14.6–15.2).

31 For example, the Classical hippodrome at Olympia, where the chariot and horse races were held, never had any evidence of seating, merely two long earthen banks parallel to and on either side of the race-track. L.D. Drees, *Olympia. Gods, Artists, and Athletes* (New York 1968), 96–100.

32 A. Boëthius, *Etruscan and Early Italian Architecture* (Harmondsworth 1978), Ch. 6, 'Hellenised Rome "Consuetudo Italica"', 136–215.

33 The amphitheatre at Cimiez (Cemenelum) has a *cavea* where a first century AD inner ring has been used as the basis of a larger, possibly early third century AD expansion of this structure. This pattern is fairly common. P.-M. Duval, 'Rapport préliminaire sur les fouilles de *Cemenelum* (Cimiez)', *Gallia* 4 (1946), 77–136; A. Grenier, *Manuel de archéologie gallo-romaine* (Paris 1958) vol. III, fasc. 2, 599–606; Golvin, #16, 78–79.

34 For example, beneath pavers of the piazza surrounding the monumental amphitheatre at Capua, the so-called Anfiteatro Campano, there are traces of an earlier structure with vaulted substructures (an earlier amphitheatre perhaps?) that was destroyed when the later amphitheatre was built (from field observation notes made on site in July 1978). The site of the earliest arena at Capua has not been identified. Such an important site for the training of gladiators in the late republic should have had such a monument.

35 *CIL* 10.852: *C(aius) Quinctius C(ai) f(ilius) Valgus M(arcus) Porcius M(arci) f(ilius) duovir(i) quinq-(uennales) coloniai honoris caussa spectacula de sua peq(unia) fac(iunda) coer(arunt) et colonieis locum in perpetuom deder(unt).* See also E. La Rocca, M. and A. de Vos, coordinamento di F. Coarelli, *Guida archeologica di Pompei* (Rome 1976), 248–55.

36 For P.A. Brunt, *Italian Manpower 225 BC–AD 14* (Oxford 1971), 305, the average size of these Sullan veteran colonies was no more than about 4,000; La Rocca et al., *op. cit.*, 37–38, estimate the size of the colony at 4,000–5,000 colonists; P. Zanker, *Pompeji. Stadtbilder als Spiegel von Gesellschaft und Herrschaftsform* (Mainz 1987), 18, gives a lower limit for the numbers in this colony at about 2,000.

37 P. Castrén, *Ordo Populusque Pompeianus. Polity and Society in Roman Pompeii* (Helsinki 1975), 88–90, points out the recent debate over the provenance of these wine amphorae. Some scholars think these amphorae are Campanian in origin, others that they originated in Tarraconensis (north-eastern Spain): *ibid.*, 89 n. 2.

38 *CIL* I².1722.

39 *ILLRP* 598, perhaps in 86 BC?

40 Castrén, *op. cit.*, 88–90: the municipal magistrates with censorial powers were called *censores*, before the Sullan colony; afterwards, they were known as *duoviri quinquennales*. During the early years of the colony, these officials were apparently not elected regularly, but on an *ad hoc* basis; it was not until the Augustan era that these magistrates were elected on a regular five-year cycle, independently from the general census. Castrén, *op. cit.*, 270–71, assigns the election of Valgus and Porcius to the year 70 BC.

41 The term *amphitheatrum* seems to have been first coined at a later date and was in common use only from the Augustan era. See Etienne, *op. cit.*, 213–20.

42 Welch, *op. cit.*, thinks that Sullan veteran colonies had foundation laws (*leges coloniae*) requiring such munificence.

43 *Venationes* often accompanied such gladiatorial spectacles. Sometimes public banquets (*epula*) and the random distribution of gifts (*sportula*) also took place as part of such a display. Other spectacles, such as chariot races, theatrical performances or athletic competitions, are also attested in fulfilment of the obligations on an incumbent politician to reward the electorate for voting him into office. F.F. Abbot and A.C. Johnson, *Municipal Administration in the Roman Empire* (New York 1926).

44 The terms *primum maenianum, secundum maenianum* and *summum maenianum* used to designate the terraces of seating in an amphitheatre (e.g., *CIL* 6.2059, 29 ff.) derive from the censor (348 BC) Caius Maenius, the conqueror of the Volsci at Antium, who for the first time in the latter half of the fourth century BC, erected such balconies on the upper floors of the *tabernae* around the Forum Romanum (Festus, ed. by W.M. Lindsay in *Glossaria Latina*, vol. 4 (1913), 134 b, 22; Pliny, *Historia Naturalis* 35.113; Vitruvius, *de architectura* 5.1.2; Boëthius, *op. cit.*, 133).

45 Vitruvius, *de architectura* 5.1.1–2.

46 The so-called *amphitheatrum minus*. Golvin #5, pp. 38: mid-first century BC construction date.

47 Golvin #1, p. 25 and Tableau 2, p. 44: late second-century BC construction date.

48 First phase of construction: Golvin #7, pp. 39–40 and Tableau 2, p. 44: first-century BC construction date.

49 Welch, *op. cit.*, 68: 'The earliest amphitheatres appear in Campania at a time when veteran colonisation had commenced there on an unprecedented scale, and this is probably no coincidence.'

50 A.N. Sherwin White, *The Roman Citizenship*, 2nd edn (Oxford 1973), 134–73, esp. 150–57. The newly enfranchised Oscans were probably assigned to the Voltinian voting tribe: Lily Ross Taylor, *The Voting Districts of the Roman Republic* (Rome 1960), 111–15.

51 Welch, *op. cit.*, 62–65.

52 Golvin #2, pp. 33–37.

53 Combining a double seat width allocation (80cm) for the podium and a normal single seat width allocation (40cm) for the *ima cavea*: see Table 2.1, seating estimate of 2,064 spectators. There seems to be no other hard evidence for this figure; most references deal with general considerations of the average size of a Roman legion, or similar approaches. The details of the seating within this zone were certainly substantially altered in the Augustan period. However, there is no evidence that the overall size and depth of the podium and *ima cavea* had been altered from its original state. Golvin, 35–36.

54 There are twelve sets of such stairways ('h' on Golvin's Plate XXIII,2) indicated on Golvin's plan of the upper parts of this amphitheatre. R. Graefe, *Vela erunt: die Zeltdächer der römischen Theater und ähnlicher Anlagen* (Mainz 1979), vol. I, 67–70, Abb. 82–83, II, Taf. 80, seems to be a more accurate and detailed survey of this part of the monument and provides a more reliable reconstruction.

55 References to these awnings use the standard phrase, '*vela erunt*'. P Sabbatini Tumolesi, *op. cit.*, 142–43. She points out that the *munera* of M. Tullius, datable to the Augustan era, did not include references to *vela*. See also Graefe, *op. cit.*, 1979, 19, 67–70 and Abb. 82–83, 186, who gives a date of the mid-first century AD for the addition of *vela* to the Pompeian amphitheatre. *Vela* were added

to the Large Theatre at Pompeii shortly before BC 3–2 as part of an addition to the upper auditorium: *ibid.*, 36–40.

56 Tacitus, *Annales* 14.17.

57 *Ibid.* 13.31.2.

58 Robert Etienne, *La vie quotidienne à Pompéi* (Paris 1966), 115–16.

59 M. Grant, *Cities of Vesuvius. Pompeii & Herculaneum* (Harmondsworth 1971), 74. However, the debate over this issue still continues.

60 Sabbatini Tumolesi, *op. cit.*, 24–26.

61 *Ibid.*, 45. A *munus* of Tiberius Claudius Verus, dated by the author to AD 61/62, when he was one of the two chief magistrates (*duoviri*), included both beast fights and athletics, but not gladiatorial combats.

62 Grant, *Cities of Vesuvius*, 26–28.

63 Tacitus, *Annales* 15.22.4; Seneca, *Quaestiones naturales* 6.2.

64 The arena-wall is represented with an imitation marble pattern on the fresco of the amphitheatre riot of AD 59 discussed above. See Figure 2.7.

65 Region V, insula 5, #3. During the period AD 54–62, the property may have belonged to the *lanista*, M. Mesonius: see Sabbatini Tumolesi, *op. cit.*, 69–74, 147–49.

66 La Rocca et al., *op. cit.*, 152–55.

67 Probably identifiable as one Pomponius Faustinus: Sabbatini Tumolesi, *op. cit.*, 74–75, 149; Castrén, *op. cit.*, 206.

68 Sabbatini Tumolesi, *op. cit.*, 149–50.

69 The presence of gladiators from both the *Iuliani* and the *Neroniani* in the same series of games given by M. Mesonius at Pompeii (= *CIL* 4.2508 = Sabbatini Tumolesi, no. 32) argues for much more than a simple renaming of an old institution.

70 Sabbatini Tumolesi, *op. cit.*, 147–49.

71 *CIL* 4.4418.

72 T. Wiedemann, *Emperors and Gladiators* (London 1992), 130–44; R. Lane Fox, *Pagans and Christians in the Mediterranean World from the Second Century AD to the Conversion of Constantine* (Harmondsworth 1986), *passim*, but esp. 663–81.

73 For the detailed inscription recording these regulations, the so-called *lex Ursonensis*, see *CIL* 1².593 = 2.5439 = *ILS* 6085.

74 Sabbatini Tumolesi, *op. cit.*, 137–38. Perhaps this decline in activity may partially reflect Nero's wider prohibition (AD 57) on the giving of games outside Rome and Italy (Tacitus, *Annales* 13.31) or may merely reflect a diversion of funding away from spectacles and towards rebuilding monuments damaged by the earthquake of AD 62.

75 Sabbatini Tumolesi, *op. cit.*, 155.

76 The definitive publication to date is that of Sabbatini Tumolesi, *op. cit.*

77 *Ibid.*, no. 32, pp. 69–74 (= *CIL* 4.2508). Provenance unknown; now in Museo Nazionale di Napoli.

78 Porta Ercolano, Tomb #17, West. = *CIL* 4.1182. See Sabbatini Tumolesi, *op. cit.*, 63–67 for this new interpretation. This monument belongs to the Claudio-Neronian period of Pompeii (roughly AD 43–62). Its frescoes have long since weathered away, but detailed drawings were made when it was uncovered by F. Mazois; see *ibid.*, Tav. III, 1 & 2.

79 Sabbatini Tumolesi, *op. cit.*, 32–44.

80 Pliny, *Historia Naturalis* 26.114–15.

81 K.M.D. Dunbabin, *The Mosaics of Roman North Africa. Studies in Iconography and Patronage* (Oxford 1978), 65–76.

82 Golvin, 44.

83 Welch, *op. cit.*, 59–80.

84 A.J.S. Spawforth, in *OCD*³ (1996), *s.v.* 'Corinth. Roman', 391. See Golvin #126, p 138. Katherine Welch has studied this monument and will be publishing her results in a forthcoming work. Another factor to be considered, when determining the date of this monument, is its potential role as the centre of transmission for the rare type of gladiator known as the *essedarius* (or British-chariot gladiator). These gladiators probably appeared for the first time at Rome during the Quadruple Triumphal games of Caesar in 46 BC. Yet by the Augustan era they are found on the island Thasos in the Aegean. Is it possible that from Rome they spread to the Caesarean colony at Corinth and from there to other eastern provinces? The role of Corinth in the early development and transmission of architectural ideas about the amphitheatre to the west, possibly via its former colony at Syracuse, deserves further

investigation, particularly the possible influences of the so-called 'Platform for Contact Sports' (see above pp. 37–39) on later monuments.

85 It is difficult to speak with certainty about the summit of the seating area (*cavea*) which usually suffers damage and degradation first and consequently is rarely well preserved in these monuments. However, on general principles, this statement is sound.

CHAPTER THREE IMPERIAL AMPHITHEATRES

1 Capua had been in decline since its public humiliation for having taken sides with Hannibal in the Second Punic War; its rehabilitation began under Vespasian and continued thereafter. Puteoli was the chief port of Rome from the Augustan era until the construction of the artificial harbours of Portus at Ostia in the delta of the Tiber under Claudius and Trajan. From this time the importance of Puteoli declined. R. Stillwell, W.L. McDonald and M.H. McAllister, eds, *The Princeton Encyclopedia of Classical Sites* (Princeton 1976), *s.v.* 'Capua' by A. de Franciscis, 195–96; *s.v.* 'Puteoli' by H. Comfort, 743–44.

2 Golvin #5, p. 38, and #153, pp. 180–84.

3 Golvin #1, p. 25 and #179, pp. 204–05; G. Pesce, *I relievi dell'Anfiteatro Campano* (Studi e Materiali del Museo dell'Impero Romano, N. 2) (Rome 1941).

4 Golvin #150, p. 169–71.

5 *OCD*[3], *s.v.* 'Verona' by T.W. Potter 1588, and *PECS*, *s.v.* 'Verona' by B. Forlati Tamaro, 968–69, both with additional bibliography.

6 Obviously intended as a pun on the traditional title for the Gallic homeland, 'Gallia Comata' ('Long-Haired Gaul'). *Bellum Gallicum* 8.50–52; Cicero, *Epistulae ad Atticum* 1.1.2.

7 The Veneti had traditionally been the allies of Rome in this region, living a peaceful existence as horse breeders and traders, particularly in Baltic amber.

8 A.N. Sherwin White, *The Roman Citizenship*, 2nd edn (Oxford 1973), 157–59.

9 J.B. Ward-Perkins, *Roman Imperial Architecture* (Harmondsworth 1981), 171–84.

10 Pliny, *Epistulae* 10.41 and 42. See also G.R. Watson, *The Roman Soldier* (London 1969), 143–46; R. Macmullen, 'Roman Imperial Building in the Province', *Harvard Studies in Classical Philology* 64 (1959), 214 ff.

11 A. Garzetti, *From Tiberius to the Antonines. A History of the Roman Empire AD 14–192* (London 1974), 126–27. Augustus first annexed these regions, but they had been administered as military zones under the command of a military governor (*praefectus*).

12 The others are Mediolanum, Patavium, Parma, Mutina, Placentia, Bononia, Luna, Lucca: see Golvin for references.

13 Ward-Perkins, *op. cit.*, 52–56, 63–65, e.g., the *Porta Maggiore*, and even the posthumous temple of the deified Claudius, completed by Vespasian after AD 70, a telling indication of the close association of this peculiar style of masonry with the emperor Claudius.

14 Suetonius, *Divus Claudius*, 41–42.

15 F. Coarelli and L. Franzoni, *L'arena di Verona* (Verona 1972), 34–37.

16 Golvin #150, p. 171.

17 This was unusual in that most surviving façades show an alteration from Tuscan to Ionic to Corinthian with height.

18 Golvin, 170, citing other Julio-Claudian parallels: the amphitheatres at Aosta (#132), Mérida (#77), Saintes (#100), and the theatres at Aosta, Mérida and the theatre of Marcellus, Rome.

19 Golvin, 170, n. 101, citing Vitruvius, *de architectura* 5.1.13.

20 Bays IV, XXXIV, XL and LXX.

21 *CIL* 5.3456: 'I/LOC(US) IIII/LIN(EA) I' = 'the 1st [?] *cuneus* or *maenianum* / the 4th tier of seats / seat number 1'. Golvin, 171; Coarelli and Franzoni, *op. cit.*, 49 f.

22 R. Graefe, *op. cit.*, 83 and Tafel 98.

23 When covered over, a person could not stand upright inside it. Golvin, 171.

24 Golvin, 171, mistakenly says that this aqueduct entered the arena from the west.

25 Golvin, 171, mistakenly says that the basin slopes gently from west to east; in fact, it slopes from north to south, where the main evacuation drainage channel lay.

26 These drains are built in the same manner (river-cobble concrete with brick levelling courses) as the interior walls of the amphitheatre. The ring-drains do not reach the northern main channel of the aqueduct, all three networks stopping short before it. The drainage pattern is from north to south.

27 K.M. Coleman, 'Launching into History: Aquatic Displays in the Early Empire', *JRS* 83 (1993), 48–74, esp. 58–60.

28 Golvin #77, p. 109–10, esp. n. 174 – dedicatory inscription of the second half of the year 8 BC. Golvin assigns this basin (not shown on the architectural plan, Plate XXX) to the initial phase of construction of the arena. It was later superseded by a more sophisticated, deeper series of substructures (actually depicted on Golvin's plan, Plate XXX) designed for supplying the arena from galleries beneath it. Golvin dates the change to the beginning of the second century AD. Professor Coleman, doubtless because of the confusion in Golvin, has mistaken the later for the earlier basin: see her Figure 3, p. 58.

29 M. Wilson Jones, 'Designing Amphitheatres', *MDAI(R)* 100 (1993), 391–442, esp. 410–12.

30 First a base line, which will become the major axis of the arena, is marked out. On this base line, two points, A and A', are placed such that the distance separating them is the same as the desired width of the arena (see Figure 3.3, A). Then using a compass, arcs are inscribed from each point, such that they pass through the other. The intersection points of these arcs, B and B', now determine the vertices of two equilateral (equal-sided) triangles, ABA' and AB'A', one above and the other below the base line (see Figure 3.3, B). Now points B and B' are connected and this line extended to form the minor axis of the arena. Point B is connected to points A and A' and these two lines extended; this is repeated with point B' and points A and A'. Now all four circular segments that will form the oval outline of the arena and *cavea* are determined, with their centres at A, A', B and B' (see Figure 3.3, C).

Having established that the width of the arena (w) should be the same as the distance between the original two points on the base line (A and A'), a circle is inscribed whose centre is the intersection of the major and minor axes of the arena such that its circumference passes through both A and A'. Where this circle intersects the minor axis are points C and C' (see Figure 3.3, C). Now, with one end of the compass fixed upon B, the other leg is extended such that the length of the arc passes through point C', inscribing an arc of this length inside angle ABA'. This process is repeated using point B' as the vertex of an arc through point A and inside angle AB'A'. Using centres, A and A', the length of the compass arc is set to such a length that the oval trace of the arena connects up smoothly.

Now having decided upon the width of the *cavea* (here at Verona, one half the length of the major axis of the arena), the outer trace of the façade of the monument can be laid out in a manner exactly similar to that above for the arena.

31 Wilson Jones, *op. cit.*, 412 and Table 3.

32 In fact, each bay measures 20¼ Roman ft. As Wilson Jones (*ibid.*) explains, the calculations involved in determining the precise circumference of an oval-shaped figure are extremely complicated and often, as here, lead to errors in estimation.

33 *CIL* 5.3408 = *ILS* 5551. Found in Verona. . . . *nis f. Po[b.] / Lucil(ius) Iustinus / equo publico, / honorib(us) omnib(us) / municip(ii?) functus; / [id]em in porticu, quae / [d]ucit at ludum public(um), [c]olumn(as) IIII cum superfic(io) / [e]t stratura pictura / [v]olente populo dedit.*

34 The reference to Verona as a *municipium*, probably not earlier than *c.* 49 BC, as well as the use of the term 'equo publico', revived by Augustus, having fallen into disuse from about the Sullan era, provide the critical dating criteria here. *OCD* ³, *s.v.*, 'equites. Imperial period' by F.G.B. Marsh, updated by G.P. Burton, 551–52.

35 Tacitus *Historiae* 2.11 ff., esp. 2.23.

36 Golvin #153, p. 180–84.

37 The construction date of the second amphitheatre at Capua is disputed. It is possible that it too may have already had two monumental amphitheatres by the Flavian era.

38 F. Coarelli, *Guida archeologica di Roma*, 3rd edn (Rome 1980), 166; Golvin, 52–53, 55–56.

39 See the list of Campanian amphitheatres in Golvin: Minturnae (pp. 251–52, Tiberian), Venafrum (#87, p. 119, Augustan?) and Sinuessa (p. 251, Augustan), all near the border with Campania; Liternum (p. 25, late second century BC), Cumae (p. 25, late second century BC), Puteoli's small amphitheatre (#5, p. 38, mid-first century BC), Teanum and Cales (#4, p. 38, Sullan era), Capua's earlier amphitheatre (p. 24, late second century BC), Pompeii (#2, pp. 33–37, *c.* 70 BC), Nola (p. 252, unexcavated, perhaps pre-Augustan phase), Nuceria Constantia (#84, pp. 116–17, Phase I: *c.* AD 60–65; Phase II: Trajanic), Abella (#3, p. 37, Sullan era), Telesia (#6, p. 38, mid-first century BC).

40 From the little that remains of the Augustan amphitheatre at Puteoli, there do not seem to have been special subterranean facilities provided to stage *venationes*.

41 Pliny, *Historia Naturalis* 8.20–21.

42 T. Wiedemann, 'This Terrible Place. The Amphitheatre and its Spectacles', unpublished public lecture in the British Museum One Day Lecture Series, October 1998.

43 The Claudian artificial harbour at Ostia was not completely successful. Tactius reports great loss to merchant shipping (some 200 ships) in it during a violent storm in AD 62 (*Annales* 15.18.3). It was not until the construction of the Trajanic hexagonal artificial harbour at Portus that Puteoli began to decline in favour of this new facility. *PECS, s.v.* 'Portus' by R. Meiggs, 731.

44 A. Maiuri, *Studi e ricerche sull'anfiteatro flavio Puteolano* (Naples 1955), 85–89, Figures 32–36: *[C]olonia [Fl]avia A[ug(usta)] / [P]uteola[na] pe[cu]n[ia sua]* (= Figure 36) the best-preserved of these inscriptions. The others, however, corroborate the *lacunae* as restored.

45 E.g., the gift of the amphitheatre at Alba Fucens by the commandant of the Praetorian Guard in Rome, Quintus Naevius Cordus Sutorius Macro, a local who had risen high in the service of the emperor Tiberius: *AE* (1957), #250 (*c.* AD 40); F. de Visscher, 'L'amphithéâtre d'Alba Fucens et son fondateur Q. Naevius Macro, préfet du prétoire de Tibère', *Rendiconti della reale accademia dei Lincei* 12 (1957), 39–49.

46 Golvin, 181.

47 For a fuller discussion of these corporation chapels, see below, pp. 77f.

48 Vespasian rewarded Puteoli's loyalty during the troubled times of AD 69. When he eventually came out on top, he granted it the status of a titular Roman colony and expanded its previously small territory (*c.* 10km^2 of coastline) by the inclusion of a substantial part of the agricultural hinterland, the *ager Campanus*, of Capua, which had taken the side of Vitellius during the civil wars. *PECS, s.v.*, 'Puteoli' by H. Comfort. See also M. Frederiksen, *Campania*, posthumously edited by N. Purcell (Rome 1984).

Leglay (*Bulletin de la Société Nationale des Antiquaires de France* [1977] inscription #4, pp. 106–109) attempts to link the dedicatory inscription of Lucius Cassius Cerealis, an important local citizen of Puteoli, in which an amphitheatre is mentioned possibly in connection with a *gladiatorium munus* dedicated to Nero by Cerealis (this part of the inscription is subject to interpretation), with this amphitheatre. Golvin convincingly refutes this attempt and correctly connects the inscription with the earlier amphitheatre at Puteoli: Golvin 153, pp. 180–84.

49 Wilson Jones, *op. cit.*, 391–442.

50 Cornice blocks and socles containing square holes (*c.* 30cm on a side) through which the masts that secured the awning (*vela*) passed. Graefe, *op. cit.*, 78–81.

51 Maiuri, *op. cit.*, 42–54.

52 To Maiuri the plan of this chapel resembled that of a monumental fountain (or *nymphaeum*): a series of three rectangles, interconnecting and progressively diminishing in width to draw one's attention to focus upon a central apse (1.72m wide) in the rear wall, where the cult statue would have stood. Maiuri, *op. cit.*; see the plans: Figure 5 on p. 25 and Figure 21 on p. 55.

53 Golvin, 337–40, citing numerous examples of *Nemesea*.

54 Those directly behind bays I, VI, LXIV and LXIX: see Maiuri, *op. cit.*, Figure on pp. 12–13, with numbering of the arcades of the façade.

55 Those directly behind bays X, LIX and LX: see Maiuri, *op. cit.*, Figure on pp. 12–13, with numbering of the arcades of the façade.

56 Arcade I corresponding to arcade LXIX, arcade VI to LXIV, arcade X to LX; only arcade LIX does not seem to have had a corresponding element in arcade XI. Nevertheless there does appear to be a strong organising principle at work here.

57 Arcades I, VI, LXIX and LXIV: see Maiuri, *op. cit.*, Figure on pp. 12–13, with numbering of the arcades of the façade.

58 Arcades X, LIX and perhaps LX: see *ibid.*

59 Beneath arcade I: Maiuri, *op. cit.*, Figure 13 on p. 42.

60 *G(aius) / Stonicius / Trophimianus* and *pa(v)imentum / sua pequnia / marmorabit*: Maiuri, *op. cit.*, 45, assigned a date, based on palaeographical comparisons, of the second century AD.

61 *CIL* 10.8059: found near Capua, this inscription mentions a Trophimianus and also Diane Tifitane (*sic*).

62 Built beneath arcade LXIX: see Maiuri, *op. cit.*, Figure on pp. 12–13, with numbering of the arcades of the façade.

63 Beneath arcade LXIV: see *ibid.*

64 Beneath arcade VI: see *ibid.*

65 Beneath arcade X: see *ibid.*

66 Maiuri, *op. cit.*, 46–47: *Pulbe / ri Amo / ri Sca / billari / orum*. Assigned date, the end of the second century AD based on the palaeographic criterion of the cursive nature of the letters. Maiuri notes the

similarity of this dedication to similar ones from Pompeii (*CIL* 4.5395) where the term *amor populi* ('the heart throb of the people') is used for popular and much-loved theatrical performers, the mimes (*mimi*) and their leaders (*archimimi*).

67 W. Burkert, *Greek Religion. Archaic and Classical*, Engl. transl. by J. Raffan (Blackwell 1985), 161–67.

68 M. Fulford, *The Silchester Amphitheatre. Excavations of 1979–85* (London 1989), 37 and Figure 20.

69 Maiuri, *op. cit.*, 35–40, Figures 8–11.

70 Maiuri, *op. cit.*, 30–35; see now also Coleman, *op. cit.*, 48–74, esp. 58–60.

71 Maiuri, *op. cit.*, 40–42: beneath the sloping vaulting of arcades III, XI, XXIII, XXXVII, XLVII and LIX.

72 Beneath arcades XXXIII and LXVIII: see Maiuri, *op. cit.*, Figure on pp. 12–13, with numbering of the arcades of the façade.

73 Beneath arcades LXIV and LXIX: see *ibid.*

74 Maiuri, *op. cit.*, 63–65.

75 *Ibid.*, 65–72. This date rests partly upon the extensive use of high quality brickwork (*opus testaceum*) in this region of the amphitheatre and partly upon the construction history of the Colosseum in Rome, better documented historically, where this zone is attested to the Domitianic era.

76 Two factors make this hypothesis probable: first, the arena is designed to accommodate chiefly beast fights (*venationes*), and second, Diana was the patron goddess of beast fighters.

77 See the excellent study by K.M. Coleman, 'Fatal Charades: Roman Executions Staged as Mythological Enactments', *JRS* 80 (1990), 44–73.

78 G. Jennison, *op. cit.*, 158–61.

79 *ILS* 1937: *Anniae / Agrippinae / uxori / C. Iuli Apolloni / decur. Romae / trib(unorum) item aedil(ium), / accens. velató, / cur(atoris) mun(eris) glad(iatorii) / tridui, hered. / l. d. d. d.*

80 F. Millar, *The Emperor in the Roman World* (Ithaca, NY 1977), 66–69. The exact significance of the term *accensus velatus* is still debated and may indeed be something of a catch-all phrase heavily redolent of antiquarian significance.

81 Apollonius obviously did not hold office at Puteoli, nor is there evidence of his being a priest in the imperial cult. Therefore, a one-off series of spectacles in honour of the emperor, perhaps in a time of crisis, seems the obvious occasion for such an exhibition.

82 M. Gavius Puteolanus (*ILS* 6333 = *CIL* 10.1785) found at Naples: *Gaviae M. f. / Fabiae Rufinae / honestissim. matron. et ra/rissim. femin., M. Aur. . . . proc. / summar. rat. uxori, M. Gavi Pute/olani IIvir., aed., cur. muner. gla/diatori quadriduo et omnibus / honorib. et munerib. perfunc. / filiae, M. Gavi Fabi Iusti s[p]lendi/diss. eq. R., augur., IIvir. II, q. II, / cur. muner. glad. et om[nibus hono]rib. et munerib. perfunc[ti sorori], res publica peq. sua oblat . . .*

83 The close linkage in the text of the inscription between the gladiatorial games with Puteolanus's 'fully discharging all honours and obligations for his daughter' leads one to believe that he wished there to be an association in the mind of the reader between these two concepts, perhaps reminiscent of the funeral gladiatorial games given by Julius Caesar for his daughter Julia.

84 L. Aurelius Aug(usti) libertus, Pylades (*ILS* 5186): *L. Aurelio Aug. lib. Pyladi / pantomimo temporis sui primo, / hieronicae coronato IIII, patrono / parasitorum Apollinis, sacerdoti / synhodi, honorato Puteolis d.d. ornamentis decurionalib. / duumviralib., auguri ob amorem / erga patriam et eximiam libera/litatem in edendo muner. gladi/atorum venatione passiva* [*OLD* = 'random, indiscriminate'] *ex in/dulgentia sacratissimi princip. / <Commodi Pii Felicis Aug.>* [Commodus' name erased and later restored], *centuria Cornelia.* For more information about this Pylades (there was more than one pantomime who bore this famous name), see *KlPauly*, Band 4, 1248, *s.v.* 'Pylades n.4'.

85 *OCD*[3], *s.v.* 'Pantomime' by A.J.S. Spawforth, 1107; J.P.V.D. Balsdon, *Life and Leisure in Ancient Rome* (London 1974), 274–76.

86 Only the lower portico survives today, but it is logical to assume that the upper also needed such treatment.

87 Maiuri, *op. cit.*, 16–20.

88 See *ibid.*, 21, Figure 4.

89 Wilson Jones, *op. cit.*, 414–16 and Figure 20.

90 However, whereas the Verona amphitheatre uses a focal-triangle of 72, 125 and 144 Roman ft., here at Puteoli, the next larger size focal-triangle composed of simple whole number ratios is found, namely 75, 130 and 150 Roman ft. And, whereas at Verona it was necessary to expand the radii of the circular segments to obtain a *cavea* façade that would accommodate seventy-two bays whose width was a simple

whole number (20 Roman ft.), here the radii were perhaps shortened so that its façade arcades achieved the same net result.

Wilson Jones scrupulously avoids forcing an interpretation of ambiguous evidence here. There are two possibilities, neither of which can now be ascertained with certainty. Either the radii of the segment circles were shortened as described in the text, or else the dimensions as originally calculated were found to produce the same result. Remember that the perimeter of an oval is a very complicated trigonometric calculation, and that the estimate of ½ (L + W) x pi = circumference, is not a precise calculation. *Ibid.*, 414.

91 Golvin #179, pp. 204–05, Plates XL and XLI.

92 Outer *ambulacra*: 4.05 and 3.75m wide; middle *ambulacrum*: 3.60m; inner *ambulacrum*: 3.56m Source: Golvin, 204–05.

93 Much of the reconstruction of this monument is based upon its striking similarities to the Colosseum in those parts that have survived.

94 All labels refer to Figure 3.7: outer ring-corridor ('C'), doubled vaulted bays with hoists; inner linear corridor ('B'); single vaulted bays with hoists; central bay ('A'); single vaulted bay with hoists; inner linear corridor ('B'); doubled vaulted bays with hoists; outer ring-corridor ('C').

95 All labels refer to Figure 3.7: outer ring-corridor ('C'); hoisting bay; (lateral corridor + hoisting bay) × 4; central bay ('A'); (hoisting bay with lateral corridor) x 4; hoisting bay; outer ring-corridor ('C').

96 Pesce, *op. cit.*

97 A. de Franciscis, *Bolletino d'Arte* serie 4, 35 (1950), 153–55.

98 Since very little now remains of the façade, this reconstruction is hypothetical. It is based upon the following evidence. The protomes exhibit three distinct scales: roughly 100, 71 and 58cm in height. The two busts *in situ* on the lowest arcade are of the 1m scale. Thus, it has been argued that the 71cm. protomes occupied the middle arcade and the 58cm protomes the upper arcade of the façade.

99 Pesce, *op. cit.*, n. 1.

100 *Ibid.*, n. 2.

101 *Ibid.*, n. 3.

102 *Ibid.*, n. 5.

103 *Ibid.*, n. 8.

104 *Ibid.*, n. 9.

105 *Ibid.*, n. 16.

106 *Ibid.*, n. 6.

107 *Ibid.*, n. 7.

108 *Ibid.*, n. 10.

109 *Ibid.*, n. 11.

110 *Ibid.*, n. 14.

111 *Ibid.*, n. 15.

112 *Ibid.*, n. 4.

113 *Ibid.*, n. 12 and 13.

114 *Ibid.*, 15.

115 *Ibid.*, 15. He cites the semilunate moulding on the Jupiter (n. 5) and Mercury (n. 9) as being similar to the Hadrianic reliefs on the Monument of the Haterii, Rome; also the manner of the representation of the mantle as thrown over the right shoulder.

116 *Ibid.*, 16, citing numerous Etruscan examples of sculptural adornment of keystones of arches with heads or torsoes, e.g., an arch at Volterra, the 'Arch of Augustus', Perugia, and the 'Porte di Giove e di Bove', Falerii. In addition, he cites related architectural phenomena: the decoration of seven arches of one of the *plutei* of the Rostra in the *Forum Romanum* with griffins'-head protomes; the decoration of the Doric-Corinthian temple at Paestum; and female heads on Corinthian capitals and Doric metopes. Pesce suggests an Etruscan origin for these too.

117 So-called no doubt from the similarity to permanent breastworks or parapets on walls, also called *plutei*.

118 *Ibid.*, n. 21, Tav. XV, *c*. The two pieces of the relief as depicted are incorrectly joined: the upper one should be several centimetres to the left. The description given is of the rectified joining.

119 This relief bears close thematic resemblance to one from the tomb of the Haterii, *via Labicana*, Rome, where a treadwheel crane is being used in the construction of the family mausoleum. D. Strong, *Roman Art* (Harmondsworth 1980), 137–40, Figure 76: late first century AD. This relief is far more detailed than the corresponding Capuan one.

120 The column bases are moulded, the shafts are unfluted, the capitals reveal only the rudiments of foliage and the architrave consists of a moulded cornice. Between the columns of the portico, in very shallow relief, is carved a pilaster with a 'modinata' base, from which springs an impost block and the beginnings of an arch.
121 Pesce, *op. cit.*, n. 22, Tav. XIV, b.
122 Graefe, *op. cit.*, 82–83.
123 Pesce, *op. cit.*, n. 17, p. 18 and Tav. XIV, a.
124 E.g., the well-known *alimenta* scene from the Trajanic Arch at Beneventum, depicting the emperor bestowing his beneficence, food relief for the poor citizens (*alimenta*), upon several cities, here represented by their turret-crowned Tyches. Strong, *op. cit.*, n. 58, Figure 93.
125 Pesce, *op. cit.*, n. 25, pp. 22–24 and Tav. XI–XII.
126 Vitruvius, *de architectura* 1.7.1: *Herculi, in quibus civitatibus non sunt gymnasia neque amphitheatra, ad circum.*
127 Pesce, *op. cit.*, n. 31 (Tav. XX, a), n. 32 (Tav. XX, b), n. 33 (Tav. XXII, b), and perhaps also n. 34 and 35.
128 *Ibid.*, n. 29, Tav. XVIII, b.
129 *Ibid.*, n. 30, Tav. XXIII, a.
130 *Ibid.*, n. 39 and 40, Tav. XXI, a and b. Another fragment represents the fully-clad Diana as huntress: *ibid.*, n. 41, Tav. XVI, b.
131 *Ibid.*, n. 43, Tav. XVIII, a.
132 Of the latter half of the third century BC: R.R.R. Smith, *Hellenistic Sculpture* (Thames & Hudson 1991), 106 and Figure 135.
133 See the excellent study in Coleman, 'Fatal Charades', 44–73.
134 Pesce, *op. cit.*, n. 42, Tav. XIII.
135 Coleman, 'Fatal Charades', 44–73.
136 Pesce, *op. cit.*, n. 37, Tav. XXII, a.
137 *Ibid.*, n. 38, Tav. XXII, c.
138 *Ibid.*, n. 46, Tav. XXIV, a: Paris is identified by his Phrygian cap.
139 *Ibid.*, n. 36, Tav. XXIII, a: identification from other more complete representations of this mythical scene, particularly on sarcophagi, cf. p. 26 n. 38.
140 *Ibid.*, n. 44, Tav. XVII, b: a Maenad in Archaising style; n. 45, Tav. XIX, a: a dancing Maenad, or perhaps one of the *archigalli*, or eunuch priests, of the Phrygian goddess Cybele.
141 *Ibid.*, n. 23, Tav. XV, b. Three possible interpretations present themselves: Mars, an oriental deity assimilated to Mars, or perhaps an example of emperor worship.
142 *Ibid.*, n. 24, Tav. XV, a.
143 *Ibid.*, n. 47, Tav. XIX, b; Pesce suggests this may have been a triad of deities originally, but without speculating on the third deity's identity.
144 *Ibid.*, n. 18, Tav. XVI, f; n. 19, Tav. XVI, d; n. 20, Tav. XVI, a.
145 *Ibid.*, n. 26, Tav. XVII, c.
146 *OCD*³, *s.v.* 'Phlyakes' by W.G. Arnott, 1172.
147 E.g., at Verona: see Coarelli and Franzoni, *op. cit.*, 34–37.
148 Pesce, *op. cit.*, n. 62.
149 *Ibid.*, n. 56; less probably the European elk (*Alces alces*).
150 *Ibid.*, n. 60.
151 *Ibid.*, n. 55.
152 A. Garzetti, *op. cit.*, 426 n. 11, for the renascent prosperity of Capua under Hadrian and the decline of Puteoli.
153 We know of an imperial breeding and training complex for elephants at Laurentum, south of Rome, probably from the time of Julius Caesar, run by an official of the imperial civil service, *procurator ad elephantos: ILS* 1578. G. Ville *La gladiature en Occident des origines à la mort de Domitien, BEFAR* No. 245 (Rome 1981), 351. The fields about the largely abandoned village of Ardea are also reported to have been used for grazing this herd: *OCD*³, *s.v.* 'Ardea' by T.W. Potter, 151.
154 See Dunbabin, *op. cit.*, 65–87.
155 Jennison, *op. cit.*, 76–77.
156 *Ibid.*, e.g. in the male bust (n. 12), Diana (n. 15) and Minerva (n. 16).
157 Esp. the male bust (n. 8), which is so reminiscent of the 'Antinous Silvanus' type of the Hadrianic era.
158 J. Elsner, *Imperial Rome and Christian Triumph*, Oxford History of Art (Oxford 1998), 28–35.

159 E.g., the Niobid Sarcophagus, Museo Laterano, Rome, of the last years of Hadrian's reign.

160 Pesce, *op. cit.*, 11 and n. 25. The statues are now in the Museo Nazionale, Naples.

161 An alternative reconstruction postulates some form of the word *propilaeum* in this lacuna, i.e., one or more monumental entranceways and columns as the additional elements contributed by Hadrian and completed by Antoninus Pius. G. Rucca, *Capua Vetere* (Naples 1828), 143.

162 *[colonia Iu]LIA FELIX AUG[usta Capua] / FECIT / [divus Had]RIANUS AUG. [restituit / imagines e]T COLUMNAS AD[di(dit) curavit / Imp(erator) Caes(ar) T. Ael]IUS HADRIANU[s Antoninus / Aug(ustus)] PIUS DEDICAVI[t].*

163 *CIL* 10.3832 = *ILS* 6309: *[colonia Iu]LIA FELIX AUG[usta Capua] / FECIT / [divus Had]RIANUS AUG. [restituit / e]T COLUMNAS AD[iecit. / Imp(erator) Caes(ar) T. Ael]IUS HADRIANU[s Antoninus / Aug(ustus)] PIUS DEDICAVI[t].* The underlined portion is the only emendation of Mazocchi's text.

164 J. Beloch, *Campanien* (Breslavia 1890), 352. Pesce, *op. cit.*, 10 n. 23.

165 Pesce, *op. cit.*, 6–11 n. 38.

166 The archaeological criteria on which this dating is based are the construction technique of brickwork (*opus latericium*) consistent with a date in the first half of the second century AD, and the method of laying down a thick raft (*platea*) of concrete to act as the foundations for the structure, which recalls Hadrianic construction methods in, e.g., the Temple of Venus at Rome and the Pantheon, Rome. W.L. MacDonald, *The Architecture of the Roman Empire. Vol. I. An Introductory Study*, Yale Publications in the History of Art 17 rev. edn (New Haven 1982), 94–96, 111–18, 154.

167 See, above, the discussion of the various reconstructions of the lacunae of the dedicatory inscription for this monument. Also Pesce, *op. cit.*, 10.

168 Pesce, *op. cit.*, 9.

169 Wilson Jones, *op. cit.*, 416 and Figure 21.

170 In detail this scheme involves the construction of a Pythagorean triangle (whose sides are in the ratio 3:4:5) (see Figure 1.11). Then the major and minor axes are projected from the sides of the triangle that form the right angle. This triangle is then reflected in the major and minor axes so that four identical, congruent (touching) triangles now occupy each of the four quadrants of the intersecting axes of the arena. By projecting the outer sides of these triangles, the four segmental arcs and their corresponding vertices are produced for the construction of the trace of the arena and *cavea*. Next a circle is inscribed whose centre is the intersection of the major and minor axes, so that its circumference passes through both vertices lying on the major axis. Where this circle intersects the minor axis, we have the ends of the minor axis of the arena. To establish the trace of the arena, the compass is set on one of the two vertices on the minor axis and an arc inscribed within the segment such that its length passes through the edge of the arena on the minor axis. This is repeated using the opposite vertex on the minor axis. Now the compass is placed on one of the vertices on the major axis and the smooth trace of the arena's curve completed by adjusting the length of the arc. This is repeated using the other vertex on the major axis. Next the edge of the façade of the *cavea* on the minor axis is determined by marking off the appropriate distance with a compass (here at Capua, equal to the width of the arena) on both sides of the arena on the minor axis. Then, having determined the position of the façade of the *cavea*, the trace is filled in as for the arena.

171 Golvin #1, p. 25.

172 Golvin, #154 and #155, pp. 184–90.

173 *PECS*, s.v. 'Arelate' by P. Amy, 87–88 and 'Nemausus' by P. Gros, 616–17.

174 *OCD*[3], *s.v.* 'Nemausus' by J.F. Drinkwater, 1033; P. Gros, *op. cit.*

175 See Golvin, 75–97 with numerous examples.

176 G. Lugli, 'La datazione degli anfiteatri di Arles e di Nîmes in Provenza', *Rivista dell'Istituto nazionale di archeologia e storia dell'arte*, NS 13–14 (1964–65), 179.

177 J.-Cl. Bessac et al., 'Recherches sur les fondations de l'amphithéâtre de Nîmes (Gard – France)', *RANarb* 17 (1984), 221–37.

178 The series began at the south and continued clockwise to the east. Numbers V, VII, X and XVI still survive. Golvin, 189–90.

179 Wilson Jones, *op. cit.*, 407 and 412–14: the piers at Nîmes are fairly precise at 8 ft. x 5 ft. each, whereas those at Arles vary from this standard by as much as 4 per cent or more (1 part in 24 or 25).

180 The origins of this architectural style may perhaps be traced to the entablatures of the porticoes of the *Forum Transitorium* in Rome, built by Domitian and completed under Nerva. See R. Etienne, 'La date de l'amphithéâtre de Nîmes', *Mélange Piganiol*, 2 (1966), 985–1010.

181 P. Amy et al., *L'Arc d'Orange, Gallia* Suppl. XV (Paris 1962).

182 Reconstructions of the seating arrangements in detail are problematical due to the partial destruction of the *cavea*. For example, Formigé reconstructs the *cavea* as follows: podium (four tiers), *ima cavea* (seven), *media cavea* (eleven), *summea cavea* (twelve). J. Formigé, 'L'amphithéâtre d'Arles', *RA* (1964:2), 128–32.

183 *CIL* 12.697: C. IUNIUS PRISCUS IIV[IR. IUR. DIC.] QUINQ(ennalis) CAND(idatus) ARE-LAT(ensium) ITEM FLA[MEN OB HONOREM QUINQUENNALITATIS? P]O[DIU]M[[S]] CUM [IA]NUIS / – ET SI[GNA DUO? NEPT[UNI A]RGENT[EA – R]EI [PUB]LICE POL-LICIT(us) HS CC(milibus) D[E SUO ADIECTIS? –] F[ACIENDA CU]RAVIT – / – [IN MUN]ERUM [ET VENATI]ON[U]M [E]DI[TIONEM?] – P(ondo?) V LUMIN(a) X [ORD]INE(es) XXXIIII [F]ORENS[IB(us) – IIIIVIR(is) AUG(ustalibus) N[AVICULAR(iis?) SECUNDUM DISCIPLI]NAM MORES[QUE] DEDIT.

Attempts at reconstruction have been made in O. Hirschfeld, 'Sacerdozi dei municipii nell' Africa', *AdI* 38 (1866), 71–82, and Formigé, 37–45, *op. cit.* (1965:1), as well as Lugli, *op. cit.*, n. 177, 166–69. P. Somella, *Rivista dell'Instituto archeologico. Napoli* (1964–65), 198–99, has demonstrated that these slabs are definitely not contemporaneous with the original phase of construction of the podium wall. They were added later. Hirschfeld, *op. cit.*, assigns a date of the beginning of the second century AD to this inscription.

184 Not 'Crispus' as in Golvin, 187, where also the citation is in error as '*CIL* 12.714'.

185 *Oxford Latin Dictionary* (1982), *s.v.* 'sevir', 1750. See also *OCD*³, *s.v.* '*Augustales*' by J.B. Rives, 215.

186 *CIL* 12.3316–3318.

187 *CIL* 12.3316 (= *ILS* 5656): N(autis) ATR. ET OVIDIS LOCA N(umero) XXV D(ata) D(ecreto) D(ecurionum) N(emausensium), N(autis) RHOD(anici) ET [A]RAR(ici) XL D(ata) D(ecreto) D(ecurionum) N(emausensium).

188 *CIL* 12.727: *familia gladiatoria* of the second century AD.

189 *AE* (1946), 162. *Not FA* (1946), 162 [= Golvin, 187, n. 288].

190 Funerary inscriptions of the first century AD: Ville, *op. cit.*, 284: a *Iulianus* and a *Neronianus*.

191 *CIL* 12.3325 (= *ILS* 5101): MUR(millo) / COLUMBUS / SERENIANUS (pugnarum)XXV / NAT(ione) AEDU(u)S / HIC ADQUIESCIT. / SPERATA CONIUNX.

192 *CIL* 12.3324 (= *ILS* 5096): MUNER(e) (C(ai) POMP(ei) MART(ialis) / ESSE(darius) LIB(eratus) / FAUSTUS. [signum = 'coronarum'] XXXVII / N(atione) ARABUS. / EUCHE CONTUBERN(alis) DE SUO.

193 *CIL* 12.3323 (= *ILS* 5095): BERYLLUS ESSE(darius) LIB(eratus) XX [= vicesima pugna], NAT(ione) GRAECUS, ANN(is) XXV, NOMAS CONIUNX VIR(o) B(ene) MER(enti).

194 *CIL* 12.3327 (= *ILS* 5120): RET(iarius) / L(ucius) POMPEIUS /)(coronarum) VIIII, N(atione) VIANNES / SIS, AN(nis) XXV. / OPTATA CONIUNX / D(e) S(uo) D(edit). It is not possible to say how many contests he fought altogether, since the number of times he was unsuccessful but spared (*stans missus*) is not recorded.

195 *CIL* 12.3332 (= *ILS* 5087): T(h)R(aeci), / Q(uinto) VETTIO GRACI/LI COR(onarum) TRIUM, / ANNORUM XXV, / NATIONE HISPAN(o), / DONAVIT L(ucius) SESTIUS / LATINUS / D(octor).

196 Care must be exercised here since a great part of the substructures of the arena of Arles has not survived, being made of wood. Hence a clear picture is not readily attainable. However, by analogy with the subterranean galleries at Nîmes which are better preserved and have been excavated, it seems that this statement is generally valid.

197 For a detailed bibliography for these terms, see D.L. Bomgardner, 'The Carthage Amphitheatre: A Reappraisal', *AJA* 93 (1989), 85–103, esp. 89 and n. 22.

198 Each arm of the cross was roughly 6m wide and 36m long. They were excavated in 1866 by Revoil: H. Revoil, *Rapport sur les fouilles de l'amphithéâtre de Nîmes* (Paris 1866), 163 ff. See also F. Mazauric, 'Les souterrains de l'amphithéâtre de Nîmes', *MémAcadNîmes* 33 (1910), 1–35. I have not been able to consult these works.

199 *CIL* 12.3315: T. CRISPIUS REBURRUS FECIT.

200 See Golvin, 184 for details of those who proposed an early chronology: Esperandieu, Jaquemin and Constans.

201 A. Grenier, *Manuel d'archéologie gallo-romaine. Vol. III. L'Architecture. Fasc. 2: Ludi et circenses, théâtres, amphithéâtres, cirques* (Paris 1958), 639.

202 Lugli, *op. cit.*, 145–93.

203 Etienne, *op. cit.*, 985–1010.

204 Golvin #154–55, 184–90.

205 J.-Cl. Bessac et al., *op. cit.*, 221–37.

206 Wilson Jones, *op. cit.*, esp. 434–35.

207 Wilson Jones, *op. cit.*, 407: the piers at Nîmes are 8ft. x 5ft. with applied pilaster 3ft. x 2ft.; at Arles some piers are ⅟₂₄ or ⅟₂₅ larger in all these dimensions.

208 Golvin #162, pp. 192–93, poorly known and dated rather haphazardly to either the Flavian era or the second century AD.

209 Wilson Jones, *op. cit.*, 412–14, Figure 19.

210 *Ibid.*, 434–35.

211 Formigé, *op. cit.* (1964:2), 37–41: AD 410 besieged by Gerontius, AD 425 by Theoderic I, AD 452 by Attila the Hun, AD 462, AD 477 by Euric III, AD 508 by Clovis.

212 Cassiodorus, *Variae* 3.44: *pro reparatione itaque murorum Arelatensium vel turrium vetustarum certam pecuniae direximus quantitatem.*

213 Formigé, *op. cit.*, 38.

214 *Ibid.*: AD 533, AD 566 Sigebert, *c.* AD 576 the Lombards, AD 585 the Visigoths.

215 Chronique de Moissac (*Dom Martin Bouquet*, I, p. 655 D): [*Karolus*] *Nemauso vero arenam civitatis illius atque portas cremari iussit.*

216 Formigé, *op. cit.*, 38–39.

CHAPTER FOUR THE NORTH AFRICAN AMPHITHEATRES

1 General surveys include J.-Cl. Golvin, *L'amphithéâtre romain* (Paris 1988), *passim* and under reference numbers given for each entry; H. Slim, 'Recherches préliminaires sur les amphithéâtres romains de Tunisie' in H. Slim, ed., *L'Africa romana* (Sassari 1984), 129–59; J.-Cl. Lachaux, *Théâtres et Amphithéâtres d'Afrique Proconsulaire* (Aix-en-Provence 1979).

2 Unfortunately the amphitheatre at Lepcis Magna, which is perhaps the best preserved and finest in North Africa, could not be studied in detail or photographed and remains largely unpublished. I am grateful to the Libyan Department of Antiquities for permission to visit this monument briefly.

    The information which I present concerning the El Jem amphitheatre is from previously published accounts. I was unable to obtain permission to study this monument. The definitive report on this monument still awaits publication.

    I am grateful to the I.N.A.A., Tunis, and to its director at the time of my investigations, Dr A. Beschaouch, and also to M. A. Ennabli, Conservateur du Site de Carthage, for their generous assistance and permission to undertake the study of the amphitheatres of Tunisia.

3 G. Rickman, *The Corn Supply of Ancient Rome* (Oxford 1980), 108–12, 231–35; S. Raven, *Rome in Africa*, 2nd edn (London 1984), 84–105.

4 Demarcated in 202 BC by Scipio Africanus's famous *fossa regia* stretching from Thabraca on the northeast Tunisian coast to the Gulf of Gabès in the south-east. Raven, *op. cit.*, 53.

5 A. Lézine, *Utique* (Tunis 1970), 66, on the evidence from aerial photographs.

6 Chiefly the veterans of Caesar's Campanian ally Sittius and his soldiers in and around Cirta (Constantine) on the western edge of the new province – a strategic buffer between it and the Mauretanian client-kingdom to the west. Appian, *Bellum Civile* 4.54.

7 Primarily Julius Caesar's Latin colonies: Carthage (Plutarch, *Vitae Parallelae. Caesar*, 57; Dio Cassius 43.50); Thysdrus (= El Jem: T.R.S. Broughton, *The Romanization of Africa Proconsularis* [Baltimore 1929], 54 f., Ch. 6; however, L. Teutsch, *Das römische Städtewesen in Nordafrika* [Berlin 1962], 85, argues for an Augustan veteran colony); Hippo Diarrhytus (Bizerte: *CIL* 8.1026 – *col. Iulia Hippo Diarrhytus*); and a series of settlements in the region of Cap Bon: e.g., Curubis (*CIL* 8.980 – *col. Iulia Curubis*), Clupea, Neapolis, Carpis. See Marcel Benabou, *La résistance africaine à la romanisation* (Paris 1976), 40–42.

8 Benabou, *op. cit.*, 43–57.

9 The Julian colony was supplemented by an Octavian colony in 29 BC: *ibid.*, 52 n. 24.

10 Golvin #95, pp. 122–23; D. L. Bomgardner, 'An Analytical Study of North African Amphitheatres', unpublished PhD dissertation, University of Michigan, Ann Arbor, 1985, Interdepartmental Programme in Classical Art and Archaeology, 252–57: however, a date later, but before the end of the first century AD cannot be ruled out.

11 Maxula: Pliny, *Historia Naturalis* 5.24; Uthina: settled by veterans of the *legio XIII* (*CIL* 8.2427;

Teutsch, *op. cit.*, 167); Thuburbo Minus: settled by veterans of the *legio VIII* (Benabou, *op. cit.*, 53 n. 30).

12 Benabou, *op. cit.*, 50–55.

13 *Ibid.*, 55–57.

14 Bomgardner, *op. cit.*, 1985, 379–84; Golvin #81, pp. 112–14.

15 Benabou, *op. cit.*, 85–96.

16 G. di Vita-Ervard, *Libya Antiqua* (1965), 29–38: the dedicatory inscription.

17 Bomgardner, *op. cit.*, 412–15; Golvin #30, pp. 85–86; R. Lequément, *Fouilles dans l'amphithéâtre de Tébessa (1965–1968)*, BAA Suppl. No. 2 (Algiers 1979).

18 Bomgardner, *op. cit.*, 304–09; Golvin #113, p. 132. See N. Duval and F. Baratte, *Les ruines de Sufetula* (Tunis 1973) for proposed origins of the city from a Flavian military camp.

19 L. Foucher, *Découvertes archéologiques à Thysdrus en 1961* (Tunis 1962), 63; L. Foucher, *La maison de la procession dionysiaque à El Jem* (Paris 1963), 101 f.; L. Foucher, *Hadrumetum* (Tunis/Paris 1964), 314 n. 1299. Golvin #25, p. 84, thinks it is slightly later, the beginning of the second century AD.

20 Benabou, *op. cit.*, 101–11, 114.

21 *Ibid.*, 113–16.

22 Ronald Syme, *Révue des Etudes Anciennes* 38 (1936), 182–84.

23 L. Leschi, *Libyca* 1 (1953), 197; *CIL* 8.18042, the earliest dated inscription found within the camp.

24 Benabou, *op. cit.*, 115–20.

25 A. Garzetti, *From Tiberius to the Antonines. A History of the Roman Empire AD 14–192* (London 1974), 395–96.

26 See the well-known rescript from Commodus concerning the *lex Hadriana: CIL* 8.10570, 14464; Benabou, *op. cit.*, 162–64.

27 Benabou, *op. cit.*, 131–34.

28 P. Leveau, 'Recherches historiques sur un région montagneuse de Maurétanie Césarienne: des Tigava Castra à la mer', *MEFRA* 89 (1977), 257–311, esp. 288–90; Golvin #46, p. 90.

29 Bomgardner, *op. cit.*, 274.

30 Benabou, *op. cit.*, 161–64.

31 Bomgardner, *op. cit.*, 404; L. Leschi, *Libyca* 2 (1954), 185–86; *AE* (1955),137 found in the west entrance to the arena.

32 Benabou, *op. cit.*, 169–71.

33 *Ibid.*, 171–75.

34 Bomgardner, *op. cit.*, 379–84; Golvin #81, pp. 112–14.

35 Benabou, *op. cit.*, 175–83.

36 Bomgardner, *op. cit.*, 317–19; Golvin #116, p. 133.

37 Bomgardner, *op. cit.*, 348–49; J. Kolendo, *Archeologia* (1973), 76.

38 Bomgardner, *op. cit.*, 281–83. Date by analogy with close resemblance in use of materials and building techniques with the Great Baths here, dated by its dedicatory inscription to AD 199: G.-C.Picard, *CRAI* (1974), 14.

39 Bomgardner, *op. cit.*, 376–78; Golvin #76, p. 97.

40 H. Musurillo, *The Acts of the Christian Martyrs* (Oxford 1972), xxii–xxiii, 86–89: text, bibliography and short commentary.

41 R. Lane Fox, *Pagans and Christians in the Mediterranean World from the Second Century AD to the Conversion of Constantine* (Harmondsworth 1986), 427.

42 *Scriptores Historiae Augustae, Severus*, 17.1; Eusebius, *Historia Ecclesiae* 6.2.2.

43 M. Besnier, *L'empire romain de l'avènement des Sévères au concile de Nicée* (Paris 1937), 45–52.

44 *BAC* (1949), 678–80.

45 W.H.C. Frend, *The Donatist Church: A Movement of Protest in Roman North Africa*, rev. edn (Oxford 1985); see also P. Brown, *Augustine of Hippo* (Berkeley 1967).

46 C.R. Whittaker, *Herodian, Vols I and II*, (LCL edn (Cambridge 1970), II, 221 n. 1.

47 Besnier, *op. cit.*, 142–46.

48 *PECS*, s.v. 'Thysdrus' by H. Slim, 919–20.

49 *Ibid.*

50 Pellissier, *RA* 1 (1844), 816 f.; A. Lézine, 'Notes sur l'amphithéâtre de Thysdrus', *CahTunisie* 31 (1960), 29–50; J. Kolendo, *Archéologia* 24 (1973), 74–80; Golvin #186, pp. 209–12.

51 L. Foucher, *s.v.* 'Thysdrus' in *Enciclopedia dell' arte antica*, vol. VII (1966), 845–47.

52 Golvin #187, pp. 212–13.

53 The probable location of their martyrdom was the, as yet undiscovered, military amphitheatre that adjoined the camp of the urban cohort(s) stationed permanently at Carthage. The problem of the location of this camp has occupied scholars since the end of the nineteenth century. Gauckler thought that he had discovered the remains of this camp on the hill of Bordj Djedid, overlooking the Antonine Baths from its lofty coastal site (P. Gauckler, *CRAI* [1904], 695–703). However, he never published his excavations in detail.

The most recent re-examination of this issue, an article co-authored by three scholars, N. Duval, S. Lancel and Y. Le Bohac, *BAC* 15–16 (1979–80), 33–89, has reached divided conclusions. Le Bohac, an expert on the Roman army, has established that two urban cohorts were stationed permanently at Carthage until the second century AD, after which time one and perhaps two remained on station. He argues for the traditional location of the camp(s) on Bordj Djedid, but also adds that the camp itself may have been more similar in form to a *villa urbana*, such as the headquarters of the night watch (*vigiles*) uncovered at Ostia, than to that of either a legionary or an auxiliary fort. Duval argues that the location may have been either on Bordj Djedid or Sayda (to the north) and stresses that the problem is still very much in play, awaiting more convincing proof before a secure attribution for the location of this camp can be made.

The martyrdom of Perpetua and Felicitas was recorded in antiquity in graphic detail in the *Passio Sanctarum Perpetuae et Felicitatis* to be found in Musurillo, *op. cit.*, 117–23.

54 Text: R. Dozy and M.J. de Goeje, eds. and trans., *Déscription de l'Afrique et de l'Espagne par Edrisi. Texte arabe publié pour la première fois d'après les manuscrits de Paris et d'Oxford avec une traduction, des notes et un glossaire* (Leiden 1866), 131–32 (112–13 in the Arabic manuscript).

55 The northern route was blocked by the Greeks, who were competing for the same resources, but using the Tin Trade Route that ran down the Rhône valley from the tin mines of Cornwall and Brittany.

56 Granted this honorific title for his conquest of Hannibal at Zama.

57 An abortive attempt was made under the Gracchi (123 BC) to settle landless Italian peasants here, the *colonia Iunonia*. Under unclear circumstances, however, the colony failed.

58 Pomponius, *De Chronographia* 1.34: *iam quidem iterum opulentia*. See *KlPauly* 4 (1979), 1039–40, *s.v.* 'Pomponius' B,5 (F. Lassèrre), for the date of composition during the reign of Claudius.

59 *CIL* 8.24586 and 14.2243.

60 Rickman, *op. cit.*, 108–112.

61 *OCD³*, *s.v.* 'Carthage' by R.J.A. Wilson, 295–96 with bibliography; *PECS*, *s.v.* 'Carthage' by A. Ennabli, 201–02.

62 Dozy and de Goeje, *op. cit.*, 131–32 (112–13 in the Arabic manuscript). No major textual problems occur in this passage. The very literal English translation and brief commentary given were kindly supplied by Mrs Helen W. Brown, Heberden Coin Room, Ashmolean Museum, Oxford.

63 This is the Arabic word 'shibr' or 'shabr' meaning 'a span', usually considered the equivalent of 9 to 9½ inches, but it is not an exact measurement in modern terms.

64 These figures assume that al-Idrisi's width for the spans is measured from one column centre to the next. Also, an average value of 9¼ inches was used in the conversion of 'spans' into feet and thence into metres. Thus each pier width would reach *c.* 1.06m and the span of each arch would be *c.* 5.99m.

65 Specialist in Roman construction technique and its dating, Trinity College, Dublin. Personal communication.

66 K. Welch, 'The Roman Arena in Late Republican Italy: A New Interpretation', *JRA* 7 (1994), 59–80.

67 A. Lézine, *Architecture romaine d'Afrique* (Paris 1961), 60–64. This statement must be treated with some caution and further research in this area may alter, or further refine it.

68 *Ibid.*, characterises this construction technique as typical of the first century AD at Carthage. During the second century, mortar was introduced and anathyrosis was abandoned.

69 Golvin, 122, underscores the speculative nature of this reconstruction owing to the poor state of preservation of these areas of the monument.

70 *Ibid.*, Golvin gives the width of this *ambulacrum* as 2.85m; my own measurements, made on site in 1977, were 3.25m.

71 Al-Bakri, *Description de l'Afrique septentrionale*, trans. de Slane (Alger 1911–13; reprint edn: Paris 1965), 105f.

72 I interpret al-Idrisi's statement that the upper storeys were unadorned to mean that the sculpted bosses were absent, not the usual applied orders of half-columns. Al-Bakri's account of the façade is in accord with this assumption.

73 Lézine, *op. cit.*, 60–64. Lézine assigns the Kedel limestone façade to the early third century AD on the

basis of the building materials used and the construction technique employed, which he identifies as close to those employed in the construction of the Odeon, traditionally dated to AD 207 (*ibid.*, 56 n.1). Recently this dating has been called into question: T.D. Barnes, *Tertullian*, 2nd edn (Oxford 1985).

74 Recorded fragments include Diana, Hercules and the Victories.

75 Père Delattre, 'Fouilles dans l'amphithéâtre de Carthage (1896–1897)', *Mémoires de la Société Nationale des Antiquaires de France* 57 (1898), 135–87.

76 *AE* (1910), #78 = *ILS* 9406 = *ILAfr* 390 = *ILTun* 1050. See M. Silvia Bassignano, *Il flaminato nelle provincie romane dell'Africa* (Rome 1974), 118 n. 23, for the dating of this inscription.

77 *AE* (1928), #4.

78 *CRAI* (1903), 106; A. Audollent, *Defixionum tabellae* (Paris 1904), 334 ff., #246–54: *venatores* = #247–51; *gladiatores* = #252, #254.

79 *Ibid.*: *apri* = #250,b; *leones* = #250,b; *tauri* = #247, #250,b; *ursi* = #247, #250,b, #253. Tablet #253 can be dated palaeographically to the second century AD; similarly tablet #250 may date to the third century.

80 Père Delattre, *op. cit.*, 136 ff.; Diana: Père Delattre, *Musée Lavigerie de Saint-Louis de Carthage*, 3 vols. (Paris 1899), II, 16, Plate III.6; Bacchus: *ibid.*, II, 22, Plate V.1.

81 *Ibid.*, II, 50 f., Plate XIII.1–2; cf. Pliny, *Historia Naturalis* 7.125; Vitruvius, *De architectura* 10.8. For the representation of a hydraulic organ in the arena on the Zliten 'Gladiator Mosaic', see Dunbabin, *op. cit.*, Appendix I Plate XX. 46, 49: of probable Flavian date.

82 Delattre, 'Fouilles dans l'amphithéâtre', 139.

83 *Ibid.*, 167 f., #90. See M. Leglay, *Saturne Africain. Histoire* (Paris 1966), 387 f., for the dedications of *plantae pedis* in the ritual of the cult of Saturn in Africa, e.g., the pair found in the Temple of Saturn at Thugga: L. Carton, *Nouvelles Archives des Missions scientifiques* 7 (1897), 367 ff.; see also A. García y Bellido, *Colonia Aelia Augusta Italica* (Madrid 1960) 28, Figure 18, another example found *in situ* in the Italica amphitheatre dedicated to *Caelestis Pia Augusta* by C. S . . . *lius Africanus et filii*; on the basis of the cognomen and the cult, this man should be a North African, perhaps even a citizen of Carthage. Unfortunately, no date has been suggested for this inscription.

84 Delattre, 'Fouilles dans l'amphithéâtre', 167, #89.

85 Audollent, *op. cit.*, 334 ff.: Mercury = #246,a; Typhon-Seth = #246,b; demon = #248,a. See also the photographs of two such tablets published by Delattre, *Musée Lavigerie*, II, 87 ff., Plates XXI–XXII.

86 J. Martin, *Musée Lavigerie de Saint-Louis de Carthage, Suppl. II* (Paris 1915), 35.

87 Delattre, 'Fouilles dans l'amphithéâtre', 139, among the few types specifically listed: Otacilla, wife of Philip the Arab (AD 244–49), Maximinus (235–38), Maximian (286–308), Maxentius (307–12), Constantius II (337–61).

88 Delattre, *Musée Lavigerie*, II, 16: the total preserved height of the Diana is 0.95m; *ibid.*, II, 22: the Bacchus measures 1.17m high. Compare the miniature figure of the goddess Ephesian Diana found near a small *sacellum* in the *cavea* of the amphitheatre at Lepcis Magna (preserved height = 0.11m): *Libya Antiqua* 1 (1964), Plate LXVIII,a. See K.M.D. Dunbabin, *The Mosaics of Roman North Africa* (Oxford 1978), Figure 53, for the association of Bacchus with *venationes* on the Smirat 'Magerius' mosaic.

89 J. Deininger, *Die Provinziallandtage der römischen Kaiserzeit* (Berlin 1965), 133f.; D. Fishwick, *Hermes* 92 (1964), 342–63; R.P. Duncan-Jones, 'The Chronology of the Priesthood of Africa Proconsularis under the Principate', *Epigraphische Studien* 5 (1968), 151–58. There is a consensus that the imperial cult was established in Africa Proconsularis between AD 70 and 72, early in the reign of Vespasian.

90 A. Beschaouch has pioneered the identification and elaboration of these professional guilds, his so-called *sodalitates venatorum*, through the study of the inscriptions and figured polychrome mosaic pavements of Tunisia. See, for example, his article 'Nouvelles recherches sur les sodalités de l'Afrique romaine', *CRAI* (1977) 486–503. For the Telegenii, specifically, see Dunbabin, *op. cit.*, 67 n. 14.

91 Dunabin, *op. cit.* 67–69; Catalogue No. Smirat 1, p. 268: the well-known 'Magerius' mosaic from Smirat.

92 Beschaouch, *op. cit.*, 486–503.

93 It was typical Roman practice that successful candidates in municipal elections showed their gratitude by making a large payment (*summa honoraria*) to the community, often to pay for *munera legitima* (gladiatorial games and *venationes*) for their fellow citizens; indeed in some communities it was mandatory to do so. A similar procedure operated upon election to the high priesthood of the provincial council. R. Duncan-Jones, *The Economy of the Roman Empire*, 2nd edn (Cambridge 1982).

Individual cities within the province provided annual contributions to the provincial assembly, perhaps sometimes topped up by funding from the emperor. Thus the entire expense would be met from a combination of private and public funding. F. Millar, *The Emperor in the Roman World* (Ithaca 1977), 375–94.

94 *Ibid.*

95 O. Hirschfeld, 'I sacerdozi dei municipii nell'Africa', *AdI* 38 (1866), 69–77; Duncan-Jones, 'The Chronology of the Priesthood', 151–58, where the inception of the *sacerdos provinciae Africae* is established as the beginning of Vespasian's reign, AD 70–72; Augustine, *Epistulae* 138.19 (Goldbacher, edn [1904]); Bassignano, *op. cit.*, 109–22.

96 Millar, *op. cit*, 389 n. 22.

97 Dunbabin, *op. cit.*, Carthage #3a of the later third century AD; provenance – a private house near the amphitheatre.

98 Probably *mel(ius) quaestura*, citing Dunbabin, *op. cit.*, 72, a favourable comparison between this series of games and the official *munera* given by the quaestors as part of their duties at Carthage.

99 For the problems concerning the actual venue for this execution, probably a military amphitheatre associated with the camp(s) of the urban cohort(s) permanently stationed here, see above n. 53.

100 The standard test for someone accused of being a Christian was to be brought before the local magistrates or provincial governor and to be asked to offer a sacrifice of incense to the genius of the emperor. Failure to do so would result in conviction.

101 Lane Fox, *op. cit.*, 435 ff.

102 *Digesta*, 50.2.3.3. See also Besnier, *op. cit.*, 45–46.

103 *Ibid.*, 51.

104 *Ibid.*, 49–50, on the evidence of Tertullian, *Apologeticum*.

105 Musurillo, *op. cit.*, xxv–xxvii, 116–31 for text and commentary.

106 G.-C. Picard, 'Les *sacerdotes* de Saturne et les sacrifices humains dans l'Afrique romaine', *Société archéologique de la province de Constantine. Receuil des notices et memoires* 66 (1948), 117–23; Leglay, *Saturne Africain. Histoire*, 313–19.

107 Musurillo, *op. cit.*: *Passio SS. P et F.*, §19.3 *etiam super pulpitum ab urso vexati sunt*; §19.5: *itaque cum apro subministraretur, venator qui illum* [*sc. Saturus*] *aprum subligaverat, subfossus ab eadem bestia post dies muneris obiit*; §19.6: *et cum ad ursum substrictus esset in ponte, ursus de cavea prodire noluit*; §20.2: *dispolitae et reticulis indutae producebantur*. Cf. the bear and bull which have been tethered together on the Zliten 'Gladiator Mosaic'; see also Seneca, *De ira* 3.43.2; G. Jennison, *op. cit.*, 60–83, 168–69, who emphasises the practical difficulties in training animals to perform in the arena. Such restraints were often necessary in spite of, or in place of, this training.

108 L. Robert, 'Une vision de Perpétue martyre à Carthage', *CRAI* (1982), 228–76, see esp. 237–46.

109 These arguments were first developed and presented in my article, D.L. Bomgardner, 'The Carthage Amphitheater. A Reappraisal', *American Journal of Archaeology* 93 (1989), 85–103.

110 Père Delattre, *L'amphithéâtre de Carthage et le pèlèrinage de Sainte Perpétue* (Lyons 1913), 15; field notes made on site in June 1977.

111 Lézine, *Architecture romaine*, 60–64.

112 Field notes of 25 July 1977.

113 Lézine, *Architecture romaine, passim*.

114 *Ibid.*, 60–64. See also n. 73 above.

115 *CIL* 8.12513; R. Cagnat, *RA* 10:2 (1887), 171–79; Bomgardner, 'The Carthage Amphitheater', 96 n. 47. This very fragmentary inscription can be assigned a date after AD 145.

116 Lézine, *Architecture romaine*, 60–64.

117 *AE* (1910) no. 78 = *ILAfr* 390 = *ILTun* 9046; Bassignano, *op. cit.*, 111, no. 13, 114, no. 8 and 117–18, 188 nos. 23–24; R. Gruendel, *Klio* 46 (1965), 351–54.

118 P. Delattre, 'Fouilles dans l'amphithéâtre', 135–87, esp. 162–63, no. 82 = *CIL* 8.24551.

119 I. Calabi Limentani, *Epigrafia latina*, 3rd edn (Milan 1974), 263–68, 275–80. Although it is possible that this numeral may refer to the amount of money spent on the construction of the monument, such usage appears relatively infrequently. See Duncan-Jones, *Economy of the Roman Empire*, 75 and inscriptions # 65, 472, 477. I thank Dr joyce Reynolds for valuable discussion of this material.

120 Calabi Limentani, *op. cit.*, 482–83.

121 Golvin #95, pp. 122–23.

122 The possibility that this inscription might actually refer to the *amphitheatrum castrense* or military

camp amphitheatre remains slight. Municipal *munera* commemorated by an inscription are much more likely to have taken place within the known civic amphitheatre's context.

123 *Scriptores Historiae Augustae. Antoninus Pius* 9; Aurelius Victor, *De Caesaribus* 13: *multae urbes reposi-tae ornataeque, atque imprimis Poenorum Carthago quam ignis foede consumpserat*, should indicate a more widespread conflagration by fire, which necessitated the extensive repairs referred to by Aurelius Victor through the generosity of M. Aurelius.

124 Delattre, 'Fouilles dans l'amphithéâtre', 142–52, #1–35, 159–62, #74–81. Colosseum *comparanda*: S.B. Platner and T. Ashby, *A Topographical Dictionary of Ancient Rome* (Rome 1929), *s.v.* 'Amphitheatrum flavium', esp. 9; see also A. Chastagnol, *Le Sénat romain sous le règne d'Odoacre* (Bonn 1966), Chs. 1–2; J. Kolendo, 'La répartition des places aux spectacles et la stratification sociale dans l'Empire Romain. A propos des inscriptions sur les gradins des amphithéâtres et théâtres', *Ktema* 6 (1981), 310–15, esp. 310.

125 *CIL* 8.12527.

126 M. Rosenblum, *Luxorius. A Latin Poet among the Vandals* (New York 1961): *venatores*: epigrams 48, 49, 67, 68; a 'podium-jumper': epigram 87; bears: epigrams 48, 49; trained hunting leopards: epigram 74. Martial's *Epigrams* is the obvious source of much of Luxorius's imitation.

127 It was not possible for me to undertake any investigations at El Jem. All materials come from previously published sources. See Golvin #186, pp. 209–12.

128 *Bellum Africanum* 36.

129 J. Gascou, *La politique municipale de l'empire romain en Afrique proconsulaire de Trajan à Septime-Sévère* (Rome 1972), 192–94.

130 Golvin #25, p. 84 and #112, pp. 131–32.

131 Beschaouch, *op. cit.*

132 See the Catalogue Entry later in this chapter, p. 175.

133 M. Wilson Jones, 'Designing Amphitheatres', *MDAI(R)* 100 (1993), 433–34.

134 *Ibid.*; Lézine, 'Notes sur l'amphithéâtre de Thysdrus', 29–50.

135 *Ibid.*

136 Wilson Jones, *op. cit.*, 420–22, Figure 23.

137 The focal triangle was 66:88:110 Roman ft., or 3:4:5 modules. *Ibid.*, 420, notes that the reduction factor was nearly 22:28 for the scale adjustment between the Colosseum and the El Jem amphitheatre.

138 Before AD 648 when this 'fortress' of Fahs al-Adjom was used as the rallying point following the Byzantine defeat during the first Arab invasion of Byzacena (roughly the south-eastern part of modern Tunisia). en-Noweiri, 'Histoire de la province d'Afrique et du Magreb', transl. de Slane, *Journal Asiatique* 12 (1841), 109, the early Arab invasions of the Sahel.

139 J.M. Abun-Nasr, *A History of the Maghrib*, 2nd edn (Cambridge 1975), 505 ff.

140 Abun-Nasr, *op. cit.*, 181–83; Lt.-Col. Hanezzo, *Bulletin archéologique de Sousse* (1911–13), 29–65, esp. 38.

141 Hanezzo, *op. cit.*, 39.

142 *Ibid.*; Abun-Nasr, *op. cit.*, 259 ff.

143 Sir R.L. Playfair, *Travels in the Footsteps of Bruce in Algeria and Tunis* (London 1877), 161.

144 Bomgardner, 'North African Amphitheatres', 379–84; Golvin, 112–14; J.-Cl. Golvin and Ph. Leveau, 'L'Amphithéâtre et le théâtre-amphithéâtre de Cherchel: monuments à spectacle et histoire urbaine à Caesarea de Maurétanie', *MEFRA* 91 (1979), 817–43.

145 Welch, *op. cit.*

146 Bomgardner, 'North African Amphitheatres', 402–07; Golvin #60, pp. 93–94 and #111, pp. 130–31; J.-Cl. Golvin and M. Janon, 'L'amphithéâtre de Lambèse (Numidie) d'après des documents anciens', *BAC* n.s. 12–14 (1976–78, 1980), 169–94, 258 f.; L. Leschi, *Libyca* 2 (1954), 171–86.

147 Gemellae (Golvin #44): Bomgardner, 'North African Amphitheatres', 399–401; Golvin, 90; J. Baradez, 'Deux amphithéâtres inédits du limes de Numidie: Gemellae et Mesarfelta', *Mélanges d'archéologie et d'histoire efferts à Jérôme Carcopino* (Paris 1966), 55–69, esp. 58–60. Mesarfelta (Golvin #45): Bomgardner, 'North African Amphitheatres', 408, Golvin, 90; Baradez, *op. cit.*, 58–60.

148 Golvin, 90; Leveau, *op. cit.*, 288–90.

149 Bomgardner, 'North African Amphitheatres', 389–93; Golvin #130, pp. 139–40.

150 Bomgardner, 'North African Amphitheatres', 238–40; field survey: June 1977; Golvin, 133–34.

151 V. Guérin, *Voyages archéologiques dans la régence de Tunis* (2 vols., Paris 1862), I, 161 f.

152 Bomgardner, 'North African Amphitheatres', 241–42; field survey: June 1977; Golvin, 94–95; Lachaux, *op. cit.*, 32–33.

153 Gascou *op. cit.*, 184 f.

154 Bomgardner, 'North African Amphitheatres', 243–44; Golvin, 212–13.

155 Bomgardner, 'North African Amphitheatres', 245–47; field survey: July 1977; Golvin, 133.

156 Augustine, *Sermones* (ed. Denis) 17.7–9.

157 P. Romanelli, *Topografia e archeologia dell'Africa romana* (Turin 1970), Ch. 5.

158 Carton, *Bulletin de la société géographique de Tunis* (1891), 12 f.

159 Golvin, 122–23; Lézine, *Architecture romaine*, 60–64.

160 Bomgardner, 'North African Amphitheatres', 271–77; A. di Vita, 'Lepcis Magna, anfiteatro-circo, relazione preliminare', *Libya Antiqua, suppl. II* (1966), 85; Golvin, 83–84.

161 G. di Vita-Evrard, *Libya Antiqua* 2 (1965), 29–38.

162 D.L. Bomgardner, 'The Amphitheater', in N. Ben Lazreg and D.J. Mattingly, *Leptiminus (Lamta): A Roman Port City in Tunisia. Report no. 1*, *JRA Supplementary Series 4* (Ann Arbor 1992), 44–47; Bomgardner, 'North African Amphitheatres', 278–80; Golvin, 132.

163 J. Gascou, *AntAfr* 6 (1972), 137–43.

164 Bomgardner, 'North African Amphitheatres', 281–84; field survey: June 1977; Golvin, 134.

165 L. Teutsch, *Revue internationale des droits d'antiquité* 8 (1961), 35.

166 G.-C. Picard, *CRAI* (1963), 124 ff.

167 J. Gascou, 'La politique municipale de l'empire romain en Afrique Proconsulaire de Trajan à Septime-Sévère', *COLLEFR* 8 (Rome 1972), 147–51.

168 G.-C. Picard, *CRAI* (1974), 14.

169 M. Leglay, *Saturne africain. Monuments* (2 vols., Paris 1961–66), I, 242 ff.

170 Bomgardner, 'North African Amphitheatres', 289–90; Golvin, 254.

171 R. Bartoccini, *Guida di Sabratha* (Milan 1927), 75–77; Bomgardner, 'North African Amphitheatres', 291–94; Golvin, 134–35.

172 P. Ward, *Sabratha* (Cambridge 1970), 46 f.

173 Bomgardner, 'North African Amphitheatres', 295–96; field survey: July 1977; Golvin, 95.

174 Broughton, *op. cit.*, 82 n. 205.

175 Based chiefly upon arguments from the evidence of its civic development and the construction techniques used.

176 Bomgardner, 'North African Amphitheatres', 297–98; Golvin, 208.

177 Bomgardner, 'North African Amphitheatres', 299–303; field survey: June 1977; Golvin, 95.

178 *Sermones* (ed. Denis) 17.7–9.

179 Leglay, *Saturne africain. Monuments*, I, 286 ff.; Leglay, *Saturne africain. Histoire*, 313 ff., 460 ff..

180 Bomgardner, 'North African Amphitheatres', 304–09; field survey: June 1977; Golvin, 132.

181 Guérin, *op. cit.*, I, 383.

182 E. Kirsten, *Nordafrikanische Stadtbilder* (Heidelberg 1961), 77.

183 Bomgardner, 'North African Amphitheatres', 310–11; field survey: June 1977; Golvin, 95–96.

184 Bomgardner, 'North African Amphitheatres', 312–13; Golvin, 209; Sir Grenville Temple, *Excursions in the Mediterranean, Algiers and Tunis* (2 vols., London 1835), I, 135.

185 Dimensions quoted are from Temple, *op. cit.*

186 Bomgardner, 'North African Amphitheatres', 314–16; Golvin, 94; R.P. Lapeyre, 'L'amphithéâtre de Thibari', *RAfr* 81 (1937), 395–401.

187 Bomgardner, 'North African Amphitheatres', 317–19; field survey: July 1977; Golvin, 133.

188 Gascou, *La politique municipale*, 182 f.

189 Bomgardner, 'North African Amphitheatres', 320; field survey: June 1977; Golvin, 257 (unable to find amphitheatre, based upon Lachaux, *op. cit.*, 126).

190 Bomgardner, 'North African Amphitheatres', 324–26; field survey: June 1977; Golvin, 135.

191 P. Quoniam, *Karthago* 10 (1959/60), 67–79.

192 H.-G. Pflaum, 'La romanisation de l'ancien territoire de la Carthage punique à la lumière des découverts épigraphiques récents', *AntAfr* 4 (1970), 111–17.

193 Based upon comparative architectural monuments on the site and the general development of the civic monuments here.

194 Based upon a comparison with the repair phase of the Baths of the Labyrinth.

195 *Terminus post quem* of AD 177–80 for inscriptions: *ILT* 720–21, 723–29.

196 Golvin, 209–12, with bibliography.

197 Golvin, 84; Slim, *Recherches préliminaires*, 136–38; H. Slim, *CRAI* (1986), 461–64.

198 Golvin, 131–32.

199 *AAT*, 'feuille Oudna', 48; Bomgardner, 'North African Amphitheatres', 353–57; field notes of June 1977.

200 Bomgardner, 'North African Amphitheatres', 358–62; field notes of July 1977; Comte d'Herisson, *Rélation d'une mission archéologique en Tunisie* (Paris 1881), 78; Golvin, 94.

201 H. Dunant, *Notice sur la régence de Tunis* (Geneva 1858; reprint edn, Tunis: S.T.D. 1975), 109.

202 Lézine, *Utique*, 66.

203 H. Slim, *Recherches preliminaires*, I, 147 and Figure 4.

204 A. Pauly, G. Wissowa and W. Knoll, eds., *Real-Encyclopädie der klassischen Altertumswissenschaft* (1893–), *s.v.* '*Ulixibera*' by M. Leglay. Wilmanns, *CIL*, Vol. VIII, p. 17, has suggested Henchir-el-Menzel as the correct attribution.

205 Bomgardner, 'North African Amphitheatres', 376–78; Golvin, 97.

206 C.H. Kraeling, *Ptolemais, City of the Pentapolis* (Chicago 1962), 14.

207 Private communication from Shimon Applebaum.

208 Bomgardner, 'North African Amphitheatres', 379–84; Golvin, 112–14; Golvin and Leveau, *op. cit.*, 817–43.

209 *Ibid.*, 278 n. 12.

210 Bomgardner, 'North African Amphitheatres', 389–93; Golvin, 139–40.

211 Based upon a stylistic analysis of the sarcophagi reused in the construction of the *cavea*: *Libyca* (1957), 133–35.

212 *FA* 9 (1954), 5349.

213 *Libyca* (1954), 277 f.

214 Bomgardner, 'North African Amphitheatres', 399–401; Golvin, 90; Baradez, *op. cit.*, 58–60.

215 P. Trousset, *Actes du XIe Congrès Internationale d'Etudes des Frontières Romaines* (Budapest 1977), 571 ff.

216 *Notitia Dignitatum* 25.

217 Baradez, *op. cit.*, 60.

218 Golvin, 90; P. Leveau, 'Recherches historiques sur une région montagneuse de Maurétanie Césarienne, de *Tigava Castra* à la mer', *MEFRA* 89 (1977), 288–90.

219 M. Leglay in *KlPauly*, *s.v.* '*Tigava castra*', Band 5, col. 824.

220 Leveau, *op. cit.*, 288–90.

221 Bomgardner, 'North African Amphitheatres', 402–07; Golvin, 93–94; J.-Cl. Golvin and M. Janon, 'L'amphithéâtre de Lambèse (Numidie) d'après des documents anciens', *BAC* 12–14 (1976–78, 1980), 169–94, 258 f.

222 L. Leschi, *Libyca* 1 (1953), 197. Sir Ronald Syme, *Révue des etudes anciennes* 38 (1936), 182–84, thinks that this transfer occurred early in the reign of Trajan.

223 *CIL* 8.18247; Gascou, *La politique municipale*, 152–56.

224 J. Deininger, *Die Provinziallandtage der römischen Kaiserzeit* (Berlin 1965), 134 f.

225 M. Leglay in *KlPauly*, *s.v.* '*Lambaese*'.

226 Bomgardner, 'North African Amphitheatres', 402–07; Golvin, 130–31; Golvin and Janon, *op. cit.*, 169–94, 258 f.

227 L. Leschi, *Libyca* 2 (1954), 171–86.

228 Kolendo, *op. cit.*, 301–15.

229 Bomgardner, 'North African Amphitheatres', 409–11; Golvin, 96; A. Ravoisié, *Exploration scientifique de l'Algérie. Architecture et Beaux-Arts* (2 vols., Paris 1846), II, pls. 56–59.

230 Teutsch, *op. cit.*, 65 ff.

231 J. Roger, *RAfr* 60 (1865), 391 ff.

232 Féraud, *RAfr* 19 (1875), 83; Ch. Vars, *Rusicade et Stora* (Paris 1898), 130.

233 Bomgardner, 'North African Amphitheatres', 412–15; Golvin, 85–86; Lequément, *op. cit.*

234 F. de Pachtère, *CRAI* (1916), 282.

235 Gascou, *La politique municipale*, 91–97.

236 De Pachtère, *op. cit.*, Syme, *op. cit.*

237 L. Robert, *Les gladiateurs dans l'Orient grec* (Paris 1940).

238 For example the rivalry between the cities of Hadrumetum and Thysdrus: Foucher, *Hadrumetum*, 145; see pp. 162–66, for reasons for believing Hadrumetum had an amphitheatre and possible locations. Undiscovered to date.

239 *CIL* 8.6995 = *ILS* 411 is the basis for the existence of an amphitheatre at Cirta: . . . *quam promisit ex reditibus amphitheatri diei muneris.* . . . Undiscovered to date.

CIL 8.8482, 20348 and also Massiéra, *BAC* (1928/29), 161 f., for the existence of a late third-century amphitheatre at Sitifis. Undiscovered to date.

240 Compare, e.g., the Hunt Mosaic of the Maison d'Isguntus at Hippo Regius (= Dunbabin, *op. cit.*, Hippo Regius, #3 (e); see also App. II for the suggested date of the early fourth century, *c.* 310–30), where the live capture of felines for the amphitheatre is depicted. The owner of the villa may have been involved in the lucrative trade in live beasts like that of the owner of the villa at Piazza Armerina in Sicily where similar mosaics are found: R.J.A. Wilson, *Piazza Armerina* (London 1983), Ch. 3.

241 See Duncan-Jones, *Economy of the Roman Empire*, 82 ff., for the sums involved.

242 Cl. Bourgeois, 'L'entrée des bêtes dans l'arène à Mactar', *BAC* (1979–80), 17–27: the Mactaris beast pens. See Jennison, *op. cit.*, 93 ff. for Latin terminology.

243 See Crema, *op. cit.*, 95–99, 203–07, 293–302, 436–41, 548–50, for an excellent chronological summary of amphitheatre construction in the empire.

244 J.B. Ward-Perkins, 'From Republic to Empire: Reflections on the Early Provincial Architecture of the Roman West', *JRS* 60 (1970), 1–19.

245 Fictile vaulting tubes and certain types of mosaic designs, notably those found at the villa at Piazza Armerina, originally came from North Africa to Sicily. Dunbabin, *op. cit.*, 196 ff.; E.H. Arslan, *Bolletino d'Arte* (1965), 45–52.

246 R. Cagnat, *L'armée romaine d'Afrique*, 2nd edn (Paris 1913), 351 ff. The amphitheatre at Lugdunum has many geometric properties in common with that at Carthage.

247 *Ibid.*, 359–64.

248 *CIL* 8.2728 = *ILS* 5795, of *c.* AD 150: a most remarkably informative inscription. Datus wanted his troubles recorded for posterity: his finest hour or his worst nightmare?

249 Pliny, *Epistulae* 10.41 and 42; G.R. Watson, *The Roman Soldier* (London 1969), 144

250 Cagnat, *op. cit.*, 215.

251 R. MacMullen, *HSCP* 64 (1959), 214 ff.

252 A. Audollent, *Carthage romaine: 146 avant J.-C. – 698 après J.-C.* (Paris 1901), 337 ff.

253 *Ibid.*, 347 ff.

254 M. Leglay, *Saturne africain. Histoire*, 313 ff., 460 ff.; G.-C. Picard, 'Les *sacerdotes* de Saturne et les sacrifices humains dans l'Afrique romaine', *Societé archéologique de la province de Constantine. Receuil des notices et mémoires* 66 (1948), 117–23.

255 See catalogue entries for details. For Thuburnica, a small amphitheatre without details was recorded here by Carton, *Bulletin archéologique de Sousse* 11 (1901), 105. It was adjacent to the local *tophet*: Leglay, *Saturne africain. Histoire*, 281; also Leglay, *Saturne africain. Monuments*, I, 274 f. See Carton, *BAC* (1908), 420–27 for details of this sanctuary.

256 A. Piganiol, *Essai sur les jeux romains* (Strasbourg 1923), 62 ff.

257 A. Pauly, G. Wissowa and W. Kroll, eds., *Real-Encyclopädie der klassischen Altertumswissenschaft* (1893–), *s.v.* 'Nemesis' by H. Herter, coll. 2360 ff.

258 Dunbabin, *op. cit.*, 65 ff.

259 J.W. Salomonson, 'Spätrömische rote Tonware mit Reliefverzierung aus nordafrikanischen Werkstätten', *BABesch* 44 (1969), 4–109, esp. 45 ff.

260 Jennison, *op. cit.*, 83 ff., for an excellent general, if somewhat out-of-date, survey of this evolution; G. Ville, 'Les jeux de gladiateurs dans l'Empire chrétien', *MEFRA* 72 (1960), 273–335, for the end of *munera*; T. Wiedemann, *Emperors and Gladiators* (London 1992), 128–64.

CHAPTER FIVE ENDINGS AND NEW BEGINNINGS

1 J.J. Wilkes, *Dalmatia* (Cambridge, Mass. 1969), 385.

2 My own calculations.

3 Golvin, 206, based upon historical probabilities, local topographical development and construction materials used.

4 Wilkes, *op. cit.*, 385 n. 1

5 *Historia Salonitana* of Thomas the Archdeacon, ed. Fr. Racki, (Zagreb 1894), c. 7 ff., cited in Wilkes, *op. cit.*, 385 n. 1.

6 *CIL* 3.1980 = *ILS* 2287 cited in *OCD³* (1996), *s.v.* 'Salonae' by J.J. Wilkes, 1350.

7 Golvin #181, pp. 206–07.

8 E. Dyggve, *Recherches à Salone* (Copenhagen 1933), II, 35–150.

9 Golvin, 213–23.

10 Golvin, 214–15.

11 This figure is derived from a comparison with the first amphitheatre at Lambaesis in North Africa, which seems to be the closest parallel available.

12 Golvin, 215–16.

13 Contorniate medallions depict gladiatorial combats among the games commemorating the inaugurations of new consuls at Rome well into the 430s and 440s. These consular games were the last vestiges of gladiatorial *munera* at Rome. T. Wiedemann, *Emperors and Gladiators* (London 1992), 158 and n. 75.

14 *Ibid.*, 159.

15 The last record of a *venatio* at Rome occurred on 1 January, AD 523, when Theoderic granted permission for the consul Maximus to provide one for his inaugural consular games: Cassiodorus, *Variae* 5.42. The last mention of a *venatio* in the amphitheatre at Constantinople (the 'Kynegion') was in January, AD 537, during the consular games of that year: Justinian, *Novellae* 105, ch. 1: cited by A. Chastagnol, *Le Sénat romain sous le règne d'Odoacre. Recherche sur l'Epigraphie du Colisée au Ve Siècle* (Bonn 1966), 62.

16 Wiedemann, *op. cit.*, 137–44.

17 *Ibid.*, Ch. 4 'Opposition and Abolition', 128–64.

18 P. Veyne, 'The Roman Empire', in P. Veyne, ed., *A History of Private Life. I. From Pagan Rome to Byzantium* (Cambridge, Mass. 1992), 5–234, esp. 208–10.

19 P. Brown, 'Late Antiquity' in Veyne, ed., *A History of Private Life*, 242–43.

20 See above, Chapter One, 17ff.

21 Wiedemann, *op. cit.*, 146–60.

22 Augustine, *Confessiones* 6.8: my own translation, slightly adapted.

23 Professor Thomas Wiedemann, personal communication.

24 P. Veyne, *Le pain et le cirque. Sociologie historique d'un pluralisme politique* (Paris 1976), 375 ff.

25 Ambrose, *De officiis ministrorum* (ed. Krabinger; Tübingen 1857), II, 109–10: *Largitas enim duo sunt genera: unum liberalitatis, alterum prodigae effusionis. Liberale est hospitem suscipere, nudum vestire, redimere captivos, non habentes sumptu iuvare. . . . Prodigum est popularis favoris gratia exinanire proprias opes; quod faciunt qui ludis circensibus, vel etiam theatralibus, et muneribus gladiatoriis vel etiam venationibus, patrimonium dilapidant suum.*

26 Cicero, *De officiis* 2.16 and 60; also *Pro Murena* 40. Both cited in Wiedemann, *op. cit.*, 137.

27 See Robin Lane Fox, *Pagans and Christians in the Mediterranean World from the Second Century AD to the Conversion of Constantine* (Harmondsworth 1986), 419 ff., for an excellent account of the persecutions of this era.

28 The precise details of what this symbol looked like are still in debate; *ibid.*, 613–16. Probably at this stage it resembled a cross (*stauros*) with a loop (like a Greek letter 'rho') on the top, later elaborated into the *labarum*, the staff of Constantine, a cross with the Greek 'chi' and 'rho' intertwined, representing the Greek word 'Christos', the 'Christ', the 'anointed one' of the Lord.

29 Wiedemann, *op. cit.*, 132–37.

30 Cassius Dio 54.2.4 and 17.4.

31 Suetonius, *Tiberius* 34.1 and 47.

32 Tacitus, *Annales* 13.31.

33 *ILS* 5163 = *CIL* 2.6278.

34 *Codex Theodosianus* 15. 12.1 [= *Codex Iustinianus* 11.44.1].

35 Wiedemann, *op. cit.*, 156.

36 R. Krautheimer, *Rome. Profile of a City, 312–1308* (Princeton 1980), Ch. 1, 'Rome and Constantine', 3–31.

37 *Codex Theodosianus* 9.40.8.

38 Wiedemann, *op. cit.*, 157: e.g., a *munus* at Hispellum in the 330s (*Codex Theodosianus* 9.40.8).

39 Wiedemann, *op. cit.*, 158 and n. 74, disagrees, arguing that the evidence from *CIL* 14.300 does not support this conclusion. Chastagnol, *op. cit.*, thinks that the decree of the emperor Honorius of AD 399 banning gladiatorial combats referred only to the African provinces, following the revolt of Gildo, and was therefore perhaps intended as a punitive measure.

40 A.H.M. Jones, *The Later Roman Empire 284–602* (Oxford 1964), 705.

41 J.P.V.D. Balsdon, *Life and Leisure in Ancient Rome* (London 1974), 251, citing *Codex Theodosianus* 2.8.19; 2.8.22.

42 Jones, *op. cit.*, 167, citing Zosimus 4.37 for Bishop Marcellus of Apamea.

43 *Ibid.*, citing Libanius, *Orationes* 30.8 ff.

44 Wiedemann, *op. cit.*, 158.

45 G. Ville, 'Les jeux de gladiateurs dans l'Empire chrétien', *MEFRA* 72 (1960), 273–335.

46 R. Rémondon, *La crise de l'empire romain de Marc Aurèle à Anastase* (Paris 1970), 159–62.

47 Chastagnol, *op. cit.*, 22, argues cogently for the end of the gladiatorial *munera* during the early years of the reign of Valentinian III, perhaps when the imperial court abandoned Ravenna for Rome: August 439–January 440. Following the earthquake damage of AD 429, the Colosseum had probably remained out of use during most of the following decade 429–438. The prefect of the city Flavius Paulus undertook major repairs to bring this monument back into use. The dedication of the restored Colosseum probably occurred during either the quaestorian games of December 438 or the consular/praetorian games of January 439. The Circus Maximus was used as the alternative venue for these spectacles.

48 Lane Fox, *op. cit.*, 669.

49 Wiedemann, *op. cit.*, 158, citing Salvian, *De gubernatione Dei* 6.10; *CJ* 3, 12.9; Justinian, *Novellae* 105, §2.

50 Peter Brown, *op. cit.*, 239 ff.

51 Either the quaestors, aediles or praetors (it varied throughout the course of the empire) were responsible for their organisation and the influx of added funding to supplement the official state subsidy provided each year.

52 He goes on to impute baser, ulterior motives on the part of the provincial governors for encouraging such spectacles: 'the governors' intentions being to win partisans to screen their irregularities' (trans. M. Grant, Penguin Classics, 1977). Wiedemann, *op. cit.*, 134, thinks that Nero may have been trying to force a greater number of games to be held at Rome in his newly-constructed amphitheatre in order to maximise his own acclaim as *editor* at home.

53 The so-called *senatus consultum de pretiis gladiatorum minuendis*. This law is known from two fragmentary inscriptions of its text, one from Spain (Italica) and one from Turkey (Sardis). The Italica bronze tablet is the more complete (= *CIL* 2.6278 = *ILS* 5163). Cf. the commentary and translation in J.H. Oliver and R.E.A. Palmer, 'Minutes of an Act of the Roman Senate', *Hesperia* (1955), 320–49, Plate 89 and the earlier work by Th. Mommsen, *Gesammelte Schriften* VIII (Berlin 1913), 499–531. For a more detailed consideration of this important piece of evidence for the history of the gladiatorial *munera*, see the Appendix at the end of this book.

54 Four *sesterces* (= 1 *denarius*) was enough money for a working man to feed himself and his family for one day. The silver piece referred to in the Bible as being paid for a day's labour in the parable of the workers in the vineyard was the equivalent of one *denarius*. Attempts to determine modern equivalents for ancient sums of money are notoriously riddled with difficulties. I prefer to work along the lines laid out above, leaving conversions to the individual. But perhaps a sum in the order of £25–35 as the modern equivalent of one *denarius* may not be too far off the mark.

55 I assume that the Augustan prohibition of not more than 120 gladiators in any single *munus* given by anyone other than the emperor himself was still in force. Cassius Dio 54.2.4.

56 F. Millar, *The Emperor in the Roman World* (Ithaca 1977), 194–95.

57 *ILS* 1412 (northern Italy), 9014 (the two Pannonias and Dalmatia), 1396 (Britain, etc. and Asia Minor, etc.), 1397 (Alexandria, Egypt).

58 The property qualification for entry into the Senate was land holdings valued at 1 million *sesterces* or more, a very considerable sum of money, perhaps equivalent to about £6 million today. Thus the sums involved may be roughly estimated at a total expenditure per year of between £375 million and £750 million, the loss of revenue to the *fiscus* being between £125 million and £190 million.

59 Wiedemann, *op. cit.*, 134–35, also rightly points out the important financial overtones of this act in light of the general climate of fiscal impoverishment due to the dual blows of a major outbreak of plague (in the 160s) and large-scale barbarian invasions along the Danubian *limes* (in the 170s).

60 See above pp. 196 and fn. 254.

61 Oliver and Palmer, *op. cit.*, 325 (basing their argument upon a passage from Eusebius 5.1.37) argue that these were a type of *bestiarius*.

62 Jones, *op. cit.*, 61 ff.; T. Frank, *Economic Survey of Ancient Rome. Vol. 5: Rome and Italy of the Empire* (Baltimore 1940), 310–421; *AE* (1947), 148–49, an important additional fragment.

63 Wiedemann, *op. cit.*, 153.

64 *AE* (1967), 549; K.M.D. Dunbabin, *The Mosaics of Roman North Africa. Studies in Iconography and*

Patronage (Oxford, 1978), 67–9; R. Duncan-Jones, *The Economy of the Roman Empire*, 2nd edn (Cambridge 1982), 250 and n. 3.

65 Jones, *op. cit.*, 1017–18 citing *Supplementum Epigraphicum Graecum*, 14.386.

66 See p. 204, for the limit of no more than 120 gladiators in any one display by a private individual and not more than twice in any year set by Augustus in 22 BC.

67 *CIL* 13.8639: *ursarius leg*[ionis] *XXX U*[lpiae] *V*[ictricis] *S*[everianae] *A*[lexandrinae]; *CIL* 13.5243 (= *ILS* 3267, from Zurich): a dedication to Diana and Silvanus by the *ursarii*; *CIL* 13.2717; *CIL* 12.533.10. A recently discovered inscription from the Danubian frontier attests *ursarii* there also.

68 A. Riese, *Das rheinische Germanien in den antiken Inschriften*, n. 556.

69 G. Jennison, *Animals for Show and Pleasure in Ancient Rome* (Manchester 1937), 140–41 citing Symmachus, *Epistulae* 5.62.

70 Beschaouch has found evidence that these *sodalitates*, in addition to their more usual activities in the arenas of North Africa, were also engaged in commercial ventures abroad, including the export of oil to Rome. See references above in Chapter Four fn. 90. I see their function much in the same light as that of the silk and spice caravan merchants who supplied goods not available within the limits of the empire.

71 A.H.M. Jones, *The Decline of the Ancient World* (London 1966), 311. For a more detailed examination of the *cursus clabularis*, cf. Jones, *Later Roman Empire*, 831–34.

72 It only cost 16 *denarii* (roughly £400) to transport a *modius* (peck) of grain all the way from Alexandria to Rome by sea (*c.* 1,250 miles): Jones, *Decline of the Ancient World*, 311.

73 *Ibid.*, 312.

74 Jennison, *op. cit.*, 151–52, citing *Codex Theodosianus* 15.11.2. Jennison points out that Hierapolis was probably being used as a central collection point before the final dispatch of the entire consignment of beasts to Rome.

75 Jennison, *op. cit.*, 151 citing Symmachus, *Epistulae* 2.76; 5.56; 6.34.3; 9.20 and 117.

76 G.W.W. Barker and G.D.B. Jones, UNESCO Libyan Valleys Survey, *Libyan Studies* 13 (1982), 1–34; 14 (1983), 69–85; 15 (1984), 1–70.

77 Jones, *Decline of the Ancient World*, 315–16.

78 P.A. Brunt and J.M. Moore, eds., *Res Gestae Divi Augusti. The Achievements of the Divine Augustus* (Oxford 1967), Section 22,3, pp. 50–51.

79 There were probably other wild beasts also exhibited, but only the numbers of African big cat species are recorded, doubtless both because of their expense to procure and their popularity with the crowds.

80 Cassius Dio 66.25.1; Suetonius, *Divus Titus* 7.3.

81 Cassius Dio 68.15.1.

82 Jennison, *op. cit.*, 83–98.

83 Jennison, *op. cit.*, 140 citing Strabo 2.5.33.

84 G. Rickman, *The Corn Supply of Ancient Rome* (Oxford 1980), 108–12, 231–35. This was at a time of threatened instability in the Egyptian corn supply.

85 *Ibid.*, 129–30 n. 40 citing *Scriptores Historiae Augustae. Commodus* 17.7.

86 E. Rodriguez-Almeida, *Il monte Testaccio* (Rome 1984). Spanish oil exports were the predominant contributor to the late imperial amphorae debris, but North African amphorae occur with a greater frequency than before.

87 Recently there has been a rapid increase in the numbers of wild boar in rural areas of France which has caused huge amounts of damage to agriculture in these regions.

88 M. Rosenblum, *Luxorius. A Latin Poet among the Vandals* (New York 1961), no. 60: *Amphitheatrales mirantur rura triumphos / et nemus ignotas cernit adesse feras. / Spectat arando novos agrestis turba labores / nautaque de pelago gaudia mixta videt. / Fecundus nil perdit ager, plus germina crescunt. / Dum metuunt omnes hic sua fata ferae.*

89 R. Delbrueck, *Die Consulardiptychen und verwandte Denkmäler* (Berlin 1929).

90 Cassiodorus, *Variae* 5.42. I thank Brian Ward-Perkins for bringing this reference to my attention.

91 Cf. Jennison, *op. cit.*, 93–98.

92 Chastagnol, *op. cit.*, 61 n. 16.

93 Jones, *The Later Roman Empire*, 162.

94 Chastagnol, *op. cit.*, 61 ff.

95 Chastagnol, *op. cit.*, 62, citing Justinian, *Novellae* 105, Ch. 1.

96 E. Gibbon, *The Decline and Fall of the Roman Empire*, (3 vols.,   ed. David Womersley, Harmondsworth 1994), II, Ch. 40, 616–17. The ordinary consulship was finally abolished by a law

promulgated in the reign of Leo the Philosopher (886–911). Jones (*The Later Roman Empire*, 533) notes that after Justinian's reign the ordinary consulship was only assumed by the reigning monarch in the first January after his accession.

97 Acacius, the father of Theodora, empress of Justinian (AD 527–48), was 'master of the beasts' at Constantinople for the Green Faction. E. Gibbon, *The Decline and Fall of the Roman Empire*, ed. F. Fernández-Armesto, Folio Society Edn. (8 vols., London 1987), V, 60–61. This seems to indicate that each of the two dominant factions, the Blues and Greens, attended to the supply and training of their own beasts for the amphitheatre.

98 The ordinary consulship at Rome came to an end in 534 under Paulinus. Jones, *The Later Roman Empire*, 533.

99 Cassiodorus *Variae* 5.42. As in earlier times, the emperor had to give special permission for exceptional spectacles. Chastagnol, *op. cit.*, 62.

100 Jones, *Decline of the Ancient World*, 102.

101 D. Keys, *Catastrophe* (London 1999), *passim*.

102 Fleas are unaffected by plague bacilli unless the temperature drops below 25°C. When this happens, the bacilli cause the flea's gut to block, starving it. It goes into a feeding frenzy before it dies. This is the scenario for transmission to humans.

103 For the detailed history of this process see C. Mocchegiani Carpano and R. Luciano, 'I restauri dell'Anfiteatro Flavio', *RIA* 4 (1981), 9–69; R. Rea. 'Le antiche raffigurazioni dell'anfiteatro', in *Anfiteatro Flavio. Immagine, Testimonianze, Spettacoli* (Rome 1988), 23–46. For the Colosseum in disuse during the sixth to eleventh centuries AD: Chastagnol, *op. cit.*, 62.

104 Cassiodorus, *Variae* 4.42: cited by *ibid.*, 61.

105 *Anonymous Valesianus*, c. 60 (*Monumenta Germaniae Historica*, 322).

106 '*amphitheatrum . . . fecit*' *Anonymous Valesianus*, c. 71 (*Monumenta Germaniae Historica*, 324).

107 *Liber Pontificalis*, I, 472. I thank Brian Ward-Perkins for bringing this reference to my attention.

108 R. Guillard, 'Etudes sur l'Hippodrome de Byzance VI', *Byzantino-Slavica*, 27 (1966), 302–06.

109 Krautheimer, *op. cit.*, 319.

110 *Ibid.*, 157.

111 *Ibid.*, 319.

112 Golvin, 207.

113 Gibbon, *Decline and Fall*, ed. Womersley, III, 1073–84.

114 Leo Africanus, *Description of Africa*, II.vi.804, transl. J. Parry, Hakluyt Society Extra Series no. 18 (London 1600; repr. edn 1963), 457.

115 I am not certain that such a work exists in English. Ernest Hemingway's *Death in the Afternoon* does not deal with the historical aspects of the development of the modern *corrida* so much as with the emotional and psychological reactions to the present reality.

116 C.M. Kelly in *OCD³* (1996), *s.v.* 'corruption', 402–03.

117 Augustine, *Confessiones* 6.8.

APPENDIX

1 J.H. Oliver and R.E.A. Palmer, 'Minutes of an Act of the Roman Senate', *Hesperia* 24 (1955), 320–49.

2 F. Millar. *The Emperor in the Roman World* (Ithaca 1977), 195.

3 Oliver and Palmer, *op. cit.*, 320, for a revised text.

4 T. Wiedemann, *Emperors and Gladiators* (London 1992), 134–36.

5 Oliver and Palmer, *op. cit.*, 325, basing their argument on a passage from Eusebius 5.1.37.

Select bibliography

J.M. Abun-Nasr, *A History of the Maghrib*, 2nd edn (Cambridge 1975).

P. Amy et al., *L'Arc d'Orange, Gallia* Suppl. XV (Paris 1962).

A. Audollent, *Carthage romaine: 146 avant J.-C.–698 après J.-C.*, BEFAR, fasc. 84 (Paris 1901).

—— *Defixionum tabellae* (Paris 1904).

R. Auguet, *Cruelty and Civilisation: The Roman Games* (London 1972).

J. Aymard, *Essai sur les chasses romaines dès origines à la fin du siècle des Antonins (Cynegetica)*, BEFAR, fasc. 171 (Paris 1951).

E. Babelon, R. Cagnat and S. Reinach, *Atlas archéologique de la Tunisie* (Paris 1892–1913).

J.P.V.D. Balsdon, *Life and Leisure in Ancient Rome* (London 1974).

T.D. Barnes, *Tertullian*, 2nd edn (Oxford 1985).

M. Silvia Bassignano, *Il flaminato nelle provincie romane dell'Africa* (Rome 1974).

M. Benabou, *La résistance africaine à la romanisation* (Paris 1976).

A. Beschaouch, 'La mosaïque de chasse à l'amphithéâtre découverte à Smirat en Tunisie', *CRAI* (1966), 134–57.

—— 'Nouvelles recherches sur les sodalités de l'Afrique romaine', *CRAI* (1977), 486–503.

A. Beschaouch, R. Hanoune and Y. Thébert, *Les ruines de Bulla Regia*, CollEFR 28 (Rome: Palais Farnèse 1977).

M. Besnier, *L'Empire romain de l'avènement des Sévères au concile de Nicée* (Paris 1937).

J.-Cl. Bessac et al., 'Recherches sur les fondations de l'amphithéâtre de Nîmes (Gard – France)', *RANarb* 17 (1984), 221–37.

H.J. Beste, 'Relazione sulle indagini in corso nei sotteranei i cosidetti ipogei', *MDAI(R)* 105 (1998), 106–18. (I have not been able to consult this source.)

A. Boëthius, *Etruscan and Early Roman Architecture* (Harmondsworth 1978).

D.L. Bomgardner 'An Analytical Study of North African Amphitheatres', unpublished PhD dissertation, University of Michigan, Ann Arbor, Interdepartmental Programme in Classical Art and Archaeology, 1985.

—— 'The Carthage Amphitheater: A Reappraisal', *AJA* 93 (1989), 85–103.

—— 'Amphitheatres on the Fringe', *JRA* 4 (1991), 282–94.

—— 'The Trade in Wild Beasts for Roman Spectacles: A Green Perspective', *Anthropozoologica* 16 (1992), 161–66.

—— 'A New Era for Amphitheatre Studies', *JRA* 6 (1993), 375–90.

Cl. Bourgeois, 'L'entrée des bêtes dans l'arène à Mactar', *BAC* (1979–80), 17–27.

T.R.S. Broughton, *The Romanization of Africa Proconsularis* (Baltimore 1929).

P. Brown, *Augustine of Hippo* (Berkeley 1967).

—— 'Late Antiquity', in P. Veyne, ed., *A History of Private Life. I. From Pagan Rome to Byzantium* (Cambridge, Mass. 1992), 234–311.

P.A. Brunt, *Italian Manpower 225 BC–AD 14* (Oxford 1971).

P.A. Brunt and J.M. Moore, eds., *Res Gestae Divi Augusti. The Achievements of the Divine Augustus* (Oxford 1967).

W. Burkert, *Greek Religion. Archaic and Classical*, Engl. transl. by J. Raffan (Blackwell 1985).

R. Cagnat, *L'armée romaine d'Afrique et l'occupation militaire de l'Afrique sous les empereurs*, 2nd edn (2 vols., Paris 1913).

R. Cagnat, A. Merlin and L. Chatelain, *Inscriptions Latines d'Afrique (Tripolitanie, Tunisie, Maroc)* (Paris 1923).

I. Calabi Limentani, *Epigrafia latina*, 3rd edn (Milan 1974).

A. Cameron, *Circus Factions. Blues and Greens at Rome and Byzantium* (Oxford 1976).

P. Castrén, *Ordo Populusque Pompeianus. Polity and Society in Roman Pompeii* (Helsinki 1975).

A. Chastagnol, *Le Sénat romain sous le règne d'Odoacre. Recherche sur l'Epigraphie du Colisée au Vᵉ Siècle* (Bonn 1966).

A. Claridge et al., *Rome. An Oxford Archaeological Guide* (Oxford 1998).

F. Coarelli, *Guida archeologica di Roma*, 3rd edn (Rome 1980).

F. Coarelli and L. Franzoni, *L'arena di Verona* (Verona 1972).

K.M. Coleman, 'Fatal Charades: Roman Executions Staged as Mythological Enactments', *JRS* 80 (1990), 44–73.

—— 'Launching into History: Aquatic Displays in the Early Empire', *JRS* 83 (1993), 48–74.

A.M. Colini and L. Cozza, *Ludus Magnus* (Rome 1962).

Chr. Courtois, *Les Vandales et l'Afrique* (Paris 1955).

G. Cozzo, *The Colosseum: The Flavian Amphitheatre* (Rome 1971).

L. Crema, *L'architettura romana*, Enciclopedia classica 12,3,1 (Turin 1959).

J. Crook, *Law and Life of Rome* (Ithaca 1967).

J. Deininger, *Die Provinziallandtage der romischen Kaiserzeit* (Berlin 1965).

Père Delattre, 'Fouilles dans l'amphithéâtre de Carthage (1896–1897)', *Mémoires de la Société Nationale des Antiquaires de France* 57 (1898), 135–87.

—— *Musée Lavigerie de Saint-Louis de Carthage* (3 vols., Paris 1899).

—— *L'amphithéâtre de Carthage et le pèlerinage de Sainte Perpétue* (Lyons 1913).

R. Delbrueck, *Die Consulardiptychen und verwandte Denkmäler* (Berlin 1929).

A. di Vita, 'Lepcis Magna, anfiteatro-circo, relazione preliminare', *Supplements to Libya Antiqua, II* (1966), 84–91.

Ch. Dubois, *Pouzzoles antique*, BEFAR, fasc. 98 (Paris 1907).

K.M.D. Dunbabin, *The Mosaics of Roman North Africa. Studies in Iconography and Patronage* (Oxford 1978).

R. Duncan-Jones, 'The Chronology of the Priesthood of Africa Proconsularis under the Principate', *Epigraphische Studien* 5 (1968), 151–58.

—— *The Economy of the Roman Empire*, 2nd edn (Cambridge 1982).

N. Duval and F. Baratte, *Les ruines de Sufetula* (Tunis 1973).

—— 'Etudes sur la garnison de Carthage. Le camp de la cohorte urbaine', *BAC* 15–16 (1979–80), 79–89.

E. Dyggve, *Recherches à Salone, tome II* (Copenhagen 1933).

J. Elsner, *Imperial Rome and Christian Triumph*, Oxford History of Art (Oxford 1998).

E. Esperandieu, *L'amphithéâtre de Nîmes* (Paris 1933).

R. Etienne, 'La naissance de l'amphithéâtre, le mot et la chose', *REL* 43 (1965), 213–20.

—— *La vie quotidienne à Pompéi* (Paris 1966).

—— 'La date de l'amphithéâtre de Nîmes', *Mélange Piganiol*, 2 (1966), 985–1010.

J.D. Fage, ed., *The Cambridge History of Africa. Vol. 2. From c. 500 BC to AD 1050* (Cambridge 1978).

J. Formigé, 'L'amphithéâtre d'Arles', *RA* 2 (1964), 25–41, 113–63; 1 (1965), 1–46.

L. Foucher, *Découvertes archéologiques à Thysdrus en 1961* (Tunis 1962).

—— *La maison de la procession dionysiaque à El Jem* (Paris 1963).

—— *Hadrumetum* (Tunis/Paris 1964).

T. Frank, *Economic Survey of Ancient Rome. Vol. 5: Rome and Italy of the Empire* (Baltimore 1940).

M. Frederiksen, *Campania*, posthumously edited by N. Purcell (Rome 1984).

W.H.C. Frend, *The Donatist Church: A Movement of Protest in Roman North Africa*, rev. edn (Oxford 1985).

E. Frézouls, 'Aspects de l'histoire architecturale du théâtre romain', *ANRW* 2,12,1 (1983), 343–441.

M. Fulford, *The Silchester Amphitheatre. Excavations of 1979–85* (London 1989).

P. Garnsey and R. Saller, *The Roman Empire. Economy, Society and Culture* (London 1987).

A. Garzetti, *From Tiberius to the Antonines. A History of the Roman Empire AD 14–192* (London 1974).

J. Gascou, *La politique municipale de l'empire romain en Afrique proconsulaire de Trajan à Septime-Sévère* (Rome 1972).

A. von Gerkan, 'Das Obergeschoss des flavischen Amphitheaters', *MDAI(R)* 40 (1925), 11–50.

E. Gibbon, *The Decline and Fall of the Roman Empire*, ed. F. Fernández-Armesto, Folio Society Edn. (8 vols., London 1987).

——, *The Decline and Fall of the Roman Empire*, ed. David Womersley (3 vols., Harmondsworth 1994).

M. Girosi, 'L'anfiteatro di Pompei', *Memorie Accademia di Archeologia, Lettere e Belle Arti di Napoli* 5 (1936), 29–55.

J.-Cl. Golvin, *L'amphithéâtre romain. Essai sur la théorisation de sa forme et de ses fonctions* (2 vols., Paris 1988). Text and volume of plates.

J.-Cl. Golvin and M. Janon, 'L'amphithéâtre de Lambèse (Numidie) d'après des documents anciens', *BAC* n.s. 12–14 (1976–78, 1980), 169–94, 258 ff.

J.-Cl. Golvin and Ph. Leveau, 'L'amphithéâtre et le théâtre-amphithéâtre de Cherchel: monuments à spectacle et histoire urbaine à Caesarea de Maurétanie', *MEFRA* 91 (1979), 817–43.

R. Graefe, *Vela erunt: die Zeltdächer der römischen Theater und ähnlicher Anlagen* (2 vols., Mainz 1979).

M. Grant, *Cities of Vesuvius. Pompeii & Herculaneum* (Harmondsworth 1971).

M. Grant, *Gladiators* (Harmondsworth 1971).

A. Grénier, *Manuel d'archéologie gallo-romaine. Vol. III. L'Architecture. Fasc. 2: Ludi et circenses, théâtres, amphithéâtres, cirques* (Paris 1958).

St Gsell, *Les monuments antiques de l'Algérie* (2 vols., Paris 1901).

—— *Atlas archéologique de l'Algérie* (2 vols., Algiers 1911).

—— *Histoire ancienne de l'Afrique du Nord*, 3rd edn (8 vols., Paris 1921–28).

—— *Inscriptions latines de l'Algérie. Tome I: Inscriptions de la Proconsulaire* (Paris 1922).

—— *Inscriptions latines de l'Algérie. Tome II, vol. 2* (Paris 1976).

St. Gsell and H.-G. Pflaum, et al., *Inscriptions latines de l'Algérie. Tome II, vol. I: Inscriptions de la confédération cirtéene, de Cuicul et de la tribu des Suburbures* (Paris 1957).

V. Guérin, *Voyage archéologique dans la régence de Tunis* (2 vols., Paris 1862).

G. Hallier, 'La géométrie des amphithéâtres militaires sur les limes du Rhin et du Danube', in *Akten des 14. Internationalen Limeskongresses in Carnuntum* (Vienna 1990), 71–82.

O. Hirschfeld, 'I sacerdozi dei municipii nell'Africa', *AdI* 38 (1866), 69–77.

S. Hornblower and A. Spawforth, eds., *The Oxford Classical Dictionary*, 3rd edn (Oxford 1996).

G. Jennison, *Animals for Show and Pleasure in Ancient Rome* (Manchester 1937).

A.H.M. Jones, *The Later Roman Empire 284–602* (2 vols., Oxford 1964).

—— *The Decline of the Ancient World* (London 1966).

D. Keys, *Catastrophe* (London 1999).

R. Krautheimer, *Rome. Profile of a City, 312–1308* (Princeton 1980).

J.-Cl. Lachaux, *Théâtres et amphithéâtres d'Afrique Proconsulaire* (Aix-en-Provence 1979).

L.C. Lancaster, 'Reconstructing the Restorations of the Colosseum after the Fire of 217', *JRA* 11 (1998), 146–74. (I have not been able to consult this source.)

R. Lane Fox, *Pagans and Christians in the Mediterranean World from the Second Century AD to the Conversion of Constantine* (Harmondsworth 1986).

R.P. Lapeyre, 'L'amphithéâtre de Thibari', *RAfr* 81 (1937), 395–99.

E. La Rocca and M. and A. de Vos, Coordinamento di F. Coarelli, *Guida archeologica di Pompei* (Rome 1976).

M. Leglay, *Saturne africain. Monuments* (2 vols., Paris 1961–66).

—— *Saturne africain. Histoire* (Paris 1966).

Cl. Lepelley, *Les cités de l'Afrique romaine au Bas-Empire* (2 vols., Paris 1979).

R. Lequément, *Fouilles dans l'amphithéâtre de Tébessa (1965–1968)*, BAA Suppl. No. 2 (Algiers 1979).

A. Lézine, 'Notes sur l'amphithéâtre de Thysdrus', *CahTunisie* 31 (1960), 28–50.

—— *Architecture romaine d'Afrique. Recherches et mises au point* (Paris 1961).

—— *Carthage-Utique. Etudes d'architecture et d'urbanisme* (Paris 1968).

—— *Utique* (Tunis 1970).

G. Lugli, 'La datazione degli anfiteatri di Arles e di Nîmes in Provenza', *Rivista dell'Instituto nazionale di archeologia e storia dell'arte* n.s. 13–14 (1964–65), 145–99.

W.L. MacDonald, *The Architecture of the Roman Empire. Vol. I. An Introductory Study*, Yale Publications in the History of Art, 17, rev. edn (New Haven 1982).

A. Maiuri, *Studi e ricerche sull'anfiteatro flavio Puteolano*, Memorie Accademia di Archeologia, Lettere e Belle Arti di Napoli, no. 3 (Naples, 1955).

J. Martin, *Musée Lavigerie de Saint-Louis de Carthage, Suppl. II* (Paris 1915).

F. Mazauric, 'Les souterrains de l'amphithéâtre de Nîmes', *MémAcadNîmes* 33 (1910), 1–35.

A. Merlin, *Inscriptions Latines de la Tunisie* (Paris 1944).

F. Millar, *The Emperor in the Roman World* (Ithaca 1977).

C. Mocchegiani Carpano and R. Luciano, 'I restauri dell'Anfiteatro Flavio', *RIA* 4 (1981), 9–69.

H. Musurillo, *The Acts of the Christian Martyrs* (Oxford 1972).

J.H. Oliver and R.E.A. Palmer, 'Minutes of an Act of the Roman Senate', *Hesperia* 24 (1955), 320–49.

G. Pesce, *I relievi dell'Anfiteatro Campano*, Studi e materiali del Museo dell'Impero Romano, N. 2 (Rome 1941).

H.-G. Pflaum, 'La romanisation de l'ancien territoire de la Carthage punique à la lumière des découvertes épigraphiques récentes', *AntAfr* 4 (1970), 75–117.

G.-C. Picard, 'Les *sacerdotes* de Saturne et les sacrifices humains dans l'Afrique romaine', *Société archéologique de la province de Constantine. Receuil des notices et memoires* 66 (1948), 117–23.

—— *Les religions de l'Afrique antique* (Paris 1954).

—— *La civilisation de l'Afrique romaine* (Paris 1959).

—— *La Carthage de saint Augustin* (Paris 1965).

A. Piganiol, *Essai sur les jeux romains* (Strasbourg 1923).

Sir R.L. Playfair, *Travels in the Footsteps of Bruce in Algeria and Tunis* (London 1877).

L. Poinssot and P. Quoniam, 'Bêtes d'amphithéâtre sur trois mosaïques de Bardo', *Karthago* 4 (1953), 155–67.

S. Raven, *Rome in Africa*, 2nd edn (London 1984).

R. Rea, 'Le antiche raffigurazioni dell'anfiteatro', in *Anfiteatro Flavio. Immagine, Testimonianze, Spettacoli* (Rome 1988), 23–46.

R. Rea, et al., 'Gli ipogei dell'Anfiteatro Flavio nell'analisi delle structure murarie: L'impianto dell'éta flavia', *MNIR* 50 (1991), 169–235. (I have not been able to consult this source.)

R. Rémondon, *La crise de l'empire romain de Marc Aurèle à Anastase* (Paris 1970).

J.M. Reynolds and J.B. Ward-Perkins, *The Inscriptions of Roman Tripolitania* (Rome 1952).

G. Rickman, *The Corn Supply of Ancient Rome* (Oxford 1980).

L. Robert, *Les gladiateurs dans l'Orient grec* (Paris 1940).

—— 'Une vision de Perpétue martyre à Carthage', *CRAI* (1982), 228–76.

E. Rodriguez-Almeida, *Il monte Testaccio* (Rome 1984).

P. Romanelli, *Storia delle provincie romana dell'Africa* (Rome 1959).

—— *Topografia e archeologia dell'Africa romana* (Turin 1970).

M. Rosenblum, *Luxorius. A Latin Poet among the Vandals* (New York 1961).

P. Sabbatini Tumolesi, *Gladiatorum paria. Annunci di spettacoli gladiatorii à Pompei* (Rome 1980).

—— *Epigrafia anfiteatrale dell'Occidente Romano, Vol. 1: Roma* (Rome 1988).

J.W. Salomonson, 'The "Fancy Dress Banquet". An Attempt at Interpreting a Roman Mosaic from El Djem', *BABesch* 35 (1960), 25–55.

—— *Voluptatem spectandi non perdat sed mutet: observations sur l'iconographie du martyre en Afrique romaine* (Amsterdam 1979).

F. Sear, *Roman Architecture* (London 1982).

A.N. Sherwin White, *The Roman Citizenship*, 2nd edn (Oxford 1973).

H. Slim, 'Les facteurs de l'épanouissement économiques de Thysdrus', *CahTunisie* 31 (1960), 51–56.

—— 'Quelques aspects de la vie économique à Thysdrus avant le second siècle de l'ére chrétienne', *CahTunisie* 45/46 (1964), 155–58.

—— 'Nouveaux témoignages sur la vie économique à Thysdrus', *BAC* 19 (1983), 63–85.

—— 'Recherches préliminaires sur les amphithéâtres romains de Tunisie', in H. Slim, *L'Africa romana* (Sassari 1984), 129–59.

R. Stillwell, W.L. MacDonald, and M.H. McAllister, eds., *The Princeton Encyclopedia of Classical Sites* (Princeton 1976).

D. Strong, *Roman Art* (Harmondsworth 1980).

S. Stucchi, *Architettura cirenaica*, Monografie de Archeologia Libica IX (Rome 1975).

L. Teutsch, *Das römische Städtewesen in Nordafrika in der Zeit von C. Gracchus bis zum Tode des Kaisers Augustus* (Berlin 1962).

C. Tissot, *Géographie comparée de la Province romaine d'Afrique* (2 vols. and atlas, Paris 1884).

J.M.C. Toynbee, *Animals in Roman Life and Art* (London 1973).

P. Veyne, *Le pain et le cirque. Sociologie historique d'un pluralisme politique* (Paris 1976).

——, ed., *A History of Private Life. I. From Pagan Rome to Byzantium* (Cambridge, Mass. 1992).

G. Ville, 'Les jeux de gladiateurs dans l'Empire chrétien', *MEFRA* 72 (1960), 273–335.

——, *La gladiature en Occident des origines à la mort de Domitien, BEFAR* 245 (Rome 1981).

F. de Visscher, 'L'amphithéâtre d'Alba Fucens et son fondateur Q. Naevius Macro, préfet du prétoire de Tibère', *Rendiconti delle reale accademia dei Lincei* 12 (1957), 39–49.

J.B. Ward-Perkins, *Roman Imperial Architecture* (Harmondsworth 1981).

——, 'From Republic to Empire: Reflections on the Early Provincial Architecture of the Roman West', *JRS* 60 (1970), 1–19.

G.R. Watson, *The Roman Soldier* (London 1969).

K. Welch, 'The Roman Arena in Late-Republican Italy: A New Interpretation', *JRA* 7 (1994), 59–80.

T. Wiedemann, *Emperors and Gladiators* (London 1992).

J.J. Wilkes, *Dalmatia* (Cambridge, Mass. 1969).

R.J.A. Wilson, *Piazza Armerina* (London 1983).

M. Wilson Jones, 'Designing Amphitheatres', *MDAI(R)* 100 (1993), 391–442.

P. Zanker, *Pompeji. Stadtbilder als Spiegel von Gesellschaft und Herrschaftsform* (Mainz 1987).

Index